19.95

W9-BBE-524

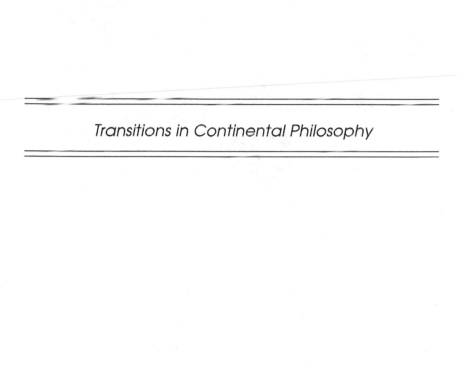

Transitions in Continental Philosophy

Selected Studies in
Phenomenology and Existential Philosophy 18

Transitions in Continental Philosophy

Edited by
Arleen B. Dallery
and
Stephen H. Watson

with
E. Marya Bower

STATE UNIVERSITY OF NEW YORK PRESS

Production by Ruth Fisher
Marketing by Bernadette LaManna

Published by
State University of New York Press, Albany

© 1994 State University of New York

For information, address the State University of New York Press,
State University Plaza, Albany, NY 12246

Library of Congress Cataloging-in-Publication Data

Transitions in continental philosophy / edited by Arleen B. Dallery
   and Stephen H. Watson with E. Marya Bower.
      p.   cm. — (Selected studies in phenomenology and existential
   philosophy ; 18)
      Includes bibliographical references and index.
      ISBN 0-7914-1849-9 (alk. paper). — ISBN 0-7914-1850-2 (pbk. :
   alk. paper)
      1. Philosophy, Modern—20th century.   2. Philosophy, European.
   3. Psychoanalysis and philosophy.   4. Feminist theory.   5. Ethics,
   Modern—20th century.   I. Dallery, Arleen B.   II. Watson, Stephen
   H., 1951–   .   III. Bower, E. Marya.   IV. Series.
   B804.T716   1994
   190'.9'04—dc20   93-1254
                                                                         CIP

10 9 8 7 6 5 4 3 2 1

Contents

Introduction

The papers collected in this volume arise from a recent meeting of the Society for Phenomenology and Existential Philosophy held at Villanova University in Villanova, Pennsylvania. As the title of the volume indicates, these papers represent a certain transition in the development of Continental philosophy. If one traces the beginnings of Continental philosophy in North America from the 1940s, and its emergence as a research program in its own right from the 1960s, one finds a project not dissimilar to its historical antecedents. It is a project that is both foundational and Cartesian at least in this respect, that it remains firmly centered upon theoretical issues in epistemology and ontology. These themes remain predominant from the time of Husserl to the period of structuralist activity in France in the early 1960s. Although discussions concerning issues in ethics, political theory, or aesthetics were not absent during this time—indeed, it was often claimed that what made phenomenological and existential philosophy interesting was the safe harbor it provided for research in these areas against the antimetaphysical and antiidealist tendencies of positivism—it remained true that here too such concerns remained, to invoke the terms of metatheory, "regional." Phenomenologists, it was proclaimed, steadfastly refused to abandon first intentions for second ones. Nevertheless, even "Continentalists," as they came to be called during this time, still seemed obliged to render first an account of ontology or epistemology to make these "regional" investigations credible. Even now there are those who speak of Continental philosophy as "coming of age" and fulfilling itself in this respect.

It is no longer clear, however, that those sorts of claims are fulfillable. Nor is it clear that Continental philosophy simply inherits such a clear and univocal research program—any more than have its theoretical competitors, for example, analytic philosophy, differing views of pragmatism, or neo-Thomism. Rather, it is perhaps more true that such constraints have themselves turned paralogical, that the outlines of such classical research programs themselves have collapsed. If, for example, we cannot do without Husserl and Heidegger, many of our colleagues, as this volume testifies, no longer feel compelled to be responsible to them or to their foundational or *Wissenschaftliche* pretensions. And this is so for reasons that, although perhaps never simply theoretical, remain nevertheless theoretical in implication. Such is, of course, always the case with paradigm changes, as historians almost everywhere have recognized. Both Husserl's and Heidegger's questions, however, although never simply irrelevant—as this volume likewise testifies—clearly no longer dominate recent thought as they once did.

It is not, of course, that there are no antecedents for such moves, even within Continental philosophy and even in its classical authors. Not only can one invoke the "romantic" or "antimetaphysical" discourses of Kierkegaard or Nietzsche, but even such an apparently "classical" figure like Scheler was not centered upon such issues. And yet, too often it is claimed that this arises simply out of a disregard for rigor. The point, however, is that "first philosophy" no longer binds. It may not be clear at all what "ethics is first philosophy" might strictly mean in this collapse, any more than it is clear what it would mean for feminist theory to make itself "foundational," but it is clear that neither of them will take second place to antecedent tracts on the hermeneutic inventory or the transcendental articulation of the categories. As the papers on Husserl and Heidegger included here likewise attest, however, this distance also facilitates a certain renewal of these classical sources, a certain rewriting and reappraisal of the movement that they themselves originate. This is perhaps most indicative of the status of this transition.

It has been said often enough that we have abandoned grand theory. Perhaps it is better to acknowledge that this too is neither true nor false. Rather, grand theory is being written "otherwise": locally, perhaps more empirically, but without turning simply reductive; without, that is, turning to empiricism. And this seems to be true whether the thought originates from Paris or Frankfurt, or from Stony Brook, Nashville, or Evanston. Now the demonstrations are woven between counterdiscourses and concrete interventions, complicated in the relationship between theory and practice—or to speak classically, in the transition *[Übergehen]* between concept and determination, idea and intuition, the ontic and the ontological, experience and judgment.

It is just in this sense that such regional discourses extend beyond their localities, that discourses on art, politics, or feminist theory impinge upon strictly delimited domains and categories of inquiry, without simply dissolving them—that psychoanalysis impacts on epistemology, art on metaphysics, ethics on its classical absorption within ontology, or feminist theory on all of these. The result, however, must be seen to be anything but reductive or totalizing in effect, for example, the "aesthetization" or "politicization" of Reason, but instead must be seen to be a transformation of those domains. And this effect again itself delimits the horizons of a certain practice of philosophy as "Continental," one that no longer can be understood to fulfill the transcendental or idealist traditions from which it emerged, but rather one that can be understood to rewrite and to challenge— often doubtless both against and despite themselves—those very resources.

We find this rewriting and challenging at work from the outset of this volume. In the first chapter of this part, which addresses political themes, Philip Buckley reflects upon the implications of Husserl's *Kaizo* articles. Buckley discusses the call that Husserl made in these articles for a renewed affirmation of the possibility of a rational life as the goal of authentic humanity and considers what role philosophers and phenomenologists may have to play in this renewal. Buckley also examines the relationship between this call, originally uttered in the shadow of Weimar Germany, and the far-ranging political and social changes that swept Eastern Europe in 1989.

Peg Birmingham's paper examines the accusations levied against Foucault and Arendt that claim that their conceptual commitments cause them to be unable to distinguish between legitimate and illegitimate uses of power. While tracing the lines of agreement that exist between these two thinkers, Birmingham argues that each has a conception of power as multiple—as in and of the plural—that gives support to an understanding of the legitimate power of law that is grounded on the principle of publicness.

The inquiry into the texts of Foucault continues in Ladelle Mc-Whorter's chapter. Focusing on the text *Discipline and Punish,* McWhorter explores the possibility that Foucault's texts may themselves be self-overcoming. While examining the suggestion that the human individual is a product of power relations and disciplinary techniques, McWhorter argues that Foucault causes us to place into question not only our will to know ourselves, but also our drive to know anything at all—even Foucault's texts.

The chapter by Stuart Barnett completes this part of the volume. In this chapter, Barnett challenges the tendency to receive Foucault's critique of subjectivity in such a way that it is understood to be in accord with a Habermasian conception of politicized self-representation. By undertaking a broad overview of the works of both Habermas and Foucault, Barnett explores how Habermas's conception of an objective reality that is free of history or historical transformation is in direct conflict with Foucault's attempts to understand the historical origins of the power relations that infuse different discursive spaces.

The second part of the volume includes papers devoted to feminist theory. It begins with a revised version of the plenary address presented by Michèle Le Doeuff. In her chapter, Le Doeuff reflects upon the concept of the "pact" that was said to exist between Simone de Beauvoir and Sartre. Here she illuminates the domineering or tyrannical role that Sartre played in both de Beauvoir's personal and philosophical endeavors. Within this work, Le Doeuff questions whether the concept of a "pact" can or does provide an example of an appropriate and fruitful mode of philosophical sociability—challenging feminists and philosophers all to reconsider their manner of interaction.

In a rich and far-reaching essay, Ellie Ragland-Sullivan discusses the foundations for and implications of an ethics based upon Lacan's psychoanalytic theory. Tracing the connections and diremptions that exist between Lacan and Freud and Aristotle, Ragland-Sullivan notes that Lacan's interest in the particularness of desire led him to explore the emergence of repetitive actions that function as a futile attempt to regain the consistency, wholeness, or unity that one feels is lacking in one's life. Insofar as these repetitions may be paradoxical, serving themselves as a barrier to change or to health, Ragland-Sullivan posits that an ethics based upon Lacanian analysis may allow us to gain the freedom to divest ourselves of inappropriate repetitive tasks and rituals and thereby allow us to attend to the recovery from both individual and societal ills.

Kelly Oliver's chapter also explores the possibility of the development of a new ethics. Focusing on the work of Julia Kristeva, Oliver examines how Kristeva has challenged the insights of Lacan that suggest, first, that language is the result of lack and, second, that there is a fundamental connection between the Father and Law. Oliver discusses how the discourses of poetry, psychoanalysis, and maternity have grounded Kristeva's inquiry into the question of alterity within identity. She also reflects upon Kristeva's conception of a "herethics," an ethics based upon love that may enable us to forego what has traditionally been a rejection or "sacrifice of either mothers or women."

In the first of three chapters that consider the thought of Luce Irigaray, Tamsin Lorraine discusses how the perception and anticipation of the experience of body boundaries influences the construction of the subject. Lorraine first describes how the masculine subject may be said to deny the experience of the merged and fluid body boundaries of the child and mother, codifying instead the experience of the woman-other under the category of the maternal-feminine who exists only to serve as an affirmation of the masculine-subject. She then explores the strategy of feminine subjectivity that can entertain the possibility of a porous relationship with the other—a relationship that eschews traditional categories in favor of an ever-changing and informing relationship with an other who is also in the midst of growth and change—and that can thereby ground a new ethics.

Elizabeth Grosz's chapter invites the reader to consider Irigaray's sometimes disturbing conception of the divine. Placing Irigaray's work on this concept into the context of her movement from a consideration of "the problematic of the interdependence, autonomy, and difference of the sexes" to an examination of the "conditions and possibilities of the modes of exchanges between the two sexes," Grosz proposes that the nature of the divine—properly reconsidered—can provide women with an ideal self-image that is perceived to be necessary for the achievement of positive interaction between men and women. Grosz's discussion of Irigaray's work on the ideas of the elemental, of female autonomy, and of sexual exchange enables her to suggest what this positive interaction might look like.

Although she approaches the questions from a different perspective, Eléanor Kuykendall continues the consideration of Irigaray's conception of the divine and the implications that it has for the possibility of the development of a new ethics. Focusing on Irigaray's reflections on the birth and the death of gods as well as on the feminine Christ, which are presented in the third part of *Amante Marine,* and on Irigaray's more recent work in applied linguistics, Kuykendall ponders how a new articulation of sexual difference could function as the cornerstone for this new ethics. In addition, Kuykendall raises interesting questions regarding the implications of Irigaray's inquiry into French linguistic practices for readers and speakers of English.

In the third part of the volume, three very different essays on aesthetics are included. Yifat Hachamovitch's rich and challenging chapter combines aesthetic reflection with a knowledge of classical and contemporary phenomenological scholarship in order to examine the lived experience of human culture and its ties to the movement of earth and sea, wind and need. Drawing upon the still life paintings of seventeenth century Spain, and examining carefully Samuel Baks's painting "Pears," Hachamovitch contributes reflections on aesthetics, metaphysics, and politics in her inquiry into the subsoil of intentional structures and constituting life.

Kristin Switala's chapter brings the philosophical debates concerning the nature and stability of a text and its interpretation into the domain of music. In her examination of the debates that surround the authentic performance and appropriate interpretation of Baroque musical scores, Switala provides insights into the inherent fluidity and multilayered nature of a (musical) text. She also discusses how historical and contextual situations, including economic and political factors, can affect the creation, performance, and interpretation of various texts.

Having touched upon the domains of painting and music, this part ends with an essay devoted to a literary form, viz., autobiography. Kate Mehuron's chapter examines Christa Wolf's autobiography in order to consider the possibilities and implications that reside in the empathetic witnessing of women to themselves and to each other. By exploring the dynamics of shame that are revealed to be at work in the telling of one's story, and in dialogue with a number of other authors including Irigaray and Lyotard, Mehuron challenges her readers to reexamine the tension and potential inherent in the attempt to reveal one's unspeakable knowledge of one's self.

The fourth and final part of this volume is devoted to ethics. The opening essay by Fred Dallmayr provides the reader with an opportunity to consider once again how the work of Martin Heidegger may contribute to current discussions of ethics and politics. In this chapter, Dallmayr presents a survey of three of Heidegger's works, the *Beiträge zur Philosophie,* the Schelling lectures, and "The Anaximander Fragment." Tracing Heidegger's consideration of the *Seinsfuge* through these texts, Dallmayr shows how this concept functions as a key element in Heidegger's consideration of the distinction between good and evil and between justice and injustice. In addition, he indicates how the ideas presented in these works can be brought to respond to some of the recent criticisms directed against Heidegger.

In the second essay focused on the work of Heidegger, John van Buren suggests how the insights gained by the young Heidegger as he attempted to deconstruct and to demythologize metaphysics can be used to come to terms with the work of the later Heidegger—especially insofar as this later work itself can be read as being in need of a certain demythologizing. Combining sweeping sketches of the thought configurations of both the early and the later Heidegger with insightful questions and challenges, van Buren indicates a path of thought that will undoubtedly prove provocative for both current and future inquiries into Heidegger's work and meaning.

Thomas Anderson's essay includes a consideration of two of the three systems of ethics that Jean-Paul Sartre presented during his lifetime. Anderson suggests that the first ethics, based primarily on the ontology of *Being and Nothingness* and articulated in the *Cahiers,* was founded upon a naive, and therefore unsatisfactory, conception of radical human freedom. The second ethics, articulated in Sartre's 1964 Rome lecture, can be seen to differ from the first insofar as it recognizes how one's physical and historical circumstances can proscribe one's freedom. While examining the different sources, goals, and methods of justification attributed to each of these systems of ethics, Anderson reveals the implications that each system has for positive intersubjective relationships.

The next chapter, by Brian Caterino, examines the work of Jean-François Lyotard. In his essay, Caterino first shows how Lyotard has drawn upon and been in dialogue with Aristotle, Kant, and Levinas as he has constructed his conception of morality. Caterino then takes a critical stand against Lyotard's (and Levinas's) work, arguing that there is an autonomous rationality in the moral realm that is rooted in the necessary intersubjectivity of those who inhabit the social domain. In addition, Caterino explores Lyotard's understanding of the role of prescriptives and descriptives in the achievement and articulation of knowledge.

Jerome Miller's essay invites the reader to reflect thoughtfully on the very possibility of an ethics and ethical behavior in the midst of postmodernism and deconstruction. Rather than concluding that these contemporary critiques have destroyed the possibility of an ethics insofar as they have done away with its foundation, Miller suggests that one should contemplate the possibility of an ethics without a foundation. Thus he proposes that deconstruction should not be viewed as something that one does to others; rather it should be understood to be something that one's self undergoes. Undergoing deconstruction, Miller argues, will allow one to face one's destitution and nothingness, not as a prelude to overcoming it, but as the first step in embracing it. Once one has embraced one's own destitution and released one's self-interest and concern for self-preservation, one is able to recognize that the good of the other has precedence over one's own good.

In the first of two chapters on Levinas, Wendy Farley considers the two primary metaphors that Levinas employs in his work: command and desire. Farley argues that, although the metaphor of command is used by Levinas to critique totalizing philosophies, it is unable to be employed positively in his restatement of ethical obligation. It cannot be used positively because it fails to get beyond the violence of dominance; command simply reverses the relationship of dominance, thereby excluding the desire for the (good of the) Other that cannot be commanded. Farley concludes that the metaphor of desire can be employed positively because desire is understood to fill one with a longing for the Other as Other, thereby preserving the asymmetry of alterity while not reestablishing a dominating or hierarchical relationship.

Jill Robbins presents the final chapter of this volume. Robbins explores Levinas's concern with the figural, both in its manifestation as figural interpretation of the Old Testament and in its manifestation as theatrical representation. While examining how the Judaic and the Christian reading of the Old Testament differ insofar as the Judaic may be said to eschew figural readings whereas the Christian overflows with them, Robbins suggests that the Christian interpretation may result in a petrification of individuals and of their relationships with others. This petrification of individuals can be characterized as a loss of face—one of whose essential characteristics is mobility—and thus can be said to do violence to the very possibility of an ethics.

As is evident from these essays, what is occurring here is an ongoing and developing discourse that both challenges and revitalizes the tradition in which it has its origin. It is not our intention to suggest that this volume captures all of the depth and breadth of this challenging transition. It is our belief, however, that these essays attest to the rich possibilities that may yet develop.

Part 1

Politics

1 Political Aspects of Husserl's Call for Renewal

R. PHILIP BUCKLEY

The dramatic events of 1989 in Eastern Europe occurred with such rapidity that even the usual flood of media wisdom was occasionally interrupted. When commentators finally caught their breath, a common motif that emerged in the description of these happenings was that they were part of some sort of general process of renewal, reform, or rebirth and, with regard to the German states in particular and Europe in general, a movement toward some sort of unity. A somewhat less heralded event in 1989 was the appearance of Husserliana XXVII—*Aufsätze und Vorträge* of Edmund Husserl from 1922–1937.[1] Nevertheless, a philosophical connection can be made between these two apparently unrelated occurrences, for in this recent volume of Husserliana appear five essays on *"Erneuerung"* —"Renewal." In these essays, Husserl himself called for a renewal or rehabilitation of the European spirit; indeed, he seeks a rehabilitation of the whole world based upon a renewed Europe. The purpose of this chapter is not to suggest that Husserl was a prophet, but rather to reconsider his appeal for renewal in light of recent history and to see, in turn, what his view on renewal might offer to a philosophical comprehension of present day changes in Europe. First, I will briefly sketch the genesis of these essays and the context within which they were written and seek a definition of what Husserl means by renewal. In the second section, I will focus on some of the communal and political aspects of Husserl's call for renewal. Finally, my conclusion will be that, although Husserl's view of European renewal displays some shortcomings, it nonetheless offers on many points an enlightening critique of some of the hidden presuppositions governing the description of the historic changes taking place in Europe.

3

Husserl's Definition of Renewal

The five essays on "renewal" were written in the years 1922–23 for the Japanese journal *Kaizo;* the title itself apparently meaning something like renewal, reform, or reconstruction.[2] The audience for this journal consisted of young Japanese intellectuals who had their eyes on the West, those possessing the same mind-set as the numerous Japanese students of philosophy who attended Husserl's seminars in Freiburg. The first essay, "Renewal—Its Problem and Its Method,"[3] sets forth Husserl's general assessment of the situation immediately following World War I and the framework of a methodology for achieving the renewal that Husserl felt to be necessary. This essay was published in 1923 in *Kaizo* and appeared in both Japanese and German. The next two essays, *"Die Methode der Wesensforschung"* ("The Method of the Investigation of Essence") and *"Erneuerung als individualethisches Problem"* ("Renewal as Individual-Ethical Problem"), the themes of which are the proper method of renewal and the role of the individual, were printed only in their Japanese translation. Two earlier essays intended for *Kaizo, "Erneuerung und Wissenschaft"* ("Renewal and Science"), which deals with the universal aspect of renewal, and *"Formale Typen der Kultur in der Menschheitsentwicklung"* ("Formal Types of Culture in the Development of Humanity"), were never published. This last essay in particular places the problem of renewal within the context of world history.

When considering these articles, it is important to keep in mind the historical context within which Husserl was writing, namely, the "deplorable situation,"[4] as he calls it in *Kaizo,* of a Weimar Germany in "political, national, religious, artistic, and philosophical chaos."[5] It is useful to recall some of the hallmarks of this difficult period. The constitution of 1919 never enjoyed enough popular support to fill the political vacuum left by the fall of the *Kaiserreich.*[6] In addition, a combination of lack of support for the constitution, traditional German regionalism, and Allied control in some sectors led to a diffusion of political power (that is, a decentralized Germany). Even at the local level, however, little consensus could be found to establish stable forms of government. Socialists, communists, republicans, monarchists, fascists, and many others not only had different political agendas, they also disagreed radically on the very form of political life.

Economically, there was the two-edged sword of the war and its aftermath: namely, the depletion of resources that had occurred and, at the same time, the collapse of the false economic rise that the war had brought to at least certain sectors of the economy. Added to this was the war debt imposed by the treaty of Versailles.[7] The economic hardships of the period are conveyed by Husserl himself in a letter from 1922 to the

Canadian Winthrop Bell, in which he complains that, due to inflation, his pay raise actually works out to be one-tenth of his old salary; he adds that, because he needed the money, he could not refuse the offer to write some articles for the Japanese journal *Kaizo!*[8] Given such a situation, combined with the personal suffering and loss that the war had brought,[9] one can empathize with the depression and confusion, as well as the resentment, felt in Germany at the time. It is this resentment that Husserl is voicing when he says that the war, in a certain sense, had continued *past* 1918, to be waged with psychological torture, moral deprivation, and economic need.[10]

It would seem, therefore, that the First World War may well be viewed as the external event pivotal to the production of these *Kaizo* articles. Pierre Trotignon claims that it was the First World War that formed a radical break with the cultural and rational heritage of Europe that had existed for twenty-five centuries. The war was a true crisis, separating Europe from the rational ideal that had guided it from its origin.[11] There can be little doubt of the tragic role that the First World War played in Husserl's consciousness of a crisis. It would be mislead ing, however, to consider this monumental event as the efficient cause of Husserl's crisis-philosophy first expressed in these *Kaizo* articles. The war and its aftermath, just as the rise of Nazism, were for Husserl *signs* of something fundamentally amiss in European civilization, signs of a sickness with roots reaching well beyond the immediate circumstances of these terrible events.

One is reminded of Spengler's contentions, expressed in the preface to *Der Untergang des Abendlandes,* that his work had basically taken shape before the war, and that he had even chosen his title by 1912. So the war was not the cause of decay, but a reflection. As Spengler says, "events have justified my theory and refuted nothing."[12] One should add immediately that, although Spengler and Husserl agree that the present situation is a sign of something, they disagree radically about the under- lying cause of this degeneration and about the nature of possible solu- tions. *Untergang,* says Husserl, is our fate only if we passively accept it as such.[13] It is to Husserl's credit that he gave in neither to the superficial pessimism that repeats itself in every age, but that grew to a crescendo in the 1920s, nor to an external analysis of the crisis that would perhaps yield easy answers. As Franco Volpi has pointed out in an excellent article entitled *"Aux racines du malaise contemporain: Husserl et la responsabilité du philosophe,"* Husserl's account deserves special attention because it attempts to discover the *primordial* roots of the contemporary malaise.[14] It is this depth that gives Husserl's analysis its lasting value.

The fundamental crisis that Husserl describes in the *Kaizo* articles is a loss of *faith*. Renewal is thus the renewal of faith, a reestablishment or rekindling of faith. The faith that has been lost is that faith that has sustained Europe since its "foundation" or origin, that is, since the Greeks.[15] This faith can be described in the first place as a belief in the possibility of rational existence. It is a sense that human life can be fully rational, a belief that all human activity can be guided by rationally established means. For Husserl, this faith also has what might be called a *moral dimension*. It is not just a belief that human life *can* be rational, but rather a belief that human life *ought* to be rational. This faith proclaims that for human life to be truly human, it must be rational. According to this faith, truly human existence is a rational existence. Thus, this faith not only proclaims that rational existence is possible, but also that such an existence constitutes a goal for authentic humanity. It is a faith in the moral sense of human culture, that is, of rationally determining values within a culture. It is thus a rational faith in morality and a moral faith in rationality.

What is this rationality, and how has the West come to lose faith in it? For Husserl, true rationality ultimately takes the form of philosophy. The trademarks of this philosophical rationality that continually appear in his thought are well known: critique, theory, ideality, omni-temporality, infinitude, method, and universality. The belief that true human life is a rational life is a belief that this life must be imbued with a sense of critique and a desire to see for oneself. It maintains that one should accept nothing simply on the basis of the tradition and that one must be willing to critique oneself and one's actions. Rationality also implies a certain attitude that is not dominated by immediate, pressing concerns and that is not interested solely in functioning, but in truly comprehending and knowing why the world and its inhabitants function as they do.

When Husserl describes in the *Kaizo* articles the "sorrowful age" in which he lives and the loss of faith in this ideal of rationality, one cannot help but sense here the shadow of the First World War. As was indicated earlier, however, the war was itself only a sign for Husserl of the abandonment of the struggle for rational existence. In the articles for *Kaizo,* Husserl attributes the primary cause for the loss of faith in the possibility of ordering life in a rational way to the lack of a science that can act as an aid in this task. It is not that science is completely absent; indeed, there exist numerous natural sciences that seem to function well and to produce results. But the science required for the direction of human life is different because the "subject matter" of such a science is different. Values belong to the realm of "Spirit," and a proper scientific approach to this realm is lacking. Again, it is not as if "human sciences," the "sciences of spirit," are nowhere to be found. Rather, they have shown themselves to be inadequate to the task of providing a proper, a priori, scientific approach to the realm of subjective, human life. Renewal of the sagging faith in the possibility of meaningful human existence is thus based on the establishment of an a priori, normative science of human subjectivity. Only by this means can the traditional faith of the West in rational, meaningful human existence be regenerated.

In *Kaizo,* the emphasis is thus not so much on the *threat* to the proper approach to spirit that arises from the tendency of the natural sciences to view everything as a fact, rather, it is on the inability of the human sciences to develop and to found themselves properly. That is, Husserl does not stress the *hubris* and self-forgetfulness of the natural sciences so much as the poor performance of the human sciences. This stands somewhat in contrast to the view in the *Crisis*. In that text, the natural sciences share the culpability for the decay. Indeed, there the self-forgetfulness of the natural sciences of their ground in human subjectivity is clearly a fundamental cause of the crisis.[16] In the *Crisis,* the source of existential alienation and discontent is said to be the inability of *all* the sciences to deliver on their promises. In *Kaizo,* the view is much more that the natural sciences are doing precisely what they must, that even the negative aspects of the technological developments within the natural sciences are overemphasized. Disappointment is felt primarily in the human sciences. As Husserl mentions in an earlier version of the first *Kaizo* article, there even existed deep-seated mistrust of philosophy due to its association with war propaganda. Still, the returning soldiers had a spiritual need. For Husserl, their numbers at philosophy lectures showed that they sought the fulfillment of this need in the true philosophy of "eternal ideas, which carry in themselves the sense of the world and human life."[17] The terrible situation is, therefore, not entirely without hope. The dire nature of the times made the need for philosophy apparent. As long as things were "going well," the question of the proper scientific approach to humanity could be overlooked. But in view of the destruction of the war and its aftermath, questioning about the nature of human life, its meaning, and its rationality becomes so acute as to be unavoidable. Thus there is what Husserl describes as the "universal call"[18] for renewal, a renewal that is led by the reestablishment of faith in the project of rational, human existence.

This brief summary of Husserl's assessment of the situation and his description of the proper method to approach the lack of faith is drawn mainly from *Kaizo* I and II. It also gives rise to numerous questions, for there seem to be some paradoxes and ambiguities in what Husserl says. For example, his approach to the lamentable situation seems ruled by what might be called the *logic of the felix culpa*.[19] That is, faith in rationality really *had* to be lost before it could be restored by the salvific act of transcendental phenomenology. Husserl seems to imply a cycle of decay and rebirth in his view of the history of Western rationality. He does not, however, give an adequate account of the necessity of this decay. A further intriguing problem worthy of investigation would be the fact that renewal is basically a renewal of faith. What role does faith play in all of this? Faith is a difficult notion for philosophy. Faith in rationality is even more difficult. A rational faith in rationality begins to sound circular, and the restoration of a rational faith in rationality by means of science strikes one as a peculiar project. Of course, everything hinges on what one means by *faith,* and this is no easy question in Husserl. Still, in the fifth *Kaizo* piece, a clue might be yielded by the discussion of religious faith and by the identification of authentic religious faith with the critical aspect of the phenomenological attitude. As tempting as these topics might be, the following reflections on *Kaizo* are guided by political philosophy. What are the social and political aspects of this renewal? How does it come about in a large-scale, communal sense? What is the philosopher's role in this overall renewal? Possible answers to these and other "political" questions can be sought in *Kaizo* III and IV in which Husserl considers in turn the role of the individual in renewal and the universal nature of "scientific" renewal.

Renewal: An Individual Task or a Societal Task?

My intention is *not* to suggest that one finds in these *Kaizo* articles a concise and clearly expressed political philosophy. Nowhere in Husserl's work does one find such a philosophy.[20] Nevertheless, it would be a false understanding of phenomenological reduction to think that phenomenologists and more specifically Husserl have nothing to say about social phenomena. For Husserl, the crisis has a societal dimension, and nowhere is this more evident than in the *Kaizo* articles. The difficulty that Husserl recognizes is that part of the crisis consists in being "lost" in the political and social world, that is, in accepting what has been given as self-evident and thereby formulating solutions to the crisis in the same worn out and sedimented concepts and language that are in fact part of the problem. Phenomenological reduction is required, not because of a lack of interest in the social and political world, but rather because Husserl wants to approach these phenomena in a new, unhindered way.

Without reduction, one runs the risk of joining the political sophists who use "socioethical argumentation as a disguise for the egoistical goals of an completely degenerate nationalism."[21] For Husserl, it makes no sense to talk about the reestablishment of rationality in political life if we have lost faith in rationality *überhaupt.* Before we can talk about acting rationally in the political and social realm, we must reestablish the belief that humanity itself is rational. Politics is by no means excluded from the project of renewal; to the contrary, the spiritual renewal that Husserl seeks may have far-reaching political consequences. Husserl says that the establishment of a science of humanity and the human community would in turn "establish a rationality in social and political activity and a national, political technique."[22] How might this be the case?

Any discussion of the social and the political involves two distinct but connected relationships: the relationship of subject to subject (the "I" to other individual instances of "I") and the relationship of the individual subject to the community of subjects (the "I" to the "we"). Neither of these relationships is without difficulty in Husserl. Regarding the first, it is well known that if one focuses on Husserl's "egology," that is, on his emphasis on the singularity of subjectivity and on such statements as "the monads have no windows,"[23] then one is confronted, to some degree, with the possibility of solipsism in his thought. The subject can be seen as a completely self-sufficient, self-actualizing, and self-subsisting entity. Husserl sometimes uses the image of a circle to describe the life of this individual "monad,"[24] because a circle safely contains everything within its boundaries or, conversely, excludes everything from its own interiority. On the other hand, Husserl also stresses relations of *Einfühlung* (empathy). Through such relations the monads do indeed seem to have windows! To be sure, the subject never has access to the subjective life of other monads in the same way that it has access to its own inner life. There is, nevertheless, an awareness of other subjects within one's own subjectivity. This intersubjectivity forms the basis for the second relationship, namely, between the "I" and the "we," for only through a type of "sharing" between individual subjects can anything like an authentic "we" emerge. Before suggesting how renewal takes place in the framework of this relationship, let me characterize this "we" more closely.

The shortest definition that Husserl gives of different sorts of communities, different sorts of "we"s (e.g., family, clubs, and somewhat more problematic, the state) is that they are "personalities of a higher order."[25] This formulation already implies the similarity and the difference between the "I" and the "we." The similarity is that the community too is a "personality," that is, it can somehow be viewed as a subject writ large. Husserl says at the outset of *Kaizo* III that the community "is a personal, one might say, many-headed and yet connected subjectivity."[26] So tight is the analogy between the individual and the community that he describes the individual and the community as an "inseparable pair of ideas."[27] In various texts, Husserl ascribes to the "personality of a higher order" all sorts of characteristics that are normally associated with an individual's personality, such as memory and even a form of corporeity. Just as an individual has a will, so too is there a community will.

It is crucial to remember, however, that to speak of the community as a subjectivity is indeed to speak analogously. The personality of a higher order is *founded* in the individuals who also form the basis for the analogy. *Higher-order* does not mean better, or first, but founded. Thus, the community is something different from the individuals who make it up, it is more than the mere sum of the individuals who make it up,[28] it is in fact something new, but it cannot exist without the individual. An authentic community will, for example, cannot exist without the willing of the individuals who make up the community. One is reminded of the nature of categorial acts that, on the one hand, are something truly new, but that are founded and exist only on the basis of individual acts of perception. The founded nature of the community is important to stress, for it goes against any notion of preexistent communal structures wherein the individual is viewed as a mere part or where the individual finds his true being. James Hart, in an article describing the elements of Husserl's theory of community, summarizes this point well:

> Husserl's discussion of the ontological features of the community as a personality of a higher order (or an analogous founded "I" of "I's") makes it clear that the "we" emergent out of being-in-one-another of wills in community is not absolutist in the sense of a prior existing founding principle which is the efficient cause of its moments/members and for which the moments/members are accidental. . . . This emergent high-order substrate, "we," as the analogous "I" of "I's", is constituted from out of a manifold of "I's".[29]

It is worthwhile to note that Husserl's position goes against a common trend that developed in antiliberal circles in Weimar Germany, namely, to treat the state as the *highest* ontological order and to see individuals as secondary.[30] Within these circles, renewal was said to begin with the renewal of the state, the individual being "renewed" through the renewal of the state. For Husserl, on the contrary, the fact that the true community is ontologically founded on individuals precludes any such view of renewal "from above."

Husserl does understand, however, that communities can diverge into an inauthentic form. This happens precisely when there is a loss of the radical independence, self-responsibility, and willingness to be critical on the part of the individual member. In *Kaizo,* Husserl names such an inauthentic form of community "an imperialist organization of will, a central will in which all single wills are focused and to which all must subordinate themselves."[31] Such an inauthentic "we" is possible only in the unphenomenological attitude of power over others. In the fifth *Kaizo* article, in which Husserl compares and contrasts religious and scientific culture, he gives the medieval church as the prime example of such an imperialist unity. Power over others is fundamentally irrational for Husserl because it takes away the very basis of true rationality: self-determination, self-judgment, autonomy, and seeing for oneself. One should add here that another unphenomenological attitude is implicated in this inauthentic "we," namely, laziness. The mere acceptance of the insights of others, the mindless taking over of the tradition or the dictates of the community, this attitude makes possible an imperialistic community. Such laziness, or as Husserl calls it in the "Vienna Lecture," *fatigue [Müdigkeit]*, is one of the major symptoms of the degeneration that he hopes to reverse.[32]

The authentic community, therefore, does not consist of either an overwhelming central will or of a group of lazy individuals. Rather, it consists of what Husserl calls surprisingly a *communistic unity of wills*, wherein there is a "consciousness of the communal goal of the common good to be pursued, of an encompassing will of which all know themselves to be functionaries, but as free, and not even a freedom which must practice renunciation, and also not subordinated functionaries."[33] The unity of will *[Willenseinheit]* that makes up the authentic community is not derived *from above*, but is arrived at *from below*. This arriving takes place through the process of sharing insights, insights that are valid and obtainable (at least, in principle) for everyone, but that are first won by the hard, phenomenological work of the individual. James Hart points out both the role played by Husserl's intuitionism and the intersubjective nature of true phenomenological activity when he says:

> although phenomenology is negated when regarded as solipsism, i.e. where what it uncovers holds only for me and not for us, and therefore although phenomenology can exist only as an ongoing building of a common good and common life, no "we" can stand for me; I cannot delegate to anyone my seeing and marshalling of evidence—an evidence whose sense is "for us all," but an "us" which is co-founded on my seeing and in no way substitutes for my seeing or asks me to trust someone else's seeing. The ideals of the institutionalization of a phenomenological culture and radical democracy draw near to one another.[34]

This citation brings us back directly to our question of communal renewal, for what Husserl intends by renewal is nothing less than phenomenological culture. Who is responsible for renewal? Those who have not yet lost sight of the goal of rational life, of philosophy as a rigorous science, namely, phenomenologists; initially, individual phenomenologists undertaking their own struggle for insight. Husserl clearly recognizes,

however, that whereas such individual efforts may bring personal satisfaction, they are insufficient to renew culture.[35] An important stage of
general cultural renewal is, therefore, for phenomenological philosophers
themselves to form an authentic community. There are, however, several
difficulties with this movement from individual renewal to large-scale
renewal.

First, there is the difficulty of philosophers themselves forming what
Husserl calls an authentic community. Husserl gives no account of the
possibility of the authentic conflict that does indeed seem to mark philosophical activity. Husserl certainly has a theory of intersubjective correction. Through the comparison of believed insights the possibility of illusion
is ruled out and the proper justification of true insights is discovered. It is
these insights, shared by individuals and justified in common, that form
the very basis for the unity of will that is essential to authentic community. While it is true that this process of intersubjective correction plays a
crucial role in communal philosophical life, it is also obvious that there
can exist a plurality of well-justified insights that do not coincide in a
common will. Husserl's view of the unicity of universal reason precludes
the possibility of unsolvable rational conflict. The existence of two (or
three . . .) distinct but equally well-justified forms of rationality is also
an impossibility for Husserl. The struggle that seems to characterize philosophical engagement can be viewed as authentic by Husserl only if it is
interpreted as part of the process of intersubjective correction *within* the
already established framework of the scientific rationality founded by the
Greeks. Any suggestion that true philosophy might *diverge* from, perhaps
even negate, this form of scientific rationality could be seen only as a
deepening of the crisis by Husserl.

Yet it could be asserted that the admission that there might be totally different *and still valid* views on a question is the *Stellungnahme*
that perhaps best prevents the philosopher from becoming a tyrant. Such
an admission of "difference" could itself be understood not as a denial of
authentic, communal, philosophical life, but, rather, as the affirmation of
such a life and as a precondition for true, philosophical existence. In this
case, of all possible communities, philosophers seem to be the group
least likely to fulfill Husserl's view of an authentic community.

Let us assume for a moment, however, that philosophers do in fact
constitute an authentic "we" as set forth by Husserl. The next question is
how the renewed faith in rationality possessed in common by this group
is to be passed on to the larger community. A possible answer, not unknown to the tradition of philosophy, is to speak of the *authority* of
philosophy. In the tradition, this authority was usually based on philosophers having insights that the majority was deemed to lack. Although
Husserl does sometimes speak of the authority of philosophers,[36] he cer-

tainly cannot mean it in this traditional sense. For the rest of the world simply to accept the insights and attitudes of philosophers clearly goes against Husserl's emphasis on personal freedom and his view that insights must always be gained for oneself. Indeed, it would be rather surprising for Husserl to suggest that a type of argumentation that is based on power and authority, a type of argumentation excluded from philosophy, could then be applied by philosophers to the world at large.

A further possible account of how the life of rationality lived by philosophers contributes to a rational culture is found in the *functionalism* that can be detected at various places in Husserl's thought. This functionalism is particularly evident in the *Kaizo* articles. Here, the cause of the crisis is described as a loss of faith in rationality that is precipitated primarily by the lack of a proper science of human rationality. This faith will be restored when the scientists of rationality (philosophers) reestablish their own method and principles. If philosophers were to fulfill their function properly, then the entire network of sciences and scientific culture in general would operate in a manner more in keeping with the scientific character that they claim. Husserl had a great deal of affinity for the functionalist approach, even within philosophy itself. It is worthwhile to recall that within his scheme for phenomenology, Husserl sees phenomenologists as being occupied with a particular region of being. Hence, each phenomenologist is to direct his or her efforts toward one specific realm of phenomena, be it toward religion, history, art, or other realms. Husserl is a great promoter of the division of labor within philosophy. Such an approach seems also to be suggested when discussing large-scale renewal.

Still, the mechanics of how a well-functioning philosophy actually entails well-functioning sciences and a well-functioning culture remain unclear. Indeed, Husserl realizes that the natural sciences "function" rather well, at least qua technique. The difficulty is that the *meaning* of these sciences has been lost; their ultimate rationality is no longer evident. This ultimate rational sense is to be recovered by rediscovering in a rigorously scientific way the origin of all science in human subjectivity. Yet it is not altogether evident how the rediscovery of the meaning of scientific activity by philosophy will actually restore the meaning within the sciences themselves, let alone within the entire culture affected by those sciences. The meaning rediscovered by philosophy must somehow be conveyed; Husserl, however, never gives a complete account of how this "conveying" might take place. It is possible to imagine that the insights of phenomenology would at least have some impact on the human sciences since both phenomenology and the human sciences are concerned with subjectivity. But the ultimate effect of phenomenology on the natural sciences remains difficult to foretell. Simply to inform biologists,

physicists, chemists, or even mathematicians that philosophers have rediscovered the original and ultimate meaning of their tasks does not seem
to achieve the profound renewal that Husserl seeks.

The functionalist approach appears even less palatable when the
crisis of culture is considered. A group of philosophers living in perfect
rationality does not make a philosophical culture. Indeed, the functionalist interpretation of the mechanics of overcoming the crisis, just as the
authoritarian interpretation, seems to go against Husserl's radical individualism and the requirement of seeing for oneself. Philosophers can
"propagate" the spirit of reason among the "laypeople"[37] only by bringing
them to see, not by seeing for them. Thus, an even more radical view is
required to account for large-scale renewal. In short, everyone must become a phenomenologist.

It does seem to be the case that, if everyone were to become a
phenomenologist, then a phenomenological culture would arise. This culture would be truly philosophical and, therefore, the true reestablishment
of the Greek-origin. The suggestion that everyone become a
phenomenologist can be understood in at least two ways. A rather extreme understanding would posit that everyone must actually engage in
philosophical activity, each person inquiring back into the origin of all
knowledge and truth in subjectivity. Everyone would have to conduct the
type of constitutive analyses of consciousness that led Husserl to produce
such an extensive *Nachlass*. As unlikely as this universal phenomenological existence might be, it also is not what Husserl expects. In the first
place, Husserl believes that to be a philosopher is a highly personal
vocation to which only a few are called. He is also very well aware that a
certain forgetfulness is necessary within the sciences. To function well as
a physicist, one cannot continually be focusing on the constituting origin
of the world that one studies. The physicist must have a certain blindness
and must maintain a certain naive acceptance of the objective world to
make any progress at all.

Yet, in a certain sense, it is this blindness that Husserl hopes to
overcome because this blindness lies at the root of the crisis. In a remarkable passage located in an early manuscript from 1887, we find Husserl's
assessment of the narrowness that allows the mathematician, in particular, and the scientist, in general, to pursue interests without paying attention to questions of foundation and meaning:

> This limitation to ever more specialized fields [that is characteristic of
> modern science in general] is nothing that constitutes value or worth. It
> is only a necessary evil. The complete researcher who strives to be a
> complete human being as well should never lose sight of the relation of
> his science to the more general and higher epistemic goals of humanity.

Professional restriction to a single field is necessary; but it is reproachable to become fully absorbed in such a field. And [the researcher] must appear even more reproachable who is indifferent even to the more general questions which concern the foundation of his science, as well as its value and place in the realm of human knowledge in general.[38]

The ambiguity of Husserl's approach to the scientist is clearly felt here. Is there a way for scientists to "become" phenomenologists and yet continue to work in their specialized domains? This is perhaps possible if everyone becoming a phenomenologist is interpreted slightly differently: it is not as if everyone must *do* phenomenology, but rather, everyone must proceed *as* a phenomenologist does.

This narrower understanding of what it means for individuals to form a philosophical culture can be viewed as a fourth understanding of the mechanics of renewal. It is thus not a question of philosophy giving authoritarian instruction, nor of philosophy functioning well on its own, nor of the entire population of the world undertaking a purely philosophical existence. It is rather that phenomenological philosophers can be seen as exemplars of how life is to be lived rationally; they are the models that show how one strives for a rational existence. A rational life involves having insight into what one is doing; it means determining for oneself a life on the basis of reason. A rational life requires the justification of each and every "position taking" *[Stellungnahme]*, it demands taking responsibility for oneself on the basis of autonomous reason.

For Husserl, the philosopher must be the example of such rational living, of such responsible behavior. The philosopher is thus a model to be emulated by the natural scientist, by the politician, by the banker, by the baker, by the sociologist, and by the lawyer. Philosophers as a group must be an example of rationally determined communal life to the society at large. In their common endeavor of working toward the establishment of the goal of rational existence, philosophers are to be the example of what a community, united in the task of determining a rational societal existence, could achieve.

Although it remains dubious whether philosophers, both individually and through their work in common, have lived up to their vocation as role models, it is also dubious whether such responsible behavior on the part of philosophers would be noticed; if noticed, whether it could be widely implemented; and if implemented on a large scale, whether this would be sufficient to cure the crisis that Husserl has depicted with such accuracy. In the first place, it must be admitted that philosophy occupies, at least formally, a more marginal position than it did in the past. Perhaps it is a sign of the gravity of the crisis that the "moral preaching"[39] philosophy is called upon by Husserl to undertake to overcome the crisis falls mostly on deaf ears. It is a crisis that, by its very nature, is not so noticeable. Things are, after all, functioning rather well; and when they do not function well, the tendency is to attribute mal-functioning to a temporary and reparable deviation rather than to something being fundamentally amiss. It is a crisis of forgetting, and forgetting implies that one is not bothered by what is forgotten due to the very fact that it is forgotten.

Some may argue that philosophy is not so marginal, that philosophers are being noticed, that the need for philosophy is being recognized. No university rector would deny the importance of philosophy, although their actions often do, and even the business world seems interested in "getting" some ethics. The language of the expressed need for philosophy, however, often betrays the very type of thinking that Husserl feels is part of the crisis. If one of the dangers of the crisis is that it can pass unnoticed, an equally great danger is that it can be noticed in a superficial way. By the rapid formation of centers for bioethics and for business ethics, philosophy may feel liberated from a marginal position. But philosophy may also slip into a type of thinking that is itself part of the crisis.

Perhaps being marginal in a culture in crisis is the best indication that philosophy is somehow being true to itself. Philosophy is "slow" and may even stand in the way of the breathtaking and blind progress that is so idolized by the sciences. Philosophy may thus be marginalized, but perhaps it should not fear this marginal position. After all, history is full of the stories of marginal movements that have had enormous social impact. Husserl himself never feared such marginality. To the contrary, one sometimes is under the impression that, for Husserl, the worse the crisis, the greater is the need for philosophy to assume its self-responsibility. The more destitute the situation, the greater is the need for philosophy to assert its truth; the more the world drifts away from philosophy, the more Husserl feels obligated to carry on the struggle. The hope issuing from Husserl's thinking about the crisis distinguishes him from the average thinker of doom. Husserl's philosophy of cultural renewal is a philosophy of a recaptured faith in reason, a faith that then can hope, against all odds, for a rational future.

Husserl's "Renewal" and the Present Day European Situation

Despite the inadequacies of Husserl's account of the mechanics of renewal, his position has much to offer. I would like to conclude by mentioning three areas in which Husserl's thought offers a positive criticism of certain popular conceptions of recent occurrences in Eastern Europe and also to point out a rather negative aspect in Husserl's call for renewal that is extremely pertinent to the present European situation. The positive aspects are the spiritual nature of renewal, the radical individual responsibility required for renewal, and the criticism of the "statist" mentality. The negative aspect of Husserl's discussion of renewal is his "Eurocentrism."

Recent events in Eastern Europe have certainly been given many interpretations. One interpretation parallels in some respects Husserl's vision of renewal. It claims a crucial role for philosophy in what has occurred. Hence, in Poland, such a view would point out the prominent role in reform played by a "Solidarity" thinker such as Jozef Tischner or, more generally, the Thomistic-realism-personalism of the Lublin school. Similarly, the signatories of Charta 77 (having found their philosophical inspiration in Jan Patocka) in Czechoslovakia would be viewed as the vanguard of a reform movement. Other interpretations are of a wholly different, and less Husserlian, nature. These view the alienation that has prompted the recent upheaval in Eastern Europe as being of a materialistic order. Certainly, here too there is much talk about political freedom. But this occurs most frequently within the context of discussions about economics. Political freedom is viewed either as the prerequisite or the result of the introduction of a market economy. The primary goal is revealed as economic renewal. Husserl would probably have nothing against such economic renewal, unless it were to be taken by people (as it has been in some circles) as authentic renewal, that is, as the renewal of human culture as such. To view economic renewal as authentic renewal would be to place the mundane over the transcendental, to remain trapped in a naturalistic attitude. It would, therefore, constitute for Husserl a deepening of the crisis. Husserl would most likely be in favor of material improvement. Such improvement, however, is neither a necessary nor a sufficient condition for the "bliss" *[Glückseligkeit]* that is the result of authentic renewal.[40] This bliss arises from leading one's life rationally, from living autonomously, regardless of, even in spite of, the material and factical circumstances in which one finds oneself. *Wirtschaftswunder* is probably not a bad thing, but it is nothing compared to the "wonder of wonders," the human subject, living in personal freedom, exercising its possibilities of rational self-judgment and self-critique. It may be true that Husserl's philosophy can be seen as *too* spiritual and idealistic, but it certainly offers a different view of authentic human life to a group of nations rushing to embrace a Western European culture that Husserl would still describe as itself requiring fundamental, authentic renewal.

It has also already been pointed out that the movement of renewal in Husserl can be described as being from "bottom to top." In general, the "revolutions" in Eastern Europe also seem to exhibit such a movement.

One should keep in mind, however, that this "bottom" or basis of renewal was for Husserl the individual. The precondition for authentic renewal could be described as the critical "position taking" by the individual. That is, the individual must have the willingness to supply justification for each of one's beliefs, and such justification can come only from radically autonomous reason. The next stage of renewal was the formation by a group of such truly autonomous individuals into a community, a "we," wherein each "I" can see and justify its own position within that "we." Given this view of self-responsibility, I wonder if Husserl might not have looked with some suspicion at the mass movement that has brought such sudden change to Eastern Europe. He might even have gone so far as to view this "people power" as a form of inauthentic "we." Mass movements do not always seem to originate in the radical, rational self-responsibility of individuals, nor do the individual members of mass movements always seem to possess a clear-sighted, rational justification for what they are doing. In short, I think that Husserl would view the happenings as too much a movement of the heart and not enough a movement of the head. I would hope that Husserl would have preferred this inauthentic "'we' of below" (people power) to the inauthentic "'we' of above" (totalitarian regime) against which it has struggled. Still, Husserl's view does remind us that there is a threat to individual responsibility in mass movements and that freedom of expression, movement, and communication does not yield, a priori, an authentic community.

Although it is true that Husserl at times views the state as a necessary constraint upon the irrational drives and tendencies of humans, that is, as a protection against disharmony within the practical realm when perfectly functioning autonomous reason is absent, ultimately he might also classify the state as an inauthentic "we." This is rather evident with regard to states that are founded on racial or cultural determinations, for an authentic community could never be based on empirical or naturalistic presuppositions nor on mere tradition. Hence, it can be surmised that Husserl would be suspicious of the role that ethnic determinations have played in the "renewal" of Eastern Europe and would probably view the ethnic violence in various countries as a sign that authentic renewal is not taking place.

It should be added, however, that *any* state seems to be a pregiven body that in some ways claims to speak for the individual and to express the individual's interests, even though the individual had nothing to do with the constitution of this entity. Thus, it is not too surprising that Husserl hints rather clearly in *Kaizo* that, with the advent of large-scale authentic communal life, there would result an *Abbau* of the state power organizations.[41] This deconstruction of the state is far more dramatic than the dismantling of the totalitarian structures that have dominated Eastern

Europe, for Husserl's implied criticism of the state applies equally well to the liberal-democratic conception of state now being imported or resurrected in Eastern Europe. James Hart has shown that even liberal-democratic institutions do not correspond to Husserl's idea of a radically democratic society, for within the state the common good is always constituted from above, even if at least part of the above are my representatives.[42] In true community, nobody can *represent* me and nobody can speak for me. There can be no delegation to elected officials of my responsibility to make decisions and no submission to the whims of a technocratic bureaucracy. The state, says Husserl, "is a unity by power, by domination."[43] This domination has a different, less harsh, and more *hidden* form in the institutions of a liberal democracy. Husserl's view of authentic communal life as the *Liebesgemeinschaft* offers the image of communal unity without such domination. To be sure, this is a distant, perhaps impossible, goal. What I have already indicated for philosophers may hold true for society as a whole: there could be such a thing as unsolvable *rational* conflict. In such instances, there may be need of arbitration from above. This arbitration, although ideally somewhat rational, may indeed be truly arbitrary. Still, Husserl's view offers both a challenge and a warning: it challenges the individual to radical responsibility for one's self and for one's place in the community and it warns against placing all our hopes for authentic self-expression and authentic "being-with-one-another" in the hands of the state.

Whereas Husserl's approach to renewal may challenge us to do some fundamental rethinking about the rational nature of our individual and communal life, his thought itself displays a certain closed-mindedness. I think this lack of openness can best be displayed by outlining his "Eurocentrism." For Husserl, the idea of a philosophical culture is a peculiarly Western idea, founded in the Greeks and nurtured in *European* civilization. By philosophical culture, Husserl understands a culture guided by a proper, scientific form of rationality. The type of rational knowledge that existed in cultures such as the Babylonian, Egyptian, Chinese, and Indian can be classified only as a lower form of knowledge by Husserl, as "pre- or unscientific."[44] The scientific rationality that lies at the basis of a philosophical culture developed exclusively in Europe. It is itself, however, not exclusive. As the ultimate form of rationality, it is universal, open to all who wish to partake in it. In Husserl's view, this is precisely what the Japanese had done. In *Kaizo* he describes Japan as a "young, fresh, green branch of 'European' culture."[45] Having joined the project of European culture, they are also affected by the loss of faith in the rationality that is the basis of that project. But a rather obvious question comes to mind: did there not exist in a culture such as the Japanese a faith in a truly "rational" system of values long before it turned westward?

Husserl's suggestion that only the revival of true, Western-scientific rationality can stand at the basis of a philosophical and hence genuine culture is highly questionable. Could it not be that other forms of rationality have something to offer to the task of a genuinely renewed world? Might not the renewal of Western rationality and the overcoming of the one-sided, narrow concept of rationality that has dominated our culture since the Renaissance be aided by interchange with such otherness? Indeed, within our own tradition there are many other forms of rationality that might serve the task of renewal. The loss of faith in the deficient scientific form of rationality could perhaps be seen not simply as a call for more complete and fully grounded scientific rationality, but rather as giving other forms of rationality a chance. Poetic, narrative, and religious forms of rationality may have much more to contribute to human renewal than Husserl seems willing to grant.

2   Arendt/Foucault: Power and the Law

PEG ELIZABETH BIRMINGHAM

Critics of Natural Law theory, which in its modern version is based on the notion of human nature endowed with inalienable rights, are often accused of being unable to give an account of legitimate authority. If one rejects the notion of human nature as a fiction, the accusation continues, there is no possibility of differentiating between the pursuit of power for private interest and the pursuit of power for the common good. In other words, the accusation charges that the rejection of human nature and natural law does not permit the possibility of thinking the political, if one means by that the debate about the legitimate and illegitimate uses of power. Two contemporary thinkers who stand accused are Hannah Arendt and Michel Foucault. Claude Lefort, for example, argues that Arendt, rejecting the concept of the rights of man by claiming that it derives from the fiction of human nature, can give no account of authority and the legitimate exercise of power.[1] Habermas charges Foucault with the same shortcoming, arguing that Foucault's rejection of human nature and his insistence that power be thought of as multiple—separated from the notion of law—allows him to sidestep the question of legitimation.[2]

Of course, Foucault and Arendt address different areas. Foucault analyzes social practices and the institutions in which they are embedded. His texts are prison documents, lists of the insane, and medical and educational records. Arendt, in contrast, analyzes more prototypic political events: the French and American revolutions, the rise of totalitarianism, and the trial of Eichmann. Yet, despite their differences, Foucault and Arendt utilize similar critical strategies. Both are interested in analyzing power and the law not from the perspective of theory, but from the perspective of specific, local events in which power is actually at work. Both

21

thinkers also are interested in understanding power and the law in a way that is not tied to the framework of sovereignty and repression.

In what follows I will examine their respective positions in view of the accusation that, having rejected the notion of human nature and having embraced an understanding of power as multiple, both thinkers are unable to distinguish between legitimate and illegitimate uses of power. This will require (1) laying out their respective positions on power understood as sovereignty and repression, and (2) suggesting that both Foucault's and Arendt's attempts to think power and law *against* the framework of sovereignty allows for thinking a principle of the legitimacy of power from out of power itself. In turn, I will argue, this allows for a way to think 'originary rights,' which avoids both the Syclla of naturalism and the Charybdis of historicism.

Foucault: Power as Sovereignty and Repression

Turning first to Foucault's critique of an understanding of power linked to the twin notions of sovereignty and repression, it is important to note that Foucault's own position changes from the mid-1970s to the early 1980s. I am specifically referring to the series of lectures and interviews that Foucault gave on power in the 1970s (published in *Power/Knowledge*), and the essay entitled "The Subject and Power," written in 1982 and published as an afterword to Dreyfus and Rabinow's text on Foucault. (The 1982 essay is to my knowledge the last essay Foucault wrote explicitly on the subject of power.)

The question that occupies Foucault in the series of interviews and essays that make up the text *Power/Knowledge* is whether power must be thought of in terms of the law. When an interviewer reminds him of an earlier statement that inverts Clauswitz's formula such that politics is understood as the continuation of war by other means, Foucault responds tentatively:

> As soon as one endeavors to detach power with its techniques and procedures from the form of law within which it has been theoretically confined up until now, one is driven to ask this basic question: isn't power simply a form of warlike domination? Shouldn't one therefore conceive all problems of power in terms of relations of war? Isn't power a sort of generalized war which assumes at particular moments the forms of peace and the state? Peace would then be a form of war, and the State a means of waging it.[3]

Of course, this is Hobbes's understanding of power at the moment that the individual leaves the state of nature (the state of war) and consents to be governed by the sovereign. Foucault is quite correct to point out that if one understands power in terms of the sovereign, wherein one gives up one's own power and consents to be ruled, then power must also be understood as repression and prohibition. In this understanding of power, sovereignty and repression are inseparable: "The key point is that to this reduction of power to the figure of the master there is linked another reduction, that of procedures of power to the law of prohibition" (P/K 139). According to Foucault's analysis, the reduction of power to law enables power "never to be thought of in other than negative terms: refusal, limitation, obstruction, censorship. Power is what says no" (P/K 139). In this schema, power takes on the pure form of 'thou shalt not':

> In defining the effects of power as repression, one adopts a purely juridical conception of such power, one identifies power with a law which says no, power is taken above all as carrying the force of prohibition. Now I believe that this is a wholly negative, narrow, skeletal conception of power, one which has been curiously widespread. (P/K 119)

Contrary to Habermas's reading, Foucault's insistence on the separation of power from the law is founded upon his understanding of the law as prohibition. If law is an essentially negative force that presupposes a sovereign whose role is to forbid and a subject who says yes to this prohibition, and further, if Foucault's project is to think power outside this relation to law so understood, then it follows that Foucault must separate power from the law. The question emerges, however, whether a different understanding of power and the law, one that is itself freed from the figure of the sovereign, might not allow for rethinking in a radically different way the relation between law and power.

Indeed, this is precisely what Foucault calls for as he continues his reflection upon the nature of power. Tracing the history of the juridical-political theory of sovereignty, Foucault argues that this same theory of sovereignty that provided for the power of the feudal monarchy was reactivated in the construction of modern practices of disciplinary power. Foucault contends that disciplinary power with its procedural techniques inaugurates a new mechanism of power that is "absolutely incompatible with the relations of sovereignty" (P/K 104). This is a new form of power exercised over human bodies that permits time and labor to be extracted from these bodies. At the same time, Foucault asserts, disciplinary power has not canceled out sovereignty with its theory of right as the organizing principle of major legal codes. This is because the theory of sovereignty helps to conceal disciplinary domination as it guarantees each person his or her sovereign rights. These two heterogeneous but inseparable views of power *together* characterize modern political life. On the one hand, power is understood as the right of sovereignty embodied in public law and the sovereign will both of the nation and the individual citizen as subject of that nation. On the other hand, power is organized as disciplinary power characterized by normalization wherein clinical knowledge is the realm of jurisprudence. The task of rethinking power, Foucault suggests, is to think a third way that relies on neither a notion of a disciplinary form of power nor the rights of sovereignty (whether of the nation or the subject of that nation).

> If one wants to look for a non-disciplinary form of power, or rather, to struggle against disciplines and disciplinary power, it is not towards the ancient right of sovereignty that one should turn, but towards the possibility of a new form of right, one which must indeed be anti-disciplinarian, but at the same time liberated from the principle of sovereignty. (P/K 108)

Surprisingly, in his indictment of Foucault in *The Philosophical Discourse of Modernity,* Habermas quotes this passage and then dismisses it as a *"vague"* reference to another form of power that Foucault himself does not think.[4] I suggest, however, that Habermas should have read on after this 1976 lecture on power, turning to Foucault's 1982 essay "The Subject and Power." In this essay Foucault begins to think a notion of power that is based on neither a theory of sovereignty nor disciplinary practices. He argues here that power exists only when it is put into action. The exercise of power is a mode of action upon the actions of others; furthermore, it must include the element of freedom. "Power is exercised only over free subjects, and only insofar as they are free. By this we mean individual or collective subjects who are faced with a field of possibilities in which several ways of behaving, several reactions and diverse comportments may be realized."[5] Foucault thus contends that slavery cannot be understood as a power relationship. Lacking the element of freedom, it also lacks power. This means that power is not a function of consent or control. In itself, Foucault submits, power can be understood neither as a renunciation of freedom, nor as demanding a transference of rights, nor as the power of each and all delegated to only a few. A different understanding of law now begins to emerge. No longer understood in terms of domination or prohibition, the law as that which *governs* the exercise of action upon other actions, a sphere of power upon other spheres of power, would have to be understood as relational and regulative. Here Foucault suggests a way to understand the law as neither domination or prohibition. I suggest, however, that we must turn to Arendt to see a fully developed understanding of this notion of power and law. In other words, Foucault's understanding of a field of action or, rather, a field of power in which the self is understood as an actor rather than a subject, places his thought in the proximity of Arendt's. Indeed, I suggest that Arendt's thinking, although in agreement with several aspects of the notion of power outlined by Foucault, goes further in rethinking the question of the legitimation of power.

Arendt: The Rejection of Sovereign Power

In his 1976 essay on power, Foucault argues: "What we need, however, is a political philosophy that isn't erected around the problem of sovereignty, nor therefore around the problems of law and prohibition. We need to cut off the King's head: in political theory that has still to be done" (P/K 121). This is a remarkable statement insofar as it suggests that, although Foucault certainly has read Arendt, he has not read her closely enough. For it is precisely the continuous task of Arendt's political philosophy to cut off "the head of the king," that is, to think a notion of power that is not linked to a notion of sovereignty and, furthermore, to think a notion of the law that is not understood as prohibition. This, in turn, allows for a rethinking of 'originary rights' freed from both naturalism and historicism.

Whereas Arendt agrees with Foucault's suggestion that the modern political realm is characterized by an understanding of power as sovereign, she goes further, showing that this notion of sovereign power is itself tied to a long tradition that has its origins in Augustine. Of course for Augustine the problem of being able to act, or more precisely, his inability to act, is tied to a will that is divided against itself. This is his dilemma: I will and I cannot.[6] A divided will is an impotent will. A powerful will, therefore, is possible only if the will is one with itself. Now Arendt points out that this conception of power, located in a unified will, is precisely the conception of power developed in modern political theory. Rousseau is the examplary figure. She suggests that Rousseau's turn to the unanimous will of the nation is motivated by the problem of the profound instability of all modern political bodies, which is the result of an elementary lack of authority. One way to solve the problem of authority, she argues, was to make the nation absolute. The legitimacy of power and the legality of the laws would reside in the will of the nation: the general will of the nation that would reflect the innate, natural goodness of each individual heart and will.

Because Augustine has already demonstrated that a divided will is impotent, unanimity is mandatory for the concept of a powerful general will. Thus, Arendt contends, the notion of the general will *must* be based upon unanimous consent: unanimity of opinion rather than a plurality of opinions. In other words, the unanimity of the general will, whose absolute sovereignty guarantees the stability of the political realm, depends upon the individual wills giving up their particular interests and consenting to be ruled by a government whose power has become sovereign *precisely because* individuals have given up their individual power.

Significantly, Foucault's analysis of the modern state echoes Arendt's. Like Arendt, Foucault also points out that this notion of an unanimous general will, ruling over an undivided social body, characterizes the modern form of the political (P/K 97–98). For both Arendt and Foucault, the existence of an absolute sovereign, in whom the identical origin of law and power is embodied, makes the law powerful and power legitimate. This does not change when the absolute sovereign is the general will of the people.

Arendt claims that the act of consent combines the principle of absolute rulership and national principles, "according to which there must be one representative of the nation as a whole, and where the government is understood to incorporate the will of all nationals."[7] Here we begin to see the emerging form of the nation-state. Indeed, Arendt claims that the modern understanding of the self as a subject who is the bearer of inalienable rights is inseparable from and informs the notion of the sovereign nation-state that gets its power from the sovereign general will of the people. In this schema, power is always associated with sovereignty and unity: the unanimity of the general will that is embodied in the figure of the ruler. Napoleon is the exemplary figure: "I am the *pouvoir constituant*" (OR 163).

Arendt suggests that the problem with this schema is twofold. First, rights are indistinguishable from the sovereignty of the general will of the nation-state. This schema does not allow for the rights of those who are not recognized as part of the general will. This leads to the second problem: at the level of the individual, one must be a national to have rights. Indeed, Arendt's critique of the modern understanding of 'inalienable rights' is founded upon this recognition that these 'inalienable rights' were from the beginning tied up with national sovereignty. And, she submits, no groups saw this more clearly than those who had lost the protection of the sovereign: "The Rights of Man, supposedly inalienable, proved to be unenforceable—even in countries whose constitutions were based upon them—whenever people appeared who were no longer citizens of any sovereign state."[8] Just as a different understanding of law, freed from the figure of the sovereign, might allow for a rethinking of the relation of law and power, so too, rather than simply dismissing altogether the notion of rights as a fiction tied to a sovereign subject, Arendt's analysis suggests that it might be possible to rethink the notion of rights from out of an understanding of power that is not tied to the notion of sovereignty.

Arendt's rejection of sovereign power has its basis in her rejection of the philosophical understanding of freedom that from Augustine onward has understood freedom as located in a subjective will. Her understanding of freedom is political, located *not* in the "I will," but in the "I am able." Thus, from the outset, Arendt's understanding of freedom is inseparable from power. In addition, the "I am able" must be understood as the ability to act in a public space, to move in a space of freedom with others. (Here Arendt is in agreement with the later Foucault who maintained that, when speaking of power and freedom, one must use the spatial metaphor.)

Moreover, Arendt agrees with Foucault that power is multiple. Power must always be said in the plural. For power to exist, there must be other centers of power. "Power comes into being only if and when men join themselves together for the purpose of action, and it will disappear when, for whatever reason, they disperse and desert one another" (OR 175). Domination, on the other hand, is the loss of power that occurs only where there is a central ruling power. Thus, the notion of sovereignty can denote strength, but it can never denote power. The principle of federalism illuminates this point. The establishment of the Union as Madison and Jefferson understood it did not take away from the power of the states, rather it provided a new source of power. Indeed, she contends, if the individual states had not existed, the Union would have had to erect them to have the power it did. This again suggests that power is generated by power and that to be powerful one must be in relation to other powers. Here we see Arendt's rejection of Rousseau's identification of sovereignty with power. Arendt argues, then, that action demands a plurality of actors and, further, that power must be understood as the only "human attribute which applies solely to the worldly in-between space by which actors are mutually related" (OR 175).

Power, therefore, denotes not only the ability to act, but action in concert with others.[9] Thus, Arendt insists that "the power structure itself precedes and outlasts all aims, so that power, far from being the means to an end, is actually the very condition enabling a group of people to think and act in the means-ends category" (OV 51). This is why Arendt argues that full blown terror, resulting in the complete atomization of the political, is the presence of an absolute violence without the presence of power. Power, present only when people act in concert, has completely disappeared. Montesquieu had already identified this problem: terror is ultimately impotent and self-destructive because it fears any and all organization and opposition, even turning against those in its own forces who might organize.[10] Arendt, going further, suggests that the difference between totalitarianism and tyranny is that the former turns against even the power of its friends (OV 55).

What then of the relation between power and the law? Or more precisely, how can we think the legitimate power of the law? I submit that Arendt's understanding of a noncentralized, nonsovereign understanding of power that is synonymous with *public* freedom and action allows for rethinking the legitimate power of the law. First, Arendt argues that the modern understanding of law, its roots in Hobbes, is contractual. She agrees with Foucault that this understanding of law as contract still views the law as dominating or coercive. Furthermore, law understood as contract is inseparable from an understanding of power as sovereign.

> [The law understood as contract is] a fictitious aboriginal act on the side of each member, by virtue of which he gives up his isolated strength and power to constitute a government; far from gaining a new power, and possibly more than he had before, he resigns his power such as it is, and far from binding himself with promises, he gives his 'consent' to be ruled by the government, whose power consists of the sum total of forces which all individual persons have channelled into it and which are monopolized by the government for the alleged benefit of all subjects. (OR 170)

Arendt argues, however, that the contract is not the exclusive foundation for the law. Counter to the contract, the law can be founded on the mutual compact. She points to compacts such as the Mayflower Compact that were made prior to the Revolution and that contained no reference to king or prince. The principle of the compact (or covenant) is the claim to power without the further claim to sovereignty. The principle was "neither expansion nor conquest but the further combination of powers" (OR 168). The compact, Arendt argues, understands the political bond in the old Roman sense of alliance that "gathers together the isolated strength of the allied partners and binds them into a new power structure by virtue of 'free and sincere promises'" (OR 170). This is very different from the contract wherein "an individual person resigns his power to some higher authority and *consents* to be ruled in exchange for a reasonable protection of his life and property" (OR 169, emphasis mine). The difference between an act of covenant and an act of consent is that the first is based on an increase of power through the recognition of otherness inspired by the principle of plurality, whereas the second is based on giving up power in the recognition of sovereignty inspired by the principle of unanimity.

The notion of law that emerges out of the mutual covenant is one that understands the law as neither sovereign nor dominating, neither commandment nor imposed standard. Rather, following Montesquieu's insight, Arendt suggests that the law must be understood as the regulator of these different domains of power. Here there is a way to think multiplicity of power with rule. Arendt again looks to Montesquieu for whom the law, "never lost its original 'spatial significance' altogether, namely, 'the notion of a range or province within which defined power may be legitimately exercised'" (OR 186–187). Because the laws are no more than the relations that exist and preserve different realms of power and are therefore relative by definition, Arendt argues that Montesquieu "needed no absolute source of authority and could describe the 'spirit of the laws' without ever posing the troublesome question of their absolute validity" (OR 189).

Thus the work of the law is not to unite, but to divide. Indeed, it is only through the work of division, and not at all through unanimity, that the political space is constituted. As Claude Lefort asserts, seemingly following Arendt's understanding of power and law, power cannot be "divorced from the work of division by which society is instituted; a society can therefore relate to itself only through the experience of an internal division which proves to be not a de facto division, but a division which generates its constitution."[11] Although Arendt would agree with Lefort, she also would stress that the internal divisions of power are regulated by a principle that necessarily stands "outside" the positive political space. It is significant that Arendt insists on the double sense of constitution as both noun and verb. In the constitution of power, the cuts of power (positive, civil laws) always need to be augmented and amended. Thus, she offers a way to think multiplicity and difference as essential to the constitution of order. Or more precisely, the order is constituted only through multiplicity and difference.

I suggest that Foucault's continuous reflection on the "outside" (and nowhere is this more evidenced than in his essay on Blanchot) also attempts to think the constitutive power of the political. He seems also to be in agreement with Arendt's demand that the constitutive power of the political remains outside the positive divisions of power as they are actually at work in various social practices and divisions.

Moreover, this demand to think the "outside" of power is precisely why Arendt insists on the distinction between the social and the political. She understands that the internal divisions that constitute the practices of the social must be regulated by something "outside" these practices. In other words, these social divisions and practices necessarily refer to constitutive political principles (principles of law and power) that not only give them sense *[mise en sens]*, but also allow for the very staging *[mise en scene]* of these practices and divisions.[12] It is precisely because social practices and divisions always already refer to this constitutive "outside" that it is impossible to localize the political within the social.

The Principle of Publicness

Arendt, however, does not relinquish the problem of the problem of legitimate political power. In other words, she does not relinquish the problem of legitimate principles of law. To resolve this problem, Arendt turns back to the discussion of power. More precisely, she suggests that the principle that ought to govern power, and the positive laws that regulate divisions of power, must be located within power itself. Here Arendt draws on the double meaning of the Greek word *arche* meaning both "to begin" and "principle." The principle of action, she argues, lies at its beginning, and it is this principle that provides the inspiration for action-power. Now, if it is the case that power is synonymous with action and freedom, and if all three terms denote the appearance of an actor among a plurality of actors in a space of freedom, then the principle that inspires power and that gives it its legitimacy must be found within power itself. In other words, the principle of legitimate power is the principle of publicness. "Because of its inherent tendency to disclose the agent together with the act, action needs for its full appearance the shining brightness we once called glory, and which is possible only in the public realm."[13] Because *action* and *power* are synonymous terms for Arendt, we can substitute *power* for *action* in the preceding passage. Arendt's analysis, therefore, suggests that legitimate power is precisely the power that allows the actor to appear in a public space with others. And this principle provides for a new understanding of the law as neither sovereign nor coercive, but instead as that which constitutes power-freedom. This principle of publicness is the principle of justice that constitutes the space of the political: it demands that the divisions or cuts of power be such that all actors are able to appear and to act. In other words, the principle of publicness demands that all positive, civil laws constitute and regulate the cuts of power in such a way that all actors are empowered. This principle of publicness answers Foucault's call for a new form of power and right that is antidisciplinarian and liberated from the principle of sovereignty.

Certainly the event of totalitarianism contributed to Arendt's rethinking of legitimate power in terms of the principle of publicness. Indeed, a distinction not often noted by Arendt's readers, but one just as important for her political philosophy as the more often debated distinction between the political and the social, is precisely the distinction between the public and the secret.[14] I would go further and suggest that this distinction between the public and the secret is prior to and informs Arendt's distinction between the political and the social. The priority of the distinction between the public and the secret is clearly seen in Arendt's analysis of Robespierre and the terror of sentimentality. The terror is located in a shift of places. The enemy of the nation no longer resides abroad, but is located within: the common enemy resides in everyone's heart. Any and all means must, thus, be used to root out any hypocrisy that this "public" space might carry within itself. I submit, therefore, that when Arendt argues that the lesson to be learned from the terror of Robespierre is the need for the distinction between the political and the social, she is really arguing for the more fundamental distinction between the public and the secret. Her analysis reveals that the terror emerges when the space of the political is no longer regulated by a principle of publicness. Her subsequent distinction between the political and the social emerges from the insight that if the political is founded upon needs, which by definition are private, it always runs the risk of negating the principle of publicness; it thereby runs the risk of replacing the political with the private, or, more precisely, of replacing the public with the secret.

This becomes even clearer in Arendt's analysis of totalitarianism, a regime characterized by the substitution of the secret for the public. Totalitarian power is located completely in the realm of the secret wherein, "the only rule of which everybody in a totalitarian state may be sure is that the more visible government agencies are, the less power they carry, and the less that is known of the existence of an institution, the more powerful it will ultimately turn out to be" (OT 403). What Arendt discovers in her analysis of totalitarianism is precisely the fundamental political distinction between power (which is always public) and violence (which in one way or another is always secret and conspiratorial). Thus Arendt points out: "The Moscow-directed Communist parties, in marked contrast to their predecessors, show a curious tendency to prefer the conditions of conspiracy even where complete legality is possible. The more conspicuous the power of totalitarianism the more secret become its true goals" (OT 414).

Although it is beyond the task of this chapter, Arendt's later reflections on labor, work, and action need to be thought from out of these earlier insights on the secret workings of totalitarianism. She clearly saw in her analysis of totalitarianism that it was precisely the powerlessness of isolated men and women (and she argues that nothing is more isolating than the laboring activity because it is activity without speech and therefore without publicness) that was the pretotalitarian moment. Arendt suggests that this isolation signaled the destruction of the public space, which, in turn, allowed for the rise of totalitarianism and its terrifying secret violence.

The principle of publicness also allows for a rethinking of a notion of rights that does not have its basis in an understanding of human nature as a sovereign subject endowed with inalienable rights. Arendt is able to reject the fiction of human nature and still think the inalienable right of the actor who in order to act must be able to appear in a public space of freedom. Though stripped of a State or stripped of a home, this funda- mental right to be able to appear cannot be stripped from the actor be- cause the first act, the act of beginning itself—the event of natality—contains both the beginning and its principle within itself. The event of natality carries within it the principle of publicness, which re- stated as the law of humanity, in which humanity is understood as the plurality of actors in a public space of freedom, demands that the actor has the right to appear. Or, as Arendt so succinctly states, the law of humanity demands that the actor has the right to have rights. Again, this is a right not predicated on an ontological notion of human nature, but rather, on the nature of power itself. The nature of power itself, under- stood as the "I am able" that is inseparable from the ability to appear in a public space of freedom with a plurality of other actors, provides the basis for 'originary rights' founded on the originary right to have rights.

This is precisely the law of humanity articulated by Kant in his essay "Perpetual Peace," and quoted so approvingly by Arendt in her Kant lectures: "Humans have it by virtue of their common possession of the earth, whereas on a globe, they cannot infinitely disperse and hence must finally tolerate the presence of each other. [For] the common right to the face of the earth . . . belongs to human beings generally.[15]

Thus, I would argue that Arendt and, implicitly, the later Foucault, who also understands power in terms of action and freedom, by providing a principle of law that regulates different spheres of power, have been able to provide a way to distinguish between legitimate and illegitimate shapes of power. Although law necessarily emerges from a different source than power, its source being the Constitution that constitutes power by staging the work of division that allows spheres of power to appear, nevertheless power and the law are inspired by the same imperative of action: the principle of publicness that demands that each actor by virtue of the event of natality itself has the right to appear, that is, the right to temporary sojourn.

3

Self-Overcoming in Foucault's *Discipline and Punish*

LADELLE McWHORTER

Prisons are veritable universities of crime. Within them young offenders learn both the values and the techniques of hardened criminals. In addition to these lessons in professional ethics and theory, aspiring criminals also get hands-on experience within prison walls, for prisons are also centers of criminal activity: drug and arms trafficking, rape, gang warfare, and murder. And, like all good universities, prisons help their proteges make the contacts they need to further their budding careers.

Few will disagree that our prison system, along with its subsidiary mechanisms, produces the conditions under which delinquency can spread and flourish. But Michel Foucault's assertion in *Discipline and Punish* is far stronger than that. Foucault is not just reiterating the familiar claim that prisons produce a medium for the development of delinquency, rather, he is claiming that our disciplinary society actually produces the delinquent self in its very being.

> It is said that the prison fabricated delinquents; it is true that it brings back, almost inevitably, before the courts those who have been sent there. But it also fabricates them in the sense that it has introduced into the operation of the law and the offence, the judge and the offender, the condemned man and the executioner, the non-corporeal reality of the delinquency that links them together and, for a century and a half, has caught them in the same trap.[1]

Delinquency itself—as a functional locus within a discourse but also as a possible form of selfhood, as a way of being, as a way of being known and of knowing oneself—arose simultaneously with and is sustained and perpetuated by what Foucault calls the *carceral system*. Delinquency and the prison system are the twin offspring of the same series of events, the same movement of power.

Foucault offers two sorts of evidence for his assertion that the very being of the delinquent is a product of a certain series of events within a network of power. First, he notes the lack of the figure of the delinquent prior to the dramatic rise in the use of incarceration as a form of punishment in Western Europe. Before the advent of prison systems with their internal hierarchies and structures of correction and their attendant psychiatric and medical knowledges and practices, legal proceedings and techniques of punishment focused primarily on an act or series of acts. Criminality was merely a matter of action, not a state of being, and punishment was its counteraction. But as a carceral system develops, we find that the central focus of judicial administration is not action, but rather self, the true being of the one who acts offensively. Actions are considered only insofar as they function to initiate contact between the delinquent and the correctional system and insofar as they are understood to be the true expression of an underlying reality. Delinquency functions as the name of that reality.

In addition to delinquency's absence prior to the widespread use of imprisonment to punish offenders, Foucault offers another piece of evidence to support his notion that delinquency is produced within a certain configuration of power relations. He points out how very useful delinquency is and, as a result, how very invested in its existence certain mechanisms of power are.

Delinquency is indirectly useful because it represents such an improvement over popular, sporadic unlawfulness. The existence of a class of people who claim illegality as their own prerogative necessarily limits the unlawful activity of the general population. Once delinquency was defined and reified, a sorting process could occur. Delinquents, unlike sporadically rowdy citizens, could be identified, watched, and managed.

Delinquency also has its direct uses. Occasionally delinquents have been used as a population and labor force to colonize conquered territories. More often, they have been used as a sort of covert labor force at home, available for employment by legitimate private businesses or various state agencies to work on the fringes of legality—as smugglers, prostitutes, odds-makers, informants, and spies. A prominent example from recent history of the direct use of delinquency by a legitimate agency is the C.I.A.'s employment of General Manuel Noriega and his underlings in Central America. But we need not look to the sensational case for corroboration of Foucault's claim. We need only consider how often prostitutes are used in the negotiation of business deals or petty thugs are employed by collection agencies. Delinquents perform valued services that result in power and profits for people whose own reputations are clean.

Delinquents are not only legally marginal laborers; they are also auxiliary police. Crime normalizes. Crime in the ghettos keeps racial and ethnic minorities frightened and disorganized; thus they cannot effectively challenge the oppression perpetrated against them by dominant social groups. The existence of thugs and thieves who confine themselves primarily to ethnic and working class neighborhoods helps to determine property values and thereby ensures continued segregation by race and class. Rapists help keep women in our "place" by literally curtailing our activities and by making us feel dependent upon the protection of men.[2]

But beyond their use as terrorists, hitmen, spies, or informants, delinquents perform another service. They serve as objects of knowledge. Foucault writes, "in fabricating delinquency, it [disciplinary power] gave to criminal justice a unitary field of objects, authenticated by the 'sciences,' and thus enabled it to function on a general horizon of 'truth'" (DP 256). In other words, certain knowledges themselves, namely the human sciences, have a direct interest in the fabrication and continued existence of their object of study, the delinquent individual.

Delinquents are so very useful, it would seem, that if they did not already exist, society would have had to invent them. Indeed, that is just Foucault's point. Foucault's target for destabilization in *Discipline and Punish,* however, it not just our carceral system. The trap is set for much bigger prey.

Enter the will to truth. If Foucault is right, we may say in outrage, then a terrible thing has occurred: people have been victimized by disciplinary powers that have created false identities for them. Whatever their "real" truth, young men and women have been prodded, pressed, and brainwashed into behaving like criminals and even into believing that criminality formed the core of their very souls. Delinquency does not exist, but for a century and a half we have all been made to believe that it does and to act accordingly, with disastrous results. Something must be done.

Let us consider this outrage and the assumptions that underlie and drive it. The first important assumption is that fundamentally humanity occurs as individuals, each with his or her own true core identity that is untouched by power except a posteriori and negatively. The second important assumption, which is interrelated with the first, is that power is antithetical to truth; this leads to the conclusion that we must be suspicious of any claim to truth if it is clear that the claim is in the interest of some power.

As bearers of a classical liberal legacy, we are predisposed to assume that whatever is traversed by power is also corrupted by it. Power, we tend to believe, distorts truth. If an event, a thing, or a way of being human cannot be separated from functions of power, then we feel fairly certain that we are not in possession of truth with regard to that event, thing, or person. Therefore, if we become persuaded that delinquency is thoroughly permeated by power, we tend to lose faith in its reality. While reading *Discipline and Punish,* then, we may begin to suspect that the truth of the individuals treated as delinquents has been lost completely beneath a truthless discursive overlay. Delinquents are not *really* delinquents, rather they are victims of oppression.

That view, however, is not likely to appeal to those of us who have known delinquents, attended school with them, worked with them, or have had blood ties with them. At times, some may seem to be victims of a system that casts them into a role in violation of their own natures. But more frequently, delinquents do not seem like victims except perhaps in some very abstract, theoretical sense; they seem, instead, like people who choose to live as they do *just as nondelinquents choose to live as they do.*

And that, given our tendency to see power as a violation of truth, should come as a fairly disturbing thought. For it implies this: either we are all victims of oppressive forces and our truth is hidden from us perhaps irrevocably, or delinquents are real beings, true beings fabricated by power.

The text pursues the latter possibility. The very being of the delinquent is a matter of production, it asserts. Furthermore, delinquency is not the only form of selfhood that may be analyzed as a production of disciplinary regimes. There is also the soldier, the factory worker, the schoolchild, and, the text insinuates, the family member. These beings, these persons, also are produced through disciplinary mechanisms. These ways of being selves are also invested and contoured by networks of power. Delinquency is far from a singular occurrence. In fact, Foucault asserts, "[t]his book is intended as a correlative history of the modern soul . . ." (DP 23). Not just delinquents, but everyone is placed in question here. *Discipline and Punish* is not a discourse about what is external to its readers and author; it is a discourse whose movement encompasses and places in question every one of us.

The first prospect was unsettling enough: that perhaps we are all so traversed—in even the most ordinary, most intimate or characteristic expressions of ourselves—by normalizing disciplinary power that we are all ignorant of our own truth, that all our efforts to know ourselves are illusory failures. But the second prospect, that the "truth" of the individual may in fact just *be* configurations of power, is far more unsettling. For how is the will to truth to appropriate and conform itself to the "truth" that there is no stable, unitary truth of the individual human soul apart from historical, productive power? We would, perhaps, rather place our hope on the first prospect and assume that we just do not have the real truth about ourselves. As Foucault's text unfolds, however, the second prospect takes on greater and greater plausibility. We are forced, by the power of our own desire for truth, to open our thinking to the possibility that the human individual may itself be a historical event, a product of power relations. We will follow this thought's unfolding through the rest of this chapter.

First of all, we willing self-knowers might ask, how could a disciplinary regime create individuality? Foucault offers a careful and convincing analysis. He suggests three mutually reinforcing modes of production of individuality: hierarchical observation, normalizing judgment, and the technique of the examination.

First we see a shift in architecture. Buildings are to function as machines in which observation may take place, for observation in itself becomes a means of control. Hospitals become machines for controlling contagion, and thus the conduct of those infected. Factories become machines for controlling production by controlling the laborers within them. Schools become machines for controlling the development of children. The form of power that invests these architectural apparatuses is not modeled after the top to bottom power of a sovereign king; power comes to function within these institutions automatically, anonymously, and continuously. "Discipline makes possible the operation of a relational power that sustains itself by its own mechanisms and which, for the spectacle of public events, substitutes the uninterrupted play of calculated gazes" (DP 177). A network of power is formed in which a certain set of spaces are marked out, across which human beings are distributed. One is identified by the space one occupies, and one is kept in that space and brought into conformity with that identity through the subtly physical, though noncorporeal, method of constant ordered observation.

Observation is closely related to normalization. Observation of persons makes possible a ranking system in which persons are compared to one another and to a set of standards. Deviation from the standards or failure to progress upward through the established ranks in the allotted time is grounds for punishment. Once such a system is in place and functioning, however, the sort of punishment it offers is simply its own reassertion. The schoolboy who fails to remember his catechism is punished by being lowered in class rank. The norm or standard that the child must attain spreads itself out both spatially and temporally in terms of gradations, expectations for progress, and physical location so that the child who fails does not violate the normalizing system or escape it, but merely remains within it, demoted, marked by its judgment. The disciplinary technique of normalization not only defines the good, the right, or the proper, but also the bad, the wrong, and the improper all on a long continuum of gradation from which there is no escape. There is no outside to normalizing networks, and there is no gap in them, only a gapless series of ranks. Within such a network every stage of development, every possible state of being, can be identified.

Finally, "the examination combines the techniques of an observing hierarchy and those of a normalizing judgment" (DP 184). Examination is the technique of differentiation; it is the mechanism for distribution of persons across a graded and gapless continuum. "In this space of domination, disciplinary power manifests its potency, essentially, by arranging objects. The examination is, as it were, the ceremony of this objectification" (DP 187). Most significant, it is the examination that first inserts the patient, the schoolchild, the soldier, or the prisoner into a system of writing. Records must be kept of the course of disease, of the progress of training, or of rehabilitation.

> Thanks to the whole apparatus of writing that accompanies it, the examination opened up two correlative possibilities: firstly, the constitution of the individual as a describable, analyzable object, not in order to reduce him to "specific" features, as did the naturalists in relation to living things, but in order to maintain him in his individual features, in his particular evolution, in his own aptitudes or abilities, under the gaze of a permanent corpus of knowledge; and, secondly, the constitution of a comparative system that made possible the measurement of overall phenomena, the description of groups, the characterization of collective facts, the calculation of the gaps between individuals, their distribution in a given "population." (DP 190)

Thus each human being, thoroughly individualized and maintained in his or her individuality, becomes a "case." He or she is both an object of knowledge and an identifiable, locatable target for power. The individual "may be described, judged, measured, compared with others" (DP 191). And, at the same time, the individual may "be trained or corrected, classified, normalized, excluded, etc." (DP 191).

Prior to the establishment of disciplinary power, only heroes—kings, generals, or saints—were marked out as individuals whose lives might be documented and who might feel themselves to be unique. Within disciplinary regimes, however, individuality is created and enforced for all persons. Self-identity is produced and persons are fixed by it, unable to transgress it. Within disciplinary systems, each person is observed, examined, judged, and documented in his or her precise degree of deviation from the norm. Thus individuality just is deviance. To be an individual just is to occupy a particular place with regard to a set of norms and to own a history of such particular occupations in a documented order. As such, individuality can exist only within a network of power relations wherein norms and hierarchies are strictly maintained. The modern individual is a creation of disciplinary techniques.

This point cannot be overstressed because our inclination will be to disregard its significance. Our own will to truth, the will that informs us in our very being, will insist upon its own object, its raison d'être: a true self-identical core of being analytically separable from and logically prior to power. Taking Foucault seriously, then, when he suggests that such an a priori self-identical core does not exist, will threaten that will's very existence.

Insofar as we *are* that will to truth, if we find ourselves thinking within the plausibility of Foucault's account of individuality, we will attempt to think the historicity of individuality as the "truth" of the individual. That move will probably occur as follows. First, we will assume that individuals exist self-identically through time. Then we will assume that the ahistorical truth of ourselves as individuals is that we were fabricated within power mechanisms and are sustained by them. We will discipline ourselves to that truth, attempt to force ourselves to identify with that truth, to become that truth, to "own" it. The *real* truth of individual selfhood, we will say, is that it cannot be understood separately from power. We will, however, maintain the reality of that truth apart from power and thus we will fail to place in question truth itself, the notion that there are stable identities that can be known apart from any context of valuation, of power.

Such a move, however, will only end in frustration because within Foucault's discourse it will not bring us to stable ground. Once we realize that the movement toward self-identical individuality is itself the move of a disciplinary regime, we must also realize that to insist that the true identity of individuality is its historicity and its location within a power regime is simply to replicate that disciplinary power. *Any* insistence on a stable identity for a human self, whether that stable identity is the identity of the delinquent or the identity of a power-traversed historical subjectivity, is a move undertaken from within disciplinary power and not in violation of it. In other words, this new claim to truth—that the individual is a creation of power—is not innocent of power. On its own terms, it is a self-violating claim.

Thus the text disrupts our move to reinstate the notion of a truth dissociated from power and refuses to allow us to leave unquestioned the notion that power and truth are mutually repulsive. Perhaps, Foucault writes,

> we should abandon a whole tradition that allows us to imagine that knowledge can exist only where the power relations are suspended and that knowledge can develop only outside its injunctions, its demands

and its interests. Perhaps we should abandon the belief that power makes mad and that, by the same token, the renunciation of power is one of the conditions of knowledge. We should admit rather that power produces knowledge (and not simply by encouraging it because it is useful); that power and knowledge directly imply one another; that there is no power relation without the correlative constitution of a field of knowledge, nor any knowledge that does not presuppose and constitute at the same time power relations. (DP 27)

We are not, so this text tells us, going to find a truth of our selves that is free of networks of power. Even the truth that we are not going to find a truth of our selves that is free of networks of power is not free of these networks.

We must cease once and for all to describe the effects of power in negative terms: it 'excludes,' it 'represses,' it 'censors,' it 'abstracts,' it 'masks,' it 'conceals.' In fact, power produces; it produces reality; it produces domains of objects and rituals of truth. The individual and the knowledge that may be gained of him belong to this production. (DP 194)

For centuries we Westerners believed that we must come to know ourselves in our ownmost truth. Only thus can we be saved; only thus can we be mentally healthy; only thus can we battle the powers of oppression that surround us in the gathering darkness. Foucault's discourse places in question our belief that there is a true self, apart from historical power networks, that we can come to know. But worse, his discourse places in question our *drive* to know. Our will to truth, to the truth of ourselves, maintains itself by asserting that there is a truth toward which it strives. In the absence of such a truth, the will to truth—which to a great extent *is* what we are—cannot remain in being.

Within the unfolding of Foucault's discourse, as we have said, the will to truth will attempt to maintain itself by asserting that the truth of self is power. But that assertion cannot maintain its own stability, for what it amounts to is an assertion that the pure core of self-identity simply is impurely self-identical, precisely because it is an a posteriori construction of power.

Furthermore, the drive to identify has already been exposed as a disciplinary drive, not a Galahadesque search for pure self undertaken in purity. To remain what it is, however, to maintain itself in its own identity, the drive to know, the will to truth cannot own itself as power; it cannot own its own creativity, nor can it own its own interestedness. If the "truth" of the will to truth is its affinity with what it has named untruth, then it is disrupted in its movement, since it is forced, compelled by its own energy, to accept as truth that it has no truth.

This, of course, is a paradox. It amounts to perpetual violation, disruption, and frustration of the drive to know. Foucault's discourse is the labyrinth in which the will to truth is led to turn against itself. It is a movement that folds back upon what moves it. It is the energy of our will to know folding back over upon itself—again and again and again. The text's movement *is* the will to truth turning against, over, and through itself. The text *is* fundamentally self-violating and self-overcoming, not just because it destabilizes the notion of self, but, more important, because it places in question the very power of the text itself. It is the text qua text that is undergoing destabilization within the text.

The thesis of this chapter is that self-overcoming is not simply to be looked for, to be located and analyzed, within Foucault's texts, but rather that Foucault's texts may be read *as* self-overcomings, as pure motion, as overcoming-occurring. Foucault's discourse runs counter to power and instigates the overcoming of certain structures of power, for example, the ascetic self; but Foucault's discourse also is power, and its truth is contingent upon and supportive of that power. Thus it is a discourse that bares its neck before its own analytic knife; it is a discourse that embraces its own mortality. In its agitative action it dissolves itself. It is a discourse that, in proper—that is, in perverse—Nietzschean fashion, ends by biting its own tail—simultaneously, of course, swallowing in advance any commentary that would claim to have offered a true account of the self-overcoming movement it manifests.

4

Resisting Subjects:
Habermas On the Subject of Foucault

STUART BARNETT

The work of Michel Foucault will no doubt continue to provoke resistance. Even where his methods are embraced, one must question whether the name of Foucault is merely serving to further precisely the discourses his studies put into question. This resistance, which is at the heart of apparent acceptance, is founded in the notion of the subject. For there remains in the reception of Foucault a commitment to a certain notion of subjectivity that is informed to a great extent by neo-Marxism's emphasis on the role of consciousness in political change. Thus the work of Foucault, which in fact presents a rigorous critique of the very idea of subjectivity, has been made to affirm that which it sought to challenge.

One of the most decisive instances of such a misreading of Foucault is one that would bring him into accord with a Habermasian notion of politicized self-representation. Such a reading perceives Foucault as offering an indication of how complex political repression can be and of how it can exert itself it in a variety of domains. Studies such as *Madness and Civilization* and *Discipline and Punish* would, accordingly, be understood as dissections of the elaborate ways in which scientific disciplines and political regimes can *deny* the ability of social classes and groups to represent themselves. Bentham's Panopticon, as discussed in *Discipline and Punish,* would be the paradigmatic example of the gaze of power that surveys and regulates any attempt at self-representation. As such, Foucault fits in neatly with a historical scheme that posits that self-representation was part of a political struggle in which we are still participating. Yet in all such Habermasian readings, the concepts of power, subjectivity, repression, and resistance do not undergo the displacement that Foucault's work has made possible and necessary. To meet the

43

challenge still presented by Foucault's work, it is necessary to examine what continues to condition the reception of Foucault.

*   *   *

Although the reception of Foucault remains informed by the Habermasian ideal of politicized self-representation, the simple notion of a social class overcoming political repression through self-representation does not do justice to the thought of Habermas. This interpretation of Habermas was instigated by such early works as *The Structural Transformation of the Public Sphere*. This work in particular had a wide-ranging impact, especially in German-speaking countries, upon cultural and literary theory. This is understandable, for it is here that Habermas discusses in detail specific cultural movements and literary genres, offering even a discussion of *Wilhelm Meister*. Yet, because of the greater commitment to sociological analysis, *The Structural Transformation of the Public Sphere* allows itself to be misread in a way that is antithetical to the larger philosophical intentions of the Habermasian project. Indeed, one might readily conclude from such a work that, although Foucault dismisses the concept of the subject, Habermas merely places the same concept in a historical scenario that asserts the political significance of a social class's efforts to establish a sphere of self-representation. This was clearly the effect of this book upon literary criticism in western Germany. There are already indications that its recent translation into English will further the effort to sanitize Foucault of antihumanism.

Such a reading does make Habermas's work more compatible with a Marxist tradition defined by the Lukácsian emphasis on the role of class consciousness in historical change. The status of the subject, however, undergoes a more thorough interrogation than this assumption would suggest. Habermas's criticism of Foucault is based on the claim that Foucault argues for a conception of the subject that is too strong. According to Habermas, Foucault is bound up in the aporias of philosophical modernity, which are, in turn, caused by the insistence that epistemology be founded upon the self-certainty of the subject. "As long as the basic concepts of the philosophy of consciousness lead us to understand knowledge exclusively as knowledge of something in the objective world, rationality is assessed by how the isolated subject orients himself to representational and propositional contents."[1] Habermas's intention is to bring to an end the subject-centered nature of philosophical modernity. As suggested here, this will require a reassessment of the subject's relation to objective reality. To attain this end, Habermas sets forth his theory of communicative action.

Habermas's aim is to weaken both the status of the subject and the self-representations a subject may make of itself. To accomplish this and to avoid the danger of relativism, Habermas must ground the subject in something that both weakens and secures its status. He finds this ground in the realm of objectivity. Objectivity describes the realm of empirical sensations and the objects that cause them. Habermas stresses in "A Postscript to *Knowledge and Human Interests*" that "[t]hings and happenings (persons and their utterances) are 'something in the world' that we *experience* or *handle;* they are objects of possible (action-related) experience or (experientially based) actions."[2] These objects exist in a real empirical sense independent of any subjective experience of them. Yet any subjective experience of these objects is grounded in the certitude of their existence. Subjective experience of these objects is, in a certain sense, undeniable. Habermas underscores that "[p]erceptions cannot be false."[3] Yet this subjective certainty is quite distinct from truth. Indeed, whether universal validity can be ascribed to these experiences is an entirely different matter.

Objectivity, then, is not to be confused with truth. Habermas stipulates an important precondition that objectivity must fulfill to be considered a possible candidate for a truth claim: "the objectivity of experience consists precisely in its being intersubjectively shared."[4] The true objectivity of perceptions resides in whether they can be expressed as claims or assertions in propositional form. The truth of these propositions, in turn, is dependent upon a possible consensus as to their usefulness and validity. Truth, therefore, is a matter of consensus about the assertions made in reference to objective experiences. "[T]he truth of propositions is not corroborated by processes happening in the world but by a consensus achieved through argumentative reasoning."[5] Habermas develops this notion further in *The Theory of Communicative Action,* where he argues that a "judgment can be objective if it is undertaken on the basis of a *transsubjective* validity claim that has the same meaning for observers and nonparticipants as it has for the acting subject himself."[6] Truth is the result of a consensus reached by subjects capable of verifying and responding to the general practicality and validity of assertions.

The concern over objectivity and truth is not peripheral to Habermas's philosophy. In fact, this distinction motivates his consensus theory of truth. Habermas plainly points out in the "Postscript" that it "was precisely in order to separate more clearly the problem of meaning constitution from that of validity, that I tried to evolve a consensus-theory of truth and to defend that theory against competing approaches."[7] Both the notions of an ideal speech situation and of rational consensus are based on this crucial distinction. The strict demarcation of objectivity from truth serves, first of all, to ensure that empirical reality is granted an inviolate autonomy. Accordingly, theories or languages cannot impinge upon reality. These media do not change reality; they only interpret it.

Habermas maintains that the "truth of a proposition can only be tested and grounded or discarded in the framework of a discourse or, more precisely, a theoretical discourse. However, the truth of a theory in no way determines the objectivity of its experiential content."[8] Thus the status of both objective reality and the experience of it are made secure. At the same time, truth is made a matter of intersubjective consensus. Truth is thereby granted a status independent of objective certitude.

In an aside directed against the movement of postempiricism that has grown out of Positivism, Habermas reveals what is no doubt the most important implication of the notion of objectivity.

> The theory languages, which undergo a discontinuous development in the course of scientific progress, can *interpret* the structures of an object domain not yet penetrated by science. They can also to some extent reformulate them. But as long as we are not angels or animals, these languages cannot *transform* the structures themselves into conditions of *another* object domain. It is always the experience of identical objects of *our* world which is being interpreted differently according to the state of scientific progress we happen to have reached.[9]

The claim of the unity of objectivity provides consensus with a stable foundation upon which to base itself. Without this foundation, consensus would never be anything but a particular, localized consensus. Because reality does not fundamentally change, our experience of it is characterized by a unity that allows itself to be axiomatized in rational discourse. The unity of experience offers an ideal speech situation the possibility of reconciling all subjects to a course of action motivated by universal interests.[10]

Objectivity grounds the status of the subject by situating it in a fixed empirical reality. All perceptions and truth claims are in some way related to this empirical reality. This reality gives propositions something to be about in a final sense. Habermas emphasizes the importance objectivity has in *The Theory of Communicative Action:*

> Only against the background of an objective world, and measured against criticizable claims to truth and efficacy, can beliefs appear as systematically false, action intentions as systematically hopeless, and thoughts as fantasies, as mere imaginings. Only against the background of a normative reality that has become autonomous, and measured against the criticizable claim to normative rightness, can intentions, wishes, attitudes, feelings appear as illegitimate or merely idiosyncratic, as nongeneralizable and merely subjective.[11]

Subjective experience is validated inasmuch as it is adequate to this objective reality. Disagreement about objective reality must be attributed to differences in individual subjective experiences. Logically, therefore, it requires intersubjective debate to winnow out the idiosyncrasies of individual subjective experience. Consensus makes it possible for subjectivity to secure the status granted to it by objective reality.[12]

Yet, as outlined earlier, there is also a realm of objectivity with regard to propositions themselves. Although objective reality is indeed inviolate, propositions regarding it are not automatically ascribed a status commensurate with their subject matter. In fact, for a proposition to be objective, it must simply be considered acceptable as a topic of open debate. Whether an objective proposition is to be accepted as a truth claim is a matter for the open and argumentative process of consensus involving all actors in a speech situation. The subject per se is weakened, therefore, because priority is given to the intersubjective space in which truth is to be achieved.

Habermas's criticism of Foucault is that he cannot admit this productive ambivalence into the notion of subjectivity. For Foucault, subjects can only be objects. According to Habermas, however, subjects can always make judgments about objective reality and set these forth as truth claims. Having done this, whatever a subject has said does indeed become an objective proposition open to criticism from any other actor in the process of consensus. Yet no subject, Habermas would emphasize, ever loses its right to participate in the communal process of self-understanding. Foucault fails to recognize that "killing off dialogical relationships transforms subjects, who are monologically turned in upon themselves, into objects for one another, and only objects."[13] For Habermas, Foucault's writings are predicated upon this assumption. Accordingly, the fact that objective propositions can be made about objective reality seals the fate of subjectivity for Foucault.

Habermas argues that Foucault collapses the distinction between these two realms of objectivity, real and propositional. This distinction is crucial for Habermas because subjectivity for him is precisely the capacity for propositional objectivity. For Foucault, subjects have no privileged status in the realm of objective reality; they are merely components of objective reality. This occurs because Foucault can conceive of the subject only in terms of the Cartesian *cogito* in search of certainty. Once this notion of subjectivity proves fruitless, the only alternative Foucault can perceive is to view subjects as objects about which objective propositions are made. In contrast with this, Habermas claims that "this attitude of participants in linguistically mediated interaction makes possible a different relationship of the subject to itself from the sort of objectifying attitude that an observer assumes toward entities in the external world."[14]

Habermas argues that the notion of consensus allows one to conceive of a realm of intersubjectivity that requires the ongoing participation of all involved subjects.[15]

*   *   *

To be one and permanent, Habermas's notion of objective reality must renounce historical transformation. Even more, it must deny local history.[16] Foucault, on the other hand, argues that the notion of reality is profoundly historical. The experience of this objective reality, likewise, does not betoken an undeniable, immediate event. Rather, experience, and anything that might lead to objective propositions, is always already informed by history. Objective propositions are so contoured by local histories into idiosyncratic speech situations that the recourse to objective reality in any particular discourse is merely a way of making an objective proposition unassailable. Foucault thus introduces history into realms that Habermas would want to be innocent of history.

Foucault's project is to develop a politics of that discursive space that Habermas would have free of both history and politics. That moment when the enunciating subject places itself in a space it believes to be free of constraints or inhibitions has a history of its own. It is this history that Foucault's work attempts to articulate. Foucault points out that his "objective, instead, has been to create a history of the different modes by which, in our culture, human beings are made subjects."[17] He explains further why the concept of the subject is of such strategic importance: "There are two meanings of the word *subject*: subject to someone else by control and dependence, and tied to his own identity by a conscience or self-knowledge. Both meanings suggest a form of power which subjugates and makes subject to."[18] Foucault seeks to analyze the particular instances in which subjects accept certain discourses as speaking the truth about themselves. He brackets the question of consensus with this comment: "the relationship of power can be the result of a prior or permanent consent, but it is not by nature the manifestation of a consensus."[19] Foucault discounts the highly counterfactual assertion that the possibility of making validity claims is an intrinsic and constant part of all discourses. Power, for Foucault, manifests itself in the imperative to make validity claims that are at the outset part of an already articulated system of disposition and action.

> [A] power relationship can only be articulated on the basis of two elements which are each indispensable if it is really to be a power relationship: that "the other" (the one over whom power is exercised) be thoroughly recognized and maintained to the very end as a person who

acts; and that, faced with a relationship of power, a whole field of responses, reactions, results, and possible inventions may open up.[20]

The realm of communicative action, therefore, is not innocent of power, but wrought through with its own histories. This is because subjectivity, like objective reality, is constituted by various political conflicts and struggles. The focus of Foucault's analysis is to articulate the process whereby subjects submit to enunciating their position in a discourse that succeeds in binding liberation to the ritual of confession.

For these reasons, the focus in Foucault's work on the ritual of the confession allows itself to be read as a refutation of the Habermasian ideal of communicative action. Contrary to Habermas, who sees in the auto-enunciation of the subject the possibility of a utopian politics, Foucault argues that the ritual of the confession, the self inscription into discursivity, forms the means by which modern power is exercised. Foucault's last work, *The History of Sexuality*, offers the clearest analysis of the politics of the auto-enunciation of the subject. For this work, unlike the earlier archaeological studies, does not easily allow itself to be misread as the depiction of the repressive forces exerted upon subjects. Rather, the very concept of the subject is at issue in *The History of Sexuality*. Here the incitement to discursivity inextricably intertwines subjectivity and subjection: "I have sought—it is my current work—the way a human being turns him- or herself into a subject. For example, I have chosen the domain of sexuality—how men have learned to recognize themselves as subjects of 'sexuality.'"[21] When the subject affirms itself in a specular relation of self-recognition, it installs itself in a political regime predicated upon precisely such acquiescence. The possibility of this self-imposed subjection has become the basis of modern power.

This concern is evident throughout Foucault's work. Indeed, the early *Madness and Civilization* provides a clear outline of the politics of the discursive space that is subjectivity. This instance is worth considering briefly, for it suggests a means of reassessing the earlier Foucault. As with the Panopticon, a much misappropriated image, the issue here is not repressive institutional force, but the inauguration of subjectivity. More precisely, the issue here is the inauguration of subjectivity *as a political event*. Thus, for example, in tracing the treatment of insanity in the age of Enlightenment and the institution of the asylum, Foucault discusses Pinel's treatment of the mad. In contrast to earlier punitive measures taken against the mad, Pinel made it crucial for the mad to recognize themselves *as mad*. The mad were made to observe the madness of others and thereby to perceive their own lack of reason.

> [T]he mad man recognizes himself as in a mirror in this madness whose absurd pretensions he has denounced; his solid sovereignty as a subject dissolves in this object he has demystified by accepting it. He is now pitilessly observed by himself. And in the silence of those who represent reason, and who have done nothing but hold up the perilous mirror, recognizes himself as objectively mad.[22]

What is essential here is that the subject recognize in itself the phenomenon that the institution has set out to discipline. The subject thereby assumes and adopts the necessity of disciplining itself.

> But the asylum, in this community of madmen, placed the mirrors in such a way that the madman, when all was said and done, inevitably surprised himself, despite himself, *as a madman.* . . . [Madness] became responsible for what it knew of its truth; it imprisoned itself in an infinitely self-referring observation; it was finally chained to the humiliation of being its own object. Awareness was now linked to the shame of being identical to that other, of being compromised in him, and of already despising oneself before being able to recognize or to know oneself.[23]

The subject becomes not only that which is known, but that which must know itself. This is, moreover, never an event that happens for the benefit of the subject. The subject becomes something that must know itself for the benefit of the political regime that makes this event possible and compulsory. The aim of this regime is to ensure that the subject is brought to monitor and control that which the regime deems necessary to monitor and control. It is not enough, however, for the subject to recognize its transgressive nature. The subject must submit to a discourse that promises to disclose the truth of itself. The subject must also submit to the necessity of administering its relation to itself. This requires the ever-renewed enunciation of what it is. In this way the subject is situated in a discursive space that requires the ongoing confession of its constantly receding and changing transgressive nature.[24]

Although this phenomenon of auto-subjection is specific to the control of the mad in *Madness and Civilization,* it is part of a larger aspect of modern power that Foucault examines in increasingly greater detail throughout his work. In *The History of Sexuality,* Foucault examines the necessity of confession in relation to sexuality. This is because

> the project of a science of the subject has gravitated, in ever narrowing circles, around the question of sex. Causality in the subject, the unconscious of the subject, truth of the subject in the other who knows, the

knowledge he holds unbeknown to him, all this found an opportunity to deploy itself in the discourse of sex.[25]

The History of Sexuality is thus not a study of sexuality per se. Indeed, Foucault would prefer to set aside the question of what sexuality in itself is. Instead, sexuality is focused upon as the ongoing principle of how subjects are made to relate to themselves in modern Western societies. Sexuality, therefore, is not approached as if it were repressed or as if it required liberation. Rather, sexuality is presented as a discourse that requires the ongoing production of its truth.[26] The truth of the subject must perpetually be examined and brought to discursivity. This confession, moreover, takes place in a discursive space that is at the outset structured to make this act of auto-subjection appear to be one of liberation.[27] Yet, as Foucault argues,

> [t]he confession is a ritual of discourse in which the speaking subject is also the subject of the statement; it is also a ritual that unfolds within a power relationship, for one does not confess without the presence (or virtual presence) of a partner who is not simply the interlocutor but the authority who requires the confession, prescribes and appreciates it, and intervenes in order to judge, punish, forgive, console, and reconcile.[28]

It will be necessary to specify the phases of the discourse of sexuality in order to characterize accurately the political regimes that benefit from the act of confession. It is clear, however, that the discourse of sexuality requires that it be articulated by the subject. In fact, its ongoing articulation *is* subjectivity. The discourse of sexuality, being perhaps the most generalized and all-pervasive discourse of the subject in the West, has come to be the principal means of bringing the subject to discipline itself.[29]

In *The Use of Pleasure,* Foucault addresses sexuality in ancient Greece. Contrary to the common perception that sexuality in ancient Greece was characterized by the guiltless pursuit of pleasure, Foucault argues that sexuality was seen as something that required a certain amount of vigilance. Given that sexuality qua discourse has always found its origins in the ruling class, the discourse of sexuality admittedly had little to say about women or slaves.[30] Instead, the discourse of sexuality organized a mode of being for the ruling class. It formulated a code of conduct in accord with an ontology of the subject. Sexuality, thus, became a domain in which one demonstrated one's mastery by displaying a mastery of oneself. Sexuality furthered the mastery of this class by making it see the necessity of mastering itself.

Sexuality in general provided access to the intelligibility of the subject's mode of being. It also provided a means of maintaining vigilance over possible actions that would not be in accord with the nature of the subject. The realm of sexuality was to include actions isomorphic to the subject's social status: "What one must aim for in the agonistic contest with oneself and in the struggle to control the desires was the point where the relationship with oneself would become isomorphic with the relationship of domination, hierarchy, and authority that one expected, as a man, a free man, to establish over his inferiors."[31] Thus sexuality was to be a veritable theater of one's social being. All sexual relations were to be a rehearsal or confirmation of one's social status. Forms of sexuality that threatened to rupture this isomorphic relation constituted problematic areas of sexuality. Sexual conduct that did not coincide with the status of the subject became a topic of reflection.[32] It is this regulated relation of the subject to itself that is the focal point of analysis for *The History of Sexuality.*

What is decisive about the Greeks for Foucault is that pleasure had a *use*. Pleasure was not, as is often asserted, pursued for its own sake. Rather, pleasure permitted and regulated the subject's relationship with itself, and this in turn regulated its functioning in the social order. A relationship with the self, Foucault explains

> is not simply "self-awareness" but self-formation as an "ethical subject," a process in which the individual delimits that part of himself that will form the object of his moral practice, defines his position relative to the precept he will follow, and decides on a certain mode of being that will serve as a moral goal. And this requires him to act upon himself, to monitor, test, improve, and transform himself.[33]

Thus while not a confession of the flesh, the Greek relationship to the self was decisive in making vigilance in the domain of sexuality necessary to participate in a political regime. It is this aspect that lends sexuality in Greek antiquity its significance for the history of sexuality. The sexuality of ancient Greece does not so much describe a decisive limit to the Christian West as announce a fundamental way in which subjects have been made to know themselves.

The transition from paganism to Christianity, then, is not characterized by a decisive break in the discourse of sexuality, according to Foucault, but by a modification of the subject's relation to itself.

> The evolution that occurred—quite slowly at that—between paganism and Christianity did not consist in gradual interiorization of rules, acts, and transgressions; rather, it carried out a restructuration of the forms of self-relationship and a transformation of the practices and techniques on which this relationship was based.[34]

The Greeks did not present a mode of sexual conduct that was antithetical to the Christianized West. Rather, the Greeks introduced the practice of the subject's reflective relation to itself in sexual matters. They set forth a sexual discourse constituted to ensure the enduring and isomorphic relation between political order and the subject's experience of itself. As a result, the shift from paganism to Christianity was characterized by an intensification of this relationship to the self. "In short, and as a first approximation, this added emphasis on sexual austerity in moral reflection takes the form, not of a tightening of the code that defined prohibited acts, but of an intensification of the relation to oneself by which one constituted oneself as the subject of one's acts."[35] The true meaning of the notion of ancient Greece's sexual freedom is perhaps the significance it held for the repressive hypothesis. Yet, in fact, the decline of paganism merely brought about a further exploitation of this new means of power. As in ancient Greece, sexuality in later pagan cultures was part of a regulation of social relations: "[t]he care of the self—or the attention one devotes to the care that others should take of themselves—appears as an intensification of social relations."[36]

Nonetheless, the discourse of sexuality began to lose its explicitly isomorphic relation to social status. As Foucault writes in *The Care of the Self:* "It is then a matter of forming and recognizing oneself as the subject of one's own actions, not through a system of signs denoting power over others, but through a relation that depends as little as possible on status and its external forms, for this relation is fulfilled in the sovereignty that one exercises over oneself."[37] Not mastery so much as self-mastery became the essential aspect of sexuality. What became necessary for the subject was that it "recognize the numerous complex conditions that must be jointly present if one is to perform acts of pleasure in an appropriate manner, without danger or harm."[38] It is this problematization of the relation of the subject to itself that becomes the basis of a new form of power: pastoral authority.

What was once required only of a ruling elite now becomes a necessary procedure for all constituents of a political regime. This decisive shift not only institutionalizes the ritual of confession, it also makes a new political power possible. Pastoral power henceforth regulates the subject's search into its innermost self for the merest sign of misconduct.

> For the Stoics, the true self is defined only by what I can be master of. . . . For the Christians things are quite different; for Christians the possibility that Satan can get inside your soul and give you thoughts you cannot recognize as Satanic but that you might interpret as coming from God leads to uncertainty about what is going on inside your soul.

You are unable to know what the real root of your desire is, at least
without hermeneutic work.[39]

No longer confined to the realm of actions, the entire space of interiority,
which was constituted by power to begin with, becomes a site of possible
transgressiveness. The vigilance of the subject went from being a self-
regulation of conduct within paganism, to being a hermeneutic of the self
within Christianity. Thus an intensification of social relations could be
achieved by subjectivity in general being conceived of as a field that
required interrogation and surveillance.

The trajectory that Foucault outlines in *The Use of Pleasure* and
The Care of the Self has, in the modern West, disseminated itself so as to
be virtually ubiquitous. As Foucault notes, "[t]he Middle Ages had organized around the theme of the flesh and the practice of penance a discourse that was markedly unitary. In the course of recent centuries, the
relative uniformity was broken apart, scattered, and multiplied in an ex-
plosion of distinct discursivities. . . ."[40] The discourse of sexuality, no
longer restricted to the ruling class, constituted a new mode of being a
subject. By encompassing virtually all subjects, this new mode permitted
power to operate precisely as subjectivity.

> [O]ne had to speak of it as a thing to be not simply condemned or
> tolerated but managed, inserted into systems of utility, regulated for the
> greater good of all, made to function according to an optimum. Sex was
> not something one simply judged; it was a thing one administered. It
> was in the nature of a public potential; it called for management proce-
> dures; it had to be taken charge of by analytical discourses.[41]

In this manner, the articulation of sexuality could become the very basis
of a then as yet undreamed of power. By means of it, power could exert
itself on the level of entire populations.

It should be stressed that Foucault does not hypostatize the concept
of power with regard to sexuality. Indeed, Foucault claims that "sexuality
is originally, historically bourgeois, and that, in its successive shifts
and transpositions, it induces specific class effects."[42] For the bourgeoisie
elaborated the modern understanding of sexuality in opposition to the
sexuality of the aristocracy. The body of the aristocrat was defined by its
blood, its lineage. The bourgeoisie appropriated the confession of the
flesh, administered by pastoral power, to establish its own class-specific
sexuality: "This class [the bourgeoisie] must be seen rather as being
occupied, from the mid-eighteenth century on, with creating its own sexuality and forming a specific body based on it, a 'class' body with its
health, hygiene, descent, and race."[43] As its power was not dependent

upon inherited land, but on real and potential physical capacity, the bourgeoisie managed its sexuality as one of its most precious resources. Because the maintenance of its power also required the physical capacity of
labor, the bourgeoisie similarly administered the sexuality of labor. Foucault describes the two phases of this dissemination of sexuality across
class lines:

> The first phase corresponded to the need to form a "labor force" (hence
> to avoid any useless "expenditure," any wasted energy, so that all forces
> were reduced to labor capacity alone) and to ensure its reproduction
> (conjugality, the regular fabrication of children). The second phase cor-
> responded to that epoch of *Spätkapitalismus* in which the exploitation
> of wage labor does not demand the same violent and physical con-
> straints as in the nineteenth century, and where the politics of the body
> does not require the elision of sex or its restriction solely to the repro-
> ductive function; it relies instead on a multiple channeling into the
> controlled circuits of the economy—on what has been called a hyper-
> repressive desublimation.[44]

It is with this second phase of late capitalism that the ritual of confession
is disseminated across class lines. Entire populations can thereby be
brought to administer themselves. Thus the isolated phenomena of reflection and confession with regard to sexuality that Foucault examines in
The Use of Pleasure and *The Care of the Self* become ubiquitous throughout society. The modern West thereby becomes characterized by what
Foucault terms bio-power. Bio-power is a regime that depends upon an
entire population administering and confessing its own sexuality. Its very
economy is dependent upon pleasure and the confession of "repression."
And although bio-power does administer populations with regard to health
and longevity, it does so only to maintain itself. For the struggle of bio-
power to maintain itself involves entire populations. It is for this reason that
the military defense of bio-power is always predicated upon genocide.[45]

* * *

Habermas might perhaps concede the validity of Foucault's notions
of sexuality and bio-power, but he would still insist that these are merely
descriptive. They refuse to admit the normative basis of their critique. In
its more popular form this question manifests itself in the claim that
Foucault leaves no room for resistance or revolution, that his analyses are
remorseless descriptions of a power made invincible. Yet Foucault has
said that "[p]ower is everywhere; not because it embraces everything, but
because it comes from everywhere."[46] Power is exerted by each individual, Foucault would claim. This is precisely what happens when the

subject confesses its transgressive nature. In such instances, however, the subject exercises this power against itself.[47] Foucault's work attempts to study how modern Western societies have come to rely on the individual subject exerting its own power against itself. This is not, as some would suggest, to argue that the individual subject has no power. Rather, it is to argue that what the subject believes to be the exertion of its power is merely the means whereby it submits to the power of a political regime.

Habermas's notion of a speech situation in which subjects confess the idiosyncrasies of their individual subjective experiences so that consensus might be established is, for Foucault, precisely how power is *exerted* in modern Western societies, not how power is *achieved*. Foucault would ask: What has made this space of enunciation possible? What is its history, its politics? Habermas would, of course, have to take recourse to objective reality to answer these questions. Foucault prevents such a strategem by persistently stressing the historicity of the subject's relation to anything that might be characterized as subjective. Accordingly, Foucault does not admit the notion of objective reality into his analyses. He thereby, admittedly, deontologizes consensus. Yet this tactic pluralizes resistance. As Foucault states, "there is no single locus of great Refusal, no soul of revolt, source of rebellion, or pure law of the revolutionary. Instead there is a plurality of resistances, each of them a special case."[48] It is toward this plurality of resistances that Foucault's work is oriented. For "it is doubtless the strategic codification of these points of resistance that makes a revolution possible."[49] Thus, Foucault's work is not simply descriptive. His work is a calculated historicization of localized resistances. As a result, Foucault's work is indeed remorseless in its analysis of how power has coopted the very notion of liberation. Yet its aim is to fiction a politics that would be predicated upon the historicity of past resistances. As Foucault says of *The History of Sexuality,* "[t]he object was to learn to what extent the effort to think one's own history can free thought from what it silently thinks, and so enable it to think differently."[50]

Foucault's work ultimately reveals a commitment to a form of resistance about which our own history can perhaps give us little information, but which thereby seems all the more imperative. His work enacts its own resistance by making it clear that it itself is yet to be made into history. For only when the ritual of confession ceases to be a means of power will Foucault's work become merely historical. In striving for this future history, one can do no better than to hope that Foucault continues to be a subject that is irresistible.

Part II

Psychoanalysis and Feminist Theory

5 Mastering a Woman: The Imaginary Foundation of a Certain Metaphysical Order

MICHÈLE LE DOEUFF
TRANSLATED BY TAMARA PARKER

"Give me Sophia, and I am Free."[1]

Feminists gathered at the Sorbonne in December 1989 to celebrate the fortieth anniversary of the publication of *The Second Sex,* thus collectively bearing witness to the cultural, political, and intellectual impor tance of Simone de Beauvoir's thought. The floor was given to militant groups and also to readers, some who had read *The Second Sex* the very year it was published and others who had read it quite recently, as they are still very young. One of the latter group, Aliénor Bertrand, a philosopher recently appointed at Nanterre, bluntly declared her rejection of the couple Beauvoir-Sartre. While sixty years have passed since the meeting of these two protagonists, it seems indeed that something has changed in couples composed of two philosophers, which are rather rare in any case. In our students' generation, the following scenario is possible: for the duration of their studies, they work together, dividing up the necessary course work and functioning as a team in this work that, by definition, is not particularly personal. Then, when the time comes for doing research—the dissertation or articles—they both carry out their own work. Thus, the less valued phase, that of apprenticeship, is shared, according to a wise principle of economy of effort, while the more creative phase finds each one with his or her own subject. Even if occasionally there is some reciprocal assistance, it is based on an agreement of mutual noninterference, especially with regard to philosophical orientations. Sartre and Simone de Beauvoir seem to have known an inverse trajectory. They did not lend each other a hand while preparing for their exams; but afterward,

59

with this thankless period finished, a certain Jean-Paul said to a certain Simone: "From now on, I am taking you in hand."[2]

In *The Prime of Life*,[3] the form of their relationship as a couple is called a *lease* and a *pact*. In this context, the two terms seem justified by the fact that the conditions of the association are explicit like the clauses in a contract, the principal clause being—come to that—transparency, sincerity, and the exclusion of lying. The memoirs of Simone de Beauvoir allow one to imagine that the purpose of this pact was to maintain the freedom of each of the contracting parties, while at the same time binding them together through the sharing of a common intellectual venture. Nevertheless, it is also Simone de Beauvoir who reports the *"je vous prends en main,"* something that is quite different from being a pact and that appears as a necessarily unilateral relationship of authority. But the agreement of mutual noninterference, which seems to be the ideal of today's up-and-coming generation, is not a pact either. It is something that has status in philosophy, at least for Rousseau, who calls it an *arrangement*—which is something else altogether. Because I need to explain this notion in order to point out certain difficulties in the question of the *pact,* I must make a detour into Rousseau.

In *Emile,* as we know, it is necessary to delay as much as possible the contact between wills. Above all else, there must no pact until maturity has been completely achieved, specifically because a good act of association presupposes one's capacity to make an agreement with oneself. In a pact, "each individual contracts, so to speak with himself."[4] Nevertheless, it is not so easy to delay the interaction of individuals. The risk is constantly present in the form of a possible *conflictual* encounter between individuals. Consider, for example, the story of the melons of the gardener Robert and the beans that little Emile thoughtlessly plants in the same place where the gardener had already planted his melons. An "arrangement" takes place, then, formulated by the gardener in this way: "if you touch my melons, I will plough your beans under."[5] What takes place in such an arrangement is strictly a matter of a negative exchange, one that presupposes a reciprocal exteriority on the part of the protagonists, that separates their activities, in this case horticultural, and that distinguishes the plot of ground that each one cultivates. Although a pact associates, this type of arrangement simply dissociates the individuals.

For Rousseau's philosophy of the "pact," this figure seems necessary indeed, because it shows that mutual independence, or reciprocal exteriority of individuals, far from occurring spontaneously (which would make any pact an absolute artifact), requires something further to remain as it is. In this case, it requires an "arrangement" based on potential belligerence. We would not understand how wills come to be fused in the pact, if we did not suppose that their separation exists only through a construct. This supposes that agglutination and encroachment are quasi-natural phenomena given proximity. The pact takes up again, dialectically, the two contradictory aspects, namely, a sort of originary confusion of the "I" and the "not-I" *and* the separation that allowed the construction of an autonomy. But this separation, once again, had been and must be artificially imposed. We can consider the first four books of *Emile* as the story of diverse strategies for creating and maintaining as long as possible an individual's insularity and for ensuring above all else that this insularity comes first, prior to the pact, so that the individual's relation to himself is structured *before* his relation to the other or others. Without the pedagogue's meticulous intervention, the being-for-itself would not precede the being-for-others; there would be from the start, and no doubt forever, a being-intermingled-with-others. The stakes, then, are considerable, because it is a matter of the *metaphysical order* and anteriority. Rousseau absolutely insists that the for-itself precedes the for-others, even if all of *Emile* attests to the opposite conviction. If one does not closely watch over it, the child will become an unfortunate being-intermingled-with-others, marked by the tyranny of one or the other. Only pedagogic artifice creates a happy insularity of the individual: the boy is given only one book to read, and this is *Robinson Crusoe.* Even the child's name contains the whole philosophical program: Emile, *aime-île* [let him love island].

I had begun with Simone de Beauvoir and Sartre; we are not as far afield from them as it seems. What I perceive as an explicit problem in Rousseau, one can find equally in Sartre, though more implicitly. And the results for Sophie, or for Simone de Beauvoir over twenty years, may well be analogous. In any case, the following doubt can be put forth: the existential system presupposes, perhaps at its base, a "tyrannical" or violent relation based on the appropriation of others. From a doctrinal or theoretical point of view, it is true, self-presence in *Being and Nothingness*[6] is designated as strictly determinable by an *internal* relation, because the "impalpable fissure" that characterizes this "self-presence" is supposed to be "intraconsciential" (EN p. 120); that is to say, it is supposed to take place within one's consciousness. In principle, the existence "for others" will come later, as a "new being which must withstand new descriptions" (EN p. 276). Certainly Sartre recognizes that "I need others in order to fully grasp all the structure of my being," and that, therefore, "the For-self refers to the For-others" (EN p. 277). But, he elaborates, "this For-others does not reside *in* others; I am responsible for it" (EN p. 276). Hence the ontological primacy of the internal and of self-presence is thereby strictly preserved from a doctrinal point of view, and one can assert, hypothetically, that this thesis has played a great role in the twentieth century's fascination with existentialism. In a letter written from Norway, Sartre speaks of "a desert island, which is me."[7] We can see this philosophy as the "cold robinsonian model" that our times perhaps need (or have needed, or will need for a long time to come . . .). The thesis of the absolute responsibility of the "I" proposes a sort of anchoring of the individual in himself[8] that can be perceived as a reassuring doctrine.

In any case, the aforementioned doctrine of the anteriority of the for-itself with respect to the for-Others in *Being and Nothingness* can be considered *philosophically unstable*. Or, once again, as in Rousseau, one can say that its very opposite is at work in it, that is to say, an archaic relation of affirmed mastery over others, of immediate domination producing the humiliation or degradation of the other. I imagine that psychoanalysts would see, in the examples I am going to give, a projection of the *drive to mastery [pulsion d'emprise]* (what Freud calls the *Bemächtingungstrieb*). From a psychoanalytic point of view, what is recounted in the second chapter ("Bad Faith") of *Being and Nothingness* is strictly coherent. This is so because an almost cruel domination over others, others being seen in this case as mere objects of the drives, *and* the construction of a mastery of stimulations or of the body itself are supposed to be neighboring, even twin, processes. An expert on the human mind surely would not tax Sartre with incoherence. On the other hand, from a philosophical point of view, to affirm the ontological primacy of the relation to the self, while supporting one's reasoning with anecdotes that presuppose a rudimentary form of annexation and subordination of the other, is a highly disputable turn, open to criticism, to say the least!

Let us begin with this remark: "'What sort of being must man be, if he is to be capable of bad faith?' Take the example of a woman who . . . " (EN p. 94). In *Being and Nothingness,* two female figures serve to explain bad faith. The first is a coquette who pretends not to understand what a man wants from her in the course of a date. The story of this scene ends with the following remark: "we shall say that this woman is of bad faith" (EN p. 93). The second is a "frigid woman" (EN p. 93), a woman who is not truly frigid (one needs only to ask her husband to be sure), but who applies herself to knowing nothing about her own pleasure. I will permit myself to recall briefly here the analysis that I proposed of these examples in *Hipparchia's Choice*.[9] The concept of *bad faith* is defined by Sartre as a "lie to oneself," an apparently internal definition, that is consistent with the principle according to which the main structures have to be defined within the subject itself. This idea, however, assumes some rather unexpected elements. To begin with, it is necessary to establish an absolute truth with respect to which there will be lies. The coquette "refuses to grasp desire for what it is," and Sartre, in the same paragraph, speaks of "raw and naked desire" (EN p. 94). As for the frigid woman, it is said that she has given "objective signs of pleasure"[10] that she works to deny afterward. *Objective* signs, desire for what *it is*, and so forth, here is a position of absolute dogmatism that is moreover taken up by a totally authoritarian attitude. Each of these "scenes" presents two consciousnesses, not just one: on the one hand, the consciousness of a woman in the process of lying to herself and, on the other hand, another consciousness that controls the absolute truth and that is sovereign insofar as it furnishes the truth of the situation. The frigid woman's husband, then the psychiatrist, then Sartre himself know, the three of them, in turn, that she is not frigid. Faced with the coquette, it is the man who is making what we call "the first moves," who knows that she knows, although she does not want to know, what he wants with her. Thus there is someone who knows better than the woman something that "she knows very well" (EN p. 94), but does not want to know, someone who substitutes his[11] own contrast, the "lie to oneself" (EN p 86). Under Sartre's pen, it is not always a woman who is shown to be dishonest. There is also a famous waiter in a café and in "Existentialism Is a Humanism," "one of my students."[12] Therefore, it is always either a woman or a man in a subordinate position, so that bad faith seems to be a speciality of socially inferior beings! In any case, if to explain bad faith one must first put someone else in the wrong, then the internal definition of the "lie to oneself" is never given.

In Sartre's life, it seems that the first person he succeeded in convincing that she was of bad faith was Simone de Beauvoir. In the *Memoirs of a Dutiful Daughter*, she recounts this, which I quote, not from the standard translation, but from Trista Selous's translation for *Hipparchia's Choice:*

> Day after day, and all day long I measured myself against Sartre, and in our discussions I was simply not in his class. One morning in the Luxembourg Gardens, near the Medici fountain, I outlined for him the pluralist morality which I had fashioned to justify the people I liked but did not wish to resemble: he ripped it to shreds. I was attached to it, because it allowed me to take my heart as the arbiter of good and evil: I struggled with him for three hours. In the end I had to admit I was beaten: besides, I had realized, in the course of our discussion, that many of my opinions were based only on prejudice, bad faith or thoughtlessness, that my reasoning was shaky and my ideas confused. 'I'm no longer sure what I think, or even if I think at all,' I noted, completely thrown. My pride was not involved, I was by nature curious rather than imperious and preferred learning to shining. (HC p. 480)

The structure of this scene in the Luxembourg Gardens is the same as that of the two scenes already described in *Being and Nothingness*. In each of these cases there is a man who knows better than a woman what she ought to think or feel. There is in this a sort of rape of the consciousness or of the subjectivity, which is not completely surprising: at the end of *Being and Nothingness,* Sartre defines knowledge as a deflowering of the object and science as rape. One could describe this as a fool's epistemology or as a morally lamentable philosophy. It is nevertheless necessary to restrain our indignation, both theoretical and ethical, in order to attempt to show how all of this builds up the Sartrian system.

From the start we will observe that the fight that took place between Sartre and Simone de Beauvoir in the Luxembourg Gardens is a scene that we already know by heart if we have read Plato. Two characters confront one another concerning the doctrine held by one of them, who finds himself forced to give an account of himself. He fails, sees his doctrine torn apart, and no longer knows what he thinks or even if he thinks, a situation known as an impasse or *aporia.* The scene recounted by Simone de Beauvoir in some way is Socratic, but it is characterized by hostility rather than by the good will Socrates thought a requirement, so it is better termed eristic. In any case, the imaginary stakes of this scene are enormous. One can say that Sartre plays at being a little Socrates or acting the stingray. Simone de Beauvoir gets trapped in the role of the not-very-intelligent interlocutor (compare Laches or Meno). The result of all this is, as she used to reply when asked her position with respect to philosophy, that she had left it to Sartre, Sartre of whom one already thought, I quote her again, that he "would someday write a work of philosophy that would count."[13] The capitulation of Simone de Beauvoir allowed Sartre to set himself up in the role of a "grand philosophe," that is to say, a "great philosopher," he who knows everything better than everyone else and who claims to be the "superconsciousness" of our century.

This scene of the destruction of a young woman philosopher is, then, the original scene of the constitution of Sartre's well-known image. From that time forward, it is not surprising that we find it rather often in his work, under various disguises. Intellectual power over a woman, knowing better than she does what is happening in her mind occurs again. In fact, it occurs not only in *Being and Nothingness,* but also in *Vérité et Existence,*[14] where a whole collection of women are made to symbolize the negative (the bad faith that is seen here as a will to not know), a negative with respect to which a superior "I" can define itself. In this posthumous text, we find again in abundance "the frigid woman." We meet another who has tuberculosis but does not want to know it, and who, I quote, "in fact, knows that she does not know" (VE p. 77). We also meet a "kept woman" in a passage that merits grammatical examination: to begin with, we have a phenomenological "I" that appears in statements of the type "I want not to know," but "I am responsible for everything before myself and before everyone, and ignorance aims to restrict my responsibility in the world. Thus, the geography of my ignorance represents exactly, in the negative, the finitude of my choice of what to be" (VE pp. 97–98). But apparently this phenomenological "I" is not the right subject to use to describe the refusal of responsibility that constitutes ignorance. Hence Sartre suddenly changes to a formal "you," a "you" that could not be the "I" of the philosopher, because it is that of a kept woman. "If society puts you in a situation where responsibilities are taken from you [the "kept" woman], you have no concern for the Truth. You receive truths from others just as you receive your money. Woman's ignorance, etc., etc.," (VE p. 98). Why is it that bad faith cannot be described in the phenomenological "I" and always requires the arrival on stage of *another person,* not the universal "I," but a particularized person, generally of the opposite sex, a "you" or a "she" whose bad faith and ignorance will be dissected by a superior gaze? This is doubtless because the relation of power with others precedes or is contemporary with the constitution of the "I." The doctrine is supposed to give an account of the history of the subject but there is a prehistory of consciousness, a prehistory that consists of the radical defeat of the other, who is condemned to understand that she (seldom he) does not control the truth of her (seldom his) own actions or thought. It is in contrast with this other, through mastery of this other, that the subject lays down the possibility of his own authenticity, that is, the acknowledgment of his mastery over (hence responsibility for) whatever happens to him. He sets himself up as transcendental by having transcended others.

From a philosophical point of view, this is a disaster. It is, in the first place, in contradiction with the affirmed metaphysical order. If the "Being-for-others" does not come in secondarily, as a "new definition," and if the triumph over others must take place for the story of self-presence to begin, then we must consider this "self-presence" as constructed on the annihilation of the other, on a violent contact with others. Basically, *Being and Nothingness* recounts a certain Odyssey of the consciousness (first we are here, then we move there), but a subtext of the same work contradicts its travel account. Along with this logical problem we must mention a problem relative to the *philosophical position.* The radical and definitive defeat of others puts an end, also definitively, to any possible debate and gives way to dogmatism. In fact, beginning with the scene in the Luxembourg Gardens and the start of Sartre and Simone de Beauvoir's relationship, everything is ready for the onset of dogmatism. They dispute and confront one another concerning the moral doctrine elaborated by Simone de Beauvoir, not Sartre's doctrine. The latter doctrine then seems to remain invisible, removed from view and also from examination, in their debate. There is no reciprocal gaze. She exposes her thought in the debate, he does not, at least for as long as she asserts her capacity to think. Moreover, Simone de Beauvoir notes that "metaphysical objections made him shrug his shoulders" (*Memoirs,* p. 477). By removing his theories from the debate so long as there is an interlocutor, he protects them from any discussion.

The role allotted to Simone de Beauvoir was not that of an interlocutor, but that of an enamored admirer and, later, that of an editorial assistant. In the biography that Deidre Bair recently wrote, we find indications from several sources that, regularly, when they met, Sartre's first gesture was to hand Simone de Beauvoir a bundle of manuscript pages, enjoining her "to deal with this"; it seems that she meticulously annotated the drafts.[15] It is true that giving drafts to friends for them to read, discussing the drafts with them, taking into account their stylistic or linguistic suggestions, this is a common practice and one of the most enjoyable parts of writing. But Sartre's authoritarian attitude is quite a different thing, and one must note anyway that, when the work to be discussed is as extensive as Sartre's, and when the task of critical reading falls on a single person, it is almost a matter of a full-time job. On the other hand, it does not seem that Sartre performed the same task with Simone de Beauvoir's manuscripts. He intervened on an entirely different level, that of their fundamental orientation. For example, just before the war, he advised her "vehemently" to put herself "in person" into her writings. De Beauvoir said that she "had the impression of receiving a great blow on the head" and that Sartre's words, as always, "raised a multitude of possibilities and hopes" (*La Force de l'Age,* vol. 2, p. 360). He intervened in the very heart of her choice of writing, almost as a director of her literary conscience, whereas she contributed to the finishing up of texts—she was an assistant, he was probably a sort of Pygmalion, a male chauvinist pig . . . malion! The terrible sentence of 1929, "From now on, I am taking you in hand" seems to have determined their relations at least until the war.

One cannot call that a pact; I have already indicated one reason for this: there can be a pact only when two or more autonomous wills (previously constituted) commit themselves one to another and each one to itself. I am even less tempted to call it a "philosophical pact" for another reason: from the moment that someone is "taken in hand" by another, one *leaves* philosophy, to the extent that one is spared (that is to say, forbidden) a certain relation to lack, a radical lack that others cannot fill and that forces one to "think for oneself."[16] One cannot accept a ready-made philosophy, as one receives a religion. Simone de Beauvoir took herself back in hand later, somewhat while reading Hegel during the war and much more while writing *The Second Sex.* But during the first ten or twenty years of their involvement, it was as if she were excluded from the philosophical project. It was not a pact that bound them, but an infernal relation through which each of them lost a great deal, I think. For her it is quite obvious, for she lost the intellectual autonomy that she perhaps had not yet had and her vocation as a philosopher. She also lost her self-respect as a woman, which she, without a doubt had never had. And, yes, I believe one can lose what one has not actually had— when one loses the humble possibility of becoming, for example, a self-respecting woman or an independent mind.

I would like to point out, however, that we did not need the recent publication of her letters to know that she was a broken woman. I referred earlier to certain appalling anecdotes in *Being and Nothingness,* I could just as well have cited many other atrocities, for example the slime that is "the sickly new and feminine revenge" of the "in-itself," or the for-itself "obscenity of the female sex," for whose analysis I have followed Marjorie Collins and Christine Pierce's pioneering article.[17] Because Simone de Beauvoir was the editorial assistant, one must consider the fact that she admitted all of this repugnant sexism into *Being and Nothingness.* And, at the very least, as a reader of that work and as still an admirer of Sartre, she made herself an accomplice after the fact. But if it is true, as the Martist maxim goes, that "a people that oppresses another is not a free people," one can say the same for the relations between individuals, here between a man and a woman. I believe that Sartre lost a great deal when he transformed Simone de Beauvoir into an admirer. He certainly won the power to identify himself with the character of a "great philosopher." But, in a certain way, it was too easy to place himself directly into the role. Before even finishing a work, he put an end to contradiction, debate, and intellectual confrontation. If the question of solipsism lurks in *Being and Nothingness,* it is because there was no longer, in his psycho-intellectual space, a veritable, independent other. There was no longer an interlocutor in the strict sense. He closed himself off in the sphere of the Same. Perhaps nothing indicates this better than this letter from Simone de Beauvoir dated July 11, 1940: "Hegel is horribly difficult, but extremely interesting, and you ought to be acquainted with his work. It is related to your own philosophy of nothingness. I rejoice while reading it, thinking precisely of introducing you to it."[18] So one could not interest Sartre in Hegel except by telling him that it was similar to his own philosophy? This fragment gives a possible clue to Simone de Beauvoir's capitulation in the scene in the Luxembourg Gardens. If she had not abandoned her intellectual independence and surrendered to Sartre's philosophy, she would have ceased to exist for him and would have disappeared into the murky exterior regions.

I am particularly pleased to say that Hegel, surprisingly enough, did something for a woman. In the midst of the French defeat, when she did not yet know whether or not Sartre had been killed, Simone de Beauvoir spent the month of July 1940 reading Hegel. Whereas Sartre constantly pushed her toward the novel, especially the autobiographical novel, Hegel rekindled in her the spark of philosophy and independence. She wrote to Sartre, without knowing if the message in the bottle would arrive, things such as the following on July 14, 1940:

> I have found a sentence that will serve marvelously as an epigraph to my novel: "To the extent that it is the Other that acts, each conscious-ness pursues the *death* of the other. . . . The relation between the two consciousnesses is thus determined: each consciousness of self must act towards the death of the other. The essence of the other appears to it as an other, as an external one, and it must overcome this exteriority. They cannot avoid this battle *because they are forced to raise this certainty of self to the level of truth.*" All at once, I felt a brief moment of intellec-tual warmth, I wanted to philosophize. (LS p. 173)

A few days later she wrote: "I would so much like for us to orga-nize a confrontation between your ideas on nothingness, the in-itself and the for-itself, and Hegel's ideas: because there are many analogies, but Hegel turns into joy that which, in your work, is gloomy and depressing. It seems to me that both are true and I would like to find a point of equilibrium between them" (LS p. 182). A *confrontation?* This is some-thing new! Unfortunately, this "confrontation" does not seem to have taken place, at least not before the writing of *Being and Nothingness*. Or perhaps the Hegelian thesis of the exteriority of the consciousness of the other was torn apart by Sartre. If so, one will never know how. But at least there is here a reclaiming of independence by Simone de Beauvoir, timid, of course, as she hides behind Hegel, but curiously rediscovering an old element of hers. Sartre had torn apart a "pluralist morality," and now Simone de Beauvoir here reopens the door to pluralism by writing "it seems to me that both are true and I would like to find a point of equilibrium between them" (LS p. 182). Such a sentence has a Leibnizian flavor. Let me mention that the "pluralist morality" she held before Sartre tore it apart might have been inherited from her work on Leibniz. And let me say no more, because we know so little about that.

What she rediscovered, thanks to 'soldier Sartre's' absence, was the humble freedom of philosophical tastes, the freedom to choose from the pantheon of the history of philosophy the author who interested her enough to detain her all day at the National Library. It was truly a return to the past, because she rediscovered the time when she was not yet involved with Sartre. "It reminds me of the old days of the 'agrégation,' and rediscovering philosophy brings my serenity back" (LS p. 171). "Rediscovering philosophy"—it might be asked why I am so certain that this was not possible except in the absence of Sartre. I can provide you with only an indirect proof: in the same letter, she wrote "I dreamt of you . . . you wanted to strangle me" (LS p. 170).

Simone de Beauvoir's reclaiming of independence was to be continued in the writing of *The Second Sex* in which she tried to understand why women find themselves in the concrete impossibility of constructing a "certainty of self," and, what is more, of raising such a certainty to the level of truth—and why, in the end, there is no battle. Sartre's consciousness pursued the death of Simone de Beauvoir's, but hers did not oppose his with a reciprocal initiative. The end of this story, I have already recounted in *Hipparchia's Choice*. Rather than return to that today, I would like to conclude with the concept of the "pact" itself. A pact between a male philosopher and a female philosopher; I do not know of any examples of such a pact and, though I always bet on the possibility of intellectual exchanges and dialogue between men and women, I do not think the pact is the form we should hope to give to philosophical sociability. My generation was certainly caught in this illusion of cooperation, relying on the creation of a common will, explicitly determined as such, and strongly engaging the individuals. The dream of combining forces sometimes focused on the life of the couple, more often it led to the founding of leagues, clubs, groups, or coteries. One can multiply the criticisms concerning this type of attitude—a pact necessarily creates a closed society, a closed space, that is non-sense from a philosophical point of view, and so on. Compare Rousseau's unbelievable defense of male circles in Geneva and the silly theory of reason related to that defense of closure.[19] One may also say that this is necessarily an illusion, because, in an intellectual association, it is false to say that "everyone's condition is equal" or that "one's winnings equal one's losses."

To all these criticisms, one can add that the concept of the pact is, in itself, a weak or dubious concept, or at least a concept that would need some revision. On the one hand, it supposes that the subject's autonomy, its relation to itself, its self-certainty, are primary givens or, in any case, that they should be previous to the moment of the pact. On the other hand, the demonstration of this same thesis, the production or demonstration of a preliminary self-presence, relies surreptitiously on a victorious and despotic relation to another, another human being who is quite often, in Rousseau and Sartre in any case, a woman. Before Emile considers whether or not he is going to enter into a pact with the country in which he is going to live—a moment that attests to his capacity to "contract with himself," before any of that, he has been promised Sophie, a Sophie practiced in submitting to the will of others, even bred for just that. If the philosophical construction of the concept of the subject's absolute autonomy supposes a sacrificed woman, then feminism has much work to do. Not only do we have to put all of our forces into the civil and cultural war that is far from settled concerning abortion, contraception, daycare, and the protection of battered women; not only do we have to create an international solidarity so that women in Moslem countries, fighting against the Code of the Family and traditionalism will not stand like a David without a sling before millions of Goliaths, and so forth; but, what is more, in the midst of these urgent concerns, we must reconsider the way in which the Odyssey of the consciousness is described by modern philosophy.

6   Lacan and the Ethics of Desire: The Relation Between Desire and Action

ELLIE RAGLAND-SULLIVAN

The ethics of Lacanian analysis is concerned both with changing oneself and teaching analysis as a potentially new "science" of the real. By working from the real, Lacan taught that one can effect ethical change for individuals in the clinic and in society insofar as each person's action leads to change in the social realm. Lacan's teaching does not consider that the unhappiness of humankind issues from medical symptoms or economic ones per se, but rather from social symptoms derived from the basic human propensity for narcissistic self-deception concerning even the best of intentions. Against the reformist programs of the ages, Lacan argues that most change is only superficial. It is on this premise that he calls for a new ethics.

Radical change can come only from reworking the unconscious history of the letter where being *[l'être]* joins the word or *lettre* of the symbolic to the real of *jouissance* that one might define as an absolute sense of one's value as a being. The presence of *jouissance* can be measured as a meaning system based on *quality* that resides alongside the empirical or *quantifiable* system of language. These may seem to be drastic propositions insofar as ethics is generally thought of as a set of criteria for human action, both narrower than and broader than the dictates of law. Etiquette, for example, is its diminutive. Most people take the acting subject for granted as being aware of its intentions and, therefore, responsible for its actions. Thus, they concentrate their inquiry on the field of actions per se or on the belief systems that give rise to action.

The premise of my chapter is that the acting subject is not, in fact, the *agent* of its action. It must surely be axiomatic that the status of the agent must be considered prior to any question of what causes action or

71

prior to deciding what action to choose. *Agent,* as I use the term here, however, does not mean the mind or will, but is considered to be a place of power.[1] In Lacan's teaching, one does not think from a place called the *mind,* a container holding knowledge. Rather, thought is catalyzed by associations made among overlapped order(ing)s of real, symbolic, and imaginary material. These compose networks of interlinked signifying chains whose base unit is the Borromean chain. The knot that links these three circles or orders spawns a realm of the particular that Lacan called the *fourth order* of the symptom.

Lacan made a further distinction between the general order that tells every person's life story in opaque and enigmatic symptoms and the particular traits of *jouissance* discernible in each person's symptomatology. To mark the idea of a general particular and an individual particular he used spelling: the word *symptom* is a borrowing from the Greek language that refers to the order itself and the medieval French spelling *sinthome* refers to the particular case, one by one.

Every person's thought is a symptom of how the real, symbolic, and imaginary were correlated in the first place by the relation of a mother's *unconscious*—thus unknown—desire for the signifier of the father's name. Not only does each person's life elaborate a story of interactions between desire (lack) and libido *(jouissance)* that appear as enigmas and impasses in language, but, even more specifically, these coalesce into constellations of culturally imposed signifiers from which we derive what we call *gender, identity,* and *being.* That disunity and disharmony afflict every human life reveals that individuals are divided. We are not the whole beings of some supposedly natural harmony between gender and identity, or between the biological organism and its sexuality.

In *Séminaire* VII (1959–1960): *L'éthique de la psychanalyse* Lacan began to develop an ethics of psychoanalysis wherein the articulation of a word is itself an act committed. When traumatic, the effects of language first constitute and then return in the order Lacan called the *real.* Careful to distinguish his ethics from those of Aristotle, Kant, Hegel, Schopenhauer, Nietzsche, and others, Lacan's ethics is based on a rereading of Freud. But he does not see himself as going beyond Freud, or even beyond Hegel. Rather, he describes his reading as displacing himself into the interior of Freud's text.[2]

First, I shall address Lacan's claim that Freud skewed centuries of philosophies in which ethics was treated in terms of the Good by introducing the pleasure principle and the reality principle into that field. Freud saw the Good as psychic health. Second, I shall take up Lacan's claim that the ethical dimension is situated in a broader historical dimension, but only insofar as the death drive arises from the real to bear on individual and cultural history. In Lacan's reading of Freud, the reality and pleasure principles are not only *not* opposed to each other, they both refer to the death drive. In *L'acte psychanalytique,* Lacan cites Aristotle's claim that the first measure of an ethics is *the fruit of an act.*[3] It is on this path that Lacan pushed his wager with action, not only by urging clinical change, but also by showing the efficacy of teaching analysis to anyone who wants to listen.

The *new* idea in Lacan's ethics of analysis arises from his concern with what causes repetition; what makes repetition so telling; what makes radical change so difficult; why historical change reflects myriad surface illusions of difference, while the *different* always comes back in new variations of old dilemmas, at least as far as ethics is concerned. Bringing back the Latin word *causa,* Lacan translated it into French as *la chose.* *La chose,* in turn, is his translation of *das Ding.* The "thing" is the *cause* of desire. I do not mean an actual thing like an object, however, but a *loss* of whatever gave prior satisfaction. We desire the return of a satis- faction whose residual *jouissance* is inscribed in the wisp of a sensation, in the slip of a memory, or in the fading of a moment. Yet, *das Ding* causes desire to seek the *repetition* of a *jouissance* that promises a re- newed satisfaction. But repetition is paradoxical, for it also serves as the barrier to change. Desire gives rise to fantasies that seek repetition via objects meant to appease the (partial) drives. Thus, fantasy also functions to impede change.

Perhaps a brief look at the various interpretations of the other ethi- cal positions that Lacan examines will help us to understand his own more clearly insofar as he claims to make a break with philosophy. In this break, Lacan places the ethical question in the field he calls the *Freudian cut.* In Lacan's logic of the cut, etymology is not his guide. The twists and turns of meaning do not concern him; rather he is concerned with the usage of the signifier for knowledge or truth (S_2) in its synchrony; and the "letter" or *l'être* of diachrony that one might call the master signifier (S_1) or the object *a* defined as that which returns to its place—not in ontol- ogy—but in the real of one's shame or *hontology.* If one thinks of the object *a* as a residue of nonsense that, nonetheless, marks the impasses of the real as they make palpable holes in language and being, one can grasp Lacan's use of the object *a* to denote a knowledge outside ordinary mean- ing. But such *jouissance* effects do not re-present themselves to con- scious memory for what they are. Rather, they appear in disconnected images, in strange uses of language, or in enigmatic feelings in the body (Lacan 1986, p. 56).

At the beginning of the *Séminaire* on ethics, Lacan separated his psychoanalytic ethics from Aristotle's. Because Aristotle's categories are universal, they always end up in an ethics concerned with *power.* Lacan's ethics bears on desire. Moreover, Lacan says that, since Aristotle, philosophy has worked by decomposition, going ever further away from explaining the *cause* of human actions. Such "complexification" for its own sake is not a Good in his estimation (Lacan 1986, p. 88). Strange to say, it is easier for people to explain away the raison d'être of power in terms of necessary authority, authority practiced for their own Good, than to admit that there is no power without the underlying desire for it. Power may stare anyone in the face in all seeming innocence. One can rationalize one's desire for power in multiple lies. It is difficult, however, to admit the narcissistic dimension in the link between power and the desire for power, in the particular ways this link governs a person's actions.

In *L'acte psychanalytique,* Lacan says that, because reason is not even rational, what *is* rational is to know what makes reason fail (Lacan, 1967–1968). *His* answer is *das Ding,* the *chose freudienne,* the cause of desire. But "it" is not what "it" was for Kant, nor even for Freud. "The thing," Lacan says, is "the passage *to* the symbolic order of a conflict between men," the passage to some place *from* some place (Lacan, 1967–1968). In the late 1960s, Lacan does not locate *das Ding in* the symbolic order, but finds it passing into that order in the form of a conflict between individuals. But where does *it* come from? What is it?

Lacan makes it clear in *L'éthique de la psychanalyse* that the "it" does not pertain to an ethics that presents itself as a science. Nor does it constitute a knowledge of what *must* be done to establish a certain adaptation in the subject that will make him participate in a given ethical order or even submit to it. Agreeing with the writers of old that ethics always bears on the issue of the "good," even the Sovereign Good, Lacan does not hope, as Aristotle did, that ethics will succeed to the point that a particular order becomes a universal knowledge whose ethics constitutes a politics that will imitate cosmic order (Lacan 1986, p. 31). Lacan notes, incidentally, that most of Aristotle's *Nichomachean Ethics* treats this question: Why, when *everything* has been done to ensure good action, does intemperance subsist?[4]

Aristotle's question is not so different in structure, Lacan claims, from the question posed by the Marquis de Sade's dilemma. That is, in what does the *jouissance* or enjoyment of transgressing law consist? (Lacan 1986, pp. 229–230). The desire for total pleasure or *satisfaction* is not such a shocking reply to the question. But Lacan points to a major problem in that answer, thereby addressing a problem that Aristotle never solved: the relation of the universal to the particular. We are inside Lacan's terms here, guided by his signifiers through the narrow passage of his meaning. Desire is not universal, he says, but entirely particular. Indeed, one need only consider the particularity of each person's dream, story, sense of humor, sexuality, not to mention many other examples, to say the obvious: each one of us is unique. Yet, we are caught in a double bind. We try to satisfy our own particular desires by obtaining *jouissance,* but we can get what we want only from others whose desire is also particular.

Desire, thus viewed, is not equatable with pleasure, but gives evidence of a structure in being that always demands something *more* than satisfaction itself. The "more" that is asked for is some proof or guarantee of one's worth beyond what love, money, fame, or social recognition can provide. In other words, there is always an impasse in trying to be whole, when the very condition of existence makes us incomplete (lacking) vis-à-vis one another. Lacan says that if desire were universal or universalizable, as both Aristotle and Freud thought, then positivistic psychology's discovery of childish pleasure in the adult, and the adult already present in the child, would have answered our questions regarding why desire remains so problematic in relation to pleasure (Lacan 1986, p. 33). For how can the child remain in the adult? And if it can, how does this give rise to ethical dilemmas of fixated memory from which repetitions in individual histories derive, as well as in history?

In treating problems of the particular by using universal categories and paradigms, both Aristotle and Freud encountered impasses where issues concerning the particular arose, whether one refers to Aristotle's generalizations about what constitutes rhetoric or Freud's later efforts to situate the meaning of dreams in a fixed code of images tied to collective human experience.[5] In neither case can the answers be derived from a model applicable to a generic "we."

As early as *The Project For a Scientific Psychology* (1895), Freud broke away from the neurological model, from the idea that an unbroken chain of physical events is causative of memory.[6] Having failed to explain the unconscious as memory or thought, Freud came up with the concepts of a pleasure principle and a reality principle that he did not know where to place. As we know, Freud eventually placed the pleasure principle on the side of primary process thinking and the reality principle on the side of secondary process or conscious thought. Lacan suggests that Freud's theory of a pleasure principle may have been derived from his philosophy courses with Franz Brentano. Brentano taught the Aristotelian theory that universal propositions were realizable via imbibing the good or sweetness (Lacan 1986, p. 39). In any case, Freud's twin principles caused as many new problems for him as they solved old ones. Not seeing *that* the tension between the two concerned the problem of how an unconscious could think, Freud opted for biological answers to explain his theory. In his second topology in which id-ego-superego takes the place of conscious-unconscious-preconscious models, Freud made the unconscious into a progressive stream of sensations that cling to the level of the pleasure principle through memories of infantile pleasures and literal bodily sensation.

In the course of *Séminaire* VII Lacan evolved his own answer to the question of what the pleasure principle *is* and what lies beyond it. He argued that Freud had set the philosophical tradition awry in showing that reality is not, as philosophers had thought, extrinsic or innate. Reality is not something already there, such as an inner predisposition to some comfort that is *itself,* whether one calls it God, the good mother, the *cogito,* the *Dasein, das Ding an sich,* the undecidable, the uncertainty principle, the trace, or the gene. Lacan read Freud as intimating that reality is not opposed to pleasure, but rather is actually threatened by it. Reality *is not itself,* then, but is precarious, deceptive, going in the direction of displeasure (Lacan 1986, p. 40).

In the *Interpretation of Dreams* as printed in 1900, Freud sought to identify symbols with perception.[7] In *The Project* (1897–1902) he tried to identify thought with neurons. But the early Freud who elaborated such correspondence theories did not know that there is a flaw in conscious thought. Indeed, he thought similar things could be the "same" as each other. Lacan calls this an identitarian error of logic or Imaginary thought. Imaginary thinking works diacritically by opposing one thing to another as good or bad, white or black, right or wrong. In this way, we think via identification with what is familiar to each of us, failing to see that such global thought arises from the love-hate that gives consistency to the particularity of our *jouissance*. Meanwhile, answers to the enigmas in individual lives, as well as to larger life questions, are strewn at the surface of our speech in details of disunity, contradiction, and impossibility.

In Lacanian theory, the order of the particular—the fourth order of the *sinthome*—tells the story in fixations or repetitions that produce an excess *jouissance*. At the point of this excess that dwells in a piece of nonsense or some irreducible residue of pain, one knows that something has gone awry within the apparent unity of a subject. In these places of impasse in language or identificatory relations, unassimilated knowledge appears in the repetition of some prior trauma that has remained present as the knotted material of undeciphered meaning. At this *point* the subject is a response of the real. There one finds an excess in *jouissance* that appears as anxiety or frustrated desire. For symptoms are repetitions that tell the story of a person's *jouissance* in terms of *das Ding* that is not sayable, speakable, or thinkable in conscious thought. But "it" is written in and on the body anyway, as the "death drive," the more than you in you that does not want your good.

Lacan argues the unthinkable. *Das Ding* as the *Dasein* or object *a* is the *agent* of thinking and acting. But this is no impersonal "thing" or project driving one toward death or old age. Rather, it is what causes our *jouissance*. When it is stuck at repeating symptoms formed early in life, one's cause links up with the death drive, supported, as such, by two kinds of meaning: on the one hand, every person is alienated into the interlocking associations of networks of signifying chains; on the other hand, the object *a* is *logically* inferred wherever one finds people seeking consistency in enjoyment, pleasure in *repeating* the past because it is known and familiar. Lacan taught that he did not mean an actual object, but "simply the presence of a hollow, a void, which can be occupied, Freud tells us, by any object. We know the agency of this void object only in the form of the lost object, the *petit a*."[8] Jacques-Alain Miller has referred to this as the *post-Symbolic real*. Miller designates as the pre-Symbolic real the object *a* that Lacan first named as the *cause* of desire; primordially repressed—and radically lost—Ur objects. Lacan argued in 1960 that the demand aspect—the "I ask this of you . . . "—of the drive disappears in primal repression,

> with the single exception that the cut remains, for this cut remains present in that which distinguishes the drive from the organic function it inhabits: namely, its grammatical artifices, so manifest in the reversions of its articulation to both source and object. . . . The very delimitation of the 'erogenous zone' that the drive isolates from the metabolism of the function . . . is the result of a cut *[coupure]* expressed in the anatomical mark *[trait]* of a margin or border—lips, 'the enclosure of the teeth,' the rim of the anus, the tip of the penis, the vagina, the slit formed by the eyelids, even the horn-shaped aperture of the ear . . . observe that this mark of the cut is no less obviously present in the object described by analytic theory: the mamilla, faeces, the phallus (imaginary object), the urinary flow. (An unthinkable list if one adds, as I do, the phoneme, the gaze, the voice—the nothing.)[9]

The loss of *jouissance* leaves a cut that inscribes itself on the body, marking the sites where we are divided between the real of loss and the desire to be whole. It is important to note that although we seek repetition of satisfactions meant to make us whole again, the objects or things sought are themselves *lure* objects. Yet we seek wherever the cut has left its mark on us, most notably in the realm of the phallus—the mark of difference itself—where we have been asked to tailor gender and desire to anatomy, even though these are not aligned with our bodies except in a series of linguistic and mimetic lies. Thus, desire functions paradoxically. It both supports the aim of unconscious fantasy to attain the object meant to compensate for the radical loss at the center of being, body, and knowledge; and it also shows the permanent split between the wish for libidinal wholeness and the myriad substitutions that hold out false promises of Oneness. Consequently, a battle wages between Eros and Thanatos where each person's most intimate *cause* is the real of *jouissance* effects that appear in the cut, there where the subject suddenly becomes an object set adrift in the void.

But experience of the void does not refer to metaphor or myth, like the negativity or emptiness of the Heideggerian vase, itself a signifier for fullness or emptiness. Lacan talks, rather, of the *real of loss* as a catalyst that makes the void a positivized negativity: a palpable, weighty presence of *nothingness* in language, being, and body. This means that the Sovereign Good of humans lies in their seeking to replace something radically lost. The aim of repetition, then, is not the object per se, but the consistency of *jouissance* by which each of us tries to eradicate the anxiety or to satisfy the erotogeneity made by the cut. The cut marks each person's body with a second kind of knowledge, the libidinal or *jouissance* meaning that constitutes each person's myth of sexuality and gender in a knowledge that is not naturally aligned with anatomy, that is not produced by the biological organism itself.

At the *jouissance* level, the subject is neither inside nor outside, the inside-outside opposition being an imaginary construction based on the visible. Indeed, the imaginary lies and proofs abound. For example, the wholeness of joy sought in experience is paradoxically appreciated, if at all, only in retrospect; in the retelling of stories, in photos, in supposing the pleasure of the moment in memory, not in reality. For the subject is in truth an *extimate* object *a,* a *semblance* of being trying to cover a void. In the holes and gaps where the subject of the unconscious surges forth in its failure to cover over the void, it appears as an object of the gaze or voice. *Jouissance* effects are not generally thought of as a knowledge, however, because they reside outside conscious thought and language in nonsense, in enigmas, in symptoms; that is, in impasses where no person is ever One with the Good that Lacan named the *primary object.*

Yet, we continually seek imaginary collusions for the purpose of giving continuity to our divided lives. The imaginary order functions precisely to give a sense of wholeness to our lives through ritualized contexts of repetition that quickly become sterile and rote, even though such rituals serve as the axis of social life. Their importance lies in the ease with which one can equate their dependability, their repeatability, with a guarantee of truth. Yet, the real—not the imaginary—is the first order for Lacan, the order of discontinuities that infer themselves into seeming unities to present a void space between the orders: real, symbolic, and imaginary. Yet Oneness or unity is a goal that seems to be sought repetitiously by all ethical systems of prescribed actions. Whether the imaginary Oneness belongs to the White Mass or to the Black Mass, to Immanuel Kant or to the Marquis de Sade, Lacan's topological logic argues that the goal sought entails a *structural* quest for union and reunion wherein the Good is supposed to reside in following the path of some "right" way.

Lacan situates ethical problems in the dimension of the real. The real blocks us, obstructs memory, bespeaks trauma. The real is the unsayable, the unrepresentable, the impossible to bear. In this sense, any freedom to be gained lies in extracting oneself from *being* painfully alienated within the language, identifications, and desires of others. Freedom from the past imposed on each of us can be measured as a distance gained in dropping the real of repetitions whose weight is the enjoyment that satisfies a drive—ultimately the drive for satisfaction as a denial of lack —in the realm of illusion and lie. Such satisfaction is achieved at the expense of the freedom of choice that begets change via action.

In *Séminaire* VII Lacan says: "The death drive is to be situated in the historical domain, insofar as it articulates itself at a level which is only definable by function of the signifying chain, that is to say, insofar as it is a guide, which is a guide of order" (Lacan 1986, p. 250). The point is this: the real in a historical chain is isolatable only because it was first inscribed on the body as a cut that creates what Lacan called a *unary trait* (Lacan, *Ecrits*, p. 314). This trait or mark is felt at the edge or rim of an organ where *jouissance* is suspended as an inertia or blockage within the unconscious that intersects with organ function.

Lacan's teaching takes a surprising turn here. We cannot get at the real in the unconscious chain by analyzing secondary process thought, nor by adapting to a reality principle that is supposedly equatable with the superego or the gaze of social law. We can address the real only by the pathways of primary process that Lacan renames as the *metonymy* that functions by libidinal displacement. Pleasure was *first* written as primary process experience of *das Ding* when the real was constituted by trauma. This primordial trauma is inscribed in the body as an Ur repression of *jouissance*. But since this *jouissance* is constituted outside spoken language, there is no name one can give it except loss.[10] Lost memories cannot be recalled. Moreover, a priori moments of loss—be they of pleasure or pain —return at all only in *a timing of the real* that marks the body. But they also return through words in a *second* memory that Lacan called the *time of reality* or the superego.

Yet, how can one recognize the return of something radically lost to memory? Lacan's answer is that "it" does not return as pleasure, but in the form of symptoms, in the form of that which *no longer* wishes one's Good. Paradoxically, "it" once wished your good, gave you pleasure, or it would not have persisted in the time of unspeakable memory as an enigmatic mark on the body. Indeed, "it" ties you to the world. Lacan's innovation in Freud's thought here is quite remarkable. We remember that the effects he calls the object *a* are not visible objects with properties one can describe a priori, although the effects have palpable—that is, "visible"—properties. Lacan says these "objects" are "essentialized" by *jouissance* effects that return as the real of a pure void that does not exist, *but that functions* anyway according to a certain logic. If Lacan is right, something is always already laid down prior to memory: some "thing," some libidinal trait that glues the world of things, words, and desires to the body, making it possible for speaking beings to build their life myths on memories lost to conscious thought.

One may well wonder how unrepresented memories can give rise to anything. Lacan argued that the real supports the fundamental fantasies that sustain our desiring quests. Moreover, one can recognize its return in the *future perfect tense of repetition* in which meaning is made in a temporal movement between anticipation and retroaction whose referent is the void. In other words the "original" cause can never be said. One knows only that some effect has caused first pleasure and then pain that build into pockets of *jouissance* effects that weigh down the signifying chain of language and identifications. The return is "known," then, as a discontinuity or rupture in a seeming unity.

But why would there be a gap between the *pleasure* of an a priori memory and a *reality* of pain that marks the second memory as reality or superego? Why would this require an ethics of psychoanalysis? Jacques-Alain Miller clarifies Lacan in this way: the agent or *das Ding* chooses, decides, and responds from the real, from the limits of a given reality.[11] Moreover, if reality is supported by unconscious fantasies, not by objective facts, then any individual is able to rationalize the ethical imperatives that he or she follows. If thought is anchored in fundamentally unconscious fantasies, then conscious meaning need not look far to place the guarantee of its doubts in the certainties of a profoundly subjective world-view. This Cartesian guarantee mis-takes thinking something with the correctness or truth of that thought. But the consequences of believing our own suppositions, even our own doubts, places us in the hands of the supreme superego. That is, the reality of our fixations causes us to identify with our narcissistic certainties, with the death thrall of our own *jouissance*. Serge Cottet has written: "The more one gives up on *jouissance,* the more demanding the superego is."[12]

Feminist theorist Teresa Brennan has written in "The Construction of Imaginary Time" that, although Freud saw the primary processes of unconscious thought as timeless, Lacan's "linguistic" turn has shown us that secondary processes give us language. Thus, "there is no warrant for the assumptions made about the nature of the primary process. For the primary process can only be known through the perspective of the secondary process."[13] But Lacan's point, as I understand it, is precisely the opposite. He does not dispense with primary process, but locates it in a different place in the Freudian opus than Freud did.

The real of loss constitutes primary process as the desire to replace something missing. The desired "object" sought in the pursuit of pleasure leads us back to the a priori fixations that, according to Lacan, ground our pursuits in the mistaken idea that *jouissance* lies in objects, people, and events. Still, the pre-Symbolic object *a* of the real starts the chase although we lose these objects that satisfy us. Referring to this experience of loss as the cut that gives rise to *jouissance*, Lacan suggests that these cuts are what Freud called *perception marks* in *The Project*. In any case, Lacan's point is this: the infant first desires *jouissance,* not objects per se. Arguing that the unconscious *is* the time of desire, Lacan says that the timing of any person's destiny is played out—repeated or not—in response to a time whose logic is neither chronological, nor linear, but that of a mother's desire as correlated to the signifier of a father's name.

But we are not aware that our conscious words and acts emanate from unconscious desire. Indeed, the timing of the unconscious is the trace of a moment, a lightning fast movement around a Möbius strip where space is defined by the time it takes to make the turn around the figure 8 shape of this topological future. In this sense, the Möbius strip is itself a mathematical representation of a psychic truth: in speech or dreams, word and image combine in an effort to re-present desire. But they always miss precise satisfaction of a particular desire because its cause is lost.[14] All that is left of the lost cause of desire is the mark of *jouissance* in language or on the body where we encounter the time of desire as the desire to repeat, rather than the "desire to know." There where desire is linked to the death drive, the subject is an object whose limits are the limits of pain in-*corp*-orated in, but not assimilated by, language.

Although the signifier is at the beginning of what is represented to us, the "drive" is historical. Prior to language, the drive begins to develop the dimension of an ex nihilo (Lacan 1986, p. 252). Most theories of ethics disregard repetition whose meaning is the pain of loss itself, even if it is manifest only in the bittersweetness of nostalgia. Put another way, repetition lies beyond the pleasure principle. Rooted in *jouissance,* repetition gives the unconscious a law of signs that guarantees that the subject is Good for nothing, is not ideal, is a "bad object" (Lacan 1986, p. 89). In other words, the real of unconscious identifications tells the story of imperfections, failures, mistakes, "original" sin. Seen thus, moral law articulates itself in whatever refuses the impossibility of the real in favor of an illusory guarantee of certainty, righteousness, wholeness. To make his point, Lacan goes so far as to argue that Kant's universal maxim for human relations (the good of one is the good of all), enunciated in *The Critique of Practical Reason* (1788),[15] and de Sade's invitation to universal debauchery (you can do anything to me, I say to you) in *La philosophie dans le boudoir* (1796) show us the same thing: the desire for a "law" to mediate the unhappiness of the human subject.[16]

Lacan's point is this: each time one makes a choice, one chooses from the real. But how can one choose from an order of unassimilated traumas? *Because* repetition determines choice, pointing to the meaning behind habit as something laid down before, both in the symbolic *automaton* and in the contingent real. In choosing, we face the object *a* again and again; an absent, yet irreducible kernal of blockage at the heart of every signifying chain. There, loss is positivized as a palpably ungraspable effect or enigma of *la douleur* at the limit. It follows, in Lacan's context, that belief systems, transference relations, and knowledge systems can all serve as the object *a,* as fillers for a bottomless hole of loss, although Lacan says the object *a* will be linked to one of the four primordial objects that become partial drives: the breast, the faeces, the gaze, or the voice. But still, no "object" of ungraspable effect eradicates the obduracy of loss as a palpable "thing" whose effects splinter language and proliferate repetitions, creating mysteries and paradoxes that send us on intellectual, aesthetic, and ethical pursuits. In fact, the humble questions behind our endeavors are these: 'Can you see me?' 'Do you hear me?' 'Is my gift enough?' and so on.

If we seek the subject's Good in *psychoanalysis,* however, do we find something new concerning ethics? Lacan says yes. He says that we find *an unnameable subject of experience* that corresponds to the *oppositions* of reality and pleasure, thought and perception, the known and unknown. Lacan claims further that ethics has always reached a dead end in identifying, and spuriously equating, two antinomical terms: pleasure and the Good (Lacan 1986, p. 44). The Lacanian object *a* is the equivalent of Freud's subject of *Civilization and Its Discontents* who experiences malaise because civilization or social law demands too much.[17] The human answers to "too much to bear" have been various counsels of goodness or perfection that paradoxically reveal the truths of lack, loss, and lies behind these counsels of impossibility. "All have sinned and come short of the glory of God."[18]

But *what* is this real order that dwells in all humans, at the heart of culture, that produces pleasure in a first moment and death effects in a second one? For one thing, it is not *das Ding* as some imaginary lure object. Rather, wherever a consistency is inferred, *jouissance* effects can be deduced, both in language and from a writing on the body. The real appears there in a disturbance in *jouissance,* replacing the unconscious that supports speech (Lacan 1986, p. 88). While the object *a* cause-of-desire supports fundamental fantasies ($\$ \Diamond a$)[19] that, in turn, form unconscious thought around ideas and ideals covering a void, *das Ding* is the effect of a pure *jouissance* of the void trying to enter the symbolic as conflict. Paradoxically, psychoanalysis opens a way to make a connection between the unbearable real and the parts of the world it touches.

But why should the entry of the real into the public forum bring discomfort into the social realm? Lacan argues that when we encounter the *jouissance* that shocks us into knowing ourselves as unhappy, we experience uncertainty in our dependencies on language and identification. The reality that each of us accommodates in fantasy does not welcome the return of the leftover residue of *jouissance* that marks us as creatures of the real, as creatures of trauma we have not surmounted. It is not surprising that Lacan would find in repetition real knots that make us sick, make us fail, make us stumble.

At the level of primary process, desire starts as a repetition—even that of a cry—meant to bring back first satisfactions. These repetitions quickly become their own raison d'être. Indeed, they seem to anchor us in our worlds. But paradoxically, even when repetition culminates in a desired pleasure, the object thought to satisfy desire was never possessed in the first place. No "object" or act can substitute for the primary loss we seek to eradicate by repeating experiences of fantasized wholeness. Rather, obsessional repetitions, repetition bearing the very structure of obsession, point to the structure in which satisfaction is tied to the real of *jouissance*. One might reasonably say that obsession *is* the structure of language and foundation of social law. Thus obsession goes against the grain of the real that anchors it, trying at all costs to avoid knowledge of the unconscious. It makes sense that repetition functions to repress memories that cannot be said because they wrack the body with the pain of affect. We seek to avoid pain, yet experience it anyway, because repetitions give us the signifiers and object *a* from which we have formed ourselves in certain fixations that define our limits.

Let us now try to understand what Lacan meant when he said that ethics emanates from one fundamental law, the incest taboo. His is not a moral interpretation of the Oedipal myth. Nor is his point a Kleinian one: that the mother, or parts of the mother's body, are in and of themselves good or bad "objects" that constitute being in the first place or that exist as those by which suffering can later be repaired. Rather, the incest taboo, in Lacan's rethinking, is a taboo against the identificatory fantasy that one can be made whole by the mother at the level where she is taken as *das Ding,* the Good. Not only is *das Ding* not a signifier, it is outside the signified, Lacan says. *Das Ding* or *la chose freudienne* means too much pleasure, an excess.

But how does such a theory influence ethics? Because of our *prochains,* our nearest and dearest can impose on us, without even knowing they do so, a burden of unbearable pain and grief. If a child is raised for the pleasure of the Other, not for the world, the weight of death in his or her life *returns* not only as that person's own deathweight, but as an affliction on society as well. Identified with the drives, rather than with signifiers of one's own, such a person is continually confronted with the pain of anxiety caused by a too present real. Such a person does not *become* a subject qua difference, a subject for others. Yet we are confronted with a difficult paradox: we take on a sense of being only by identifying with our *semblables*.

The ethical dimension of a call to psychoanalysis comes from this truth: we pay too great a price in suffering when we find our consistency as a Oneness or wholeness in a supposedly "natural" symbiosis with another, our guarantee. But *symbiotic* does not mean Oedipal. Even the incest taboo is a lie. Incest *is* possible. Lacan uncovers what is *impossible* or taboo in incest: the Oneness it forbids. When two persons function *as if* they were one, the structure of psychosis is constituted in a foreclosure of the founding law of difference that creates a "good enough" identity on which a social link that respects the other can be built. The symbiotic failure of structure reveals the impasses that constitute incest on the slope of a demand for wholeness, rather than on the desiring axis of admitting a *lack*-in-being.

Whatever form a relation to the mother's body might take in a nostalgic romantic fantasy of plenitude, or in some Sadean destructive fantasy of social revolution, any decision, action, or choice that one makes repeats the dilemma of choosing, anchored as it is in the real of repetitions. Symptoms do not announce anything other than the presence of real knots in a story, a memory, a body. But knots return as resistances that paradoxically defend the death drive. Ego stories are told as signs of hope eternal, conquering victories of the success of merely willing change. These narcissistic illusions unveil the human refusal to give up our belief in the Good. Indeed, the ego revels in the illusion that the other—or Other—has our Good in mind.

Freud opined that psychoanalysis had not promoted the importance of moral issues. Lacan countered with the claim that psychoanalysis had to concern itself with ethics because the primary object is lost (except in psychosis); yet we negotiate it as if it were there, reify it in narcissistic ideologies and nationalisms (collective massifications of a subject) all based on equating static *jouissance* with our Good. Lacan's master discourse is the field of language in its function of keeping us from seeing the oscillating relation between fantasy and desire that language *represses* and pretends is not there. Language gives material to a logic of the imaginary that prevails in conscious thought. Lacan says that the temptation to tame the Other and the loss at its center with interpretations of wholeness and closure is irresistible. We do this by our relations to things and to others, basing most of our ethical systems on a high evaluation of the Other, our *semblable*. Theories of altruism, equality, a group good will, philanthropy, and expansions of the Goodness of Youness abound. These run counter to the limit that ethics always encounters: too much suffering.

And suffering has persisted throughout the lives of all people, in all historical eras. That its precise character always returns to issues concerning man's inhumanity to man or to impasses of private pain or suffering denied, gives the lie to any theory of a natural goodness in humankind, or to any idea of a natural harmony between fellow beings. De Sade pushed this limit to its extreme to proclaim what Lacan calls the *truth* of *metipsimus;* myself, the same, the same-ty of others. "Love your neighbor as yourself," says the Bible.[20] Lacan translates this to mean "love the image by which your ego was formed" (Lacan 1986, p. 230).

We need an ethics of psychoanalysis because we constitute each other first in the name of love and then love only that in others which reflects ourselves. In every subject, effects of *jouissance* reside at the interior of a void and appear as a rapid oscillation between nothingness and being. Our most intimate part is "that." It is not surprising, then, that Lacan views conflict between people as the intervention of the real in the symbolic. Intersubjectivity is gone. Master-slave power relations are gone. We are at the bottom line of survival where each person creates his or her world in con-*form*-ity with his or her *jouissance*. There one has a sense of being as a sense of "being" best or worst, loved or hated, all or nothing. Guilt lies in between: guilt for falling short of ideals. When one's narcissistic *jouissance* is momentarily appeased by a voice or a gaze, the time of satiation is already over. Repetition returns to mock us with the impossibility of sustaining the position of Oneness that bespeaks unity with the semblance of a Sovereign Good.

What appears instead is desire, referring to the "substance" of old: the Good of the subject. Lacan argues that Freud sidestepped the idea of defining the Good in terms of a morality or a set of laws by finding the Sovereign Good at the level of the pleasure principle, there where the mother is the forbidden good. And with this idea, Lacan thinks Freud reversed the foundation of moral law, although he did not solve the problems he uncovered (Lacan 1986, p. 85). Unlike Freud, Lacan viewed the problem of ethics as emanating from how desire is structured, how we are constituted by others to evolve into rigid selves to which we quickly become blind. If *jouissance* is absolute, nondialectical, a pure nonutilitarian real that wishes nothing except a dumb, nonsensical, blind repetition that functions only to satisfy the drive—the drive *to be* . . . seen, heard, fed in a familiar way so that each of us recognizes who we *are* in terms of who we were—then the drives are aligned with the death in repetition. Our belief that we will be *cognized* in terms of being *re-cognized,* made whole by repeated pleasures, refuses to accept that those repeated pleasures no longer give pleasure. Like the reality of fantasy, aligned as it is with the ego, *jouissance* sides with narcissism. And both validate the fixity of symptoms in whatever prefers consistency and familiarity over the Good of constituting desire anew, in giving birth to change, to action.

The analytic ethical act consists, then, of finding a way to stop identifying with the death in one's symptoms, to call a symptom by its name so that one can drop its deadly weight. One has much to gain by doing this: the freedom for action, the freedom to break out of static rituals that prevent us from working on individual or social problems. The difficulty is enormous, requiring as it does a separation of the ego (one's ideals) from the symptom. This can occur only when we tell the truth about ourselves. But telling the truth requires that we transcend our own narcissism with its roots in *jouissance.* The task is almost impossible. Because the real is already divided from conscious memory, *jouissance* effects appear in symptoms, speaking the enigmatic language of incomprehensible nonsense, illogic, and pain. But if one succeeds in making a split between the ego and the symptom, this change shifts the emphasis toward ethical speaking on which ethical action can be based. Psychoanalytic "speaking well" means calling something by its correct name. This is the only route by which a re-*form*-ation of the ego can occur. Freud's famous formula *"Wo es war, soll Ich werden"* takes on a new meaning.[21] Where *jouissance* or *es* dwelt as the emptiness of *jouissance* speaking in the place of power, an ethical word may be spoken instead. This kind of speaking bases action on lack, rather than on the grandiosity of narcissistic pretention.

The analyst uses the cut to punctuate an analysand's speech so that she or he can actually hear what has been said. This kind of cutting into speech puts the analysand in touch with the real of *jouissance* where it intersects with desire. In the terms of mathematical topology, hearing what you *actually* said in an auditory blind spot is the equivalent of the point where the Möbius strip crosses itself. This is like the double buckle of the signifier that cannot signify itself (Granon-Lafont, pp. 3–4). Thus, the paradoxical solution to the ethical dilemma posed by our depending on our own repetitions that we have lost from sight or hearing means that the analyst has to cut into language or desire at the place the patient is enjoying. Such action is ethical action that "knows" the subject is an object, a *das Ding.* At this point the subject *is* an excluded interior of the hypothetical real of its own psychic organization. It is that in life which is already dead, but insists in our language and flesh as the real of the enigmatic symptom. Given this view, one could well agree with Lacan that the *weight* of duty in Kant's *Critique* parallels his own idea of the real weight constituted by a subject's *jouissance* (Lacan 1986, p. 130).

But how can such an ethics concerned with the triumph of *new* desire over *old jouissance* help us live in the world? Is this not just another version of Camus's *"Il faut imaginer Sisyphe heureux"*?[22] That is, must one *pretend* that Sisyphus is happy *[faire comme si; faire semblant]*? No. Lacan's argument is quite simple. To live by the death scripts that fixate us as imaginary objects or *semblants* is unethical. But to know how to escape this bind requires a new kind of knowledge: a confrontation with the fictions that make up our truths by taking account of the fact that we were deceived by intimates and will be again, that there is always a failure of correlation or correspondence between symbolic-imaginary expectations and the responses we get back from the real (Lacan 1986, p. 123). Any alleviation of the traumas that first caused the losses we try to deny and eradicate, whether they concern sexual difference or social discrimination, gives each person the chance for some freedom. And the effects of individuals working for the Good, rather than for their own narcissism, have a necessary social value.

In a Lacanian ethics we know that we will not be loved (enough). We know that neither our Good nor our goods will bring final happiness or change. So we have to try another path. This other way opposes the pain of truth to the lies by which we justify our lives as good, meaningful, and benign. One effect of telling the truth of our pain, of recognizing that we are not finally curable, nor will we ever be whole, is the attenuation of the brutality exercised on all of us by cultural ideals we emulate and seek to imitate.

Lacan finds the ultimate horror at the barrier of desire where the idea of the Good is itself a barrier separating us from it. Put another way, we love our symptoms more than ourselves. We love the fixity of consistencies more than truth. Another barrier that stops us from making radical change is the aesthetic phenomenon or sublimation: a pleasure taken in the beautiful. The beautiful, in turn, seems true. Whatever one finds to be true, one finds beautiful. Given this Keatsian paradox, Lacan remarks upon the beautiful as dwelling closer to evil than to the good (Lacan 1986, p. 256). The master discourse, which is Lacan's name for repression, closes out the truth that can set one free in preference for the repetitious lies on which the death drive lives.

Of what, then, should one be cured? One should be cured of the illusions produced by ideals and fantasies because they *fix* us on the path of death, keeping us imprisoned in repetitions that place us in double binds. The real in the symbolic is a deathweight that skews our vision so that we must find beauty in what we do or think. In this way, we unconsciously defend our right to hurt ourselves, as well as others, because we cannot think or see outside our own formations. The paradox is that we survive at all only because we make ideals of the forms from which we live. Ming vase or tomato soup can—it makes no difference. Lacan's point is that changing the real—the impossible or contradictory—is so difficult, the freedom to reconstitute desire so elusive, that our only hope for a bit more distance from what perturbs us lies in smashing our dreams of completeness, in breaking with them, in emptying out our illusions of being. This requires breaking with that in you that is *more* than you, that excess in *jouissance* that claims bits and pieces of one's life as its price for the stranglehold of familiarity and consistency.

This ethics is hard because it asks us to work against the grain of the normative in desire and in being, not against ideology. In analysis another person is required to sit in as a symbol of the silence in your *cause*. This enables you to speak the unspeakable, the alienation between your desire and your *jouissance*. Lacan's texts go a long way toward exercising a similar effect on his readers. A text, however, is not an analyst. But Lacan's analytic teaching can enable a person to create new action, both at the individual and group levels. This is because Lacan's teaching asks people not to give up on their desire or their *jouissance*. When Lacan first spoke, only a few people attended his seminar. As people heard his teaching, the numbers grew into the hundreds and thousands. The "Lacan effect" has touched many countries since his death in 1981; this effect in and of itself is a proof of action, as well as of an injunction to act. But what is the cause? Is this, as some say, a cult effect that produces "true believers"?

I say no. Lacan shreds traditional notions of "truth" and "belief" in as thorough and radical a way as has ever been done by anyone. But, and this is perhaps a paradox, he speaks from the place of truth that is the place of human suffering. He teaches that freedom derives directly from an awareness of precisely how the real makes each of us suffer, a "knowledge" we practice every day. Insofar as *jouissance* is the agent of our speech, behavior, and the choices that produce our actions, Lacan's ethics of psychoanalysis is not a new set of prescriptive laws or standards for behavior. There are no new gods, least of all the god of narcissism. Rather, his is a *new* ethics that breaks with epistemology and ontology. Lacan's *hontology* enjoins us to seek the truths behind our individual lies rather than the answers that make us seem ideal or at least close off anxiety. The truth behind all social lies is the godlike power of man's inhumanity to man. These lies constitute the rationalizations and denials we live by to justify what cannot be justified. They are unethical, in Lacan's teaching, because they are impossible to bear. Lacan, thus, gives us a new subject of lack, a new object of limit, and an injunction to live with less attachment to our symptoms because—and this is crucial—our masked pain makes us harm others as we harm ourselves.

7   Julia Kristeva's Speaking Body

KELLY OLIVER

> Our philosophies of Language, embodiments of the Idea, are nothing
> more than the thoughts of archivists, archaeologists, and necrophiliacs.
> Fascinated by the remains of a process which is partly discursive, they
> substitute this fetish for what actually produced it. . . . These static
> thoughts, products of a leisurely cogitation removed from historical
> turmoil, persist in seeking the truth of language by formalizing utter-
> ances that hang in midair, and the truth of the subject by listening to
> the narrative of a sleeping body—a body in repose, withdrawn from its
> socio-historical imbrication, removed from direct experience.[1]

These lines from the introduction to Julia Kristeva's doctoral dissertation,
published as *Revolution in Poetic Language,* indicate her project to bring
the speaking body back into structuralism and phenomenology. Kristeva
argues that both structuralism and phenomenology engage in necrophilia
insofar as they deal with a "sleeping" silent body. To bring the body,
replete with drives, back into our philosophies of language, Kristeva
employs two very different strategies. Most theorists who are familiar
with Kristeva's work focus on only one of those strategies.

Kristeva is best known for her semiotic-symbolic distinction. She
developed the notion of the semiotic element in language to bring the
body back into the very structure of language. Kristeva argues that language is composed of two heterogeneous elements, the semiotic and the
symbolic. The semiotic element is associated with the sounds and rhythms
of language. She argues that, because these sounds and rhythms are primarily associated with the sounds and rhythms of the maternal body, the
semiotic element of language is also associated with the maternal body.
Most theorists concentrate on this first strategy with which Kristeva attempts to bring the speaking body back into language by arguing that

bodily drives make their way into language through the disruptive, but necessary, force of this semiotic element.

Kristeva, however, employs a second, perhaps more interesting, way of bringing the speaking body back into philosophy of language. Her tactic is to reinscribe language in the body, arguing that the dynamics that operate the symbolic are already working within the material of the body and the presymbolic imaginary. She concludes that these dynamics must therefore be material or bio-logical as well as symbolic. In other words, her strategy is to trace the signifier through the body to reinscribe, at the same time, the body in language.

Kristeva argues that the logic of signification is already present in the material body. For signification to take place, we must be able to differentiate objects. We must be able to separate ourselves from other things. Lacan suggests that it is during the mirror stage that the infant first begins to separate itself from its mother and from other objects. At this stage the infant begins to enter language. In the mirror stage, the child sees its image in the mirror. It realizes that this image is connected to itself. Yet it also must realize that this image is different from itself, a mere image. So begins the process of representation. For Lacan, because the infant, in this moment, sees the separation or gap between its body and this mirror image, it becomes ready to enter language.

Kristeva further argues that the logic of this situation is already operating within the material of the body prior to the mirror stage. In fact, she maintains that Lacan cannot really account for the infant's move to language with his fantasy of the mirror stage. For Kristeva, without what she calls *material rejection* we cannot explain the transition from the presymbolic to the symbolic. We cannot explain what motivates the move through the mirror stage to the symbolic. Lacan, of course, gives the castration threat as the motive. But to experience this threat in the first place, the child must take a position as a subject in the mirror stage. It must recognize that it is its image but not its image. It must "see" the gap between its body and its image, the other. Kristeva persuasively argues that this move is already symbolic. The mirror stage already requires a negation of the other in order to identify oneself as a subject-self. Negation is already a judgment. A judgment is made only from a position. It is already symbolic. In other words, in Lacan's account, we seem to be moving in circles: the child takes a position as subject so that he can negate his image in order to take a position as subject. "To say 'no' is already to formulate syntactically oriented propositions that are more or less grammatical" (RPL 122). For Kristeva, rather than prefiguring the symbolic, then, the mirror stage would already appear to be symbolic.

How then do we get to this symbolic in the first place? If the mirror stage is already symbolic, then we certainly cannot use it as an explanation for the onset of the symbolic. Kristeva argues that the only way to explain the transition from presymbolic to symbolic is to acknowledge the material element that is heterogeneous to the symbolic. Rejection is not unique to the symbolic.[2] Rather, it operates first in the semiotic body. To illustrate this, Kristeva reinterprets Lacan's account of Freud's Fort-Da game. Whereas Lacan sees a negativity that functions through the metonymy that marks the beginnings of symbolization,[3] Kristeva sees a negativity that is still primarily gestural and kinetic: the bodily act of throwing and retrieving the reel (RPL 170).

Negativity moves through the symbolic because it moves through the corporeal. It operates in living matter prior to the symbolic (RPL 123). And, for Kristeva, negativity does not primordially act as lack, as Lacan suggests, but as excess. If the symbolic is merely founded on a lack, then there is all the more reason for avoiding it altogether, that is, for taking refuge in neurosis and psychosis. In Kristeva's account, however, material negativity is founded on excess. Anality is the primary example. When there is too much, some must be expelled. The separation comes not from lack, but from excess. In anality, rejection precedes the symbolic (RPL 151). Moreover, in anality, separation and rejection are pleasurable (RPL 151). It is important to note that not only anality, but also orality, causes pleasure. This will be an added motivation for speaking. As Kristeva describes it, the move from presymbolic to symbolic is not motivated purely by a castration threat or sense of lack. Rather, it is excess that moves the child into the realm of the symbolic. And although this excess leads to a privation, for Kristeva, it is pleasurable. This is why we speak. In fact, Kristeva argues that if the motive for entering language was based on lack and threats, then why would we not refuse to leave the safe haven of the maternal body to avoid this world of threats. In other words, why are we not all psychotic?

Not only is separation inherent in anality and orality, it is also inherent in the act of birth itself. Birth becomes the quintessential act of separation whereby one body is violently separated from another in order to be. "Abjection preserves what existed in the archaism of pre-objectal relationship, in the immemorial violence with which a body becomes separated from another body in order to be. ... Significance is indeed inherent in the human body."[4] Birth also becomes an example of the material logic of rejection. In fact, the maternal body is chock full of rejection and alterity. In addition, for Kristeva, the maternal function performs a kind of rejection in relation to the infant.

In traditional psychoanalytic theory, it is the paternal function that provides a prohibition that leads the child away from the maternal body and into the world of symbols or society. Kristeva, however, argues that prohibition is already active in the maternal function. She claims that

within the maternal function there is a "law before the law." Before the
infant enters language, the mother has complete control over that infant's
body. The mother regulates what goes in and monitors what comes out.
She gives and takes away the breast. Kristeva suggests that this regulation
prefigures the paternal prohibition that sends the child to language. So,
once again, the logic of language is already operating on a material
level.

Kristeva's suggestion that the logic of separation is already operating within the material body has important implications for psychoanalytic theory. First, the entrance into language is the result of a pleasurable
excess and not a Lacanian lack. Second, the paternal function is severely
undermined by the notion that separation is found within the body and
prohibition is found within the maternal function. So, Kristeva begins to
break the connection between the Father and the Law, thereby opening up
the possibility of alternative third parties who can fulfill the "paternal"
function.

In addition, Kristeva's thesis that material rejection is both logically and chronologically prior to Oedipal separation works in tandem
with her thesis that language is composed of two heterogeneous elements,
the semiotic and the symbolic. Her analysis of material rejection links the
semiotic with this presymbolic bodily drive force. This allows her to set
up her account of the dialectic between the semiotic and symbolic elements
that make up language. For Kristeva, language is the result of a dialectical
oscillation between these two elements. This oscillation is the movement
between rejection and stasis, separation and recuperation, difference and
identity, the logic of which is found within the material body. In *Revolution in Poetic Language,* Kristeva describes how this dialectical oscillation leads from one level to another. Eventually the material oscillations
give rise to the speaking subject. So, this is not a static oscillation; rather,
it is a productive oscillation that crosses ever new thresholds due to the
dynamic tension between rejection and stasis, semiotic and symbolic.

Kristeva's own writing seems to be governed by this logic of oscillation between rejection and stasis, difference and identity, semiotic and
symbolic. For example, in *Revolution in Poetic Language* (1974) and
Powers of Horror (1980) Kristeva emphasizes rejection, difference, the
semiotic element. Yet in *Tales of Love* (1983) and *Black Sun* (1987) she
emphasizes stases, identity, the symbolic element.[5] And in her latest writing, *Strangers to Ourselves* (1989), she emphasizes the difference within
identity.[6]

Kristeva claims that in all of her writings she is concerned with
discourses that break identity. She wants to focus on crises in signification, places where identity breaks down. She is concerned with alterity
within identity. Three of the discourses that have been central to her

writing are poetry, psychoanalysis, and maternity. All three of these discourses, in different ways, point to crises within identity.

Poetic language, for Kristeva, points to the signifying process itself. With its attention to sounds and rhythms, as well as to meaning, poetry points to the heterogeneity of language. It shows that language is composed of two elements, meaning and nonmeaning. Both of these elements are necessary for language to exist. Poetry, then, shows that language is produced as much through nonmeaning as meaning. In the process of showing the signifying process, poetry points to a subject in process. Kristeva says that any theory of language is also a theory of the subject. If, as Lacanian psychoanalysis suggests, the subject is the result of language, and language is heterogeneous, so too is the subject. Poetry, claims Kristeva, shows the subject in process—on trial. It shows that both the subject and language are made up of something heterogeneous to meaning; both are dynamically produced by semiotic drive force. So, neither meaning nor the subject is ever fixed or unified.

Kristeva argues that poetic language is revolutionary because it is a "reversed reactivation" of the contradiction between the semiotic and the symbolic. She calls it "reversed reactivation" because in poetic language the semiotic disrupts through the symbolic. Therefore, it is reversed. That is to say that we encounter the semiotic through the symbolic in spite of the fact that the semiotic gives rise to the symbolic. The encounter with the semiotic is reversed. Moreover, it is not some sort of sublimation of the semiotic within the symbolic; rather, it is a reactivation of the contradiction between them. Therefore, Kristeva's dialectic is not a Hegelian dialectic.

The Hegelian logic would describe the semiotic as thesis, the symbolic as negation of thesis, and the return of the semiotic as the negation of the negation of the thesis. In Kristeva's dialectic, however, there is no negation of negation. The appearance of the semiotic in poetic language is not a Hegelian negation of the symbolic's negation of the semiotic. Rather, it is a reactivation of the very contradiction between semiotic and symbolic. And, for Kristeva, it is this reactivation that is revolutionary insofar as it shows the process of signification. It shows the alterity within the identity of both language and the subject.

The second discourse that shows alterity within the identity of both language and the subject is psychoanalysis. In fact, for Kristeva, psychoanalysis, unlike poetic language, can do more than show the process. Psychoanalysis can elaborate the process. She argues that unlike poetic language, literature, or religion, psychoanalysis is an elaboration of the signifying process. Whereas literature and religion are merely cathartic insofar as semiotic drives are discharged through them, psychoanalysis can describe those drives.

Kristeva suggests that, although literature and religion are mere antidepressants, what we need is a counterdepressant. Psychoanalysis, she argues, is this counterdepressant. Literature and religion merely treat the symptoms of depression. Psychoanalysis treats the cause. This is how Kristeva explains her increasing interest in psychoanalysis. For her, it is the only place where theory and practice forcefully come together. The analytic session is theory in practice and the living practice of making theory. In the analytic session, theory and practice cannot be separated. Kristeva also suggests that she turned to psychoanalysis out of her interest in the places where language breaks down. She is interested in the extremes of language—the child's acquisition of language and the psychotic's loss of language, the before and after of language.

Like poetry, psychoanalysis points to alterity or difference within identity. Psychoanalysis is concerned with alterity within the subject, the unconscious as other. Just as Kristeva brings the speaking body back into language by putting language into the body, she brings the subject into the place of the other by putting the other into the place of the subject. This is why the subject is never stable, but always in process—on trial. Just as the pattern of language is already found within the body, the pattern and logic of alterity is already found within the subject.

> This process could be summarized as an *interiorization of the founding separation of the sociosymbolic contract,* as an introduction of its cutting edge into the very interior of every identity whether subjective, sexual, ideological, or so forth. This in such a way that the habitual and increasingly explicit attempt to fabricate a scapegoat victim as foundress of a society or a countersociety may be replaced by the analysis of the potentialities of *victim/executioner* which characterize each identity, each subject, each sex.[7]

In her latest writings, Kristeva emphasizes the ethical and political implications of postulating that the social relation is internal to the psyche. She argues that it may be possible to imagine an ethics that is not merely prohibitive or restrictive, an ethics that is not merely the result of legislation. For, if the social relation is interior to the psyche, we do not need to explain how it is that we can relate to an other radically outside of ourselves. The social relation is not a relation between two radically autonomous subjects who must then relate through the law. Rather, the logic of the social relation is within the subject.

For Kristeva, this social relation can be founded on love rather than prohibition. It is a matter of living with, and learning to love, the return of the repressed. She suggests that if we can learn to live with the return of the repressed in ourselves, then we can learn to live with the return of the repressed in our society. If we can learn to love the stranger in ourselves, then we can learn to love the strangers outside ourselves. The other, then, is not so radically other. And ethics may be possible.

The first model of this other who is not so other is found in the experience of maternity. For Kristeva the maternal body is possibly the most troubling example of difference within identity. The maternal body is the very embodiment of the subject in process–on trial.[8] Before the umbilical cord is cut, who can decide? Is it one or two? The maternal body is neither one nor two. It throws all identity and difference into crisis. Kristeva suggests that maternity provides an example of a love outside of the law that can found an ethics that is not merely prohibitive.

Late in *Tales of Love,* in a piece written prior to the rest, "Stabat Mater," Kristeva imagines this outlaw love.[9] She imagines the mother's love for the child, which is a love for herself but also the willingness to give herself up, as the basis of a new ethics, "herethics" (TL 262–263). To imagine this "herethics," Kristeva suggests that it is necessary to listen to the mother and her music. She claims that motherhood needs the support of a mother's mother (even in the person of a father, or imaginary father) (TL 227). The mother's oscillating union-disunion with her child recalls her own union with her mother. When we listen to Kristeva, the mother, we see that her mother is present in her own motherhood: "Recovered childhood, dreamed peace restored, in sparks, flash of cells, instant of laughter, smiles in the blackness of dreams, at night, opaque joy that roots me in her bed, my mother's, and projects him, a son, a butterfly soaking up dew from her hand, there, nearby, in the night. Alone: she, I, and he" (TL 247).

The love that founds "herethics" is a daughter's love through identification with her mother. A mother's love is her reunion with her own mother, not only as a third party, but also as herself. The child's transferential identification with the imaginary father, then, is an identification with its mother's reunion with her mother. It is this union that satisfies, that makes one complete. What does a mother want, especially in childbirth? She wants her mother. "The Paradox: Mother or Primary Narcissism," the subtitle of "Stabat Mater," points to the mother as the site of the primary identification that Kristeva calls the *imaginary father.* If the mother loves an Other, it is her own mother. And she loves her mother not only as an Other, but also as herself, now the mother. This love that is narcissism, "the inability to love," within patriarchal analysis is the basis of Kristeva's "herethics."

Herethics is an ethics that is founded on the relationship between the mother and child during pregnancy and birth. This ethics sets up one's obligations to the other as obligations to the self and obligations to the species. This ethics is founded on the ambiguity in pregnancy and birth between subject and object positions. Kristeva calls pregnancy an *institutionalized psychosis:* am I me or it?[10] The other cannot be separated from the self. The other is within the self. It is not in its place—the place of the other. It is, rather, in the place of the subject. This inability to separate self from other is a symptom of psychosis, the fundamental psychosis upon which any relationship is built. Pregnancy, says Kristeva, is the only place where this psychosis is socially acceptable.

The mother's relation to the child as other, then, is not a relation to the phallus and, by definition, unfulfillable desire:

> For a mother . . . [t]he other is inevitable, she seems to say, turn it into a God if you wish, it is nevertheless natural, for such an other has come out of myself. . . . The "just the same" of motherly peace of mind, more persistent than philosophical doubt, gnaws, on account of its basic dis-belief, at the symbolic's allmightiness. It bypasses perverse negation ("I know, but just the same") and constitutes the basis of the social bond in its generality, in the sense of "resembling others and eventually the species." (TL 262)

The mother's other, rather than the unreachable Other, the phallus, is a natural other. "Turn it into a God if you wish," but it is not transcen-dent; it is real. The mother has bodily proof of this. For the mother, this relationship with the other is not a struggle for recognition. It is not a battle—either me or you, subject or object. The child really is and was part of the mother's flesh. And her own flesh exists for the sake of the child, because, at the limit, the child does not and cannot "exist for itself." This other is not yet autonomous; it depends on the subject. As such, it threatens the "allmightiness" of the symbolic that requires an autonomous and inaccessible Other. Within Lacanian theory, it is this inaccessibility that opens the gap between signifier and signified and that produces the symbolic. The mother, however, gains access to what is off limits. She 'knows' better. She knows that there is no transcendent Other, no phallus. The other is the flesh of her flesh, natural, loved. She knows that the Other is not transcendent; rather, it is within.

Whereas the perverse negation, the fetishism, necessary to maintain the symbolic ("I know that the word is not the thing, but just the same. I know that the other is not me, but just the same.") constitutes the social bond through force, the Law of the Father, the mother's "just the same" is its reverse.[11] The mother negates the symbolic, even while ensuring its generation. She realizes that the other is the same, that the gap is not absolute. In the face of the symbolic and its transcendental signifier, she says "just the same, I know." The mother's "just the same" constitutes the social bond through love, not force. This "just the same," however, threatens to do away with difference and "it can crush everything the other [the child] has that is specifically irreducible" (TL 263). In other words, it threatens to do away with the symbolic. It threatens psychosis. This is why even if the symbolic denies the existence of the mother, she cannot, for the sake of her child, deny the existence of the symbolic. She must wean the child. She must instigate the break-up of their primary symbiosis. She must be silent about what she "knows" because she knows better (TL 260).

The child must separate from its mother to be an autonomous being. It cannot remain dependent on her. It is the mother's love, however, and her love for her own mother, a narcissistic love from generation to generation, that supports the move into the Symbolic. This love fills language with meaning. Is it possible, then, that the primary narcissism is repressed because it is a reunion with the mother's love that is founded on, yet mistaken for, a union with the mother's body? In the traditional psychoanalytic story, primary identification with the mother is repressed due to the paternal law against incest. Could the father of the law be wrong? Perhaps primary identification is not with the mother's body, but with the mother's love. Could this be some primordial transference from body to love that constitutes the first identity?

It is possible to read Kristeva as taking us deeper into the maternal body in her writings in order to set up an ethics founded on maternal love. In her earlier writings, she is concerned with recovering a repressed maternal body that is associated with the child's relation to its mother's breast. Later, she becomes concerned with the abject maternal body that is associated with the child's relation to its birth and the mother's "sex." Recently, she is concerned with the imaginary father, which I read as a screen for the mother's love, associated, as it is, with the child's relationship to its conception and the mother's womb. The imaginary father provides the support necessary to allow the child to move into the symbolic. This can be read as a move from the mother's body to the mother's desire through the mother's love.

In her earlier writings, for example, in *Revolution in Poetic Language*, Kristeva is concerned with introducing the semiotic as a maternal, material, logic of rejection that prefigures the Law of the Father. This maternal semiotic law before the law is associated with the mother's giving and taking away of the breast. The mother regulates the ins and outs of the child's body. Following Freud, Kristeva suggests that the infant identifies with the breast in a reduplication that prefigures identification proper in the mirror stage. The infant's incorporation of the breast sets up a pattern that will be repeated in the infant's incorporation of the speech of the other (TL 26). Kristeva's purpose in developing this theory is to explain how the child begins to "recognize" difference that gives rise to its "recognition" of its own identity prior to the mirror stage. She tries to explain what motivates the child to move away from its mother's body and into the world of symbols.

Kristeva proposes that the child must "abject" its mother in order to separate from her. The experience of abjection is one that calls into question borders. Certainly what is at stake in the child's autonomy and separation from its mother are borders, the borders of self and other. The prototypical experience of abjection is birth itself. Recall the following quote from *Powers of Horror:* "Abjection preserves what existed in the archaism of pre-objectal relationship, in the immemorial violence with which a body becomes separated from another body in order to be. . . . This means once more that the heterogeneous flow, which portions the abject and sends back abjection, already dwells in a human animal that has been highly altered. . . . Significance is indeed inherent in the human body" (PH 10).

Birth is an unruly border, a fragile border between two bodies. Within Kristeva's analysis, the mother's sex represents this border. She has taken us from the surface of the mother's body, the mother's breast, toward the inside of the mother's body. She takes us further inside the mother's body with her notion of the imaginary father. Kristeva proposes that the imaginary father provides the support necessary so that the child can abject the mother's body and move into the symbolic.

Staying within the framework of traditional psychoanalysis, the child, according to Kristeva, can overcome the abject mother only through a paternal agency (MGB 263). Although this paternal agency brings with it the need to symbolize (PH 118, 44; 1981 314), however, it is not Lacan's authoritarian father. Rather, for Kristeva, it is an "Imaginary Father," a loving father. As it turns out, this father is not really a father or not only a father. It has no sexual difference (TL 26). It is a combination of the mother and the father, the "father-mother conglomerate" (TL 40). The identification with this conglomerate is the vortex of primary identification that sets up all subsequent identifications including the ego's identification with itself (TL 33).

Kristeva's imaginary father can be read as a metaphorical or *imaginary* reunion with the maternal body that takes the place of the real union with, and dependence on, the maternal body. Kristeva asks us to follow her back beyond images of the nourishing semiotic maternal body, and the abject image of birth, to the first possible image of a life: conception. The fantasy of the imaginary father as the conglomerate of mother and father can be read as a fantasy of reunion with the mother's body, which takes the place of the real union that must be lost so that the child can enter language. The child's identification with the conglomerate mother-father can be read as an identification with its conception. It is a transference to the site of the *jouissance* of the primal scene.

Through the immediate transference with the imaginary father, the child undergoes a transference to the site of maternal desire, which Kristeva claims is the desire for the phallus. It is an identification with the father whom the child imagines took part in the primal scene. But it is an identification with this imaginary father only insofar as he represents the phallus that satisfies the mother's desire. The child, then, is identifying with the imaginary father entering the mother; it is identifying with a reunion with the mother. It is identifying with her *jouissance*, her satisfaction. Through its identification with the imaginary father, the child, in the imaginary, can re-place itself back inside its mother. It can re-place itself in the mother's womb. This imaginary identification with the mother's body provides the support needed to lose the real identification with the mother's body and to move to an identification with her desire, which is a move into the symbolic.

Kristeva's analysis of the child's fantasy of the primal scene in *In the Beginning Was Love* suggests this reading. There she says, in another context, that the child identifies with the father as a protection against a fantasy too much for the child to bear: "that of being supernumerary, excluded from the act of pleasure that is the origin of its existence" (BS 42). Perhaps the fantasy of the imaginary father enables the child to insert itself into the primal scene. Through the figure of the father, the child can take pleasure in a (re)union with the mother. In addition, through this fantasy, the child can take pleasure in the beginnings of its existence, an existence founded on (imagined) pleasure rather than lack. Kristeva suggests that imagined pleasure may be more of an incentive to leave the maternal body than the Oedipal father's threats of castration.

On the surface of Kristeva's texts, we see an archaic transference from the abject mother to the imaginary father, which, like Lacanian theory, requires sacrificing the mother for the sake of the father (TL 41). Reading "against the grain" of her texts, however, it is possible to see an archaic transference that does not sacrifice the mother to the father. It is possible to see an archaic transference from the mother's body to the mother's desire through the mother's love. The semiotic body is abjected if necessary, but only for the sake of what motivates the bond in the first place: maternal love. This is not (yet) the metonymic desire for the phallus; rather, it is what Kristeva calls the metaphor of love. In terms of the phallocentric discourse, this love is narcissism without a properly alien Other. Alterity is within. Yet without this narcissism, Kristeva's "primary narcissism," the mother's "narcissism," discourse is empty, meaningless, mourning the loss of love.

We can read Kristeva's analysis of the maternal function as a challenge to the paternal function within traditional psychoanalytic theory. Although it is true that we need to abject the maternal body to separate from it and become subjects, we do so in order to love our mothers. For it is only when we can separate from the maternal body that we can love the mother, or anyone else. Yet, this move away from the maternal body is supported by the mother's love. In addition, it is motivated by elements already present within the maternal function. In my reading of Kristeva, the third party that is necessary so that the child can separate is already operating within the maternal function. The mother is, after all, primarily a speaking being. She is already living within, and for the sake of, the symbolic order.

Kristeva challenges the traditional psychoanalytic notion of the paternal function as the Law of the Father or the "no" of the father. She argues that there is a maternal semiotic law before the law. She also presents a loving mother-father conglomerate without whom there is no motive to move into language. So Kristeva redefines and breaks down the traditional notions of the maternal and paternal functions. The association between the paternal and the law has been problematic for feminists and Kristeva has succeeded in severely undermining that connection.

More important for feminism, Kristeva has suggested that Western culture needs a new discourse of maternity to counteract misplaced abjection. She suggests that the existing discourses on maternity, Christian and scientific, do not allow us to abject our mother's bodies without abjecting all women.[12] She argues that, in Western culture, abjection has been misplaced onto all women or all mothers. Neither Christian nor scientific discourse can account for the necessity to abject the mother's body without also abjecting the mother herself. Kristeva is especially interested in the Catholic discourse of maternity that centers around the Virgin Mary.

What Kristeva describes as the "cult of the virgin" has been used by a paternal symbolic to cover up the unsettling aspects of maternity and the mother-child relationship (TL). The "cult of the virgin" controls maternity and mothers by doing violence against them. The virgin's only pleasure is her child who is not hers alone, but everyone's; yet her silent sorrow is hers alone. Kristeva maintains that the image of the virgin covers over the tension between the maternal and the symbolic.

In the biblical stories, the virgin is impregnated by the Word, the Name of the Father, God. This, argues Kristeva, is a way of ensuring paternity and fighting off the remnants of matrilinear society. After all, it is the name of the father that guarantees paternity and inheritance. For her, the cult of the virgin is the reconciliation of matrilinearism and the unconscious needs of the primary identification with the mother, on the one hand, "and on the other the requirements of a new society based on exchange and before long on increased production which require the contribution of the superego and rely on the symbolic paternal agency" (TL 259). This symbolic paternal agency, then, both guarantees, and is founded on, the exchange and the control of women and children through the Name of the Father.[13] The mother is a threat to the symbolic in two immediate ways. Her *jouissance* threatens to make her a subject and suggests the impossible other of the other. In addition, she not only represents, but is a strange fold between culture and nature that cannot be fully incorporated by the symbolic (TL 259). The symbolic, however, attempts a complete incorporation of the mother with her strange fold and her outlaw *jouissance* through the cult of the virgin, First, the virgin birth does away with the "primal scene" and the mother's *jouissance* that might accompany it. The virgin's is an immaculate conception. For Kristeva, this fantasy of the immaculate conception is a protection against a fantasy that is too much for the child to bear: "that of being supernumerary, excluded from the act of pleasure [the primal scene] that is the origin of its existence."[14] So, rather than be excluded from the mother's *jouissance,* the child excludes the mother's *jouissance* with the fantasy of the immaculate conception. This is all the more striking with Kristeva's claim that "virgin" is a mistranslation of "the Semitic term that indicates the sociolegal status of a young unmarried woman" (TL 236–237). The *jouissance* of the young unmarried woman is a *jouissance* that is not confined within the social sanctions of marriage. It is an outlaw *jouissance* that does not come under paternal control, the remnants of a matrilinear society where the resulting child can take the name only of the mother. The *jouissance* of this young unmarried woman and her 'bastard' child present a threat to the paternal function of the symbolic. The image of the virgin, however, controls this threat. The virgin has no *jouissance* and her body is marked with the Name of the Father. There is no mistake about paternity here in spite of the fact that in the biblical story Joseph becomes Mary's husband.

The power of the mother in a matrilinear society, the power of the child's primary relationship-identification with the mother, and the power of the mother as the authority over the child's body are all condensed into the symbol of the virgin mother. The mother's power is brought under paternal control. For Kristeva, it is domesticated: "[i]t is as if paternity were necessary in order to relive the archaic impact of the maternal body on man . . . in order somehow to admit the threat that the male feels as much from the possessive maternal body as from his separation from it— a threat that he immediately returns to that body" (MGB 263).

Man returns the threat to the maternal body through the cult of the virgin. The maternal body is allowed joy only in pain. Her body has only ear, milk, and tears (TL 248–249). The sexed body is replaced by the "ear of understanding," the Virgin Mary of the Catholic Church (TL 257). In this way, the virgin covers over the maternal fold between the biological and cultural. There is nothing biological going on here. The virgin covers over both the bodily connection between mother and child and the separation of child from mother that gives way to its entry into the symbolic. The virgin's maternity, and her relation to her child, is purely spiritual. Otherwise, the god-child is contaminated.

Kristeva suggests, however, that the silent ear, milk, and tears "are metaphors of nonspeech, of a 'semiotics' that linguistic communication does not account for" (TL 249). So the virgin mother becomes the representative of a "return of the repressed" semiotic (TL 249). Although the virgin can control the maternal semiotic, it cannot contain the semiotic. For Kristeva, Christianity, with its virgin birth, both unravels and protects the paternal function (IBWL 40). Like sacrifice, the violence of the semiotic returns within the very ritual that attempts to repress it. The maternal semiotic is focused in the symbol of the virgin and its threat to the symbolic order is thereby controlled.

The virgin's child is not just her symbolic substitute for the penis à la Freud, or the phallus à la Lacan. Rather, the god-child is the Phallus and as such it cannot satisfy a *mother*—she knows better. The god-child, strangely enough, is Freud's fantasy. For Freud, the child is the woman's satisfaction. And what of the mother? What of her satisfaction? Kristeva suggests that Freud's account of motherhood as being either an attempt to satisfy penis envy (baby = penis) or a reactivated anal drive (baby = feces) is merely a male fantasy. With regard to the complexities of maternal experience, claims Kristeva, "Freud offers only a massive nothing, which, for those who might care to analyze it, is punctuated with this or that remark on the part of Freud's mother, proving to him in the kitchen that his own body is anything but immortal and will crumble away like dough; or the sour photograph of Marthe Freud, the wife, a whole mute story . . . " (TL 255).

So, traditional psychoanalytic theory cannot properly account for maternity. Kristeva argues that, because within Western culture we are left with only the religious discourse on maternity, which is itself inadequate and crumbling, women are "abjected." We all must separate from our mother's bodies to become autonomous subjects. To do this, for Kristeva, we must abject the maternal body. Without an adequate discourse on maternity that allows us to separate the maternal "container" from the mother herself and from women in general, however, abjection is misplaced onto mothers and women. Kristeva partially accounts for women's oppression by locating it in this misplaced abjection. In Western culture, our discourses of maternity conflate the maternal body with the mother and woman.

This is why, in "Stabat Mater" and in other essays, Kristeva begins to suggest another discourse on maternity, one in which the mother is "alone of her sex" (TL 256). The mother is not synonymous with woman. To separate from the maternal body is not to separate from woman or even the mother. Rather, in Kristeva's scenario, we separate from the maternal body in order to love the mother, women, and all others.

Ultimately, then, Kristeva attempts to bring back the speaking body, which takes us deeper into the maternal body, to bring to light the complexities of the maternal function. She emphasizes the maternal function, which is far more than Freud's "massive nothing." She listens to the music within the maternal body and thereby recovers a body that is sacrificed within Western patriarchal culture. She recovers the maternal body with all of its complexities to reckon with the necessary separation from that body that does not have to result in the sacrifice of either mothers or women. In fact, she argues that the relation of the child, especially the daughter, to the mother and her body can be the foundation for a new ethics—one that is not enforced by law. This outlaw ethics is an ethics based on love of an other who is never fully in the place of the other because she is always already the stranger within ourselves. Kristeva calls for an embrace of the return of the repressed maternal function so that women in their difference(s) can be embraced within Western culture.

8

Irigaray and Con(fusing) Body Boundaries: Chaotic Folly or Unanticipated Bliss?

TAMSIN LORRAINE

In *"Les Couleurs de la Chair,"* a talk given to a seminar on psycho-analysis published in *Sexes et Parentés,* Luce Irigaray says that the patient undergoing psychoanalysis risks suffering from sensory deprivation.[1] This may sound strange at first. How could psychoanalysis deprive a patient of her sense perception? After all, an analysis is a matter of talking, not shock treatments or a lobotomy. Presumably, if anything changes it will be the patient's understanding of her experiences, not the experiences themselves. But then, to assume that would be to forget the history of psychoanalysis that originated with cases of hysteria and the so-called abnormal sense perceptions such cases entail. The risk of sensory depri-vation that Irigaray speaks of, however, is not a distortion of sense exper-ience due to a buried trauma. It is a deprivation induced by the analysis itself. In reconstructing a patient's history in speech in the particular situation of the analysis, the patient may lose perceptual nuances she experienced at the time of the actual history. If the analyst is not sensitive to indications of a kind of perceptual instability caused by the physical set-up peculiar to the analytic scene, the patient can become uprooted from her body and her history, and thus become an automaton with an artificial story.[2] The job of the analyst, according to Irigaray, is to enable the patient to represent her perceptions, thus rendering the chronological time of her story into a simultaneous present, thereby liberating a possi-bility for a creative composition of these representations into a new per-spective. An analysis is complete when the patient's capacity to compose imaginatively a sort of painting with these representations has been rein-stated, and she is able to establish creatively new perspectives between her present, past, and future that harmonize her perceptions.[3]

Irigaray's warning about the risk of sensory deprivation presented by an analysis sets the tone for how I will be presenting her notion of sexual difference in this chapter. Although she makes free use of psychoanalysis in telling a story about masculine subjectivity and although she adds to that story in her attempts to give a positive characterization of what might constitute feminine subjectivity, she does so in the context of engaging us, her readers or listeners, in our own process of representing our perceptions and creating new perspectives that resonate with our embodied experience. Just as an analysis that imposes an artificial history on the analysand is a failed analysis, a reading that imposes on the reader a prescription of what it should mean or feel like to be a masculine or feminine subject in our culture would be a failed reading. Irigaray invites us to try out new stories, to attend to our responses and to our own perceptual dissonance as we do so. We are thus led to ask: What words resonate for us? Where is there movement? What invites a response? What part of the story that she creates for us releases energy by representing sensations that allow us a richer, more articulate understanding of who we feel ourselves to be? And what new perspectives will we form in response to her invitation?[4]

With these questions in mind, I will explore Irigaray's notions of sexual difference, the maternal-feminine, and the original matrix of our embodied existence in the bodies of our mothers, particularly as they emerge in her two books, *Ethique de la différence sexuelle* and *Sexes et Parentés*. In doing so, I will touch upon the boundaries of conventional categories, including categories by which we encode our bodies.

Attuning ourselves to perceptual dissonance, paying attention to subtle sensations, and attempting to speak with words that will amplify those sensations rather than with words that other people will readily understand opens up a conceptual space for new perspectives about ourselves and our relationship to the world and others. On the one hand, attending to fuzzy sensation-ideas and half-thoughts can lead to mad ramblings and speech so idiosyncratic and localized that it holds no meaning for anyone except the speaker.[5] On the other hand, language assimilated to symbolic codes with wide social acceptance can become so alienated from its roots in sensory experience that it becomes increasingly meaningless, with dangerous consequences for our values and our lives. Psychoanalysis, and Lacanian psychoanalysis in particular, holds that subjectivity is an activity of positioning oneself in symbolic structures conditioned by the unconscious and a personal history extending back to infancy. A psychoanalytic approach toward language would insist that a merely verbal understanding of how one wants or needs to change is not enough. Language is permeated with embodied experiences in the context of personal histories unique to each individual. To change ourselves in the present, therefore, often involves reconstituting our histories and our bodies in the process. Irigaray's notion of sexual difference gives us a way to rethink our corporeal origins in the mother, and thus to rework our histories and to rethink our strategies in constituting identities from the perceptual flux that grounds them.

The psychoanalytic story that Irigaray inherits from Lacan says that if you are male, the paternal law guarantees you a mother substitute.[6] That is, as long as you abide by the rules that govern social meaning structures as they stand, you will become a subject worthy of obtaining an object to replace the mother you lost, the mother that same law made taboo. The reward promised by the paternal law for compliance is that this object will satisfy you in the way your mother once did, but without blurring the boundaries laid out by the categories and concepts of conventional meaning. You can have your cake and eat it too: the bliss of a plenitude of sensation where you and your mother are the whole world with nothing lacking and where you are your body in continual and completely spontaneous response to the body of another, and yet you are discrete, defined, and self-identical from moment to moment, a socially recognizable and acceptable human being. Although, from the Lacanian view, this bliss is based on an illusion and this reward is forever deferred, leaving the masculine subject forever in search of the object that will finally satisfy him, the lure of this possibility enables desire.

In Irigaray's reading of this story, the masculine object, to ascend to the status of a subject who can wield symbolic codes and rest assured that he will eventually receive a mother substitute, must disassociate himself from his original mother and the satisfaction he found with her. To abide by the paternal law, he must overcome his attraction to his first home here on earth, that of his mother's womb. To achieve this, he ignores the fact that he emerged from the body of another and instead traces his origins to God or abstract ideals such as "human nature." He turns away from the vagaries of perceptual flux to found the meaning of his existence in something above and beyond embodied existence, something eternal, immutable, and perfectly complete. A return to the world of body confusion and body sensations that defy categorization is thus rendered a dangerous undertaking that runs the risk of a failure of subjectivity or a plunge into the abyss of chaotic fusion.[7] To admit the shadowy realm of inarticulate sensations can present only a disorienting distraction to a subject bent on deducing his identity and his meaning from an ideal of self-sufficient perfection.

The denial of body entanglement with the mother has on-going effects. In Irigaray's view, contemporary symbolic structures favor a masculine subjectivity that would deny the mother's material contribution to his identity. One example of this is the priority given to the father's name both in marriage and in the naming of children. In the privileging of the masculine surname, the connection between father and son is emphasized. This masculine genealogy is further supported by the law, by religious symbolism, and by language. Tracing history through a masculine genealogy reduces woman to the maternal function of providing first her body to house the self-contained fetus and then her sexual and emotional services to provide a home for the growing child and the self-sufficient man. In Irigaray's reading of the Lacanian story, masculine subjectivity posits woman not as *woman,* but as the maternal-feminine—she who does not constitute her own place in a genealogy, but who is there to house *him* in a genealogy that connects father to son.[8] Thus, the trajectory proper to her is written out of the story; woman as mother substitute, as the maternal-feminine, is there to serve his growth and his transcendance; she exists solely as a function of a masculine genealogy.[9]

In "The Fecundity of the Caress," a reading of Levinas,[10] Irigaray discusses the effects that this masculine version of subjectivity has for love between a man and a woman. Here she evokes the dangers of the active male lover turning his female beloved into an object by which to touch himself. Unable to ground himself and his identity entirely in the abstract realm of social meaning structures, he turns to his female beloved for an embodied response to his caress. But because he has rejected his body sensations as irrelevant to his essential self, he relegates his beloved to the role of other: the shadow or double of himself upon whom he projects what he cannot bear in his own identity. As a subject who is already "fixed" according to paternal law, he controls his relations to the world and to others and closes himself to any initiation from the unknown. He refuses to perceive that his beloved comes to him with a subjectivity rooted in a trajectory through space-time proper to her. She opens herself to him, freely responding to his caress; he appropriates her response to illuminate himself and his path without responding in return. "Opening herself up to the most intimate point of her being, to the most profound depths of her inwardness, but not retouched and sent back to the most sublime part of herself, she gives way to a night without end" (p. 251). He takes away the visibility she offers him without responding to her subjectivity in return, thereby sending her down into a nocturnal abyss so that he can voyage toward an autistic transcendence. In the process, he loses the opportunity for a different kind of love relationship in which both create and recreate one another in a space where both have places. In this different kind of relationship, "there is no longer any image . . . , except for that of letting go and giving self. With the hands among other ways. Sculpting, shaping, as if for the first time, on the first day. . . . The lovers meet in one moment of this incarnation. Like sculptors who are going to introduce themselves, entrust themselves to one another for a new delivery into the world" (p. 237).

Although, in this essay, Irigaray evokes lovemaking as a time that can either plunge lover and beloved into a nonnuptial of autistic transcendence and nocturnal regression,[11] or a time where receptive openness can actually re-create body boundaries for both,[12] we can extend this notion of refiguring body boundaries into more mundane contexts. Woman as the maternal-feminine can then be seen as providing a prop for re-creating one's body boundaries not only in the context of lovemaking, but in other contexts as well.

To secure his denial of his mother's material contribution to his creation, the masculine subject needs to disassociate himself from matter in general and from his own embodied existence in particular. And yet, without sense experience he could have no subjectivity at all. Although the masculine subject of Irigaray's story needs to posit himself as a self-identical entity with fixed body boundaries, his sense of his body is as contingent and subject to dissolution as his sense of self. That is, his body is no more a substance that can found him than is the thinking "I" of Cartesian philosophy. Body boundaries and a sense of oneself as embodied are continually reconstituted through sense experience. One way this occurs is in interpersonal contact. When an individual is with someone who notices and responds to his body cues in addition to the conventional meaning of his speech, that individual feels reaffirmed as having a body that is perceptible and to which people react. He thus confirms a base or anchor for his belief in himself as a self with a history.

This kind of bodily affirmation is not only reaffirming, it is creative. When someone listens to the subject attentively, registering reactions to the subject's speech with a receptive body, the subject can notice things about what he has said that he had not thought of before. Even if the person listening to him is barely cognizant of the content of his words, she can provide him with new insight by her bodily responsiveness to such things as the tone of his voice and the stance of his body. We have all experienced this kind of bodily responsiveness. But despite being able to recognize that we feel better after speaking to some people rather than others—regardless of the intellectual content of the conversation—we devalue the impact of that embodied response in our on-going process of self-constitution and self-transformation.

The masculine myth is that subjects can have a secure place in a broader network of social meaning that can be repeated according to the rules of that meaning, and yet the masculine subject exists as a body that never experiences the same thing twice. How is this possible? One strategy for securing a self that is recognizable over time is to relegate the spontaneous response and formlessness of embodied existence to women and to assume that, when a subject goes to the nourishing support of a feminine other with no fixed place of her own, he is making *her* respond to *him*. Thus, the masculine subject can represent himself as a self-sufficient and already formed subject that is merely looking for confirmation of an identity that has remained the same—or at least some core part of which has remained the same—whereas she is the formless, shapeless one who reflects effects produced by him.

Women playing out this role of other act as matter, the mute bodily response that supports the story of the self as agent, the agent who appropriates her bodily response as a reaction to and reflection of his power in the world. The possibility that she is also a body in the world that evokes a response, that she has a story of her own, a perspective unique to her spun out of her own body, is thus cancelled; she is assimilated to his story in which she affirms-confirms his agency by being reduced to a response to him. He thus preserves his boundaries intact. There is no synergistic connection where it is no longer clear who is the subject and who is the mirror reflection, who is the doer and who is the object. The masculine subject can thus keep his experience of himself and the other properly contained in anticipated categories; he can assume that his body is the point of origin for the interactions that occur between the two. Woman as other becomes one of the mirrors by which he can affirm himself as having this kind of body substance and thus as having self-originating agency and power.[13] Woman as the maternal-feminine thus grounds masculine subjectivity by providing a sort of conceptual container for the ambiguities of his own embodied existence.

In Irigaray's view, women are different from men in at least two important ways. One, they cannot objectify their mothers in the same way because it entails denying their own subjectivity, because they are, after all, themselves designated mother substitutes.[14] Two, language and symbolic meaning structures as they are currently constituted in our culture privilege and support masculine subjectivity.[15] That is, current symbolic structures support the confinement of women to a "maternal-feminine" where their only function is to be the mother substitutes that affirm masculine selves.

Feminine subjectivity thus leans toward another kind of strategy that could be given further support with a feminine imaginary and symbolic. Woman, too, would like to make sense of her own embodied history, her own trajectory through the world unique to her, apart from the trajectory of any given masculine subject who might want to incorporate her into his story. Feminine identity, an identity that respects her trajectory as her own, would entail giving a different kind of account of the relationship to the mother and to the origins of one's bodily existence within the mother.

For the feminine subject to articulate a feminine symbolic, she might interrogate her mother, not as the maternal-feminine that gave her her first home, but as a woman with an embodied history peculiar to her that is irreducible to a concept of the maternal-feminine.[16] For this feminine subject, there could be no such thing as a mother substitute; there could be only one's own history with a particular other with whom one once shared a physical intimacy that transgressed all body limits. Thus, one is not diverted into finding a lost object to recapture a moment that is blurred in the nostalgia of the forever lost and forbidden. Instead of denying the blurring of body boundaries in the context of growth and becoming in which one first took shape, the feminine subject could rediscover that context to ground new experiences of body confusion that would enable self-creation without the risk of self-obliteration. Reworking her relationship to her origins in the body of another could enable porous receptivity to the embodied presence of another in the here-now that would allow for intensification of perception and the bliss of unanticipated response to another.

In a reading of Aristotle,[17] Irigaray explores representations of our original home in our mother's womb to open up an alternative symbolic space. Psychoanalysis provides us with a story about our early childhood experiences, thus releasing elements of our embodied experience by giving them representation that we can incorporate into our current personal histories. But in incorporating such a story into our personal histories, we can maintain the notion that we were always clearly separate from our mother and from our mother's body.

But what if we were to go back further? What if we were to peruse the image of living inside of another, surrounded by mucous membrane that we share?[18] How might this disturb our stories about body boundaries? What sensations might pursuing such stories release? Are there times right now when we feel less sure about our body boundaries than we might want to admit? Are there moments when the envelope is transgressed by porousness, a receptive perception of the other, and the fluidity and permeability of body membranes?

Instead of denying her origins in the body of another, the feminine subject would reconceive her origins as a time of profound body confusion. In the womb, one could become two only in the context of a continual refraction, disintegration, and reformation of body boundaries that were never fixed or secure, but were continually renegotiated in an oscillation of body response. Instead of reducing the mother to the maternal-feminine, this feminine subject would recognize the space-time trajectory proper to her mother's history and the crucial role that her mother's particular trajectory had to play in her own formation. Thus, the feminine subject would not reduce her mother to body-matter that grounds identity by reflecting back to her the various effects of which she is capable. This mother would not provide the background against which the more important story of the subject's own development could unfold. This mother has an identity with effects as profound as the subject's that disallow reduction of the mother to a supporting role. The meaning this subject gives her mother and herself would emerge from points of contact between them that are not predicted in advance with notions about who or what either one of them is or what it means, for example, to be a mother or a woman.[19] Instead, the feminine subject would allow a continual suspension of categories of thought that admits unanticipated categories, perhaps "nonsense" or "madness" according to conventional (paternal law-governed) thought, to express the everchanging relationship of two subjects who come into mutually informing contact at various points of their two stories.

The masculine subject that reduces his mother to the maternal-feminine posits her as an entity that exists to nurture him. In overlooking his mother as woman, this subject contains the phenomenon of his embodied existence and all the confusion and wonder that is entailed in the concept of the maternal-feminine. He then renders the threatening murkiness of his origins in the body of another controllable by emptying the concept of his origins of sensory experience and by denying the particularity of his mother's body, his own response to her, and his continued body muddlement. The masculine subject who would respect sexual difference would recognize and acknowledge his mother as a subject in her own right. He would not reduce her to a concept—settled and done with, familiar, already said, already explained. He would not take her—or nature or his embodied existence—for granted. He would awaken to his own senses. He would find another way to defend against the fear of dissolution in the infinity of sense perception.

One of the fears precipitated by postmodernist critiques of the self is that, without an agent, there are no grounds for social critique, effective political commitment, or progressive change. My account suggests otherwise. The point of reference for an alternative conception of agency would not be one's own body as self-contained initiator of action, but the moment of response when two subjects join in an act of mutual creation. The subject would not repeat himself as an identical subject in isolation from others, assimilating the other into dead matter upon which he, the agent, presses himself to get a mechanically predictable response. And the other would not be mere otherness. Instead, the mirror would be alive, a living mirror that, in responding to the subject, would change what he is, what he has come to think of himself as being. In this kind of moment no reflection would ever be a mere reflection of the identity that the first subject presented, but would always be a mutation of himself, until, as he looks in the mirror, he no longer knows where she stops and he begins, until the gap between them has closed and there is only one mucous membrane shared between them. In such a moment of contiguous contact his pattern breaks down, the repetition of the same does not hold, he becomes confused because nothing is what it was, nothing is fixed, he cannot fix her with respect to himself or vice versa, and in the oscillation of response between them where there is no agent working on an object, but where both are mutually attentive, responsive, and creating, they become one in a space-time, where all is growth and becoming with no fixed point.

In this kind of interaction, both subjects would recognize that they are not merely agents having an effect, but that they are continually in process in and through interaction with a world that shapes, forms, and creates them as they respond and shape, form, and create to and with it— with no core, no part of them left untouched to orchestrate this process, but everything in process, flux, change.

In Irigaray's view, the identity of the same, that is, concepts and categories, the already-said, is usually given precedence when we communicate with language. In and through her work she asks us to attend to another kind of moment. This moment would give precedence to opening up body-based feelings, bringing feelings to full flowering in the present without saying in advance what they are or should be, but focusing on whatever and wherever there is movement and life, something different, something that comes from the here-right now,[20] Here one is not searching for some*thing,* finally, that one is trying to replace, for example, *mother* as the lost object.[21] What one wants is no more or less than living contact that inevitably involves growth, change, movement, and the breakdown of binary opposition in the oscillation of response in which neither the one nor the other is subject or object, but, if anything, both are both at once.

Irigaray's invitation to represent an alternative, feminine relation to origins in the mother does not refer us to a prediscursive reality.[22] What she is asking us to do is to remember with the body. What images invoke the kind of living response she asks for? What resonates in the here and now in a way that releases as yet unsignified experiences of the body? Remembering the body in the act of communication entails a continual openness to the present that has not yet been codified, an embodied receptivity to language that goes beyond taking the self and others as assimilatable to the same and instead responds with porous wonder to ways in which conventional categories might be broken down in present responses.[23]

The new ethics that Irigaray calls for would be one that honored moments similar to the ones that we have been exploring. To know who I am I have no choice but to respond to and to be responded to by others in a present where I continually renegotiate the boundaries between myself and my world as I continually change shape. Thus, I am whoever I feel myself to be for that moment in time, in that situation, according to whatever codes I may be informed by or put to use. Instead of being structured by a fixed identity, for example, gender identity, I allow myself to be structured by a convergence of consciousnesses which brings to bear upon this moment and space completely different sets of encoded experiences, thus allowing different words and descriptions than I had perhaps anticipated to mediate the event of that point of contact. In interactions where all the subjects involved allow the meaning of that event to be unanticipated and unanticipatable, each receives and is informed by the meaning of others instead of assimilating that meaning to the same, to his or her already formulated categories. Thus all together allow the bliss of a new meaning shared by all that none had anticipated.

The authenticity of such a moment would lie not in whether or not a given subject was able to repeat some notion of a "true" self, but in the pleasure of an experience. It is in the sheer physical contentment of getting the words right, the words that articulate body language and build upon it by developing that articulation in the broader social context of intersubjective experience, that we build crucial links between the microcosm of individual embodied experiences and the macrocosm of a social whole of embodied subjects. Such a language would not only reach deep down into the nuances of personal histories, but would also stretch across the broad spectrum of shared history.

The implicit message of Irigaray's work is that confused body boundaries lead to self-dissolution only if one equates such body confusion with a complete loss of boundaries. The psychoanalytic-influenced story she tells gives us some clues as to why one might make such an equation. It also provides suggestions for how we might open ourselves to alternative possibilities. These alternatives constitute a new way of thinking about the self, subjectivity, and agency that could enable the kind of openness to one another that would allow us to create collective visions that would resonate for us all.

9

Irigaray and the Divine

ELIZABETH GROSZ

Irigaray's recent writings on the divine have evoked shock, outrage, disappointment, and mystification in her readers. To many, she seems to have succumbed to the most naive essentialist reliance on religion to overcome or to provide solutions for women's socio-political and psychical oppression. In this chapter, I will defend her against these accusations by explaining how this recent interest is directly linked to her on-going critique and displacement of the founding concepts of Western philosophy. Her analysis of discourses of the divine is not altogether different from her analysis of psychoanalytic theory. Her fascination with the divine is foreshadowed in her earlier writings; but more particularly, it is the center of a cluster of loosely related interests. Among the more significant linkages are those she posits between (1) the domain of ethics (which, I would claim, is based on a reading of Levinas's notion of ethics as an encounter with alterity); (2) her notion of God and the divine (derived from her readings of Feuerbach, Levinas, and Schüssler-Fiorenza, among others); (3) her notion of the elements or the elemental (based on her reading of Empedoclean ontology and the later Merleau-Ponty); and (4) her notion of sexual exchange, an exchange based on irreducibly different sexes as partners (derived from her bringing together of the structuralisms of Levi-Strauss, Saussure, Marx, and Lacan). I hope in this chapter to outline briefly the points of intersection and realignment of these concepts in her recent writings,[1] and also to indicate some of the ways in which this recent work continues, yet transforms, her earlier work on psychoanalysis.

Irigaray's (earlier) work on the borders of psychoanalytic theory—one ear in its ambit, the other outside, listening to what it cannot hear—provides if not a method, strictly speaking, then at least a series of questions that can with equal relevance be asked of any form of (patriarchal) knowledge. Her question, if it can be reduced to one, is this: given that this body of knowledge or mode of representation presents the interests of only one sex, how would such knowledge look if it were able to represent adequately women's interests? This question is directed to psychoanalysis in her writings of the 1970s: if Freud and Lacan provide conceptions of sexuality, the drive, desire, the object, the unconscious, and so forth only from the point of view of masculinity, then how can these masculinist accounts be reread from other perspectives so that women's autonomy is a real possibility? How can psychoanalytic texts be read as both *necessary,* insofar as they explain the present structure and recent history of women's social subordination, and *insufficient,* insofar as they provide no way of questioning, let alone transforming, this social subordination? She demonstrates that the very texts and language of psychoanalysis simultaneously reveal its investments in male domination, yet allow alternative readings, readings that remain contrary to or different from its received interpretations. Like all texts, psychoanalytic texts (even the unconscious itself) are not inert objects controlled by their authors. Texts are material objects, and as matter, they are available for a very wide range of uses, potentially infinite readings.

A text's "viscosity," its materiality, its superabundance regarding an author's intentions, and its resistance to ownership is seen by Irigaray as a counterpart to the resistance or recalcitrance of the female body and sexuality in patriarchal culture. This parallelism or, in her terms, *isomorphism* between bodies, especially women's bodies, and texts is not random: for it is only insofar as female bodies are textually inscribed that they are constituted as lacking. It is only through textual incision that men are constructed as phallic. Thus a transformation in modes of writing is the condition of a transformation in modes of corporeal inscription and thus a transformation in bodies themselves.

If the broad question of sexual difference, autonomy, or specificity characterizes and informs all of her writings, her philosophical and political goals seem to have undergone an inflection. Her broad goal in the 1970s was the interrogation of phallocentric texts through the articulation of a repressed femininity. In the 1980s, her new interests can be summed up in the title of her 1984 text, *The Ethics of Sexual Difference.* She has moved from the problematic of the independence, autonomy, and differences of the two sexes, to that of examining the conditions and possibilities of the modes of exchange between the two sexes. *Speculum* and *This Sex* were necessary starting points; they were necessary to make clear both how knowledges have defined woman as man's other and how conceptions of masculinity or, more commonly, humanity are dependent on the silencing and denigration of femininity. The assertion of women's irreducible differences from men is only a preliminary stage in a transformation in social, theoretical, and representational relations. While a prerequisite, by itself it cannot engender new kinds of relations between the sexes. Establishing models and procedures whereby the two sexes, considered in their irreducible specificity, can be partners in a relation of exchange rather than exploitation implies the possibility of an exchange guaranteed not through the interchangeability of exchanging subjects (subjects presumed to be the same), but between subjects acknowledged as different. An entirely different mode of economy follows. Her more recent writings are an attempt to rethink models of exchange based upon difference not sameness, based upon recognition and acceptance of the sexual otherness of the other, the interaction of a dual sexual symmetry.

I should state at the outset that I do not believe that Irigaray is advocating a return to the model of piety and devotion offered by the well-worn feminine emblem, St. Teresa.[2] This would simply reinsert women back into the confines of men's modes of self-worship guaranteed by a God built in their image. Nor is she concerned with resurrecting or creating female goddesses from a mythic prehistory. Her concern with the notion of the divine or God is, rather, part of a project of creating an ideal self-image for women, an ideal to which women may aspire and through which they may make cultural artifacts—as men have created ethics, religions, sciences, and forms of life and love under the justification and authority of God. Irigaray is explicit in her rejection of these patriarchal traditions and representations of God and the divine:

> Man found a way to avoid this finitude in a *uniquely* masculine God. God created him in his own image. . . . He scarcely limits himself in himself, amongst his selves: he is father, son, spirit. Man did not let himself be defined by another genre: feminine. His only God was to correspond to the human type which we know is not neutral as far as the difference of sex goes.[3]

Indeed, Irigaray is scathing about what Lacan calls *good old God*, for this concept has enabled men to disavow their debt to femininity and, especially, maternity. Because men can present God as the Ultimate and Divine Creator and because they can regard themselves as formed by Him in His image, they have effectively contained women outside the sphere of the Divine while relying upon women's resources. She sees the Catholic Church, and, by implication, all patriarchal religions, as forms of women's oppression.

> When this minister of God only, of God the Father, pronounces the words of the Eucharist: 'This is my body, this is my blood' according to

the cannibalistic rite which is secularly ours, perhaps we could remind him that he would not be here if our body and our blood hadn't given him life. . . . And that it is us, women-mothers, whom he thus gives to be eaten.[4]

In place of patriarchal religion, Irigaray advocates neither a role-reversed female-dominated religion nor a more encompassing, truly "human" model. She refuses to abandon the category of the divine, as many others in the twentieth century have; instead, she attempts to tie notions of God and the divine to women's struggles for personal and social autonomy, thus politicizing them. She attempts to formulate the conditions of an entirely new way of envisaging the divine.

Far from thinking that we should continue the process of deification on the pattern of our ancestors and their totem animals, that we should make a regression back to the siren goddesses, in particular against the men gods, it seems to me that we certainly have to incite a return to the *cosmic,* but at the same time asking ourselves why we were stopped as we were becoming *divine.*[5]

As in her relation to psychoanalytic theory, her relations to Christianity remain ambivalent: she neither accepts in wholesale terms nor does she reject outright the discourses associated with either institution; instead, she tries to utilize their own insights against their pronouncements to highlight the limitations of each. Thus just as she uses Freud's notions of repression and the unconscious to show what of femininity psychoanalysis must repress, so too she uses what she considers are the real insights of Christianity against its manifest misogyny. For her, Christianity offers a model of "the respect for the incarnation of all bodies (men's and women's) as potentially divine: nothing more or less than each man and each woman being virtually gods."[6]

As she makes clear, however, "this message, especially as it concerns women, is most often veiled, obscured, covered over."[7] If Christianity makes explicit the fact that "spiritual becoming" and "corporeal becoming" are one and the same thing,[8] Christianity must, in fact, be seen as a form of the *cultivation* and not at all as a renunciation of the sexual. Christ is not only a God, but a God incarnated in human (here, male) sexual form. It is only by the purification and neuterization of Christ's corporeality that women's corporeality can be posited as the locus of sin. Moreover, although providing clues, hints as to what a divinity for women might be, Christianity must ultimately remain inadequate for women insofar as it is modeled on a Father-son genealogy, one in which women are either ignored or reduced to the status of mother. Only when the relation of mother and daughter can be conceived as divine, only insofar as woman can become divine in and of herself, and not simply as mother, wife, or lover, will a notion of divinity appropriate to women become possible. To understand Irigaray's notion of the divine, we must examine three themes in her writing that are intimately bound up with divinity: her conceptions of the elemental, of female autonomy, and of sexual exchange. I will look briefly at each.

The Elemental

The metaphoric play of the elements is part of Irigaray's continuing strategy of developing a model or theoretical paradigm to enable women's subjectivity, desire, and social place to be autonomously designated. It is part of her search for a corporeal or "charnel" philosophy appropriate to the body and situation of women. If, as she has argued in *This Sex Which Is Not One*, models based on physics, chemistry, biology, or evolution are all implicated in a rampant yet rarely recognized phallocentrism, then it is necessary to depart from these paradigms—while recognizing their historical role in forming our self-understanding—if women are to be understood on less constricting models. Her metaphor is based on her reading of the pre-Socratics, particularly Empedocles.

For Empedocles, the fundamental principle of being is endless change, infinite becoming. Matter is the arrangement of four different types of unchangeable particles; all objects are the result of their intermingling. The alliance each element makes with the others is described by Empedocles as love or attraction; conversely, material objects are destroyed through hate or strife. The unity of things is thus a consequence of the plurality and harmony of their elements. Love is the intermingling, the harmonious coming together, of differences. Empedocles's representation of the four elements provides an apposite metaphor of the meeting of different substances, a perilous provisional union of differences that, through Love, can yield unpredicted productivity—a rich metaphor for the possibilities of autonomy and interaction between sexually different subjects—a kind of heterosexuality without heterosexism.

In utilizing the terminology of alchemy, Irigaray turns to a prehistoric or protohistorical world-view, one preceding the imposition of a "reasoned" science, in both ancient Greece and Medieval Europe. She turns to a logic of interactive forces operating as combinatory particles; a logic of transmutation and thus, like the dialectic, a logic of *becoming*. Earth, air, fire, and water, the primal elements, combine in varying degrees to create the (significatory) structure of reality, both individual and collective. The elements constitute the "ingredients" of a type of subjectivity and "faculties" within a subjectivity—for example, their particular combinations constitute what were called the *passions*—as well as of the relations pertaining to the social and natural world: "I wanted to go back to this natural material which makes up our bodies, in which our lives and environment are grounded: the flesh of our passions."[9]

To defend her against the anticipated and usual charges of essentialism,[10] it needs to be said clearly that her use of the four elements represents a fable or mythic unfolding of a fantasied, an impossible, origin, to be read in the manner of Freud's *Totem and Taboo* or Nietzsche's *Thus Spoke Zarathustra,* rather than as historical "archeology." They have a discursive rather than a referential status. In the case of the elements, resonances with the later writings of Merleau-Ponty must also be recognized. Like Irigaray, he uses that emblem of the four elements to rethink carnality, the flesh, outside its traditional binary terms in which mind is opposed to body, self to other, and nature to culture. The flesh is the "most elementary" of terms, comprising the subject and the world, the subject in and as the world: "The flesh is not matter, is not mind, is not substance. To designate it, we should need the old term 'element' in the sense it was used to speak of water, air, earth and fire, that is, in the sense of a *general thing.* . . . The flesh is in this sense an 'element of Being'."[11]

The elemental, in sum, provides Irigaray with a language in which to represent a materiality and a corporeality outside the traditional patriarchal framework and more acceptable for representing women's corporeal-material existence. Her argument relies on an earlier account of the patriarchal debt to maternity, to women's abilities to reproduce, that remains the silent support of patriarchy. Her concept of the four elements provides a corporeal foundation for the creation of an account of a *transcendental* or *divine* order, which she believes is necessary for articulating an autonomous femininity: such a transcendence is the condition, as de Beauvoir almost recognized, of women's elevation from the category of other to the status of subject.

God and the Divine

In Irigaray's writings, the notion of God (or gods) functions to anchor several interrelated concepts. God is the ontological framework of our understanding of reality and the conditions of perception of this reality in each of us: God is the framework for the genesis of space, time, and their "contents" (persons, nature, elementary particles) that are named and constituted as distinctive particles by God's acts of division and categorization, by his speaking and naming them. God is thus, as Descartes recognized, the source and justification of (Western) knowledge. Second, God provides a framework and a horizon for the constitution of the subject's identity as a subject. Third, God provides an ideal of perfection, a becoming that is particular to each sex. Irigaray does not use a concept of God as a static, frozen image, but as a "sensible transcendental,"[12] that is, as a term designating a material process of completion and integration, a movement always tending toward, becoming, its own ideal. And fourth, God is an emblem of a supreme form of alterity that institutes ethics: one can love the other only if one also loves oneself and (a) God: "Gods are necessary and linked to the constitution of an identity and a community."[13]

Irigaray's God is neither naturalistic nor personal, neither forgiving nor judgmental. God is not the totality, unity, origin, or purpose of the world, but the principle of the ideal, a projection of the (sexed) subject onto a figure of perfection, an ego-ideal specific to that subject, a mode of self-completion without finality. God is the condition of men's finitude, their identities as law-abiding subjects, and their being situated in a *genre*. Irigaray plays on the full resonances of the term *genre:* a term able to summarize men's domination of personal and familial structures (*genre* as "genus," "family," or "humankind"), of knowledge (*genre* as "kind," "manner," or "sort," the imposition of categories), of cultural achievement (*genre* as "style," "aesthetic type"), and of social relations (*genre* as "fashion," "taste," or "style").

> Man can exist because God helps him to define his *genre,* to situate himself as a finite being in relation to the infinite. . . . To set up a genre, a God is needed. . . . Man did not let himself be defined by another genre: feminine. His only God was to correspond to the human type which we know is not neutral as far as the difference of sex goes.[14]

God is the term necessary for positioning one's finite being both in the context of other finitudes (sexual, social, terrestial) and in the context of the infinite. God provides the genre, the context, the milieu and limit of the subject, and the horizon of being against which subjectivity positions itself. For this reason, Irigaray refuses to abandon the language of patriarchal religion, although she retains a distance from it. The position of God as ideal and horizon needs to be retained as a political, aesthetic, and ethical ideal:

> If women lack a God they cannot communicate, or communicate amongst themselves. The infinite is needed, they need the infinite in order to share *a little?* Otherwise the division brings about fusion-confusion, division and tearing apart in them/her, between them. If I can't relate to some sort of horizon for the realisation of my genre, I cannot share while protecting my becoming.[15]

Her use of the concept of God is thus an inversion and displacement of its theological or religious sources. God serves as an image or metaphor of *being situated in space and time* as a subject of a particular kind and of *the capacity for an autonomous identity,* insofar as the subject aspires to a perfection that is the actualization of its potentialities. In this sense, her work must also be seen as the culmination of an ethical and ontological project fundamentally initiated by Spinoza. God represents being positioned in a place: social, natural, interpersonal. God, then, is not a personage regulating, governing, or judging these positions nor one's mode of occupying them. God is a name to describe the possibilities of awareness, and transcendence, of these positions.

If God represents, inhabits, the celestial order and men and women are fundamentally terrestrial, Irigaray is fascinated with exploring the middle ground between, somewhere between the divine and the human, the bird and the fish, man and woman: the angel. The angel is the messenger of the divine, a messenger who announces divine events: proclaiming the union of the sexes (in marriage) and the productivity of sexual exchange (particularly in birth but also in death). The angel always traverses and displaces distinct identities and categories, being a divine union of contraries:

> the angels tell of a journey between the envelope of God and the world, the micro and the macrocosm. They announce that this journey is accessible to the body of man. And especially to women's body. They represent and speak of another incarnation, another *parousia* of the body. Irreducible to philosophy, theology, morality the angels appear as messengers of the ethics evolved by art—sculpture, painting or music—without which something other than the gesture which they represent cannot be said.[16]

Yet, although the angel signifies the possibility of a bridge or path between heterogeneous orders (divine-mortal, male-female), it remains traditionally *disembodied,* sexually neuter, intangible, a form of the unity of sexual diversity never incarnated, never material. They move between one order and another, but occupy neither. They are thus able to act as images or models of a possible occupation of a middle ground by the two sexes in their meeting. These two sexes, although seeking the status of the angelic or divine, would not become *neutral* or *neuter,* but would retain their sexes in their marriage. Her ideal union of the sexes involves the corporealization of the angelic, an attribution of a body and a sex to that always moving, shimmering being. The *embodied* that is, the sexed angel, may represent the possibility of a divine—nonencompassing—union. It thus represents the possibility of a *sexual ethics.*

A sexual or carnal ethics would require that the angel and the body be found together. A world to construct or reconstruct . . . from the smallest to the greatest, from the most intimate to the most political, a genesis of love between the sexes would be still to come. A world to create or recreate in order that man and woman can again or finally cohabit, meet and sometimes remain in the same place.[17]

Thus, for Irigaray, the divine is not simply the reward for earthly virtue, all wishes come true; it is rather the field of creativity, fertility, production, an always uncertain and unpreempted field. It is the field or domain of what is new, what has not existed before, a mode of transcendence, a projection of the past into a future that gives the present new meaning and direction. The divine is a movement, a movement of and within history, a movement of becoming without *telos,* a movement of Love in its Empedoclean sense.

Sexual Autonomy and Exchange

The question of sexual difference has been displaced in Irigaray's more recent writings in favor of the postulation of an exchange between the sexes. Although she sees that women require unmediated, positive relations with other women, she also sees that it is necessary for women to be able to enter relations of exchange with men without sacrificing their positive self-conceptions. The question of the *meeting* of the two sexes is one that preoccupies her here. How can a meeting between the two sexes take place? If the sexes are characterized by *irreducible* difference—morphological, reproductive, biological, psychological, social—how can a *common ground* or meeting place between them be formed? What ground between them, what commonness left untouched by phallocentrism, enables them to speak, to understand, to share, to create?

This problematic of the unity in the heterogeneity of the two sexes underlies her explorations of the divine, the theological, and the philosophical. It is a concern that has occupied her work since the 1980s. In rather bald terms, she states her preoccupation with the productivity of the couple:

I think that man and woman is the most mysterious and creative couple. That isn't to say that other couples may not also have a lot in them, but man and woman is the most mysterious and creative.

Do you understand what I am saying: people who are sexually different and who create a different relation to the world.[18]

Very often this mysterious creativity is narrowed into the creation of a child, a "symbol" of love between the sexes. Yet the fecundity of the exchanges between the two sexes cannot and should not be reduced to procreation; for it is the fertility necessary for the production of a new world as much as for a new life.

This meeting and mingling of the two sexes is, of course, not without its perils and dangers, particularly for the woman. On the one hand, there is always a danger of a regression to stereotyped heterosexuality. Here the woman once again conforms to a logic that oppresses her, when she takes on the role of "opposite," other, or counterpart to the one. On the other hand, she also risks remaining on a parallel with, yet never meeting, her "other"—each sex living in its own homosexual economy without a point of mediation between them, each talking *at* and not *with* the other. She has written about the risks involved in women opening their feminity to a relation with men's masculinity—the risks of fusion, engulfment, absorption, anger, hatred, invasion. In a very moving and personal discussion of passion, Irigaray ranges over the emotional responses effected by interpersonal commitments to heterosexual exchange:

> It was at breakfast. We separated at your work time. You gave me something to do for the day. I asked you for that. I will flee outside myself in you. Also the outside world. I cannot stay in the world. I am in it and not in it. I don't escape from you, me, us, towards some other, no. . . .
>
> You absorbed me or you come back again to me to protect yourself from [death]. When I suffer, you are hurting in me, I think that you have abandoned your mortal limits. That my risks are redoubled to carry you in me. Redoubled? Or infinite? Overwhelmed by a peril beyond my life. Nothing that can save me without you outside of me.[19]

Irigaray asks how to establish a time and place, subjectivities and positions, whereby the two sexes can touch each other without loss or residue. Where one is not autonomous at the expense of the other, where one does not occupy the negative and the other the positive poles of a fixed opposition. Where there is mutual recognition, mutual caressing, the satisfaction of the needs of both. Such a relation cannot exist if either sex has no positive identity, no relation of autoeroticism or positive evaluation of their bodies, and no positive relation to members and ideals of their own sex. These are necessary preconditions that, in the case of both sexes, though in quite different ways, have remained out of reach. Men, for example, to retain a positive identity have had to relinquish a bodily autoeroticism. In renouncing the polymorphous pleasures of the rest of the body for the singular pleasures and benefits bestowed on a phallic organ and subjectivity, men have given up the realm of the corporeal and forced women to occupy it for them. Women, in contrast, relinquish their homosexual, particularly their maternal, connections and thus the possibilities for a positive, autonomous self-conception in remaining the guardians of the men's corporeality. They have, consequently, given up their own.

In "Divine Women," Irigaray seeks to create at least some of the conditions necessary for women to develop an autonomous self-conception. Among the necessary conditions is a concept of God and the divine, that is, a historically possible future. For it is only if women have their own concepts of the divine that a divine fecundity between the sexes may occur. The love of God, for her, is a love of the self, and this self-love is the prerequisite of love of the other. Self-love implies recognizing from whence we come (from women-mothers, all of us), where we are now (politically, philosophically), and a future in which we can become more than this (which Irigaray calls *God*). "God holds no obligations over our needs, except *to become*. No task, no obligation burdens us except that one: become divine, become perfect, don't let any parts of us be amputated that could be expansive for us."[20]

Irigaray announces the threshhold of a new era of relations between the sexes, which has the potential to supercede all social, sexual, and significatory relations in a transvaluation and transfiguration of existing religions. Her project, like that of the angel, is to announce the birth of a new epoch, a new type of exchange and coexistence. The meeting of two *different beings,* the open acceptance of a different subjectivity, has yet to occur. When it does, it will open up knowledge, social practices, productions, even life and death themselves, to a new set of values and meanings.

Her model of a relation between the two sexes that may accede to the divine involves the postulation of each having its own place, its own specifications, features, needs, desires, and corporeal identities. It implies that each sex has accepted its own finitude, has accepted what the other's position has to give and what it is able to receive from the other without loss to itself. The maximization of the capacities and latent or undeveloped skills, a trajectory toward actualization of potentials that may otherwise not be revealed, continuous self-completion, these are some of the transformations that may occur in a meeting of differences. An *economy of the gift* may occur without the presumption of an underlying identity between giver and receiver, who must reciprocate with a symbolically identical gift. This is an economy that is all circulation with no real exchange. No exchange because there is no heterogeneity between giver and receiver, no stretching of either position so that it may touch (upon) the other. Ritual exchange functions always to ensure (temporal) sameness. An exchange that genuinely involves taking and giving implies disparate identities, disparate needs, between which different gifts may or must circulate.

Irigaray attempts to outline some of the ingredients of a model of exchange that acknowledges the two different sexes as both givers and receivers. The "gifts" thus exchanged can be communication or language, sexual pleasure, the satisfaction of mutual need, a child, a home (place), a position that affirms its participants in the process of producing something new. Sexual difference heralds the era in which women and men are not neutralized under a universal or androgynous "humanity" abstracted from the sexed body; but rather, one in which production can be seen to be the contribution of women and men, and one in which men and women, through their difference, find a commonness between them.

> How can one mark this limit of a place, of the place, except by sexual difference? But, in order for ethics to be possible, it is necessary to constitute a possible place to live for each sex, each body, each flesh. Which supposes a memory of the past, a hope for the future. Memory assures a bridge of the present, and disconcerts the the symmetry of the mirror which annihilates the difference of identity.
>
> This needs time, space and time. And thus, perhaps we are again passing an epoch where *time should redeploy space.* New morning of the world? Recasting immanence and transcendence, especially through this *threshold* which has never been questioned as such: the feminine sex.[21]

Her exploration of God, the celestial, and the angelic as the intermediary between the mortal and the immortal are tropes, images, or representations that Irigaray reclaims in struggling for women's autonomy. They are the names of ideals that have been stolen from women and that must be stolen back. If God and the divine provide the horizon for self-idealization, a model to emulate, then reclamation of the names and attributes of patriarchal religion is a necessary condition for identities determined by sexual difference. God is the Other in relation to which each sex, each subject, is positioned. In constructing a God using the shadows of one's own image, Irigaray believes that the seeds or possibilities of a divine fecundity or creativity may blossom. This is not a religious conversion, a leap of faith; it is a political and textual strategy for the positive reinscription of women's bodies, identities, and futures in relation to and in exchange with the other sex.

10 Irigaray's *Amante Marine* and the Divinity of Language

ELÉANOR H. KUYKENDALL

At the end of *Amante Marine,* Luce Irigaray counters Nietzsche's description of Dionysian eros and Apollonian distance by describing a *Logos* incarnate, but of a divinity fluid and not locatable as such, and with a feminine Christ.[1] In *L'oubli de l'Air,* Irigaray questions Heidegger's *Logos* as a dwelling house of Being that neglects sexual difference, masked as neutrality. In *Ethique de la différence sexuelle,* Irigaray responds to Nietzsche and Heidegger again by proposing a conception of language of her own in which "[t]he *there is* gives way or place anew to a 'we are' or 'we become,' 'we dwell' together. This creation would be our chance, from the humblest of daily life to the 'greatest,' opening to a *sensible transcendental* coming to us through us, of which *we would be* the mediators and the bridges."[2]

We whom Irigaray's divine *Logos* visits, transform our impersonal "There is," *"Il y a,"* into first-person avowals, incarnating an ethic in the forms of words we use to speak among ourselves. Through our linguistic transformations we perpetually dislocate and relocate our relationships with those others whom we so engage. What we create of the transcendental in linguistic performance is incarnate in the forms of words we use. So Irigaray argues. She challenges us to change the way we speak and write, to re-create an ethic of sexual difference in which we speakers and writers address and refer to one another, not as equals, but as equivalent beings differently gendered.

But how can we speakers and writers transcend what we know in a specific language, such as English, while we are speaking or writing it? Irigaray's answer, briefly, is that sexual difference, sensible or perceptible in differently gendered linguistic structures, transcends them in its

129

implicit moral imperative: to recognize and honor this difference, which is universal, in all speakers and writers. Because languages like French everywhere presuppose the masculine and obscure the feminine, recognizing sexual difference also resurrects the feminine, permitting divinely inspired contact with one another, through which we become subjective by also honoring the subjectivity of others.

In the first two parts of the chapter that follows I will examine aspects of these two claims in seemingly disparate works, *Amante Marine,* which criticizes Nietzsche, and an article in linguistics. I conclude by briefly considering some possible complications of a contradiction in part of Irigaray's linguistic claim discussed in her recent *Sexes et genres à travers les langues.*[3]

The Feminine Christ of *Amante Marine*

Irigaray divides *Amante Marine,* like its predecessor *Speculum of the Other Woman,*[4] into three parts. *Amante Marine* first retells Nietzsche's *Zarathustra,* imitating its style, but criticizing its conceptions of master-slave morality and Christianity. The second and central section of *Amante Marine* rewrites and explains the poetic experiment that precedes it, this time offering the cognitive arguments that Freud and Lacan, as well as Nietzsche, assume that morality requires separation and distance and that this requirement is destructive. In the third and final section of *Amante Marine,* Irigaray turns to *Logos* as divine, deconstructing the stories of the births of Dionysius and Apollo into patriarchy, then celebrating Christ's resurrection as feminine rebirth.

I will say no more here about the first two sections of *Amante Marine,* but will turn directly to the third section, which begins as a reply to Nietzsche's *On the Birth of Tragedy.* There Irigaray recounts the births of Apollo and Dionysius, both sons of Zeus, both rescued from accidents befalling their mothers before their birth; both thus twice-born. But their personalities contrast. Dionysius is drunken, ecstatic, possessed of erotic vision; he is the god of eros. Apollo is clear, remote, possessed of reflective genius; he is the god of love. Nietzsche, retelling their story, had proposed that a combination of the attributes of Dionysius and Apollo, eros and love, was necessary for tragedy.

Irigaray, in contrast, reads the births of Dionysius and Apollo as patriarchy's usurpation of the feminine power to give birth. Eros and Love together fail to produce a unity, for these are also destruction and distance, together. Dionysius, in his erotic striving, remains but "the baby still in the cradle" and Apollo, in his distant amorous reflection, but "the twin brother." Dionysius and Apollo cannot complete one another because they are each half, but not of the other. Their mother is missing.

Irigaray recounts that Dionysius, drunken god of eros, was born of Zeus; rather, he was twice-born. Rescued from his mother's womb after lightning had killed her, he was sewn into the thigh of Zeus who, delivering him, became both mother and father to him. Nor is the birth of Dionysius the only birth attributed to Zeus. Athena, goddess of wisdom, sprang, not from his thigh, but full-grown from his head. The births damaged the children, as well as the mother. Dionysius remains emotionally in the cradle, striving always for ecstatic union to take the place of the fusion that he could not have with his own mother, recreating in each destructive encounter the death of his own mother, victim of his father's jealousy. Athena, whose birth from the head of Zeus evades the mother completely, appears to have no sexuality and incarnates only masculine virtues.

Dionysius will be surrounded by women reduced to the function of mother and nurse, who will die that he may live. These women help give title to *Amante Marine*. They are marine in the amniotic fluid of their mother's womb, marine in the supposed formlessness of their creation. But as mothers, they are goddesses of a love that culminates in their killing:

> Love is that which, by separating them from themselves *[elles-mêmes]*, draws them to suffer such agonies that the end of their divine destiny is accomplished. And from him whom they adore, they receive passage into the beyond.

> From him whom they give life, they receive death. If he is the son of the God.[5]

Apollo, also son of Zeus, is also twice-born. Assisted from the womb by his twin sister Artemis, who remains a virgin devoted to his service, Apollo, too, will depend on women devoted to his service. But Apollo, god of love and the sun, will keep these women at a distance:

> Apollo takes into and upon himself the mirror *[miroîr]* that is his sister so that he can give birth to the dream of beauty. Being of fire and ice, for a moment he holds in balance the contrasts between thunder and frost, the too hot and too cold, the too immediately present and the forever distant. His glory still shines out, like the glow of a rising sun. But it dazzles *[miroîte]* so, without burning, that it must already be made of ice *[glâce]*.[6]

Irigaray's pun on *glâce, mirror,* and *ice,* distant and cold, repeats an image of separation implicit in the mimicry of the mirror. As Apollo mimics his sister in reflecting her beauty, Dionysius, in drunken abandon, mimics a female lover's polymorphous sexuality. Zeus, of course, mimics the mother herself.

Although these myths support culture's mimicry of feminine power as the veiled, distant object of men's striving, the imitation fails, Irigaray contends, for Apollo and Dionysius fail to complete one another. They lack not Zeus, representing the masculine, but the very feminine power that they imitate so poorly. What escapes these imitations is that, to the extent that they succeed, they obliterate the separation between mother and infant that patriarchal ethics imposes. In approaching the feminine, patriarchal ethics loses its ground: "This game of mimicry protects and seduces, and the third term would be sometimes mother-nature, sometimes woman-sister. By dissimulating, assimilating himself therein, or by assimilating them, he [the god] becomes them and they become in him. Mutation in which the difference of the (male) one and the other disappears."[7] Replacing separation with fusion, unformed matter, the sea, amniotic fluid, Irigaray portrays nature as part of the self rather than separate—feminine.

To elaborate on this vision, Irigaray turns to a radical restatement of the Christian myths of birth, crucifixion, and resurrection. Here she asks, not why male religions postulate the deaths of the mother or of the feminine so that the god might live, but rather, how to tell the story in reverse. What if the god died so that the mother might live? And what if we retold Christ's death, deconstructing both Christian and Nietzschean interpretations of it, as a death that he died, and from which he was reborn, so that the mother might live? In this retelling, Mary was not impregnated through the destructive striving of eros, but beyond its laws, nor was she killed so that the infant might be born. In her body the abstract Word became feminine flesh as a manifestation of love. Christ then, unlike Dionysius or Apollo, is innocent of injury to the mother.

Irigaray then asks: "does not the Christ—second son of Adam, innocent son of the Father—manifest the tragic destiny of love and desire imprisoned in a single body?"[8] But Irigaray also asserts that this feminine Christ, supposed by patriarchal religion to have no sexuality, manifests his own erotic power. This power is neither the destruction of Dionysian eros nor the icy distance of Apollonian love:

> The god does not brutally enter into a body, only to throw it off at once, leaving it to madness and the death of a boundless passion. He does not hide behind an unending series of appearances that ease the pain of

living by giving mortals a chance to gaze upon an alien perfection. He is not made known only through writing.

He is made flesh. Continues on in the flesh. Closes with and is close to himself, from within a living body. That can be affected by *pathos—his* own and that of others.[9]

In other words, incarnation radically reinterpreted provides a spiritual model for reciprocity and mutual recognition. It redefines both subjectivity and the self-other relation.

Because Christ, not the mother, is killed, the crucifixion again manifests the force of patriarchal institutions that, Irigaray says, secrete this force. How then can crucifixion redefine subjectivity? Irigaray answers that Christ, like Apollo and Dionysius, was also twice-born. "It was necessary for Christ to be made into a corpse in order for the resurrection to reveal, in him, the flesh that overcomes the walls of tombs. Necessary double resurrection."[10] Twice-born in obliterating the separation between spirit and matter, Irigaray's Christ incorporates not only a new subjectivity, but also a new self-other relationship blurring the separation demanded by patriarchy. He transcends it in the double movement of a rebirth that is resurrection, taking care of the (m)other, so that the spirit is "Not, this time, the product of the love between Father and son, but the universe already made flesh or capable of becoming flesh, and remaining in excess to the existing world."[11] The resurrection of a feminine Christ also recognizes and honors sexual difference. Thus Irigaray's *Logos*, divine language, helps establish an ethics. Irigaray presents this ethics more concretely in the form of very recent research on sexual differences in uses of subject pronoun in French.

Je and *tu*: The Self and the Other

The Same wears two masks: maternity and patriarchy. Patriarchy rises anew in each utterance of the self-identically gendered grammatical subject, officially neutral but covertly masculine, imposing that masculinity upon speakers of both sexes. So Irigaray argues in her psycholinguistics research, as in a paper published in a special issue of the linguistics journal *Langages* in 1987.[12] This work in linguistics, in which Irigaray has been intensely engaged, parallels the very differently presented utopian writing of *Amante Marine* in its concern for the recognition of gendered, feminine subjectivity.

In "L'Ordre sexuel du discours," Irigaray reports the results of three groups of women and men speaking French: psychoanalytic patients c agnosed with hysteria or obsessional neurosis; healthy adults of both sexes visiting a clinic; and university undergraduates in the social sciences. All three groups showed sexual differences in their use of the French language. I want to discuss one example, the use of *je* and *tu*, whose analysis mirrors the mythology retold in *Amante Marine*.

Irigaray begins this analysis by asserting that hysteria is culturally feminine, whereas obsessional neurosis is culturally masculine. If so, we would expect women and men with obsessional neurosis to speak similarly, and men and women with hysteria to speak similarly. But this is not the case. Although typically hysterics are women and obsessional neurotics are men, male hysterics and female obsessional neurotics suffer their illnesses differently, each retaining the speech patterns characteristic of their sex.[13]

Studying female hysterics and male obsessives, Irigaray proposes that their speech patterns vary characteristically (but not immutably) by sex. The hysteric characteristically uses the second-person pronoun, often displacing the first-person subject entirely, as in *"Est-ce que tu m'aimes?"* or even *"Tu m'aimes?"* The obsessional neurotic characteristically uses the first-person pronoun, often displacing the second-person object entirely, as in *"Je me demande si je suis aimé."* Thus 42.6 percent of the group of seventy-five utterances of hysterics used *je* as the subject; and 29.3 percent used *tu*. But among eighty utterances of obsessional neurotics, 62.5 percent used *je* either explicitly or masked as *it [il]* or *qui;* no obsessionals at all used *tu* or *vous* as subject.[14]

What philosophical point can we draw from such a study? Restricted as it is to psychoanalytic patients, further limited by the ethical requirement to preserve the psychoanalytic patient's secrecy, this study of hysterics and obsessional neurotics suggests that women and men culturally engage different ontologies: men are subjects alone; women are subjects with others or not at all. Irigaray had also suggested elsewhere that the hysteric, not having been loved enough, lives out that absence; the obsessional neurotic, too much loved, turns toward himself.[15] The hysterics of Irigaray's psychoanalytic study thus resemble Dionysius in their striving toward another; the obsessionals resemble Apollo in their reflective distancing from the other. What about ordinary French speakers?

In *"L'ordre sexuel du discours"* Irigaray also reports the results of two other studies conducted not on psychoanalytic patients, but on visitors to a prenatal clinic and on undergraduate social sciences students. The first group, consisting of twenty women and twenty men, were given the task of producing sentences containing the word *célibat*. The second group, four subgroups consisting of eighty-three women and forty-seven

men, were given the task of producing sentences containing the words
ennui, lui, and *dire.*

In both studies, men far more often referred to themselves, either
directly with *je* or indirectly with *l'homme* or with the neutral *on.* In the
first group, five men used *je,* but no women did. In the second group 25
percent of the women used *je,* 18 percent *elle,* and 44.5 percent *il;* 31.9
percent of the men used *il,* 34 percent *je,* but only 8.5 percent *elle.*[16]
Moreover, the topic of discourse, designated by *célibat* or *ennui,* was far
more often masculinized by the men than by the women talking about
remaining unmarried or dealing with everyday annoyances.[17]

The speech of normal women and men in Irigaray's studies thus
mimics the speech of hysterical and obsessional psychoanalytic patients;
and, it again evokes the ontology of Dionysius and Apollo. But until
recently Irigaray offered no specific ethic of language use, save the appeal to use a *je* or *I* that "speaks its sources."[18] In *Je, tu, nous,* however,
as the title suggests, she does specifically describe ways that women
speaking with and about one another might use specific grammatical
forms to refer in the feminine gender, though the French language often
conceals the feminine, as we have seen.[19] Irigaray's psycholinguistic re-
searches are deconstructive, not constructive; and she has carefully limited her conclusions from them to spoken French, remarking that
grammatical divisions manifest themselves differently in different languages, so that each language must differently interpret its output. How,
then, is this concrete proposal to use a *je* or *I* that "speaks its sources" a
"sensible transcendental"? And what, finally, *is* a "sensible transcendental," anyway?

The "Sensible Transcendental" and the Divinity of Language

Irigaray's "sensible transcendental"[20] is not to be found in the facts
of ordinary use, but in an imagined alternative. The "sensible transcendental" is incarnation of the divine—of Christ's death and resurrection;
of maternity; and even as Irigaray suggests at the end of *Amante Marine,*
of the speaking subject—within language itself.

Yet Irigaray's studies of spoken French suggest that its actual use
does not support such incarnation, as we have just seen. Can her conception of language conjoining the feminine with the divine, resurrect the
feminine subjectivity that, according to her psycholinguistic researche
spoken French obliterates? If Irigaray's tales of the births and deaths
gods in *Amante Marine* offer the prospect of resurrecting femi

subjectivity, portrayed by a feminine Christ, the prospect of that resurrection must be more than an apocalyptic myth. What Irigaray is offering is also an ethic with a transcendental starting point, differently conceiving relationships among ourselves according to models drawn from actual feminine experience, such as maternity. Moreover, by reinstating these models in *Amante Marine,* Irigaray is also resurrecting an ancient and lost matriarchy in which divinity originates in the feminine as she has again recently reaffirmed.[21]

In that Irigaray's Christ is both feminine and a sexual man, he incarnates difference, as well as the divine. Language becomes divine when it also incarnates difference, allowing conversation that is otherwise impossible. Divine *Logos* becomes not flesh, though, but voice, inscription, or electric charge. This incarnation holds the always potential contradiction of gender difference in a tension that reaches a critical point in linguistic translations, as from French to English. It is at this point that Irigaray's conceptions of the linguistic subject and an ethics of sexual difference coalesce and sometimes clash. I want to end with one example of such a clash that Irigaray herself acknowledges, but whose interpretation demands more work.

In *Sexes et genres à travers les langues,* which Irigaray edited in 1990, several members of a research team translated some of her psycholinguistic experiments on the French language into English and Italian. One of these experiments was a translation of the same series of exercises reported in the second section of this chapter, in which Irigaray had found that in spoken French the use of the first-person *je* or alternatives such as *il* (for "it") or *on* are chosen by a majority of the men, but not of the women. Two different teams of researchers found that speakers of American and Canadian English do not use *I* in the same way as the French speakers of Irigaray's study; they also found that a slight majority of women, rather than men, speaking English used *I* instead of alternatives.[22]

Irigaray acknowledges the discrepancy, but her assessment of it leaves unresolved a larger and ongoing problem in our own understanding of her conception of incarnation or, to be more direct, embodiment. Is Irigaray's incarnation of the feminine in speaking and writing a matter of some biological essence, as many English-speaking commentators have suggested? Irigaray emphatically denies this.

Belonging to a sex signifies neither an assignment to an immutable truth nor a pure adherence to biology. It is physiology and the cultural interpretation of it. One cannot erase the other nor the other the one: we are bodies and culture, bodies more or less cultured. On the contrary, what is important is that the bodies of the different sexes have equivalent subjective and objective rights.

If she rejects biological essentialism, does Irigaray also reject the kind of substantialism implicit in her conception of language as incarnation? It appears not. In a later essay in the same volume assessing the results of the English-language research, Irigaray concludes that there is a "partial intersection"[24] between the responses of American and Canadian women speaking English and men speaking French. She writes, "American women say 'I' more but, by this 'I,' they often erase their feminine identity, the qualities of the world and of human relationships which can refer to it."[25] Thus it appears that Irigaray is here arguing that American and Canadian versions of the English language impose a masculine subjectivity upon all of us who use the first-person pronoun.

Irigaray's ethical conception of communication and her epistemic conception of subjectivity seem to me, as a native speaker of English, to be in conflict at this point. The relationship between her ethics and her linguistics needs elaboration to sustain her vision of femininity as a divine intervention in language and our uses of it with one another.

Part III

Aesthetics

11   The Earth That Does Not Move

YIFAT HACHAMOVITCH

The earth does not merely subside beneath the hammering of civilizations, it fascinates and converts the structures of experience, it murmurs
below and within the demotic of everyday life, speaking not only through
our farms and our bestiaries, but through all the surfaces we have pinned
down, all the technologies implicating its elemental support, all the materialities that bind the life-world to a particular order of things.

How can we map out and reconnoiter the pregiven world without
accounting for the wild body of the earth and the ways it has worked
itself into the very hides of everyday phenomena? Our life-worlds are
moored to this durable geographical subsoil; their very pregivenness is
an effect of its slow-moving history.

The tension between the wild body of the earth as it "existed at the
beginning" and "the nature which (springs) forth for us in the nexus of
community"[1] is not resolved in a historical inquiry, but activated and
reactivated each time a ruin surfaces from a pregiven world, each time a
"natural" object makes its historical debut. A return inquiry must redefine
the vital horizon of the archive, seeking its voluminosity in the very
possibility of the *longue durée* to inscribe the life-world from within, to
collude with fresh superstructures and old vegetation, to draw men to the
sea, and to bind men to the soil.

What is broadly termed *an infrastructure* in economic discourse is
not merely the equipmentality of a world constructed "below" the spaces
of culture, society, and science, it is what substructs the lived experience
of space and binds that entity "which is always and in each case its own
'there'"[2] to the particular possibilities of a particular earthly region. My
work attempts to reconsider this earthly substructure, to show how things
themselves shape the structures of experience that cultures and civilizations

hand down as traditions, as rituals, as archaisms, as symbolic systems, and to demonstrate how a world's material structures, its vegetation and stones and swamps and roads, serve as the subsoil of intentional structures, the subsoil of the constituting life.

Material life is propelled by memory as well as scarcity; the vestibules of a civilization drawing its life from the sea are not merely entrances into the more elaborate living spaces wherein culture and art weave themselves into consciousness and representation. The processes of hunger, fascination, and seduction are always and already at work at the entry ways and at the ports, in the very appropriations of material life, in its specific hungers, in the shape of its discoveries. An ontology sensitized to the materiality of things must take into account the selective mechanisms at work even as an enclave of rural civilization begins to appropriate, classify, and represent new elemental realities to itself.

In its investment of everyday objects with inherited passions, a culture betrays its own archaisms. The historic deposits of cultural experience can be sited alongside a culture's long distance dreams, which yield up its past in the shape of material fixations. A history of everyday life would disclose not only the elementary structures that lie at the basis of a world's commensality, but its hungers, its uncertainties, and its terrors: the backgame it plays with civilization. There is a deep sounding to the life-world: it speaks with the tongues of the *longue durée,* even as it collaborates with new elements, implicates new rhythms, resonates within newly crafted spaces.

Already in the fifteenth and sixteenth centuries, the canonical blended and allayed with the mundane objects of exchange, infusing the plenum of everyday life with religious voluminosity. Consider the brightness of the apples spilling on the darkened soil in Nunez de Villavicencio's *Boy with Two Dogs.* Or Murillo's *Cuisine des anges,* which depicts a spacious monastery kitchen, its vessels of brass, its pots, dishes, and basins, its earthenware jugs and sparkling white plates, while dinner is prepared by angels. In the *bodegones* of seventeenth century Spain, the genre of paintings that mixes still life representations of fruits, vegetables, and kitchenware with portraits of simple people, gathered over tavern fare, materiality itself deepens, becomes reflective, and swells with meaning. Old values resonate through domestic utensils, sacred spaces are regenerated by the shapes, the colors, the objects fetched through mercantile exchange. The fascination and seduction of market life is evident in pictures such as *The Beggar Boy, Two Peasant Boys Eating Grapes and Melon, Woman Usurer, A Peasant Girl Selling Fruit, Peasant Girls Counting Money.* These everyday people and things are in part collective representations: they betray a new preoccupation with objects unloosed not from the soil, but from the trappings of a society bent on exchange, a life-world retooled by the equipmentality of money. Here human geography displaces natural geography; the realities of a civilization that changes little or not at all for the duration of centuries—its vegetables, fruits, its rustic figures—are deployed along the new axes that divide Seville, as they divide all Mediterranean cities with oceanic dreams. Here the things of an earth that "does not move," its savoys, its celeries, its oranges, its peasants, its primitive tools, are seen within new groupings· the bodies of old men are supping on a tavern meal, the peasant becomes a streetbeggar. The vegetables appear side by side with the gold of the New World, the apothecary becomes a *bodega*—a seaside tavern.[3] In Velázquez's *Las Lanzas,* the sky itself betrays its dependence upon the lapis lazuli accessible only through a merchant's design, even as one of the oldest Spanish fixtures reappears as a "veritable *reja* of lances."[4] By reconnoitring the slow moving history of material life through everyday objects that link social space to the *longue durée,* we come to recognize them as geo-ontological sedimentations, icons that reconstruct the earth so that it becomes a place of memory. A transcendental history must reconsider everyday life on the basis of these icons, wherein the essential becomes manifest only through and by virtue of its historical dress.

Braudel's reconstruction of Mediterranean life may be viewed as a serial *"bodegón"* in which the *"tenebrissimo"* of the *longue durée* serves as the backdrop of everyday phenomena. The food and drink and palaver of short-term conjunctures are illuminated against the permanent forces that weigh upon day-to-day life without its knowledge. It is through the flesh of things that the sea itself enters into the consciousness and self-consciousness of the peninsulas; with the things brought by the sea comes money, gold, silver, Spanish coins *de a ochos reales.* The new measures that they impose upon a mentality emerging from its feudal swamp intertwine with the seamless surface of an everyday life still gauged to the time of olives, wheat, and grapes. The being that takes over the sea as its burden and its mood is also and already the being that lives in bondage to the plants of civilization.

Each time the marketplace is discovered, it presents a particular earth as its basis and a particular configuration of things as concrete possibilities of a life-world. It is a collapsible structure, as unbound as the stands and stalls of a bazaar; yet as an ontological region, it surfaces from the deep structures of history. For the small ships of the Mediterranean navigating the sea by hugging the coastline, the marketplace was discovered again and again by taking space in. Through the repeated movements of trade, through the crablike movement along the coast, in that "again and again" of *costeggiare* sailors "buying butter in Villefranche, vinegar at Nice, oil and bacon at Toulon or travelling from one seaside inn to another, dining in one and supping in the next,"[5] a port became an accentuated "indicator" of the marketplace.

The marketplace stretched itself across and through moveable bodies, it projected itself as always and already something to be discovered through the next cargo and the next ship and the next wave. Humanity "made room" for it in the life-world: it was had in advance of any actual installation, its path charted by memory and hunger. It was bound to its earthly underpinnings, yet it mapped out at a distance a world further outside than any object could ever be.[6]

The road, the sea route, and the trade route surface from within the market space as the sum of the real possibilities that "belong to the extension of empirical concepts." These concepts are still and always bound to this world, but bound in such a way that they can produce, spontaneously, in intuition, what is not bound to this world: a future thing, a thing not yet, winter wheat. The road is the "whence" and the "whither" that remains in darkness while the things themselves show themselves in the "that it is" of things.

The chance encounters depicted by the *bodegón,* its simple people—talking at the table, over bread and wine—are structures of a Mediterranean in which even the stillest figures are all, somehow, on their way[7]—always and already bound to the road, the sea route, this trade route, from which history recovers them. The road both replenishes and transforms rural life by articulating its archaisms as objects of exchange. In trading, Dasein exists in a mode of being that delineates not only the Mediterranean marketplaces of the past—finite historical spaces—but *the marketplace that in its (omni)temporality surfaces at each and every moment as that temporalizing space in which Being finds itself as thrown and the world disclosed as a sea.*

How can we understand the temporality of the market on the basis of a space of thrownness, a "mood of the earth," a sea, within which what is thrown is both thrown and throwing?[8] Consider the *mausim,* a deep structure of the Mediterranean life of trade, which throughout the Muslim countries means both fair and seasonal festival, and which was also used to describe the periodic winds that blew from the Indian Ocean.[9] This wind "unfailingly regulated sea-voyages in either direction in the Far East and the warm seas, thus precipitating or interrupting international encounters between merchants. . . . Every year, the monsoon brought to (Mocha), (the) Red Sea port (which was later to become the great centre of the coffee trade) a certain number of ships from India, the East Indies and the nearby coast of Africa, laden with men and bundles of goods" (CCII, 126–127).

Market space is first an attunement to the fates, a fateful conjuncture simulated and dissimulated by winds, sea, and tides, before it is a court that adjudicates over the "things themselves." To this fateful space belongs thrown being, a being bound to things that are themselves "thrown" temporalizations of various earths. As Braudel notes: "pepper, gum lac, benzoin, cotton cloth (woven with gold thread or painted by hand), tobacco, cinnamon, nutmeg, cloves, mace, camphor, porcelain, musk, diamonds, indigo, drugs . . . the perfumes and gums of southern Arabia" (CCII, 127). All these were carried by two ships arriving from Dabhol in India in 1621, with 300 traveling merchants all coming to sell in the port of Mocha, awaiting the arrival, from the other direction, Suez, of one ship, with Spanish pieces of eight, woolen cloth, coral, and goats-hair camlets. Market space is an ever-collapsible temporal structure, an "attunement" that marks the meeting of ships, a fair.

"If the ship from Suez failed to arrive on time, the fair . . . was threatened. The merchants from India and the East Indies deprived of their customers, would have to sell their goods at any price, for the monsoon remorselessly put an end to the fair even if it had not properly begun" (CCII, 127). The temporality at the basis of the fair is an omnitemporality. It is the possibility of historicality itself as the appearing of the "there" to which Being is attuned. It is, however, nothing outside of the history in which it displays itself, i.e., the empirical temporality in which it discloses itself and lets itself be threatened. Is this *mausim,* which is both a wind and a season, a possibility of movement toward a marketplace and that marketplace itself, the "sense" of the marketplace in general, the "sense" of all marketplaces?

The omnitemporality of the marketplace maps and preconnoiters the temporality at stake in the judgment. Its "ground" is a horizon of possible thing-experiences that are validated through and across constituting acts. These "thing-experiences" are earthly sanctions of intentionality structures. They lie at the hinge between objectivities that are absolutely "free" and bound to no particular space, no particular earth, or what Husserl describes as "objectivities of the understanding," and things that in their bindedness surface only through the web of their embeddedness. By focusing on the sea as the highway of these intentional structures, we are able to navigate the essential boundaries of an earth that begins and ends in movement.

As a phenomenon that spills over the boundaries of a physical space, the sea breaks through traditional archival trappings. It reveals at once both the "deep spontaneity" of a human boundary and its factical compliance with the horizon prescription of a particular historical space with its empirical overall style. To reconnoiter the human spaces that have been carried along in its wake, drawn into its orbit, and fertilized by its repeated infiltration is to recover a historical field of possible objects, possible experiences, and moveable bodies. It is to recover an exposed hyletic surface that constitutes the voluptuous residue of repeated figuration, repeated ecstases, that hovers in between the boundaries of the ph geographer and those of the human geographer. Yet it is more than the durable surface of the earth upon which Being makes its mark, it is the earth itself as a moveable body: the result of decomposition, constantly being renewed and prepared for use, capable of being modified and of taking on different forms. Aesthetic contact, geometric contact, cultural contact, as well as that tradition of "I sell you nuts, you sell me plums," is made through and across this residuous hylos, this crust; any deformation, any disfiguration, any vague shape, is a commentary on the earth itself.

The Emulation of the Pears

Look at Samuel Bak's *Pears*. Consider for a moment a particular phenomenon, a pear, for example, the pear in Bak's painting. How was it transported to this treeless terrain? How did it come to duplicate itself across the surfaces of a reflective horizon? How did it come to breed and multiply its voluptuous shape so that each cloud would bear its representation? These painterly objectifications make manifest the process by which an essential structure irrupts from the mind of an intuiting subjectivity and communicates itself across an intersubjective landscape. Consider the way this seamless everyday object spills over the boundaries of a particular skin and projects its recognizable form upon the visible surfaces of the surrounding world. It is not obvious that this genesis proceeds from the mute fixture docked on the bushes of the painting's foreground. It is not obvious that the direction of influence is from the earth to the sky—for how can we know that an object appearing on dry turf was not originally rendered in imitation of the vague repetitions of the clouds? And is it not possible that the pear-shaped clouds are themselves reflections of a deeper composition, embedded in the rocks strewn across the landscape? Their ovular forms are, after all, also typified by pears. Their residuous shapes may be symptomatic of long-term geographical mutations that have traced their effects upon an earthly surface.

How can we talk about the way the universe of things is decomposed and recomposed without accounting for the collusion of the material surfaces of a pregiven life-world with the intentional structures of a consciousness always and already ahead of itself in its projective thematization of the concrete contents of experience? How can we trace the spectacle of the suddenly ripe fruit without referring to a more primordial hunger?

We bear witness to an intentional act across and through the spontaneity of its objects. Phenomena pin down the intentional structure experience by disclosing the multiple surfaces of things as they appear

to us, by exhibiting *them* whole. The vague iterations of pears are the usurious effects of the *original* engendering[10] *[Erzeugung]* of an essential type made *voluminous* in the flow of a lived experience *[Erlebnis]*. Their flow of *protentions* and retentions (the receding cloud-pears, the pea*-shaped rocks at *the* foreground) manifests the unfolding of an ever w* ening horizon *wherein* the object exhibits itself through an alteratio* perspectives.

The *perspectives* of the shape and also of its color are diffe* each *is* in this new way an exhibiting of—of this shap* color. . . . In running their course they function in such a way as to form a sometimes continuous and sometimes discrete synthesis of identification, or, better, of unification. This happens not as a blending of externals; rather, as bearers of 'sense' in each phase, as meaning something, the perspectives combine in an advancing enrichment of meaning and a continuing development of meaning, such that what no longer appears is still valid as retained and such that the prior meaning which anticipates a continuous flow, the expectation of 'what is to come,' is straightway fulfilled and more closely determined. Thus everything is taken up into the unity of validity or into the *one, the* thing.[11]

As phenomena, the pears are noematic variations. To each one belongs a noetic perspective, a tacit intentionality, a consciousness fixed on its own idealization. The phenomenal pears are generated by a "free imaginative variation of the world and its shapes [that] results only in possible empirically intuitable shapes and not in exact shapes" (CES, 49). In each profile variation that characterizes the spontaneous production of an object whose vague shape is not yet ideal, in that "again and again" of its historical debut, an eidetic boundary makes itself felt. In the painting, the horizonal phenomena conform to the intrinsic content of an eidetic intuition of an object that is neither mathematical nor ideal. What is revealed in the horizon of "idealized bodies" are shapes ever experienced and experiencable—what is perceived in each eidetic structure traced by an intentional act is not isomorphic with the body of a still life.

Things 'seen' are always more than what we 'really and actually' see of them. Seeing, perceiving, is essentially having-something-itself *[Selbsthaben]* and at the same time having-something-in-advance *[Vorhaben]*, meaning-something-in-advance *[Vor-meinen]*. All praxis, with its projects *[Vorhaben]*, involves inductions; it is just that ordinary inductive knowledge [predictions], even if expressly formulated and 'verified,' is 'artless' compared to the artful 'methodical' inductions which can be carried to infinity through the method of Galilean physics with its great productivity. (CES, 51)

With respect to the microscopic taste for displaying these "methodical inductions" in pictorial space, one should contrast the still life in k's painting with the traditional (Dutch) practice of opening, slicing, shattering the thing, to reveal to our sight the productivity "behind" ppings, the mechanism of its "nature." Bak offers us the interior or ide not by cutting into the thing itself, but by disclosing the narcis-ake at the basis of its image, the montage of emulation that dem-its rigor as a cause.

The painting manifests an experience of emulation caught up in the very things that it connects. The clouds are converted by the emulation of the pear, but do not elude the movement of their "natural" dispersion in time, their mode of succession. Their deployment and rotation belong to the order of celestial objects, but their shapes conform to an essential intuition of an earthly structure, projected onto the horizon. Emulation both converts and fascinates its horizon; it organizes the surfaces of experience at a distance while maintaining the archaisms of a territory in circulation.

Yet is this not how a thing, any *thing*, comes to be thematized as a *type*? Is it not a rule of the experiencing gaze that it comes to dwell only upon objects that reconstitute their own kind? That short of this, it will take upon itself the task of duplication and thus generate, again and again, the same invariances, the same shapes, the same essential structures, the same types? How, except through a historical reconstruction, are we to separate the powers of conversion and fascination wielded by materialities that have communicated their shapes across history from the spells cast upon the life-world by scientific objects? These, too, are still and always caught up in the rocks, the clouds, the chiaroscuro of a horizon. As Landgrebe points out,

> [T]he perdurance of the unity of the thing throughout the diversity of perspectives—allowing one to speak of one's sensuous perception—is still not sufficient to authorize one to speak of a real, material thing. It still could be a phantom. The real thing is differentiated from the phantom in that it is borne out as identical in its causal connection with other things, in the influences which it experiences from them and which it exercises upon them. . . . We cannot say whether or not a supposedly individual perceived thing, taken for itself, is on par with what is real. (PEH, 158)

What is implied by the emulation of the pears, yet omitted by the mathematical objectifications of the natural scientist, is that *one sees always more and other than what commits one to an explicit intentional place*. The persistance of an eidetic structure in the face of an endlessly open world horizon betrays a life-world always and already bound by idealizations. It is by virtue of their function as habitual objects that idealized types come to dominate a perceptual repertory and resonate beyond the threshold of the space proper to their validation. Patrick Heela proposes that the carpentered environments of modern societies reflec perceptual repertory dominated by a Euclidean geometrical model.[12] visual spaces are fashioned by the essential "types" of Euclidean g etry in such a way that their invariant geometrical structures c serve as indices by which we measure and map non-Euclidean phenomena. The voluminosity of perceived things is not a quality inherent in space, but a quality imparted to space by the rigid bodies that invest it with their shape and measure, and in light of which it comes to be perceived in a uniform way.[13]

For Husserl, the logical accomplishments of science determine from the very start the world of our experience. For the scientist, the world becomes a mathematical manifold, a horizon of constituted objects whose meanings are quantitatively determinable. But these mathematical projections and their meaning-determinations are not essential structures belonging to the world as such.

The possibility of measuring and remeasuring the world, of spreading the world out as a mathematical manifold, of gutting the palpable materialities of our world and transposing them into idealized shapes—is this not the possibility of a map?[14] Yet, if "to understand geometry or any given cultural fact is to be conscious of its historicity, albeit 'implicitly'" (CES, 370), how is it possible to know a type in its historicity without considering the way it became a habitual object for a world, without thinking back to the first merchant who imported sugarcane or coffee or pears? without reconstructing the history of that "again and again" that transformed an unmapped highway into a sea route? without recalling the repetition of that inspired and essential act that mistook a levantine breeze for a trade wind? A life-world ontology would reconstruct these repetitions as deep structures of a historical space that is disclosed alongside the things it makes thematic as types. What is disclosed is disclosed not as a historiological fact, but as an "enduring possession, ever at one's disposal because it can be reproduced, and apprehended again, a repetitive process."[15]

In *The Crisis,* Husserl asks us to consider the motivation of this mapmaking effort: what propelled this dream of a map of nature, and how did this dream come to weave itself into the skins of our everyday phenomena? How do we account for the things themselves in terms of a life-world already mathematicized, which offers itself in the garb of ideas?

To authorize an essential reading of the pregiven life-world, a world still sensitized to the loom of phenomena on experiential horizons, Husserl launches a return inquiry—an inquiry that is capable of navigating space *before the plough.* Yet a historically sensitized reading of the life-world suggests that the ploughing of the earth precedes and determines the conceptual divisions of a scientific sensibility. An intentional analysis of ed spaces reactivates the *human* horizons of an earth that do not con- to the "*true*" frontiers of an earth surveyed by the physical geogra- "Technical exploitation, investment, population movements, are so many forms of energy affecting the land. But this land does not remain inert. It contains undying forces both material and human."[16]

To discover the essential shapes of a lived space is not to discover space before the plough, it is only to discover a space before a particular plough: it is to discover an earth ploughed by repeated comings and goings of peasants, merchants, transhumants, and sheep. It is to discover an Italy still draining her swamps or a Mediterranean ploughed for the duration of a sea crossing. Did not the slow moving history of Mediterranean life lay out *our* channels of communication, relaying in the rhythms of its shifting sands, in the cooing of its olives, discursive structures that still orchestrate our reflections and practices, the fealties of our everyday life?

The earth that was bound by juridical means was *that earth that a priori does not come from itself:* its measures were genealogical. The Palestinian *carruca*,[17] the Arab *faddan*,[18] the Latin *mansus,* and the French *jour(nal)*—all corresponding to the amount of land that can be plowed in one day *[jour]*,[19] mapped out the oldest emotions, the oldest fealties: they were fealties to the earth as the ideal object of transmission.

As the most universal, the most objectively exhibited element given to us, the earth itself is what furnishes the first matter of every sensible object. Insofar as it is the exemplary element (being more naturally objective, more permanent, more solid, more rigid, and so forth, than all other elements; and in a broader sense, it comprises them), it is normal that the earth has furnished the ground for the first idealities, then for the first absolutely universal and objective identities, those of calculus and geometry.[20]

By aligning all forms of fealty to the earth, the plough secured space to an order of succession in reference to which the moveable earth became a measure of legitimacy: the more earth one had, the more legitimate one was. The earth mapped out by ploughs does not appear, it descends; geometry is the very logic of this descent. As the "basis body," the earth "is the ground for the first idealities, the first objective identities, those of calculus and geometry."[21] It is the first plane, the first space of law, *the first space of writing*. All the failures of representation lie in this first failure, this first analogy. A ploughman is a scribe, he is the hand, but he is not yet a mouth,[22] not yet a geometer.[23]

Each plough institutes its own science.[24] Thus the image it sows is experienced in the world in the very instance of its essential juridica failure. The again and again of the first ideating acts, of grinding edge smoothing surfaces, trying to realize preferred shapes,[25] is the again a

again of a failure, the again and again of an earth "in which the ideal
object settles as what is *sedimented* or *deposited*,"[26] an earth in vassalage
to practical judgments, to the *c'est ecrit* of the law. Moreover, in the
Mediterranean world, *it is not that one plants things because the earth
does not move, the earth does not move because one plants things.*

The Mediterranean soil, with its infertile limestones, its rare deposits of loose soil, and the thin layers of its topsoil, which only the modest
wooden swing-plough can scratch, is at the mercy of the wind or the
flood waters. Only man's constant effort has perpetuated the arable land.
It is because the earth moves that the peasant is and must be bound even
more tightly than a spinning girl holds her needle, for

> if the peasant's vigilance should be distracted during long periods of
> unrest, not only the peasantry but also the productive soil will be de-
> stroyed. During the disturbances of the Thirty Years' War, the German
> peasantry was decimated, but the land remained and with it the possibil-
> ity of renewal. Here lay the superiority of the North. In the Mediterra-
> nean the soil dies if it is not protected by crops: the desert lies in wait
> for arable land and never lets go. It is a miracle if it is preserved or
> reconstituted by the labour of the peasants. Even modern figures prove
> this. Apart from forests, pastures, and specifically nonproductive land,
> cultivated land in about 1900 represented 46 per cent of the whole in
> Italy, 39.1 per cent in Spain, 34.1 per cent in Portugal, and only 18.6 per
> cent in Greece. On Rhodes, out of a total of 144,000 hectares, 84,000
> are still uncultivated today. On the southern shores of the sea the figures
> are even more disastrous. (MMW, 243)

Because *the earth itself cannot be a fatherland,* the regeneration of political desire for earth must be sought elsewhere: in the normative structures
that are transmitted across and through the distance of a ploughshare, in
the forms of bondage that every civilized plant recreates,[27] in the structures of care through which every juridical category makes itself loved.

> Theoretically, the *carruca* was a rectangle 2 × 3 (16 × 24 *cordes*).
> Nothing was more abstract than these proportions. No cultivated land
> ever had such proportions—they were the creation of the human mind.
> And yet, it was not just an abstraction. The concept had roots in agricul-
> tural reality. The surface corresponded to an area of arable land suffi-
> cient to nourish a household at a given moment. But in this case we
> would expect *carrucae* of different sizes, according to the quality of
> climate and soil. But Crusader documentation has a uniform *carruca.*
> The reason is obvious. We are dealing with a fiscal measure, which also
> explains the fact that its component units *(cordes, toise)* were estab-

lished by legislation and preserved in the royal *Secrète*. As such its use was first and foremost fiscal, namely that of an entity of taxation, a fiscal notion of a household tenure unit. For the administration, the whole kingdom, so to speak, was composed of regular rectangles, a kind of chessboard with regular squares. (PAC, 191)

The history of the plough is the history of the instrument through which the law, and thence, geometry, contracts our being, in the sense of *contraho: it pulls out.* The earth that does not move is issued through and across these contractions. "[B]y absolutely virtualizing dialogue, [the law] creates a kind of autonomous transcendental field from which every present subject can be absent" (EHG, 88). The ploughman disappears, what remains is an earth mapped out by law. The metal rod disappears, what remains is a standard, a canon, a ruler. The primordial intentional act disappears, writing disappears, what remains is what is written—an earth that does not move, a chessboard of regular squares, a kingdom of rectangles.

It is the very *illegibility* of the things themselves, the illegibility of the surfaces inscribed, divided, and multiplied by law—the illegibility of the wild body of the earth—that reinstates the law, and thence, geometry, as the only court of measures that adjudicates over "the things themselves." The things themselves, the olives themselves, the bodies themselves, become legal instruments in the classical dogmatic sense of *instrumentorum:* they are instruments to which faith becomes attached *[de fide instrumentorum],* instruments that validate or invalidate, in advance, a traditional yield of material life, and thus a traditional yield of emotions. The rule of faith extends itself beyond the physical terrain by prolonging itself through it.

The law sanctions and completes an originary illegibility by reproducing itself through and across each measure of earth: each field of soil is its field of imperatives, each division of the harvest is its form of homage. In the lordship of Tyre, Prawer tells us, "In three areas planted with olives, each evaluated at two local *carrucae*—one has forty olive trees, another twenty five, and the third forty again" (PAC, 160). Each moveable object carries alongside it its measure as a prescription, but the measures themselves belong to the world, they are forgotten as measures. "Olive trees need a given amount of space for their growth and in the first case mentioned above the olive trees were newly planted, which implies that such needs were calculated" (PAC, 191). The harvest, not the earth, is divided; or rather, it is the harvest that allows men to divide the earth in relation to space. Thus in the Latin Kingdom of the Crusaders, the taxation of cultivated crops was not calculated in relation to the area, but in relation to its products or to the number of trees.[28] It is through the flesh of things that an institution binds the logical terrain, which it occupies for its own calculations. As juridical objects, things always and already disclose a certain commensurability of a life-world that gave them their founding. This commensurability is totemic: we are instituted through the teacups and soupspoons of our grandmothers. We are instituted through the pressing of the olives. The earth is scaffolded by legal fictions. The instruments themselves, the images themselves, the measures themselves are already in place, already repressing, repeating, and instituting the emotional life of the subject. They become the structures of care through which the life-world accumulates validity.

A slow moving history of material life would reveal that such "validation" takes place day in, day out through and across the instrument of instruments, subjectivity, and its sad passions *[passions tristes],* its usage of, its adhesion to, the things through which the law has always and already worked its measures. It would map out the boundaries of an *earth that begins and ends in instruments:* eggs and fish and sugar, stones and roads, shops and stalls, slices of cheese, coffeecups, and tablespoons. It would reconnoiter the *longue durée* of the law through which the things themselves become signs.

What is decisive for the navigation of this history is not the object per se, but the possibility of revealing the object through the multiplication of its powers in the worlds built around it, the practices that surround it, and its potential to transform Being-in-the-world into its servant and its scribe. Thus it is precisely the question *"what binds an object to Earth, to Mars, to Kansas?"* that would bring to light the bound and binding nature of human constitution in general, while disclosing the *pathos* of the earth as a commentary on the law, demonstrating, with Husserl, that the "manifold acquisitions of earlier active life are not dead sediments,"[29] but living institutes of a juridical intentionality that perpetuates its measures through the enduring commentary of everyday objects, through all the "innocent" instruments[30] of account that convert the things themselves into structures of fealty, structures of care, structures of political love.

12 A Postmodern Musicological Approach to the Authentic Performance Debate

KRISTIN A. SWITALA

Currently raging in musicology and the philosophy of music is the debate concerning the authentic performance of old music. Since 1870, when the playing of Baroque music reemerged as fashionable, thousands of books, articles, program and score notes, and performance treatises have been published, each attempting to present the correct way to play pieces from the Baroque period. Since 1970 alone, over 100 articles dealing with *one* aspect of this issue—namely, the proper interpretation and realization of ornaments known as "grace notes"—have appeared in musical journals.[1] In this chapter, we will be concerned with how musicologists and philosophers have been using seventeenth and eighteenth century musical treatises to claim that there were basic laws of Baroque performance and that, by returning to these treatises, we can definitively establish how Baroque pieces are to be authentically performed.

This process of examining original Baroque texts and the history of their interpretations and editions, however, problematizes theories of authentic performance. As I shall show in this chapter, the Baroque scores, treatises, and tables published from 1580 to 1730 are often unclear, contradictory, poorly edited, and together produce *no* unified theory of performance procedure. In other words, the authentic performance debate undercuts its validity by resting upon an unstable, nonunified foundation. In the first section of my chapter, I will examine many of these Baroque treatises and the current claims for and against authentic performance by Godlovich, Kivy, and Young. As we shall see, the problem emerging from this debate concerns an inadequate formulation of "the musical text." In the second part of my chapter, I will take up this issue and provide an alternative to the traditional model of the musical text. I will present a "field model," or one that seeks to delimit the fields, institutional codes, and power relations that constitute the musical text. By means of this new understanding of music, we shall see how the conditions for the possibility of the authentic performance debate emerged and why they must undercut their own validity.

Baroque Ornamentation:
The Authentic Performance Debate

The Baroque Texts

In his 1676 treatise on performance practice, Thomas Mace warned, "whatever your Grace be, you must, in your Fare-well express the True Note perfectly, or else your pretended Grace, will prove a disgrace."[2] How grace notes are performed can alter the entire sound of a piece, by shifting rhythm and accent and by adding or deleting certain tones. Grace notes [appoggiaturas, ports-de-voix] are small accents or frills added to the basic notes of a musical piece to decorate, enliven, or augment the sound. In twentieth century scores, grace notes appear as smaller notes

attached to regular-sized notes:    . In most seventeenth and many

eighteenth century scores, however, these little notes [petites, agrements] did not appear at all. The performer was expected to insert them in appropriate places. To assist the player in this task, many composers included tables of ornaments and explanatory texts at the beginning or the end of their compositions. These tables listed the composer's chosen figures and what each one symbolized. For example, J. S. Bach (1720) lists the following grace symbols alongside their names and indicates how they are to be played:[3]

Such tables can be found in the works of major performers, theorists, and composers such as Simpson (1659), Chambonnières (1670), Locke (1673), Mace (1676), Loulie (1696), Purcell (1696), and most composers of the early eighteenth century.[4]

Although the performer was expected to reveal both talent and good taste by improvising from the basic score, the number of composers who sought to *regulate* free ornamentation increased throughout the seventeenth century. By the time of the Classical period (late eighteenth century), most ornaments were written out in full. The tables of ornaments no longer appeared, and Baroque music dropped out of the concert repertoire. For 100 years (roughly from 1770 to 1870), no readily available treatises, or even brief commentaries, on how Baroque performers used to interpret Baroque scores were published. During the Romantic period, interest in Baroque music began to reemerge. Musicologists and performers were baffled by either the bare notes or the strange symbols that remained in the few editions of Baroque scores in which these symbols had not already been removed. Then in 1893 Dannreuther wrote the first part of his seminal musicological work, *Musical Ornamentation.*[5] After examining the earliest surviving editions of musical scores and treatises by forty-nine composers of the 1580–1730 period, Dannreuther provided translations of their instructions on the performance of ornaments and listed several of their tables of ornaments. Thus began the quest for original Baroque manuscripts and the ensuing debates over authentic sources and interpretations.[6]

The problems surrounding the authentic performance of old music are manifold. Primarily, musicologists do not possess the original manuscripts or first editions of most of the works examined. In a few cases, such as Mace (1676), d'Anglebert (1689), Couperin (1716–1717), and Bach (1720), readily accessible facsimiles of the first editions have been published.[7] These facsimilies are in fact photocopies of the original publications, printed on more durable paper. Some of these facsimiles, however, are of later editions. For example, the copy of *Les Pieces de Clavecin* by Chambonnières is of the 1760 edition, not of the 1670 edition. It is not known how many changes were made to the text during this ninety-year period. Establishing the reliability of various manuscript copies and later printed editions is crucial for the authentic performance debate, because there is much evidence that copyists and editors often mistranslated or applied the rules of their own period to the symbols and notations of a piece from a previous age.

Many examples of conflicting or confusing data exist. One of the most famous examples of editorial changes is the 1888 Brahms and Chrysander edition of Couperin's 1713 table of ornaments. In this case the realization, that is, the way of being performed, of a particular ornament was unchanged, but the symbol itself was replaced. Facsimiles of Couperin's prints show that he used the sign ᴫ for the *pincé;* Brahms and Chrysander substituted the more fashionable sign ⊥ of the nineteenth century.[8] Twentieth century musicologists search through scores of documents, attempting to determine which symbols are original ("legitimate") and which are later modifications ("illegitimate"). Thus, they would conclude that even though the *realization* of Couperin's *pincé* is the same in the 1713 and 1888 editions, the Brahms and Chrysander edition is inauthentic, because the *symbol* is not the same.

The problem plaguing the authentic performance issue, however, goes deeper than that of conflicting or varying versions. Attempts to define Baroque performance procedure in the definitive, authentic manner in which it was originally performed are doomed before they begin. Analyses of the surviving Baroque texts reveal that there was no single, uniform way to interpret ornaments. Not only does each composer provide his own table of ornaments, but these tables conflict with each other. For example, Simpson (1659), Muffat (1690), Loulié (1696), and Dieupart (1720) identify the ornament "back-fall" or *"coulé"* quite differently:[9]

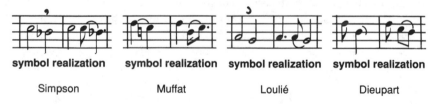

symbol realization	symbol realization	symbol realization	symbol realization
Simpson	Muffat	Loulié	Dieupart

The realization of the *port-de-voix* also varied from composer to composer, as evidenced by Hotteterre (1707), Couperin (1713), Dieupart (1720), and Rameau (1731).[10]

symbol realization	symbol realization	symbol realization	symbol realization
Hotteterre	Couperin	Dieupart	Rameau

One factor preventing the uniform systematization of ornament interpretation was the changing translations of terms between French, Italian, German, and English. For example, although Caccini's (1602)

"esclamazioni": 𝄞 is the early seventeenth century Baroque vocal

version of Diruta's (1583) Renaissance instrumental *"clamationi"* :

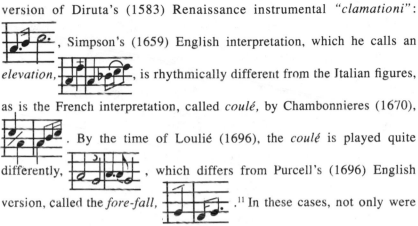

, Simpson's (1659) English interpretation, which he calls an

elevation, , is rhythmically different from the Italian figures,

as is the French interpretation, called *coulé,* by Chambonnieres (1670),

. By the time of Loulié (1696), the *coulé* is played quite

differently, , which differs from Purcell's (1696) English

version, called the *fore-fall,* .[11] In these cases, not only were

the translations of the symbol's names different, but their realizations were variable.[12]

Perhaps these disagreements did not bother the Baroque musician as much as they frustrate the contemporary performer of old music. Saint‑Lambert (1702) states, "if the choice of fingers in playing the harpsichord is arbitrary, the choice of *agrements* [ornaments] is no less so. Good taste is the only rule that must be followed."[13] It appears as if the musicians of the Baroque period played pieces as they deemed appropriate and in good taste, rather than frantically concerning themselves with the multitude of conflicting data on ornamentation, which brings us to the issue at stake.

The Authentic Performance Debate

The current debate over the authentic performance of Baroque music attempts to identify certain laws that are applicable to scores with ornaments written in as well as to scores without printed ornaments. Dolmetsch, one of the founders of the "purist" movement, declared that "none of the rules for the correct performance and interpretation of seventeenth and eighteenth century music laid down in this volume can be regarded as a matter of personal opinion, since all are supported by documentary evidence drawn from the writing of musicians of the period."[14] As more evidence from original manuscripts and first editions emerged, however, those who rejected the notion of a definitive way to perform Baroque music began to argue against the purists. In his discussion of the later twentieth century prolific publication of ornament tables, Anthony (1974) stated that "we have become over-zealous, perhaps even puritanical in our attempts to apply rules of ornamentation derived from these tables. . . . [O]ften one cannot help feeling a rigidity in [the] approach that converts a correct manner of application to *the* correct manner."[15] In other words, the conflicting material in the Baroque texts caused some musicologists and philosophers to question the legitimacy of "laws" of authentic performance.

By the late 1980s, the debate arising from this issue shifted to a more theoretical argument concerning the nature of the musical text. In his discussion of theories of authentic performance, Kivy (1988) provides seemingly insurmountable arguments against the possibility of realizing the composer's original intentions or of reconstructing the original sound of a piece of old music. Of the latter problem, he states, "Clearly, a performance will sound differently to different auditors: differently to an educated listener than to an uneducated one; differently to an Italian than to a German; and, most importantly, differently to *me* than to a contemporary of the music. For *I* can hear a piece of music as anticipating the harmonic techniques of Brahms or Wagner; and Bach could not."[16] Although people certainly will interpret what they hear in different ways, depending upon their particular cultural contexts, the purist would argue that the *sound itself,* if performed on original instruments and expressly following the textual markings, will be authentic. Godlovitch (1988) argues precisely this point against Kivy. He states that "the presence of scoring directions and other bits of hard evidence leave no doubt that the composers of early music had certain specific resources in mind."[17] An authentic performance of old music merely requires careful attention to the composer's intentions, as revealed through particular notations and directions, and a strict following of performance practices "typical of the period."[18] This way, the original sound of old music can be re-created, regardless of who hears it.

Godlovitch's purist's arguments may seem compelling to anyone not actively involved in historical-musicological research. Recall from our analysis of Baroque texts, however, that there exists a mass of conflicting data on the types of ornaments, their symbols, their realizations, and their translations into other languages and editions. Contra Godlovitch, there appears to be no "typical" way to play an ornament during the Baroque period. Also, when Godlovitch states that "respectful editors stand back and let the past speak now as it spoke then—at least as far as the score goes,"[19] a philosopher like Young (1988) can respond, "there is no more an innocent ear than there is an innocent eye."[20] Young argues that the seventeenth–eighteenth century sound of a Baroque piece could not be duplicated today, even if musicians were to use original instruments and were instructed on how to play. For example, even if we had information on how to produce air vibrations that exactly matched the air vibrations produced by Rameau or Couperin, Young explains that "not having the experiences and beliefs of earlier musicians, today's musicians cannot vibrate air precisely as early performers would."[21] In other words, the reconstruction of Baroque music can be approximate, but it cannot be an exact science because the musical text is not a static entity that remains unchanged or pure in essence over time. Any argument that maintains that fundamental rules exist for performing old music, or that a musical work has an essential purity or identity, fails to take into account multiple fluid aspects of the musical text. An alternative description of the musical text is necessary and is the focus of the next section.

The Musical Text: A Field Model

A critical problem with traditionalist or purist conceptions of the musical text results from their exclusionary tactics. These tactics seek to constrain a particular musical text to the score or to the score plus additional information about a period in music, such as treatises and instructional manuals. As we have seen, this is the project of Dolmetsch and of Godlovitch. Godlovitch asks, "shouldn't there be a sense of 'musical work' which is consistent with a work's retaining its full identity across differences in scoring, key, interpretive directives, and so on, and yet be more complex than, say the idea of 'sameness of theme'?"[22] The idea that a work retains its "full identity" is the problematic issue. This notion presumes that in some sense the musical text possesses a singular, unchanging identity. But what constitutes the musical text? The score provides symbols for the production of music, but it produces no musical sounds on its own. The performance produces musical sounds, but is based on the notation of the score. Either the score or the performance might be considered to be the musical text for any particular piece of music. There is also commentary to consider, for commentary both binds and serves as a mediator between performance and score. The musical text might even be the combination of all these things. The question facing us is whether *textual analysis* is appropriate, or even possible, for musical works of art. Through a description of the codes operating in the field of interactions between score, performance, and commentary, I will show how the conditions for the possibility of textual analysis of music and the issue of identity in music emerge.

Beginning with a basic model, Figure 12.1 illustrates the field in which score, performance, and commentary function. This complex diagram can be explained by examining each of the three main points of reference: the score, the performance, and the commentary. The score is composed of symbols that the performer translates into sounds; this results in the performance. The commentary is important for two reasons. First, every performance is accompanied by a commentary of some sort; this may be in the form of program notes, interviews, inserts or jacket

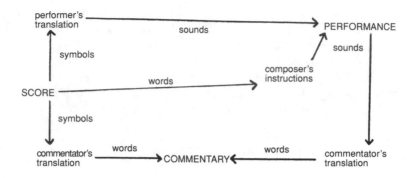

Figure 12.1

information, or narrative introduction. The commentator translates the performance's sounds into words. Second, commentary in the form of musicological analysis of the score translates the symbols of the score into words. This type of commentary can also exist on the printed score itself: the title. In placing a title onto a piece of music, the composer provides a fragment of commentary. Titles such as *L'Impatience* (Rameau), *The Tempest* (Purcell), or *St. Matthew's Passion* (J. S. Bach) translate the notes into words. They provide a context into which the symbols can be placed and understood. But this placement of symbols must be mediated through the performance for the musical effect of the title to occur. The player reads the words of the title, which provide a guide for how to play the piece.[23] The lovely melodies in one of Corelli's pieces take on new meaning for the performer when the title, *Pastorale,* accompanies the notes. The title suggests a certain style of breathing and smoothness of tonguing to the players. Similarly, Playford's title, *Packington's Pound,* suggests an approach quite different from a pastorale. In these cases, the title as commentary interacts with the notes as symbols of the score and with the performance to produce sounds laden with a particular meaning. Score, performance, and commentary operate together in this system to produce a musical piece.

Operating simultaneously in the previous grid, however, is the system shown in Figure 12.2. In this system, the directions of influence are reversed. The performer's translation of the score may have an impact on the score in two ways. First, the player may edit the piece, according to preferences or personal (instrumental) demands. For example, flutist Jean-Pierre Rampal edited J. S. Bach's collected flute sonatas, which are widely used by students and professionals today.[24] He altered certain notes and passages so that the piece would sound better on the modern (Boehm)

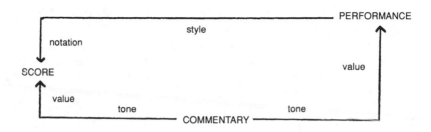

Figure 12.2

flute. Because Bach was familiar with recorders, rather than with flutes, the case could be made that Rampal's edition is better suited to the instrument. Composers themselves often edited their own works after hearing them played for the first time.[25]

The second way in which the score may be changed by the performer was discussed in the first section of this chapter. Performers of the Baroque period were expected to add ornaments to the bare scores. For example, the score for Telemann's *Sonata in F Major for F Recorder and Clavichord* contains very few ornaments:[26]

This line indicates the recorder part; it appears rather simple and bare. To a Baroque recorder player, however, that line might sound like this:

The trills, grace notes, and mordents do not appear in the score, yet the player might translate that bare notation into a florid, exciting performance. After the Baroque period, when instruments such as the recorder and clavichord were replaced by the flute and piano and Baroque music went out of style, players were not trained in the art of ornamentation; consequently, these flourishes disappeared from performances, as previously discussed.

During the twentieth century the upsurge of interest in Baroque music has produced an entire range of second-order commentaries, those that comment on seventeenth and eighteenth century commentaries, as well as numerous critical analyses and reviews of attempts to interpret

Baroque music. Whenever a particular commentary or critique gains definitive status, the scores and performances of a work are altered to fit this dominating view. When new commentaries from the Baroque period are found, the scores and performances will again be translated, based upon the new information.[27] New twentieth century commentaries that gain acceptance and dominant status also produce pressure to update critical editions of texts. The tone of these commentaries, whether favorable to or critical of certain playing methods and notation, will directly affect the value of a particular edition of a piece and of particular performances. Once the value is changed for the worse, for example, depreciating an edition based on new information concerning symbols for depicting grace notes, the score will be changed and players will perform the piece differently.[28] This process is continuous in the field; it simultaneously intersects with the translation of symbols to sounds, sounds to words, and symbols to words, as described in the first field.

Intertwined with or enmeshed within these two translation systems, a third system operates in the field of the musical text, see Figure 12.3. The meanings and value structures of the second system fold back upon themselves in the third system. In other words, the direction of influence is reversed. New editions of scores increase or decrease the value of certain commentaries, as do new performances. The performances themselves might be reappraised and given new values by new editions of scores, and the newly edited scores would be reevaluated based upon the sounds produced in the performances. If a score is edited to be "closer to the original intentions of the composer," and the performance approximates the "original sound," and the sounds are *terrible,* then commentaries will tend to intervene and depreciate the score or the performance.[29] From these three systems the instability of the score, performance, and commentary becomes apparent. The relational systems, the systems of translation operating in this field, constantly reverse the directions of

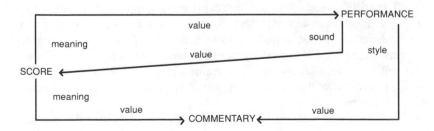

Figure 12.3

value and authenticity and constantly uproot the static authority of any particular score, performance, or commentary.

Because the interrelations between score, performance, and commentary, along with the functions of translation operating within the systems in the field, do not provide a stable text to examine, let us turn our attention to the signs of the score itself to describe how and what it communicates. As seen in the first system, the signs of the score are the symbols of written musical language. In their production and appearance, they translate the music in the composer's or editor's mind into notations. These notes and other markings communicate specific tones, harmonic structures, and phraseology to the performer or commentator who can read music. For those who cannot read music, these symbols indicate nothing other than the fact that, as a whole, they form a piece of music. The musician, musicologist, or historian can determine from the particular configurations the piece's general form (concerto, symphony, tone poem), its ensemble form (quartet, trio, solo), and often the period of its composition. All of these items are communicated by the symbols of the score to the musicologist; they are communicated without the necessity of hearing a performance. They do, however, rely upon the intervention of a history of commentary known by the musicologist, a history that

provides these symbols with contextual meaning. For example,

communicates nothing to either the performer or the reader without the accompanying (and usually previous) knowledge of a commentary that explains the symbol as indicative of a concert B^b. Because humans interpret most things via language, it is necessary to translate symbols such as these into words for the score to communicate anything to the student who is just learning how to read music or how to play an instrument.[30]

Although the musicologist or performer may get a general sense of the piece from the score alone, exactly how the work *sounds,* what affects it produces and what level of intensity or beauty it reaches, cannot be known merely from the notations on the page. Composers work out their pieces at the piano, for example, to hear what the music sounds like.[31] Taken as a self-contained, pure entity, untouched by the imposition of words or sounds, the essential score, as the musical text, conveys no music. By neglecting performance and commentary, and by privileging the original score as the ultimate legitimating factor for a piece of music, traditionalist and purist interpretations *displace* the musical text. The text they support, the essential structure of the notation on the page, is neither anything musical, nor anything that can be discussed using words. This means that, in purist terms, we cannot talk about the musical essence of a work.

Yet certain musicologists and philosophers make claims about the essential nature of the score. They search for original manuscripts containing tables of ornaments, as well as for first editions of scores, that can be used as evidence to support a particular edition or ornament table as the legitimate ("true") edition or ornament table. These items, as legitimate, are supposed to reveal the essence of the piece.[32] Purists claim that they show, via the piece's foundation, the composer's original notation, what in the piece really is real and unchangeable over time.

To understand how this view emerged, and how it maintains itself, several interstices of power, several institutional codes, must be uncovered as they slice through the multiple fields of the musical text. These are shown in Figure 12.4. The ability of performers will directly affect not only what is performed in concerts, but also how composers write their pieces. For example, Baroque composers did not use accidentals (the insertion of sharps and flats not in the key signature) in Baroque recorder music to the extent that composers of modern flute music do. This is partially because the modern flute has special keys that allow for easier fingering of accidentals in rapid passages. Recorders do not have keys and the finger combinations for passages with many accidentals are quite difficult. Only the best recorder players can perform such passages smoothly.

The quality of performers intersects with economic limitations. When money is not available, budding musicians cannot afford to pay for instructional lessons. Similarly, professional musicians must limit their practice time, so that they may work at other jobs to supplement their incomes. Economic restrictions exist for performers today, just as they did in the Baroque period. Because of increasingly restricted budgets, the pieces selected for concert schedules today are in part determined by the organization's economic situation. "Safe" pieces, such as Vivaldi's *Four Seasons* or Beethoven's *Fifth Symphony,* are often chosen over new American compositions, although this trend has shifted during the past five years (1988–1992).[33] Economic limitations influence not only what is performed, but also what is composed. When new American works were

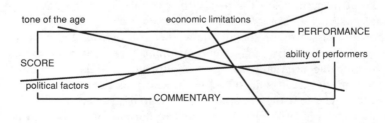

Figure 12.4

shunned by symphonic organizations, the number of American composers who could make a living at writing new music dwindled. Audience acceptance also directly affects this factor. During periods when chromatic dissonance was heard as grating and unpleasantly irritating, audiences responded by not attending performances. This resulted in the loss of income for symphonic organizations; hence certain compositions were eliminated from concert repertoires.

Political factors also influence what is composed and how composers and musicians work. One of the most famous examples of this occured during Stalin's reign in the Soviet Union. Artistic works had to support the government's directives and express the themes of a hard-working, struggling, but victorious, people. This affected the types of works produced and performed in that country.

Political factors can also reflect the general tone of an age, that is, what is viewed as important during a particular period in history. For instance, in the field of literature there is currently a movement to return to the original manuscripts of certain works to determine whether the author to whom they are attributed actually wrote them and, if so, what the author's original intentions were. In the case of Shakespeare, for example, results from such inquiries will determine the status of many of "his" works. Certain plays, or editions of plays, will be regarded as illegitimate and therefore will be excluded from the Shakespearean repertoire. The contemporary debate over the authentic performance of Baroque ornaments is similar. It emerges out of a twentieth century concern with the instability of interpretations and seeks to ground things in an essential stability. This essential stability is designed to provide an unchanging identity as the basis of the work, regardless of the forces acting upon the work before, during, or after its composition. The essence of the work is to remain the same. The problem with this view is that it fails to recognize itself as a twentieth century concern, as a view that has a particular context and mode of operation in a particular temporality and spatiality. Instead, it claims universal status and, against its own evidence, claims that Baroque music was governed by rules that musicians learned and consistently applied.

Conclusion

The musical text is far more complex and multilayered than the purist's conception of the static original score can take into account. The profusion of movements between score, performance, and commentary, as they are intersected at various levels by political and economic forces, produce constantly shifting structures that constitute the field of a Baroque text. Moreover, this fluid state of the Baroque text is viewed by purists (ironically) as an essential aspect of its authenticity.[34] The elements and lines of power pulse through this system, never remaining static or constant, except in the fleeting moments when they are constricted by institutional forces, such as in the exclusion of certain scores. In the case of Baroque ornamentation, the purist's ideology overturns itself by claiming universality while having been established on an unstable, inconsistent ground that was contextually produced. The conditions for the possibility of the authentic performance debate have been produced by the tone of our age and by many other intersecting forces in the field of the musical text.

13 The Ethics of Reminiscence: Reading Autobiography

KATE MEHURON

The most truly autobiographical moments occur not in expressions of triumphant separation but in descriptions of the way the book itself attempts to resist its own writing.

Barbara Johnson, *A World of Difference*

Consider the autobiography that has been read to be the affairs of someone's heart gone public. This chapter offers a reading of Christa Wolf's *Patterns of Childhood*[1] that will attend to some philosophical implications of the heart's exposure to public scrutiny. I view this particular autobiography as exemplary with respect to a certain tension that Barbara Johnson has articulated. In "My Monster/My Self," Johnson writes, "*Frankenstein* can be read as the story of autobiography, as the attempt to neutralize the monstrosity of autobiography. Simultaneously a revelation and a cover-up, autobiography would appear to constitute itself as in some way a repression of autobiography."[2] I read Wolf's autobiography as exemplifying this tension between narratively *indicating* the unspeakably felt monstrosity of the self and the specific repressive effects of *narrating* or *exhibiting* the self to the other.

This chapter shows the "heart" of Wolf's text as allusive toward primary scenes of monstration: original scenes dramatizing the de-formation or defectiveness of the self. The allusive figures in Wolf's reminiscence indicate a retinue of shame's defenses. Shame, allusively exhibited yet repressed by figurative device, is elided in a manner illustrative of Lyotard's concept of the *differend:* the unspeakable affect that has not, or cannot, find its idiom within the specific hegemony of genres ruling the narrative.[3] I do not cease to wonder: Is shame *ever* dissociable from the monstration of sexual difference?

Perhaps the unspeakable drama of violation indicated by shame is excluded by genres of phenomenological description or political resistance—for the terrorism of the heart violences a subjective landscape of "not being able to be." In my reading of *Patterns of Childhood,* I develop an understanding of this type of violation, a violation in which the *topos* of the heart is the desolate closure of the "not yet." Such violation inscribes that one has always been defective; the *is not,* or is, only *as* annihilated. One's subsequent monstrosities (defenses) neutralize, yet proclaim, that unspeakable knowledge; they re-monstrate over and over.

This autobiography reminisces scenes between women, especially between mother and daughter: each mirroring the other in a nondialectical engendering of self. Jane Gallop evokes the temporal and nondialectical character of this *mimesis* in her reading of Lacan's theory of the mirror stage. She writes,

> "My history," subjective history, the history of a subject, is a succession of future perfects, pasts of a future, moments twice removed from "present reality" by the combined action of an anticipation and a retroaction. . . . Since the entire past and present is dependent upon an already anticipated maturity—that is, a projected ideal one—any "natural maturation" (however closely it might resemble the anticipated ideal one) must be defended against, for it threatens to expose the fact that the self is an illusion done with mirrors.[4]

In Wolf's recounting, the *mimesis* between mothers and daughters occurs on the register of language. Idiomatic utterances undergo systematic prohibitions of affect by familial norms of expression, as well as by the coercive enunciative practices enforced by the Third Reich. *Patterns of Childhood* suggests that certain violations of the self's potentialities are bequeathed between generations of women. Wolf depicts the ethical impasse of a woman's destiny; her fate is charted by her inheritance of a "succession of future perfects" from her mother, yet the impasse is inseparable from totalitarian ideology. In my reading of Wolf's autobiography, I show how this ethical concern is central to her memory-work. I urge readers, however, to imagine the disruption of this ethical impasse by women's collective practices of mourning: re-monstrance (suffering, elided by hegemonies of familial and totalitarian discourses) converted to remembrance (ideological critique and self-creation) by the patient work of empathetic witnessing.[5]

A Problem of Reading

Again, consider the autobiography that has been read to be the affairs of someone's heart gone public. Having gone public, the essence of autobiography can be spoken only equivocally. The "we" who read the autobiography are the witnesses who provide an arena for its appearance; the autobiography's realm of phenomenality is made determinate by "our" imaginative investments. An autobiography's reading is thus a public event in which the other bears witness to an other, but the event of reading also exceeds political coding. In the *polis*, bearing witness to someone's word or deed is appropriately accompanied by political judgment; tribunals are in order. But the public space is not simply the political. If the autobiography is given only a political reading, the danger lies in the creation of a tribunal gathered to adjudicate affairs of the heart.

If the activity of bearing witness to the other is fundamental to any experience of solidarity, then the autobiography's role in creating solidarity is problematic. For example, Hannah Arendt, in "The Social Question," warns against the danger of political solidarities founded upon public confession.[6] Such solidarity tends to be self-defeating to the degree that it cultivates a profound suspicion toward the inward motives, intentions, and *pathos* of its members. One can never be inwardly pure enough and, more significantly, one can never completely mediate the intimacy of the heart in one's efforts to exhibit transparently its *topos* to another. In light of Arendt's critique, feminist readers must think anew about women's confessional writing as a constitutive activity in the self-definition of women's oppositional communities.

Rita Felski notes an additional self-defeating dialectic implied in this public aspect of women's autobiographical writing practices.[7] On the one hand, feminist identity politics has partially relied upon the value of literary intimacy or the shared process of self-discovery through the exploration of inner feelings suppressed by patriarchal, gender-oppressive prescriptions of women's duty and self-sacrifice. On the other hand, the effort to satisfy the yearning for intimacy, authenticity, and immediacy to the other through the literary vehicle of autobiography is frequently undermined by the vehicle itself. The self's indeterminacy, lack, and *complicities* with gender-oppressive symbolic codes is rendered poignant by the fictive adventures of the pen in its embellishments of one's pasts and passions. The validation inherent in being read by others collapses all too frequently into tribunals of self-castigation.

Hence, a benevolent context of reception cannot be guaranteed, nor can solidarity be definitively established on the basis of the shared *pathos* of the partially disclosed hearts of a feminist community of readers. Rather, one's literary disclosures constantly risk repudiation or phallic cooptation; yet I propose that this risk is clearly worthwhile given the ethical possibilities proferred by writing's mute appeal. I will elucidate these possibilities in the latter sections of this chapter. Presently, let us think, for a moment, the equivocality of the *we:* the *we* of manners can indict the autobiography with indiscretion; the *we* of the regime can outlaw the autobiography as subversive; the *we* of the scholarly community can judge the autobiography to indulge in anecdotal trivia;[8] the *we* of "our" solidarity find the autobiography to be unfaithful to the cause. Another reception, the philosophical *we* in Lyotard's sense, gives a reading that "denies itself the possibility of settling, on the basis of its own rules, the *differends* it examines." Lyotard promotes a version of philosophical thinking that seeks the limits of the rules of genres under scrutiny and usage. Philosophical thinking heeds the *differend* unheard between genres of discourse. It commends the anecdote to a public space differing from the one legislated by the social world of manners, the political realm of governmentally enforced tribunals and oppositional solidarity groups, or the romanticist project of autocharacterization. Such a reading is a "waste of time."[9] "We" philosophical readers constitute a public space that uses time differently than the calculative, economic space that uses time either constructively or not, wastes time or gains time, succeeds or fails.

Reading autobiographical prose temporizes in ways that, if described, lend themselves to Derrida's articulation of the impossible recuperation of the past in the present: the "deferred effect" of the trace, which cannot lend itself to a phenomenology of consciousness or presence.[10] The wasted time of autobiographical reminiscence is occasioned by the nonlinear, vertiginous effect of our efforts to heed the person idiomatically portrayed. In this regard, Phillip Lejeune writes,

> The first person, then, always conceals a hidden third person, and in this sense every autobiography is by definition indirect. . . . It is as if in autobiography, no combination of the personal pronouns could "fully express" the person in a satisfactory manner. Or rather, to put it less naively, all imaginable combinations reveal, with differing degrees of clarity, the nature of the person—the tensions between impossible unity and intolerable division and the fundamental schism which turns the speaker into a fugitive.[11]

If we assume the untimely and unmanageable temporizing of autobiographical reminiscence, then readers are faced with the interminable task of listening to the text's personal idiomatics. Readers may encounter the vertigo of an infinite summons gestured by the person herself, the fugitive of the text. Nothing guarantees the possibility of such an ethical moment, a moment in reading that chooses to attend to the remains of the other.[12] To listen: an inefficient, errant practice of pacing to and fro, waiting, the meticulous affirmation of fragments that always presage the incomplete. The vertiginous horizon of this type of listening is doubled in autobiographical production: the writer also engages in the interminable task of reading the hieroglyphics of her self.[13] One temptation, in the face of such vertigo, is to "do justice" to the text: to adjust its "complex agony."[14] Rather than doing justice to Wolf's autobiography, I will attempt to heed the "complex agony" implicated in heeding the fugitive, outlawed by the judicative impulse of autobiographical genres to hold the self accountable.

The Maternal Function

"Women have always lied to each other."
"Women have always whispered the truth to each other."
Both of these axioms are true.
"Women have always been divided against each other."
"Women have always been in secret collusion."
Both of these axioms are true.
                    Adrienne Rich, *On Lies, Secrets, and Silence*

In addition to her insight that autobiography represses itself *as* monstrosity, my reflections will assume, with Barbara Johnson, that the authorial function in literary production always coincides with the metaphorics of literary maternity. The maternal function, in this sense, is a metaphorical structure common to the writerly stance of both male and female authors.[15] What differs in each case is the gendered appropriation of literary maternity, revealed in the performative dimension of the text.[16] Autobiography doubly displays the metaphorical impetus of literary maternity, dramatizing both the author's gendered appropriation of literary maternity in general and the author's maternal style toward one's literary self as the child *of* one's self. To highlight the maternal function in Wolf's autobiography, I refer to this text's structures of address and figurative invocations.

Patterns of Childhood stumbles at the outset in its structures of address. Initially, Wolf narrates that she cannot find her voice. The problem is resolved as she decides that the writer of this text will be addressed in the second person, *you,* and the child sought in remembrance shall be addressed in the third person, *Nelly.* This is a "usable beginning" (PC 22), in which she claims to have found the person who will remember, the one "who has learned to see [her]self not as 'I' but as 'you'" (PC 118). Jolted by a vivid dream into this recognition of the person who will remember as she writes, Wolf is freed to acknowledge that this person will be an "intruding stranger" pursuing the child's innermost secret; the encounter will involve the unenviable "feeling of embarrassment in front of a child" (PC 119). Paul de Man, in "Autobiography as De-Facement," comments on the problem of narrative voice and asserts that autobiographical address depends upon "the fiction of an apostrophe to an absent, deceased, or voiceless entity, which posits the possibility of the latter's reply and confers upon it the power of speech."[17] The indirect structures of address in *Patterns of Childhood* perform the incessant displacement of any direct reply of one person to another in the course of this remembrance. The indirection enacts the stillbirth of each, for no one is summoned into animation by the address of the other. Each speaks, but retains an embarrassed silence in the face of the other.

Rather than commencing by a dialogical interplay between textual voices, remembrance is initiated by place-memory. The author takes her husband, her daughter Lenka, and her brother Lutz on a journey to Germany, Nelly's childhood habitation during the Third Reich. Visitation excites reminiscence, which exceeds the recollective imagination.[18] A life-world of the past is resuscitated in the present by the embodied return, and the world of childhood evoked by corporeal visitation begins to stir ominously: "the feeling that overcomes any living being when the earth starts moving underfoot is fear" (PC 24). Past dwellings reminisced by visitation manifest as sites of de-formation. Wolf muses that to write a "model" childhood is to write a showpiece, etymologically related to the "showing" of a monstrosity. She is interested in "the hordes of half-men, half-beasts within" (PC 36). The author brings her witnesses; Lenka is the only one whose gaze is remarked throughout the text and whose subjectivity is conjectured. The others speak for themselves; Lenka speaks for herself, is watched, and her secret thoughts and feelings about Nelly are surreptitiously guessed by her mother. There are few direct questions between the two. Wolf writes to herself, "You've learned that Lenka never answers a direct question unless she wants to, and you're secretly hoping that you'll find out about Lenka by way of Nelly" (PC 20).

Therefore the scene of writing and reminiscence is also the lived scene of embarrassed, indirect self-exposure between mother and daughter. The tension operative in the mother-daughter dyad at the site of deformation can be viewed as a specific *mimetic* tension, well-described by Irigaray's version of the feminine imaginary as it is rehearsed within phallocentrism. Also to the second person, Irigaray writes, "You look at yourself in the mirror. And already you see your own mother there. And soon your daughter, a mother. Between the two, what are you? What space is yours alone? In what frame must you contain yourself? And how to let your face show through, beyond all the masks?"[19] Irigaray, in this passage and in *Speculum of the Other Woman,*[20] performs a *mimesis* in prose that intends to ironize, hence exceed, the dyadic fusion between mother and daughter, the latter signifying the failure of one to heed and bear witness to the other.[21] Such a failure is portrayed as the stasis obtaining between those who can find identity only through playing the mother to the other within masculinist Symbolic codes that systematically prescribe the nature of the "feminine" as that which is excessive. The mother-daughter dyad is the site of a reciprocal imaginary identification with one another's devalued status that forecloses empathetic witnessing. Within this phallic Symbolic framework, to renounce the maternal function and its implication of static fusion with a "feminine" other is to face a "mourning with no remembrance. Invested with an emptiness that evokes no memories."[22]

Irigaray shows us that the specularity imposed by phallocentrism's subsumption of feminine difference to the same of "Lack" decrees that recognition between women inevitably entails specular reversals valenced by contempt, or at least by indifference. "You move toward a future which is lacking."[23] Her mimetic style of writing performs an irreverent ludic play with the maternal function that promises to wrest free of the phallic constraints associated with every single woman's *mimesis* of maternity (SO 77). The register of ludic play is inclusive of diverse writing practices such as satire, aphorism, dialogical address, hyperbole, and so on. The implicit promise offered by such fictive irreverence is the possibility of temporizing the self differently by performatively enacting an ideological critique through writing. This is the difference wedged between the "succession of future perfects" bequeathed by phallic maternity and the enunciative distance from one's "feminine" self achieved by ironizing the Symbolic codes within which that self is formed.

Hence the ethical ambiguity involved in women's efforts to bear witness empathetically to one another is illuminated by Irigaray's exploration of the specular dangers associated with moments of recognition between women. I suggest that the possibility of an ethical relation between women is proffered *specifically* with the effort to bear witness to one another. This effort implies a philosophical attentiveness to the remains of the other or to the *differend,* the truant affect that signifies wrong incurred. The ethical ambiguity involved in recognition is the possible violation of one another's futurity suffered through the judicative impulse to *represent* the other, hence to fixate the other's identity (or lack thereof) for the enhancement of one's own. *Patterns of Childhood* dramatizes a relentless pursuit of the question posed by Irigaray's *mimesis:* to what extent can the literary maternity rehearsed in the memory-work between mother and daughter, between women, wrest free of phallocentrism's icy decrees that we are "no one" to each other? "With your milk, Mother, I swallowed ice."[24] In Irigaray's theater of "feminine" affect, the extremities of complete consumption between women and the desolations of phallic mirroring of the "nothingness" of one to the other both repress and replicate originary violations of the self in her capacity to be and to be esteemed.

> Each becomes the other in consumption, the nothing of the other in consummation. Each will not in fact have known the identity of the other, has thus lost self-identity except for a hint of an imprint that each keeps in order the better to intertwine in a union already, finally, at hand. Thus I am to you as you are to me, mine is yours and yours mine, I know you as you know me, you take pleasure with me as I take pleasure in the rejoicing of this reciprocal living—and identifying— together. (SO 196)

Christa Wolf's impulse to "do justice" to her childhood and to hold herself accountable is also the impulse to distinguish retroactively mother from daughter and the woman in each from her phallic and ideological identity.[25]

Shame and the Collapse of Ethical Possibility

Wolf notes that her sense of accountability is assuaged through the purgative task of honestly remembering and admitting Nelly's character and felt subjectivity. Thus Wolf writes that memory is "a repeated moral act," which, although riven by fantasy, stores reality "intricately coded" (PC 143). But to the extent that one admits that the act of memory is premised on a hieroglyphics of the self, one must react with utmost suspicion to the *writing* of the remembered self: "you realized that you had to fear memory, this system of treachery; that by seemingly exposing it, you'd actually have to fight it" (PC 152). Wolf's project of autobiographical accountability strives to meld the second and third persons into the first, achieving "a candid, unreserved 'I'" (PC 349). The project unleashes an authorial tribunal of the heart: "Nelly is nothing but the product of your hypocrisy. It stands to reason that anyone who attempts to change a person into an object in order to use that person for a confrontation with the self has to be hypocritical if he later complains that he can no longer expose himself to this object; that it's become more and more incomprehensible to him" (PC 211). Within this tribunal, Nelly is twice pitied: first, as a dupe in the self's hypocritical drama of deceiving itself concerning its motives to write and, second, as the child whose inviolate subjectivity is probed by the prying pen and ruthless drive toward exposure on the part of the authorial adult.

In addition to the authorial prosecutor, another figure of justice predominates in Wolf's reminiscence. The author is on a first-name basis with her own mother. The latter appears regularly as "Charlotte" and twice as "Cassandra." In Christa Wolf's novel *Cassandra*,[26] Cassandra is depicted as the mythic protagonist empathetically witnessing to her own and her countrywomen's received violations within a masculinized Symbolic order. Cassandra "sees," but is not heeded by that regime; her fidelity to the task of finding an idiom for the "dreadful torment" of her own dissenting *pathos* invites the specters of punishment, humiliation, and loneliness: "then my resolution was formed, smelted, tempered, forged and cast like a spear. I will continue a witness even if there is no longer one single human being left to demand my testimony" (C 22). The mythic Cassandra transgressively perceives the institutional conspiracy of Troy, bent on concealing its civic fragility from itself. In *Patterns of Childhood*, Charlotte splits into Cassandra as she witnesses her daughter's addiction to Nazi rhetoric:

> An authentic declaration by Dr. Goebbels, with reference to the so-called Anschluss, the incorporation of Austria into the German Reich: 'At last the Teutonic Empire of the German Nation has come into being.' Nelly had sat by the loudspeaker listening to the delirium of joy bursting forth in a city named Vienna, a jubilation that could no longer be distinguished from a howl, which rose as though a force of nature were exploding, but which moved Nelly's inner depths in a way no force of nature had ever moved her before. . . Charlotte Jordan, who wasn't able to take proper care of her children because of the damned store, promised to smash the radio to bits; the girl was going off her rocker. (PC 164)

Charlotte is notified of her husband's conscription and transmutes from the mother to the woman: a figure of dissent, of transgressive vision.

> Cassandra behind the counter in her store; Cassandra aligning loaves of bread; Cassandra weighing potatoes, looking up every once in a while, with an expression in her eyes which her husband prefers not to see. Everything we do is an accident. An accident, this husband of hers. These two children about whom she has to worry so much. This house, and the poplar in front of it, completely alien. (PC 165)

I suggest that we read the splitting of Charlotte into Cassandra as a metaphorical gesture that figuratively ambiguates the scene of women "doing justice" to one another, and, further, that ambiguates the issue of one woman "doing justice" to her self. The Charlotte-Cassandra figurative axis can be read to signify two differing registers of accountability. The first, Charlotte as the maternal figure of Nelly's childhood, indicates Nelly's early sense of accountability as justice, the weighing and measuring of right and wrong, good and bad. The second, Charlotte *alias* Cassandra, signifies the woman's resistance to familial structures of terror as well as to the Third Reich's civic spaces of terrorism. "Charlotte to the mailman: 'The hell with your Führer.' . . . In other words, Nelly's mother was deserting the Führer. Her father must go to war" (PC 168).

Charlotte's "justice" consists in executing a familial reign of terror. Here I use "terror" in the sense developed by Arendt, extending it to cover familial coercive practices. Totalitarian terror destroys the space between individuals, removing the boundaries required by positive law and the liberties that ensure plurality. Terror bereaves individuals of "the source of freedom which is given with the fact of the birth of man and resides in his capacity to make a new beginning."[27] Nelly's mother enforces the unity of affect and the annihilation of Nelly's inwardness, terrorizing the author's childhood self. Wolf writes,

> Perhaps what mattered was to enlarge her own secret realm. Because, unknown to herself, this child's straight, truthful mind—to me, you're as transparent as a pane of glass, Charlotte used to say to her daughter—had designed secret hiding places to which she could retreat alone. Other people's prying is at the root of secretiveness, which can develop into a need, finally into a habit, and produce dangerous vices and great poetry. (PC 57)

Charlotte is "the secret reader of her daughter's diary" (PC 226), as well as the one who mediates the family's demand for absolute "happiness." I emphasize that she *mediates*, because the requirement of univocal affect is simultaneously exacted by authorities from beyond the familial borders.

Subsequent to Nelly's seventh year and to her hearing the words "concentration camp" for the first time, her father, Bruno Jordan, has "happily" donned the cap of the National Socialist Navy storm troops.

> [T]he overflowing happiness of the parents—overflowing onto Nelly— must have been composed of the following elements: relief (the unavoidable step has been taken without having had to be taken on one's own); a clear conscience (the membership in this comparatively harmless organization—the Navy storm troops—could not have been refused

without consequences. What consequences? That's too precise a question); the bliss of conformity (it isn't everybody's thing to be an outsider), and when Bruno Jordan had to choose between a vague discomfort in the stomach and the multi-thousand-voice roar coming over the radio, he opted, as a social being, for the thousands and against himself. (PC 42–43)

"Happiness," the prized affect of the Jordan family, is enforced through the compression and crowding out of affective discordance. Nelly is submitted to coercive language practices on both sides of the border between family and regime. "Words like 'sad' or 'lonely' have no place in the vocabulary of a happy family; as a result the child begins early to assume the difficult task of sparing his parents. To spare them misfortune and shame" (PC 23). Nelly's schoolteachers contribute to "happiness"; "glitter words" that bespeak nonhappy inward states are reprimanded, and interrogative, declarative, and exclamatory sentences are studiously avoided (PC 58, 39). In Lyotard's terms, a wrong is constituted by the elision of the *possibility* of utterance, inflicted by the hegemony of genres. As such, it is a damage accompanied by the impossibility of proving the damage.[28] The wrong inflicted on Nelly is shown in the telling, but not asserted:

> The child refuses to talk. Let's hope that whoever gets hold of her will not exploit her helplessness, as so easily happens. . . . Your heart is pounding. You realize to what extent your century has revived the old invention of torture, in order to make human beings talk. You're going to talk. Every sentence, almost every sentence in this language has a ghastly undertone which the heart, that simple hollow muscle, signals obstinately. (PC 48)

Whether civicly or familially, it is through mechanisms of humiliation that the interruptive and fertile chaos of discordant affect and insight is compressed and homogenized. *Patterns of Childhood* exhibits a full range of de-formative techniques of shame brought to bear on Nelly. The autobiography shows how the institutionalized terror of Third Reich pedagogy constitutes a civic space in which these techniques are visited upon the self's insightful capacities.

Such capacities are premised upon a discordant *pathos* that, if heeded, can yield what Cassandra terms the *vital smiling force:* a way of taking account of the other and one's self that exceeds disjunctive and universalizing valuational thinking (C 106). Martha Nussbaum's "perceptive equilibrium" captures, in ethical language, Cassandra's metaphor.[29] This is the notion of practical judgment informed by feeling in which universal prescriptive formulations are viewed as insufficient to cope with the complexity of particular situations. Nussbaum elaborates perceptive equilibrium to be a sort of situational attunement in which "bewilderment and hesitation may actually be marks of fine attention."[30] The evoked stance includes the "willingness to be incomplete, to be surprised by the new . . . to surrender invulnerability, to take up a posture of agency that is porous and susceptible of influence."[31]

We should not underestimate the degree to which marks of "fine attention" can be destroyed, or appropriated, by intersubjective and introjective shame mechanisms. Feminist thinker Christina Thürmer-Rohr elaborates the cooptation of women's ethical perceptivity in "Love and Lies: 'My Beloved Children'."[32] Thürmer-Rohr provides a provocative reflection about the formative effect of her Nazi father's letters upon her own childhood capacity for affective truth telling. She both confirms Wolf's re-creation of the discursive practices of lying that erode women's capacities for bearing witness and emphasizes the way in which fine-tuned perceptions become *complicitous* within the discursive regime of National Socialism with its ideology of the ideal "feminine" role within the family. Wolf's autobiography shows that terror's favored rhetorical tool in the Third Reich is the systematic coding and humiliation of the "feminine." The latter is the product of ideological reification into gendered assignments of the (masculine)active–(feminine)passive dichotomy. The inferiorization of "feminine" passive-receptivity follows.[33] Herr Warsinski, the teacher that Nelly loves, or wishes to please, "notices everything" and scrutinizes which of the girls wash their chests in ice-cold water "to steel themselves, as befits a German girl" (PC 100). Nelly fails to steel herself and cannot muster the strength to keep her arm raised in salute to Hitler's adage "My will is your faith" (PC 99). Herr Warsinski says that a German girl must be able to hate Jews and Communists and other enemies of the people. Nelly's defect lies in that her hatred of Jews and Communists "isn't quite as spontaneous as it should be—a defect that must be concealed" (PC 128).

The rich anecdotal texture of Wolf's autobiography exhibits civic and familial scenes that reify sexual difference and systematically humiliate those to whom an inferiorized femininity is attributed. Such gender-oppressive rituals, inclusive of coercive language practices, perform mythopoetic gestures that re-present the self as originally defective. From Nietzsche we gain an understanding of the valuative dimension of mythopoetic gesture, which is always, even in its most reactive sense, an artistry of the self. The dynamic of shame becomes, in this text, an instilled modality of bearing false witness to the self: an artistry of affective *lying* to oneself and to others. The inculcation of this modality may have its

basis in the phantasmic dimension and may thus be reliant upon an ultimately *failed* dialectic of the self and other that ceaselessly requires repetition to sustain its illusion. Wolf's achievement resides in simultaneously
showing the ontological fragility of these traits and the long-lasting,
intergenerational severity of their effects in the civic and familial realms.
She writes,

> *Verfallen*—a German word.
> A look into foreign-language dictionaries: nowhere else these four, five
> different meanings. German youth is addicted—*verfallen*—to its
> Führer. The bill drawn on the future is forfeited—*verfallen*. Their roofs
> are dilapidated—*verfallen*. But you must have known that she's a
> wreck—*verfallen*.
> No other language knows *verfallen* in the sense of "irretrievably
> lost, because enslaved by one's own, deep-down consent " (PC 288)

Wolf shows that the ritualized inculcation of shame temporizes the closure of the self's porosity to the other and to its own affirmation, terrorizing the self to bereavement of its "not yet." The presentation of the
defectiveness of one's self to the self translates into the future perfect: "I
have always already been monstrous." *Patterns of Childhood* shows the
intertwining of this modality with the monstration of sexual difference.

I suggest that "feminine" shame is the peculiar addiction to
phallocentric recognition, which has always already inferiorized receptivity as "feminine." Certain ethical possibilities borne by this inferiorized
quality are also subsequently foreclosed: perceptive equilibrium, or the
fine-tuned perceptive capacity to heed the other, and the capacity for a
"no-saying" judgment that can sharply separate the self from complicity
in deceptive familial and civic discursive practices. Nelly's "feminine"
shame functions as a mask that distorts her capacity to heed her own
inward dissent from institutionalized equations of accomplishment and
invulnerability. Her female mentor, Julia Strauch, who favors words like
devotion, leads an exemplary life, immersed in Nordic heroic legends.[34]
Julia is Nelly's first love, and the author recalls, "Nelly's first experience
of love was that of captivity" (PC 220). Under Julia's tutelage, Nelly
learns with horror of the "Wells of life," where SS men couple with
idealistic German women to produce racially pure children. Nelly apprehends, nearly simultaneously, that Julia hates being a woman and that
she herself, in her discordance with this ideal, can continue to win
Julia's esteem only by a web of deceit: "looks, gestures, words, lines that
lay within a hair's breadth of her true emotions, without fully blending
with them" (PC 225). Lenka, Wolf's daughter, is taken to peruse Nelly's

tenth-grade biology books, removeable only by special authorization at
the House of the Teacher pedagogical center. Paging the contents that
depict inferior races—Semites, Middle Easterners—the daughter is wordless, hands the book to her mother, and expresses no desire to see it
again. Wolf muses to herself, "You had the feeling that she was looking
at you with different eyes that day" (PC 8).

The Jordan family members are inter- and intragenerationally embarrassed by one another. Charlotte initiates Nelly into her recurring dream
of her failure to please her grandfather. Her "blame consists in her refusal
to publicly sing with her grandfather's drunken, tone-deaf display" (PC
51). Charlotte tells Nelly about the incident of the kowtow in her childhood. This incident features Charlotte's father, who is close to losing his
job on the railroad due to drunkenness. The children are scrubbed clean
for Railroad Inspector Witthühn's visit. The image of a trustworthy family is to be conveyed, hence the children, upon a signal from their mother,
are to sink to their knees before the inspector. Nelly's inward embarrassment is expressed: "The daughter wants to believe that her mother has
never forgiven her father for this episode. But she'd rather not talk with
her about it. She feels that it is improper to relive the shame of the child
who would later become her mother" (PC 85). Last, I note Charlotte's
embarrassment, from the beginning of their marriage, at Bruno's defective alcoholism. In one memorable scene, Charlotte bars him from her
bed, cutting him short with a single word: *derelict*. Later, while he is still
a prisoner of war in the Soviet Union, she calls their union a "good
marriage" and, while showing family photos, insists "We always got along
well with one another" (PC 123).

Writing and Empathy

Inter- as well as intragenerational embarrassment and public sham-
ing rituals bespeak a *differend* outlawed by familial and national codes of
masculinized propriety. This, coupled with the hyperbolic maternal requirement of self-exposure coded as "honesty," conspire to conceal a
woman's prior, unspoken apprehension. This apprehension is Cassandra's
transgressive insight: the futility and fragility of proprieties deemed "masculine" by the Symbolic system of National Socialism. National Socialist
ideology punishes fragility and susceptibility to the other by the institutionalized politics of contempt, yet rewards "feminine" vulnerability to,
and identification with, male others within the politics of the family.
Charlotte *alias* Cassandra, in order to acknowledge her prophetic insight
into the bankrupt Symbolic system of National Socialism and into her

husband as falling short of the masculinized Symbolic ideal, must "see" through her own complicitous web of self-deception that is maintained by introjective shame mechanisms.

It is not a coincidence that Charlotte becomes Cassandra *as* she apprehends her daughter's love of, or captivity to, phallic recognition. Nelly's leadership position in the Hitler Youth is re-membered as follows:

> "Ambition," "self-importance"—those are tried and true catchwords with a ring of sincerity and it isn't being claimed that they do not apply, at least in part. But that's just it: only in part. And it's the remainder, not covered by ambition or self-importance, that is interesting. . . . The third catchword might be: "compensation." . . . Nelly was involved in a compensation deal, and it could almost be assumed that she knew it, because she was crying as she defiantly railroaded her mother into giving her permission. Recognition, and comparative security from fear and from overwhelming guilt feelings are guaranteed, and she in turn contributes submission and the strict performance of duty. (PC 194)

Readers witness Charlotte's (*alias* Cassandra) fearful exclamation: "To think that it means that much to you!" (PC 195). In such passages, Wolf's memory-work employs fictive strategies to revise the icy mandates of the past toward the future: to divide the woman from the mother, to heed the remains of the child.

Likewise, fictive strategies are used by Irigaray to engage the past in the present, thus to temporize the future differently. Although the literary gestures of Wolf and Irigaray are vastly different, I suggest that both reveal the potential for a kind of resolute witnessing that can be enacted by the authorial pen and corresponding readerly acts, "tempered, forged and cast like a spear" (C 22). Irigaray parodies, thus differs from, the ultimate "feminine" addiction to phallic recognition that stands as an obstacle to an empathetic witnessing of the self's re-birth. She writes,

> How could "God" reveal himself in all his magnificence and waste his substance on/in so weak and vile a creature as woman? She has so often been humiliated, and every particle in her being seems but decay and infection. *Waste, refuse, matter.* Thus she will abase herself over and again in order to experience this love that claimed to be hers, and pass again through those imaginings that forbid her to respond. She takes on the most slavish tasks, affects the most shameful and degrading behavior so as to force the disdain that is felt toward her, that she feels toward herself. (SO 199)

This parody exhibits the ultimate abjection implied by the duplicitous *pathos* of shame. Irigaray's styles show, through indirection, how women's complicitousness with the phallic myth of "feminine" defectiveness is both performed by "us," yet remains a secret to "ourselves." Her parody conveys how "feminine" shame turns away from transgressive moments of insight and indulges the farce of gender-oppressive Symbolic codes; how shame preserves the abjection of the self in its addiction to the other's recognition.[35]

Arguably, such parodic indirection too easily complies with the hegemony of masculinized discursive codes that manipulate women's efforts to bear witness to memories of gendered and sexual monstration, rendering "us" fugitives to "our" selves and to each other. In this view, women are better served by projects such as the "political phenomenology of the emotions" called for and undertaken by feminist philosopher Sandra Bartky.[36] Similarly, Thürmer-Rohr's efforts to testify, by memory-work, to the specific imbrication of women's sexual and political complicity under patriarchal regimes eschews the dangers of the indirect voice. In this view, indirection can be only an obstacle to the work of testimony. I believe, however, that testimony involves a complex dynamic of listening to the repressed subtext of outlawed affect, no-saying to "feminine" phantasmic identifications, and resolute rejection of the self's temporal closure fashioned by enslavement to the future perfect tense offered by patriarchal ideologies. To assent to this dichotomy—the indirect voice *or* the prosaic political critique of the emotions and memory—is to ignore the very problematic of witnessing itself. This problematic is eloquently stated by Shoshana Felman in the context of her discussion of Paul de Man's complicities with National Socialism in "After the Apocalypse." She writes, "given this fatal political mistake, given such a radical failure of vision, such a lapse of consciousness experienced early in one's life, how can one *wake up?* What would waking up mean? . . . How not to compromise the action and henceforth the process, the endeavor, of awakening?"[37] To rule out the empathetic potential of parody and other indirect writing styles would presume that those who have suffered the traumas of ideological regimes can somehow "wake up" to a transparent cognitive, affective, and ethical relationship with one's past in the present. Thus would the metaphorics of light and clarity supersede the use of fictive strategies to sketch the contours of what remains mute. I suggest that the work of empathetic witnessing, whether performed in readerly and writerly acts or in conversations involving memory-work, requires a radical distrust of the obvious and a commitment to discursive strategies that can performatively reveal the myriad ways in which the self has been formed by, and continues to be subject to, the heteronomy of ideology.[38]

I therefore affirm the risks of women's diverse writing practices as implicitly interruptive of the fate of the self. Jane Gallop captures writing's disruptive effect:

> Somehow the avoidance of tragedy depends upon a retroactive effect reversing the internal impetus that lunges forward, a retroactive acceptance of one's foundations (whether concepts or self) as fiction. Such an acceptance might mean an openness to revision, rather than a rigid defense against the recognition of fictionality.[39]

Wolf's autobiographical account embodies this sort of retroactive acceptance and risks that the ethical task of resolute writing may reproduce yet another defective child. Casting one's spear into the past may only consolidate the fictions animating shame into the literal case: justice wielding decideability. Or, it may perform Cassandra's fidelity to a secret that "encircles and holds" her together. She muses, "There is something of everyone in me, so I have belonged completely to no one, and I have even understood their hatred for me" (C 4). Wolf's efforts to recuperate "stranded affect" from the specular vertigo of phallic recognition invites "we" readers to witness the labor of mourning wherein the judicative view of alterity as "something which demands a solution" is abandoned.[40] What sort of maternal style, what solidarities, are implicated by those who gather to listen to the unspoken within the elaborate coding of the violated self? Perhaps that other style of recognition is figured by Arisbe's friendly visit to the mythic Cassandra who remembers,

> Apparently she believed it was up to me to free myself from madness. I heaped filthy abuse on her for that. She gripped the hand with which I was trying to strike her and said sternly: "Enough self-pity." I was silent at once. People did not talk to me that way.
>
>   "Come to the surface, Cassandra," she said. "Open your inner eye. Look at yourself." (C 61)

Part IV

Ethics

14 Heidegger on Ethics and Justice

FRED DALLMAYR

Ethics has come into vogue again. After the long interlude of positivism or empiricism, attention has shifted again—at least in academic circles—to questions of moral rules and right conduct; while, under the spell of the fact-value split, the latter had been regarded simply as matters of emotive preference, normative considerations today have reemerged as legitimate topics of philosophical (and not merely psychological) inquiry. Although welcome as a reaction to positivism, philosophy's return to ethics, however, has not been a homecoming free of conflict. As it happens, the return has rekindled deep quandaries or dilemmas that had lain buried or submerged during the reign of positivism.

Even a cursory glance at contemporary ethics shows a battleground of competing if not incompatible doctrines, most of which draw sustenance from (strands in) traditional metaphysics. Thus, according to a prominent doctrine, ethics basically coincides with the formulation of universal rules or principles, rules that are either grounded in reason as such or else are derivable from argumentation in a universal discourse. Beholden in some manner to Kantian thought, this view clearly revives problems endemic to rationalist ethics: first, how abstractly (or noumenally) conceived rules can be relevant at all to concrete human practice, and second, how rules can be transferred to specific instances without engendering an infinite regress of rules for the application of rules. In response to these dilemmas, another approach, sometimes styled "virtue ethics," stresses character formation in concrete historical contexts or traditions, thus centerstaging moral conduct. Yet, in the absence of a full restoration of (Aristotelian or Thomistic) metaphysics, the legitimacy of such contexts or traditions remains opaque. To bypass this restorative need, recourse is occasionally taken to "nature" and "natural inclinations" as a basis for a substantive (nonprocedural) ethics; but how can nature still be invoked in the face of its disenchantment by modern science? In an age of technology and scientific biology, how can we still do what "comes naturally?"[1]

Ethical doctrines thus abound and continue to proliferate—but so do their intrinsic problems or perplexities. In large measure, contemporary ethics resembles a confusing Babel of tongues, a fact lending support to ethical skepticism (which is another doctrine or approach). In the following, I propose to turn for some guidance to Martin Heidegger's opus. This proposal, at first blush, is likely to seem odd or counterproductive. As is well known, Heidegger has never written a book or treatise devoted specifically, under these headings, to questions of "ethics," "justice," or the like. On the contrary, his work is widely reputed to be rich in ontological speculation, but entirely barren or unhelpful regarding moral conduct or social equity (this barrenness being perhaps the result of his speculative bent).

In part, this assessment seemed to be endorsed or legitimated by Heidegger himself, particularly in his *Letter on Humanism* where ethics, or the demand to formulate an ethical theory, was specifically subordinated to the "question of being." The situation is further complicated or aggravated, perhaps beyond remedy, by Heidegger's pro-Nazi sympathies at the beginning of the Hitler regime, a topic that dominates much of contemporary literature. According to some observers, these sympathies were not temporary or passing in character, but formed an integral staple of Heidegger's mental framework or world-view for the rest of his life; although only incipiently present in his early writings, this ingredient emerged into full bloom in 1933 and subsequent years, irrespective of the so-called *Kehre* (or turning) in his thought.[2] In view of the monstrous immorality and injustice of the Nazi regime, however, a monstrosity epitomized by Auschwitz, how can anything ethically instructive or salutary be expected from Heidegger's pen? Given his embroilment with the Nazi regime, must his work not be regarded as a seedbed of disease, rather than as a resource for ethical recovery or renovation?

Admittedly, this background overcasts my proposed undertaking, but it does not completely foil or deter it. Being mindful of warnings and danger signals may actually induce greater attentiveness to textual nuances, thus preventing summary verdicts. For my own part, I have for some time been wary of summary pronouncements, particularly the reduction of thought to ideological slogans.[3] In Heidegger's case, this wariness has been steadily deepened by the ongoing publication of his works, especially his lecture courses and treatises dating from the Nazi period (as part of the *Gesamtausgabe*). As it seems to me, these publications throw an entirely new and revealing light on the *Kehre* in his thought, which, in turn, provides new cues or guideposts for the reading of both his earlier and his later texts. Most important for my undertaking, these writings show a growing alertness to ethical questions—where ethics denotes not simply private morality but the broader arena of social equity (a field traditionally thematized under the label of *justice*). Again, as previously indicated, the concern here is not with a full-fledged or formalized ethical theory—which is nowhere offered or attempted—but rather with clues or suggestions for a transformative and nondomineering way of human life (including its social and political dimensions).

The following pages pursue these clues, or suggestive markers, by concentrating on writings conceived during the phase of the *Kehre* (the Nazi period) and its immediate aftermath. The first section takes its departure from the magnum opus of that era, the *Beiträge zur Philosophie,* and next turns to a Schelling lecture offered roughly at the same time. As will be shown, both texts adumbrate a vision of equity—articulated under the heading of "ontological joining or juncture" *[Seinsfuge]*—that then serves as a yardstick for the distinction between good and evil. The second section proceeds to an essay of the early postwar period, the so-called "Anaximander Fragment," in which the notion of ontological joining is explicitly linked with the issues of justice and injustice, of right (or righteous) and aberrant modes of life. In a concluding section, I compare Heidegger's outlook with trends in contemporary ethical theory, and particularly with recent poststructuralist initiatives, and assess its broader significance for social and political life.

I

Contrary to his speculative reputation, and to his own occasional disclaimers, Heidegger's entire opus is suffused—from beginning to end—with ethical preoccupations. Standing firmly opposed to scientific objectivism, his thought necessarily was led to undercut the positivist fact-value dichotomy and its attendant neglect of human conduct. Thanks to the publication of his early Freiburg and Marburg lectures, we now are familiar with his Aristotelian leanings at the time, particularly with his retrieval of prudential judgment (or practical-contextual *"phronesis"*) as an antidote to abstractly scientific theory constructions.[4] Although important as a gateway to later formulations, however, the long-term relevance of these leanings is rendered dubious or problematic by the programmatic "destruction" of Western metaphysics announced in *Being and Time*—a program that was bound to affect the metaphysical underpinnings of Aristotelian ethics.

In *Being and Time* itself, ethical considerations are manifest (or can be inferred) in notions like "resoluteness," "authenticity," and the "call of conscience," to say nothing of the role of "care" and "solicitude" seen as key emblems of human *Dasein*. Notions of this kind are frequently given a narrowly "humanist" or subjective-individualist reading—a construal that shortchanges the work's ontological thrust, epitomized in *Dasein's* openness to "being." Still, even when subjectivism is avoided, it is difficult to deny a certain existentialist flavor pervading *Being and Time,* a flavor tending to privilege individual decision or authenticity (and perhaps private morality) over concerns with social and ontological equity.[5] In this respect, the Nazi experience—including Heidegger's individual involvement with the regime—seemed to induce a rude awakening whose repercussions reverberated throughout all dimensions of Heidegger's lifework. Without delving into biographical detail, the experience (I believe) furnished one of the motive forces triggering his much-discussed *Kehre*— which provisionally may be defined as a transformative move occurring simultaneously on the philosophical and practical-social levels.

My ambition here is not to offer a comprehensive account of the *Kehre*—an exceedingly complex task that perhaps is still beyond reach (given the state of the *Gesamtausgabe*). For present purposes, I shall limit myself to a few selected works that illustrate the general direction of the transformation. No work is more suitable to this endeavor than *Beiträge zur Philosophie [Contributions to Philosophy],* a study comparable in weight to *Being and Time* and functioning as the crucial link or juncture in Heidegger's entire opus (connecting earlier and later phases). Written during the heyday of Nazi might and self-confidence (1936–38), *Beiträge* is remarkably free of the ideological zeal marking its context. In fact, the entire study is a call away from dominant metaphysical or ideological formulas—and an invitation to a new and different beginning *[anderer Anfang]* for which its pages seek to prepare a tentative ground.

In sharp contrast with prevailing nationalist exuberance, the book persistently stresses a stark and sobering fact; namely, the "abandonment of and by being" *[Seinsverlassenheit]* characterizing contemporary life, an abandonment nurtured in turn by a long-standing "oblivion of being" *[Seinsvergessenheit]*. The basic mood or tuning pervading the study is a subdued sobriety befitting the situation of ontological abandonment or withdrawal; preserving its subtle nuances, this mood is circumscribed variously by such terms as *awe [Erschrecken], reserve [Verhaltenheit], reticence [Scheu], premonition [Ahnung],* and *renunciation [Verzicht]*—although reserve is said to be the midpoint joining these terms together. As one should note, however, sobriety in the face of being's withdrawal does not simply signal despair or a leap into nihilism; on the contrary, far from betraying negativism, being reserved means to recognize or honor "being" precisely in its mode of refusal *[Verweigerung]* and thus the intimate intertwining of being and non-being. According to *Beiträge,* this recognition is the exit route from traditional metaphysics (and its ideological offshoots) and the gateway to the "other beginning"—a gateway eluding human fabrication or control.[6]

It is precisely in exploring this shift or transit that *Beiträge* first introduces the notion of an ontological juncture or joining *[Seinsfuge]*. Basically, the broad move from metaphysics to postmetaphysics, from the "first" to the "other" beginning, is presented as a process of joining or rejoining or, in musical terms, as a "fugue" *[Fuge]* with interlacing parts and voices. According to the study, four major parts or "joints" constitute the *Seinsfuge* as it is experienced in our age; namely, first, the "sounding" *[Anklang]* revealing being in its mode of absence; second, the "play" *[Zuspiel]* alerting to the tension between different beings; third, the "leap" *[Sprung]* signaling the exit from metaphysics; and fourth, the "grounding" *[Gründung]*, meaning *Dasein's* insertion into the happening of being and non-being. The last step, in Heidegger's portrayal, is chiefly the work of "impending" or "future-oriented" individuals *[die Zukünftigen]* whose thought is open to the distant echoes of a "last god."

As one should note and as Heidegger repeatedly emphasizes, *Seinsfuge* must not be confused with a totalizing "system" or framework, that is, with a structure encompassing a set of positive-empirical elements or subsystems. What prevents such totalization is the present-absent status of being, implicit in being's withdrawal—which entails that "grounding" is also an "un-grounding" and the "leap" also a leap into non-being or the "abyss" *[Abgrund]*. In terms of *Beiträge,* being as displayed in *Seinsfuge* is not an entity or essence, but rather a source of *agon* or contest; namely, the contest between presence and absence, revealment and concealment—or else the interplay of "world" and "earth." Regarding the ethical or ethical-political implications of *Seinsfuge,* *Beiträge* tends to be parsimonious—except for some comments on power, violence, and authority. As a happening of being, we are told, *Seinsfuge* opens up a realm of "freedom" marked or buttressed by "authority" *[Herrschaft]*, in the sense of an enabling potency. Sustained by such potency, this realm has no need of power and "violence" *[Gewalt]*—which, by contrast, are definitely required for the maintenance or alteration of empirical conditions under the aegis of human domination.[7]

In discussing *Seinsfuge* and its difference from "system," Heidegger explicitly alerts the reader to other writings of the same period in which the notion is more fully elaborated: particularly to the lecture course of

1936 entitled "Schelling: On the Essence of Human Freedom." Dealing with Schelling's conception of human freedom in all its dimensions, the lecture course examines a number of topics not directly relevant at this point, including the distinction between ontological freedom and the metaphysical doctrine of "free will" and the relation between pantheism and "fatalism," or unfreedom. For present purposes, the chief importance of the course resides in its endeavor to correlate *Seinsfuge* with the question of good and evil.

Following Schelling's transcendental-idealist vocabulary, Heidegger portrays *Seinsfuge* as the intertwining of "ground" *[Grund]* and "existence" *[Existenz]*—where *ground* signifies the dark embryonic latency of God or being, whereas *existence* denotes God's fully developed and "spiritualized" manifestation in creation. Schelling himself designates the juncture as "difference" *[Unterscheidung]*, a term that clearly anticipates and resonates with Heidegger's own notion of "ontological difference," referring to the nexus of being and beings. Departing from a stable ontology of substances and also from Aristotle's view of a "prime mover," Schelling in his treatise on freedom (of 1809) sought to grasp the dynamic differentiation in God and hence the temporal quality of the divine. In Heidegger's words, "Schelling wants to accomplish precisely this: namely, to conceive God's self-development, that is, how God—not as an abstract concept but as living life—unfolds toward Himself. A *becoming* God then? Indeed. If God is the most real of all beings, then He must undergo the greatest and most difficult becoming; and this development must exhibit the farthest tension between its 'where-from' and its 'where-to'." The where-to is captured by the term *existence* construed as the stage of revealment or self-manifestation of the divine, whereas *ground* points to the stage of latent concealment and obscurity: "Seen as existence, God is the *absolute* God or simply God Himself. Viewed as the ground of His existence, God is not yet actually Himself. And yet: God 'is' also His ground." Differently put, ground is that in God which is "not God Himself but the ground for His self-being."[8]

In Schelling's account, ground and existence are not simply identical, nor are they fully divorced; rather, their juncture exhibits a unity in and through difference, that is, a togetherness in and through contest. Most important, ground and existence are not component parts of a "system" or entities that jointly would constitute "the thing called God." *Ground* means the latency or not-yet-being of God and thus harbors in itself a "not" or "non-being"—which resists integration into a synthesis, without coinciding with pure negativity. "One forgets to consider," Heidegger observes, "whether the 'not' or 'not-yet-existence' of the ground is not precisely the feature which renders existence positively possible, that is, whether the not-yet is not that element where-from self-manifestation or self-transcendence proceeds. One forgets that what becomes is already grounded in and as the ground." Thus, divine becoming does not signify a mere departure from or annihilation of the ground, but on the contrary: "Existence lets the ground be as its ground." This letting-be or juncture also affects the temporal character of becoming—which does not involve a simple succession of stages measured by ordinary clock time. Ground and existence are not separated as past and future, but are interlocking temporalities joined together in a differentiated simultaneity. The notion of simultaneity, Heidegger comments, does not mean that past and future vanish and melt into a "pure presence," but rather that they maintain themselves as past and future and "coequally join with the present in the full richness of time itself." Becoming thus does not yield stagnation or the submergence of distinct temporal modes in a "gigantically enlarged Now"; instead, it occurs as the unique juncture of "the inexhaustible plenitude of temporality." It is in terms of the unity of this differentiated dynamic, the lecture course adds, that one has to conceive "the correlation of ground and existence."[9]

The differentiated linkage of ground and existence is also the ultimate source of the distinction between good and evil—the latter seen as a crucial emblem of human freedom. According to Schelling, divine becoming aims at progressive spiritualization, that is, at the revealment or self-manifestation of God as spirit. This revealment, however, requires an otherness or a foil in which spirit can fully manifest itself. As Heidegger comments, "There must be something other which is not God Himself but which harbors the possibility for divine manifestation. Thus there must be something which originates in God's innermost core and shares His quality as spirit and which yet remains separate or distinct from God. This other being is man (or humankind)." For Schelling, man as creature is rooted in nature and thus in the "ground" or latency of divine becoming; at the same time, however, he or she is the receptacle of divine revealment or the locus where God's "existence" becomes most fully manifest. Because God as spirit is also the epitome of freedom, divine self-manifestation can occur only in a receptacle or conduit sharing God's qualities, that is, in an otherness constituted as free being. "This means, however," Heidegger says, "that the conditions of possibility for the manifestation of the existing God are simultaneously the conditions of the possibility of good and evil, that is, of the kind of freedom in which and as which human *Dasein* exists." The notion of evil at this point does not signal a deficiency or pure negativity, but rather an outgrowth or corollary of spirit, that is, of human freedom in its partnership or reciprocity with divine freedom. More important, good and evil are not simply matters of human choice or decision, but instead occupy an ontological status by being anchored in existence as the manifestation of spirit and, still more specifically, in spirit's manifestation against the backdrop of nature's "ground." In this sense good and evil refer back to ontological juncture or *Seinsfuge:* "The demonstration of the possibility of evil hence must take its departure from the *Seinsfuge* as source of this possibility."[10]

In God or divine becoming, as stated before, ground and existence are correlated in a differentiated unity or tensional harmony—with the accent on harmony. In the case of human freedom, a similar correlation prevails, but with a different accent. If the correlation or juncture were precisely the same in God and in humankind, the two could not be distinguished—thus yielding either a simple anthropomorphism or pantheism and foiling the goal of divine manifestation (in otherness). In Schelling's own words, "If in man the identity of the two principles (ground and existence) were just as inseparable as it is in God, no distinction could emerge, which means: God as spirit could not become manifest. Thus, that same unity which in God is indivisible must in man be divisible— and this division is the possibility of good and evil." In Schelling's account, as paraphrased by Heidegger, ground and existence are "free" or freely variable against each other and not yoked together in an indissoluble teleology. In human *Dasein,* spirit's manifestation can reach fulfillment—to the point of intellectual conceit; at the same time, however, *Dasein* can seclude itself in the opacity of its peculiar ground or nature— to the point of denying the clarifying or illuminating drive of spirit. Thus, *Dasein* embraces both dimensions seen as polar extremes: "the deepest abyss and the highest heaven." To the extent that seclusion in the ground means *Dasein's* enclosure in its peculiarity or selfishness, and to the extent that spirit intimates unity or harmony, the polar tension pervading *Dasein* can be viewed as permitting the rebellion of self-centeredness against the openness of letting-be, or of self-will against universal will. As Heidegger comments, "Since human self-will is still linked to spirit (as freedom), this will can in the breadth of human endeavor attempt to put itself in the place of the universal will; thus, self-will can . . . as particular-separate selfishness pretend to be the ground of the whole. . . . This ability is the capacity for evil."[11]

The insurgence or arrogance of self-will does not mean the cancellation of *Seinsfuge,* but only its distortion or perversion into disjointedness. In asserting its supremacy, self-will does not deny the unifying thrust of spirit; rather it arrogates this unity or wholeness to itself. In this manner, the correlation of ground and existence gives way to onesided usurpation. In Heidegger's words, "In elevating itself above universal will, self-will precisely wants to be the latter. Thus, this elevation yields a distinct mode of unification . . . but a unity which is a perversion of the original constellation, that is, a perversion of the wholeness of the divine world where the universal harmonizes with the will of the ground." Following Schelling, the lecture course speaks in this context (in lieu of divine becoming) of "the becoming of a reverse or inverted God, of an anti-spirit" and hence of a rebellion against "primal being." Again, reversal or perversion should not be seen as simple deficiency or negativity, but rather as an assertive negation—more precisely, as a negation that usurps and swallows up the place of affirmation. *Seinsfuge* as such, one may recall, is not merely an ontic-empirical but an ontological juncture, that is, a juncture of being and non-being—but one in which being and non-being are conjoined by letting each other "be." By contrast, in the reversal of *Seinsfuge*—which is a synonym for evil—non-being (or the negation of wholeness) appropriates the entire juncture, thus substituting itself for being. Negation, Heidegger notes, is here "not simply the rejection of something existing," but it is "a No-saying which usurps the place of the Yes." With this usurpation, dissonance holds sway in lieu of tensional consonance, rupture and denial in lieu of sympathy. In Heidegger's vocabulary, what happens is "the reversal of *Seinsfuge* into disjuncture or disjointedness *[Ungefüge]* where ground aggrandizes itself to absorb the place of existence."[12]

As an outgrowth of *Seinsfuge* and its disjuncture, good and evil are not simply human preferences or options among other preferences; instead, the capacity for both is constitutive of the being of *Dasein*, reflecting its insertion in some form or other in *Seinsfuge*. "Humans alone," the lecture course states, "are capable of evil; but this capability is not a human property or quality. Rather, to be capable in this sense constitutes the being of humans." More precisely stated, *Dasein* as such is neither good nor evil, but capable of both. On the level of sheer capability or possibility, *Dasein* hence is an "undecided being," hovering precariously in "indecision" *[Unentschiedenheit]*. Yet, as a really living being, *Dasein* has to exit from indecision and empty possibility and enter the contest or struggle between good and evil. Entering the latter contest means to confront the arena of "decision" *[Entscheidung]*, which, however, is not an arena of arbitrary choice and hence not a warrant for pure "decisionism." In Schelling's account, the transition from capability to living reality is governed neither by arbitrary whim nor external compulsion, but by an ontological bent or disposition *[Hang]* that inclines human conduct in one way or another. Without such a bent or inclination, Heidegger comments, decision would be sheer contingency occurring in a vacuum, but never human "self-determination" in freedom, a self-determination proceeding from an inner need or necessity of *Dasein* (thematized as "resoluteness" in *Being and Time*). In the case of evil, Schelling traces the ontological bent to a "contraction of the ground"

[Anziehen des Grundes], that is, to a self-enclosure of particularity that
terminates indecision, but in such a manner as to provoke divisiveness
and disjuncture. On the other hand, goodness follows the attraction of
spirit or existence, which in the most genuine form is the attraction of
eros or love *[Liebe].* "Love," we read, "is the original union of elements
of which each might exist separately and yet does not so exist and cannot
really be without the other." Love, however, is not simply unity or identity, but rather a unity in difference or a unity that lets otherness be—
including the contraction of the ground and the resulting disjuncture:
"Love must condone the (independent or contrary) will of the ground,
because otherwise love would annihilate itself. Only by letting this independence operate, love has that foil or counterpoint in or against which it
can manifest its supremacy."[13]

Although separated by decision or "decidedness" *[Entschiedenheit],*
good and evil are not merely polar opposites or reciprocal negations—
just as *Seinsfuge* and disjuncture do not simply cancel each other but
remain linked in and through their reversal. As Heidegger emphasizes,
following Schelling, *Dasein* involves a capability and decidedness not so
much for good *or* evil as rather for good *and* evil—which is the heart of
human freedom. *Evil* in this sense means that manifestation of both good
and evil, just as *goodness* implies the appearance of both. This view
stands in stark contrast to a moralistic or value-oriented outlook according to which *good* is what "ought" and *evil* what "ought not" to be. In
terms of the lecture course, the *and* linking good and evil does not have a
moralistic tenor "as if the alternatives were an ought and an ought-not";
rather, "manifesting itself in living reality, evil in human life is simultaneously a display of goodness and vice versa." From the vantage point of
Seinsfuge, evil is not simply a reversal or negativity, but rather a present
absence or absent presence—in the sense that self-will preserves the trace
of ontological wholeness even in its negation and perversion. By the
same token, goodness evokes as its counterpoint and condition of disclosure the rebellious presence of evil. Contrary to moralistic construals, the
notion of juncture reveals that "good and evil could not conflict if they
were not already constituted as opponents, and that they could not *be*
opponents if they did not reciprocally condition each other and thus were
not ultimately related in their being." All this does not mean that good
and evil are equivalent or the same—which would deny precisely their
difference. Evil remains evil in the sense of a perversion of goodness,
and goodness finds itself confirmed in the counterforce of evil. Far from
supporting indecision or undecidability, *Seinsfuge,* in the end, attests to
the superior bent or attraction of goodness. In a phrase that summarizes
Schelling's conception, but is not alien to Heidegger's thought, "The will
of love takes precedence over the will of the ground, and this precedence

and eternal decidedness—that is, the love of being for being—this decidedness is the innermost core of absolute freedom."[14]

II

Although commenting faithfully and in detail on Schelling's treatise,
Heidegger did not necessarily endorse his idealist metaphysics, particularly his teleology of nature and spirit and its connection with subjectivity. Given the latter teleology, ground and existence were at least
potentially dichotomous—notwithstanding their asserted juncture or correlation. Heidegger's lecture course refers repeatedly to the shortcomings
of Schelling's metaphysics. These defects, he notes, emerged most clearly
in the later work where the elements of *Seinsfuge*—ground and existence—became "not only less and less compatible, but were polarized to
such an extent that Schelling relapsed into the rigid tradition of Western
metaphysics, without achieving a creative transformation." Equally problematic was the anchoring of ground and existence, non-being and being,
in a realm of absoluteness, more specifically a domain of "absolute indifference"—a conception bypassing the finitude and event-character of being
(what Heidegger came to call *Ereignis*).[15]

Not surprisingly, Heidegger during the same time turned increasingly from German idealism and metaphysics to the dawn of Western
philosophy in the pre-Socratic period in an effort to retrieve a
premetaphysical mode of thought that could serve as guidepost to an
"other" beginning (or postmetaphysics). In the decade following the
Schelling study, several lecture courses and essays were devoted to pre-
Socratic thinkers, particularly to Parmenides, Heraclitus, and Anaximander,
and to their conceptions of oneness, *logos* (construed as language), and
truth *[aletheia]*. In the present context I want to turn to an essay of the
immediate postwar period, "The Anaximander Fragment," where the notion of *Seinsfuge* is taken up and developed with specific reference to the
issue of social (and cosmic) justice or equity.

The essay deals with a saying ascribed to Anaximander that
Heidegger terms "the oldest saying of Western (or Occidental) thought."
In its customary and literal translation the saying, or fragment, states:
"Whence things have their origin, there they must also pass away according to necessity; for they must pay penalty and be judged for their injustice, according to the ordinance of time." Read in this manner, the
statement is cryptic and elusive. Moreover, there is a traditional
preunderstanding of pre-Socratic thought that additionally hampers access. Dating back to the early Peripatetic school, this preunderstanding
forms an integral fixture of Western metaphysics and still reverberates in

Hegel's history of philosophy. According to this view, the pre-Socratics were basically nature-philosophers, where *nature* is contrasted with culture, politics, and the like; given this focus, their speculations about nature were later corrected and vastly refined by Aristotelianism and ensuing advances in physical science. From the vantage of science and historical teleology, the pre-Socratics thus are condemned to the status of precursors and hence to obsolescence; for later, more "highly developed" modes of knowledge, their relevance becomes increasingly dubious outside of the range of antiquarian interest.

Heidegger's essay radically challenges and inverts these premises. Historicism or historical antiquarianism, he asserts, means "the systematic destruction of the future and of our historical relation to the advent of destiny or mission *[Geschick]*." Far from relegating them to fossils of the past, the essay presents pre-Socratic sayings as anticipations of a distant and impending future. "The antiquity marking the saying of Anaximander," we read, "belongs to the dawn of the beginnings of the Occident or evening-land *[Abendland]*. But what if the dawn outdistanced everything late; if the very earliest far surpassed the very latest?" In that case, the history of the West or evening-land might involve an evening heralding another dawn. In the same sense, we, as the latecomers or late-born of an advanced civilization, might simultaneously be the heralds of another beginning. "Are we the latecomers that we are?" Heidegger asks, "But are we at the same time also the precursors of the dawn of an altogether different age, which has left behind our present historicist conceptions of history?"[16]

Given metaphysical prejudgments, the translation of Anaximander's phrase cannot proceed directly or literally, but must venture a leap, a "leap across a gulf (or abyss)"—which is not just a gulf of two-and-a-half thousand years but the distance separating us from premetaphysical thought. The first thing to be noticed in this venture is the mingling or intertwining of domains carefully segregated in later philosophy. Although presumably focused on natural phenomena, the phrase speaks of justice and injustice, of penalty, retribution, and judgment; thus, moral and juridical notions get apparently "mixed in" with the view of nature. As Heidegger observes, the fragment does not actually speak of "things," but rather of "beings" *[ta onta]* in their multiplicity. Beings, however, do not only comprise "things" in the sense of objects, and especially not only things of nature: "Human beings too, the utensils produced by them, and the situations and circumstances effected through human action or omission—they all belong among beings; and so do demonic and divine 'things'." Hence, the Peripatetic-metaphysical prejudgment regarding Anaximander as a nature-philosopher concerned with natural matters is "altogether groundless." With the removal of this prejudgment, the notion of an indiscriminate and illegitimate mingling of domains becomes likewise untenable. Anaximander speaks indeed of justice, judgment, and penalty—but not in a manner as if these terms were borrowed from specialized academic disciplines called *ethics* or *jurisprudence*. In the dawn of Greek thought, such disciplines did not exist, which does not mean that early Greece was "ignorant" of law and ethics. Translation of the fragment thus requires a complex leap, above all the abandonment of misconceptions like these: first, "that the fragment pertains to naturephilosophy"; second, "that moral and juridical notions are inappropriately mixed in," involving a borrowing from "the separate domains of physics, ethics and law"; and finally, that the phrase reflects a "primitive experience which views the world uncritically or anthropomorphically and hence takes refuges in poetic metaphors."[17]

In referring to beings *[ta onta]*, Anaximander's fragment strikes an "ontological" theme—a theme that, though lying at the heart of Western philosophy, is nonetheless thoroughly opaque. *Being* and *beings* are terms steadily used, but with little or no reflection; commonly they are employed to signify only the broadest or vaguest generalities. In Heidegger's account, we use the terms as something "approximately intelligible," as part of the common stock of knowledge operative in ordinary language; even when familiar with their Greek precursors, we usually invest no more in their meaning than "the complacent negligence of hasty opinion." For Heidegger, to be sure, the terms are far from empty concepts; rather, they are key or code words of Western thought and history. Being and beings, he notes, are intimately entwined or conjoined, in the manner of concealment and revealment or disclosure. More specifically, being reveals or manifests itself in beings, but in doing so it tends to screen or conceal itself from view. The latter tendency has marked the development of Western metaphysics, where concern with beings has emerged as the dominant focus, while shuffling being aside. As Heidegger comments, beings here "do not step into the light of being; the unconcealment of beings—the brightness granted to them—obscures being's light." Differently put, "As it reveals itself in beings, being itself withdraws." This withdrawal, however, should not simply be seen as a deficiency or lacuna, but rather as an emblem of being's absent presence, of its disclosure in the mode of concealment. Using terminology reminiscent of *Beiträge*, the essay states that, in withdrawing or retreating, being "holds its truth in reserve. This keeping in reserve *[Ansichhalten]* is the early form of its revealment" and "its early sign is *a-letheia*," meaning un-concealment coupled with concealment. Still in the vein of *Beiträge*, Heidegger adds: "Concealment (of being), however, persists under the aegis of reticent refusal *[Verweigern]*."[18]

In embarking on his own translation or interpretation, Heidegger starts by probing further the meaning of "beings" [ta onta] as employed in the first part of Anaximander's fragment, which speaks of their origin and passing away. As he points out, origin [genesis] and passing away [phthora] should not be read simply in an evolutionary or teleological sense, but rather against the backdrop of concealment and unconcealment. Accordingly, the first term signifies the arising or coming-forth of a being from concealment or hiddenness into the light of unconcealment; correspondingly, the second term denotes not simply decay, but a being's retreat or withdrawal from unconcealment into sheltering concealment. In Heidegger's words, genesis is "the coming-forth and arriving in unconcealment" whereas phthora means "the departure or withdrawal out of unconcealment back into concealment. The 'coming forth' and 'withdrawing to' happen or occur in the space of disclosure between concealment and unconcealment." Anaximander's fragment, in its first part, thus speaks of arrival and departure or of the interplay of hiddenness and manifestation. To elucidate the sense of this interplay, Heidegger turns briefly to a passage in Homer's Iliad that, in referring to the seer Kalchas, notes that he was able to perceive present as well as future and past things or beings [eonta]. Presentness in this context means the manifestness or arrival of a being in the open region of unconcealment in which the being lingers for a "while" [Weile]. Past and future are likewise present in a sense, namely, outside the range of unconcealment or in the sphere of absent presence. Nonpresent being, we read, is "the absent or absently present; as such it remains essentially related to the presently present insofar as the latter either comes forth into or withdraws from the region of unconcealment." Thus, even the absent is present in a fashion, namely, by leaving as absence its present trace in unconcealment. Presence or presentness against this backdrop is merely an interval between arrival and departure, manifestness and hiddenness. What arrives into presence lingers or "whiles" [weilt] in disclosure while already preparing to withdraw into concealment. Hence, presence lingers "in arrival and departure," as the "transition from coming to going." The seer Kalchas perceived this interlocking of presence and absence, an insight that enabled him to be a soothsayer or "truth teller" [Wahrsager].[19]

Having explored the first part of Anaximander's fragment, Heidegger turns to the second part, focusing initially on the crucial term injustice [adikia]. It is at this point that his exegesis reinvokes the notion of Seinsfuge and its correlate of disjuncture. Quite independent of juridical usage, adikia, he notes, means basically that something is out of order or out of joint. In this manner, however, the term implicitly refers to a proper order or juncture, that is, to "justice" or dike as an emblem of Seinsfuge. In Heidegger's words, "The presentness of beings implies a certain juncture *[Fuge]* together with the possibility of being disjointed. Everything present lingers or stays for a while *[Weile]*—which latter means the transitional arrival into departure." Thus, presencing happens "between coming-forth and passing-away" or "between a two-fold absence" (or absent presence). This "between" or "in-between" is precisely the juncture *[Fuge]* into which every lingering presence is joined from its arrival to its departure; in both directions, presencing is inserted or welded into absence—an insertion that constitutes its proper juncture. Lingering or "whiling," however, can also turn into disjuncture. Instead of arriving into departure, a present being can try to prolong and to solidify its stay; having arrived into presence, it can insist on its presentness, seeking to transform "whiling" into persistence or perdurance. At this point, Heidegger notes, presentness "perseveres in its presencing, extricating itself from its transitory state. It aggrandizes itself into the selfish stubbornness *[Eigensinn]* of persistence, no longer caring about other modes of presence." In this manner, presentness leaves or abandons juncture and enters into a state of disjuncture *[Un-Fuge]*, which is the basic sense of injustice or *adikia*. Disjuncture in this context is not only an alternative kind of juncture but a counterjuncture or inverted juncture. An outgrowth of stubbornness, disjuncture signifies in fact a rebellion or "insurgence" of presentness in favor of "sheer continuance" or perdurance. Differently put, "Presentness happens then without and in opposition to the juncture of the passing while."[20]

Anaximander's saying does not only speak of disjuncture, however, but also of penalty, judgment, and the like—terms whose meaning so far is hazy. Regarding the passage usually translated as "paying penalty," Heidegger fastens onto the Greek text, which actually talks of something like "giving juncture" *[didonai diken]*. How should this phrase here be understood? *Giving*, he points out, does not only mean giving away; more genuinely, it denotes giving in, conceding, letting happen or be. "Such a giving," he writes, "lets another being have what properly belongs to the other. What properly belongs to every being, however, is the juncture of its passing stay *[Weile]* which joins it into arrival and departure." Properly joined into this interval, every being savors and rightly savors its presence without necessarily lapsing into the disjuncture of stubborn persistence, which remains a possibility and temptation. Differently phrased, being as such is not synonymous with disjuncture or injustice *[adikia]* because it is always already inserted into *Seinsfuge*, which lets it happen and which it lets happen in turn. Conversely, injustice does not absorb or overwhelm being because *adikia* is not strictly a negation or a vacuum, but rather justice itself in its mode of withdrawal or in its absent presence. Returning to Anaximander, the passage in question therefore may be rendered in this sense: that being (every being) allows juncture or justice to happen in the fact of disjuncture and even in the guise or mode of disjuncture. In Heidegger's words, "It is not in *adikia* as such nor in disjuncture that the presence of a present being consists, but rather in the *didonai diken . . . tes adikias,* in the letting-be of juncture. . . . Present being is present insofar as it lets itself belong into the non-present."[21]

What still remains unexamined in the second part of the fragment is the allusion to a judgment of sorts. In the Greek original, the reference is not so much to judgment as to estimation or *esteem [tisis],* which Heidegger initially translates as consideration or considerateness. By dwelling in *Seinsfuge,* every being grants to other beings considerately their passing stay; by contrast, stubborn self-persistence involves inconsiderateness toward others. In this stubbornness, Heidegger writes, "present being aggrandizes itself vis-à-vis or against others; neither being heeds or respects the lingering stay of the other. Thus, present beings are inconsiderate toward each other, each dominated by the craving for persistence implicit in or intimated by their presence." Still, Heidegger finds *consideration* too pale or nondescript to convey the full strength of the Greek term. Hence he replaces *considerate* and *inconsiderate* with the more poignant, though unusual, pair of *reck-ful* and *reckless*—noting that *reck [Ruch],* deriving from the Middle High German *ruoche,* corresponds roughly to the notion of "care" *[Sorge]* as employed in *Being and Time.* *Care,* he states, means being concerned with or attentive to the being of others; such attentiveness, however, is conveyed by the term *reck [Ruch* or *tisis].* In Heidegger's exegesis, the two aspects of allowing juncture to happen and showing "reck" or care are closely connected insofar as the latter derives from the former. "Insofar as beings," we read, "do not entirely dissipate themselves into the boundless conceit of self-aggrandizing persistence, by trying to eject each other mutually from the space of presencing, to this extent they let juncture be *[didonai diken].* And insofar as they let juncture be, they also already show or grant to each other 'reck' or care in their mutual relations *[didonai . . . kai tisin allelois].*" Justice *[dike]* and care *[tisis]* thus are related consequentially: "If present beings let juncture be, this happens in such a manner that, in their passing stay, they show care or 'reck' to each other. The overcoming of disjuncture occurs through the granting of care."[22]

The final passage not yet translated is the phrase *according to necessity* in the first part of the fragment that corresponds to the concluding *according to the ordinance of time.* In Heidegger's exegesis, the phrase refers not so much to necessity as to the background or nourishing soil in terms of which beings are able to let juncture happen and to show each other care. This background, however, is the "being of beings" or the happening of disclosure and concealment as such. Looking more closely at the Greek term usually rendered as "necessity" *[to chreon]*, Heidegger notes that it derives from the Greek word for hand *[cheir]*, with the result that the phrase actually has something to do with handling, being-to-hand, or handing over. Far from denoting an external necessity or constraint, the phrase then refers to "the handing over of presence, a handing over which grants or concedes presence to beings, but in such a manner that it keeps beings in hand, guarding their presence." Looking for a German equivalent for the Greek term, Heidegger (somewhat boldly) proposes the word *Brauch,* which, in its original meaning, signifies an ability to savor, to enjoy, to delight in a being's presence and autonomy without possessiveness or radical separation (thus guarding its stay). Enjoyment in this case, however, is no longer viewed as a human capacity, but as a quality of being itself in its relation to beings—which is a relation of handing over and keeping in hand. *"Brauch,"* we read, "hands beings over into their presence, that is, into their passing stay *[Weile]*; it dispenses to beings their portion of this stay. The latter, in turn, is grounded in the juncture *[Fuge]* which joins present beings into the twofold absence of arrival and departure." Together with juncture, there looms up for beings the possibility of disjuncture, as well as the contrast of care *[reck]* and recklessness. These prospects are ultimately anchored in the intertwining of being and non-being, where the latter is not a simple denial, but inscribed in the former. As Heidegger concludes, "Enjoining juncture and care, *Brauch* hands over beings into their presentness or present stay. This conjures up the constant danger that passing presence is congealed into sheer persistence. Thus, *Brauch* also permits the handing-over of beings into disjuncture"—which (we should recall) is only the trace of juncture seen as dispensation of *Brauch*.[23]

III

The discussed writings clearly have manifold implications for ethics as well as for social and political thought; they also help to correct (I believe) one-sided polemical dismissals of Heidegger as a Nazi ideologist or as a persistent apologist for fascism. In my view, the writings can actually be read as an indictment of Nazism to the extent that the latter aimed at an imperial dominion of the world based on racial-biological grounds. As presented in "The Anaximander Fragment," juncture and hence justice *[dike]* means the readiness to let others "be" and to attend to them with considerate care; by contrast, disjuncture or injustice *[adikia]* involves the insurgence of selfish conceit bent on monopolizing permanently the space of presence while shuffling others out of the way. Seen from the vantage of *Seinsfuge,* Hitler's Third Reich, scheduled to last for a "thousand years," was the epitome of disjuncture and injustice as well as of murderous recklessness. In terms of the Schelling lecture, however, disjuncture *[Ungefüge]* is also the emblem of "evil," the latter viewed not merely as a personal-moral deficiency but as an ontological perversion, as a rebellion against the structure of *Seinsfuge*. Again, Hitler's Reich in its extreme destructiveness was an embodiment of such ontological evil (independent of, or conjointly with, the individual perversities of its agents). Yet, the issue of disjuncture and injustice persists beyond the collapse of Nazism, though perhaps in less aggravated fashion. Today's world is marked by the contrast between West and non-West (or between North and South), where the West is only a small island in the vast ocean of the non-West, although it manages to monopolize the bulk of the world's economic and industrial resources. Is there not still an issue of disjuncture and injustice, now on a global scale, to which Heidegger's writings remain pertinent?

Apart from this stark political relevance, Heidegger's arguments insert themselves pointedly into ongoing debates about ethics and justice, to which I alluded at the beginning. As previously indicated, contemporary ethics is largely a battleground between Kantian rationalism and neo-Aristotelian virtue ethics—leaving aside the skeptical variant; in broader political terms, the distinction corresponds roughly to that between liberalism and communitarianism. In the language of academic moral theory, the conflict is commonly expressed in opposing pairs, such as these: deontology versus teleology, procedural form versus substance, universalism versus particularism. Although alluring as conceptual categories, the ethical import of these notions remains elusive and confusing.

In the case of rationalist ethics, given the strict separation of "is" and "ought," moral maxims and phenomenal experience, how can universal imperatives be at all transposed into the domain of practical conduct? Premised on the cancellation of teleology and ontology, how can "deontological" rules at all impose their "ought" or "must" on the realm of being? Quandaries of this kind confirm the merits of virtue ethics— but without necessarily vindicating its metaphysical assumptions. As has frequently been noted, classical—including Aristotelian—ethics is predicated on a substantive ontology (or ontology of substances) wherein each element or being is assigned its proper place and status in the universe. Couched in terms of moral conduct, *right action* here means action appropriate or fitting for a person's station and duties in life—a conception that readily supports social conservatism. As is well known, functionalist sociology offers a theory of agency where role performance is strictly tailored to the efficient functioning of the overall system (which, no doubt, is a caricature of classical ethics). The crucial aspect neglected by functionalism and substantive ethics is the dimension of freedom—

ontologically speaking, the correlation of being and non-being. By anchoring his argument in this correlation, Heidegger intimates a postmetaphysics bypassing the form-substance, norm-experience dichotomies. Moreover, in linking justice closely with *Seinsfuge,* his perspective bridges or undercuts the gulf between "rightness" and "goodness" or between "justice" and the "good life."

Still in the domain of ethical theory, the reviewed writings are liable to counter misconceptions that frequently beleaguer Heidegger's work. One such misconception—triggered chiefly by passages in *Being and Time*—holds that his thought sponsors at best a minimalist and noncognitivist ethics, more specifically a moral "decisionism" grounded in arbitrary will. Human *Dasein,* in this view, involves basically a choice or option between "authentic" and "inauthentic" modes of life—unless choice is abandoned in favor of inscrutable dispensations of fate or "destiny" (offered as translation for *Geschick*).[24] Heidegger's lectures on Schelling should dispel this decisionist reading, given the emphasis there on *eros* or inclination as ontological mentors of ethical conduct (grounded in *Seinsfuge*). To the extent that such conduct does involve "decision," the lectures explicitly differentiate that element from both sheer willfulness and fatalism: "Pure arbitrariness fails to supply a motivational basis for decision; external compulsion, on the other hand, does not furnish a motivation for its presumed target, namely, (free) decision." In countering or correcting decisionism, the same lectures also take exception to its flip-side or counterthesis: that of ethical-ontological "indecision" or "undecidability." As mentioned before, Heidegger presents the relation between juncture and disjuncture, or between good and evil, not simply as equivalent alternatives between which one might maintain a stance of neutrality or indecision. Instead, *Dasein,* he insists, cannot in actual life remain neutral, but must "exit" from indecision. This exit route is again paved by inclination and, more important, by a certain preponderance or weight built into *Seinsfuge*— in the sense that evil is not simply the negation of goodness, but rather the absent presence of goodness, just as nonbeing is the absent presence of being. To repeat a previously cited passage, "Love's will takes precedence over the will of the ground, and this precedence and eternal decidedness—that is, the love of being for being—is the innermost core of absolute freedom."[25]

Curiously, both decisionism and indecision or undecidability are sometimes blended today in (versions of) poststructuralism. In seeking to dismantle "foundationalist" metaphysics, poststructuralist writers occasionally drift into a no-man's land where being and non-being, ground and abyss, as well as good and evil, appear radically exchangeable— unless preference is directly given to abyss over ground or to anarchy over *arché*. Thus, Derrida's texts sometimes speak of the exchangeability or "undecidability" of metaphysical and ontological categories, including the dimensions of disclosure and concealment, presence and absence. Exchangeability, however, signals sameness or indifference—which neglects precisely the differentiation or differentiated correlation of these dimensions. As it happens, "difference" or differentiation is at the same time the hallmark of poststructuralism (and deconstructionism)—where difference often signifies or is synonymous with decision, struggle, or "incommensurability." Under the influence of a radical Nietzscheanism (stressing will to power), poststructuralist texts sometimes portray human relations entirely under the aegis of conflict and *agon*—to the point of canceling junctures or common bonds; in an effort to exorcise "totality," system, and homogeneity, these texts sometimes end up by celebrating particularism and atomistic dispersal. Heidegger's writings likewise extol difference, but a difference that is not equivalent to antithesis or mutual negation; although bypassing system or identity, they portray struggle as reciprocal entwinement. To quote again from the Schelling lectures, "According to the old saying of Heraclitus, struggle is the basic principle and moving force of being. But the greatest struggle is love—which provokes the deepest contest precisely in order to be and display itself in its reconciliation."[26]

Returning to political connotations, Heidegger's writings are far from neutral undecidability—although they are equally removed from ideological partisanship. The closing paragraphs of "The Anaximander Fragment" insert the discussion of justice and injustice squarely into the present global context—which is marked by the steadily intensified struggle for planetary dominion or control. The entire thrust of the essay is directed toward finding antidotes to this scenario and hence resources for an "other" beginning. The distant saying of Anaximander, Heidegger observes, becomes accessible only if we ponder the "disjointedness" *[Wirrnis]* of the present age. Wherein does this disjuncture consist? "Humans," Heidegger responds, "are on the verge of leaping onto the entire earth and its atmosphere in order to harness for themselves the powers of nature in the form of energy and to subject the course of history to the managerial plans of a world government." What is lost in this reckless move toward dominion is *Seinsfuge,* which means the willingness of humans to let juncture be and to be careful with one another as well as with nature and being. "Rebellious *Dasein,*" the essay states, "is incapable to say or acknowledge simply what *is*—to say what it means that anything *is*. Rather: the totality of beings is the target of a single will of conquest—while the simplicity of being is buried in complete oblivion." In this situation, antidotes cannot simply be fabricated or engineered; instead, their availability depends on the bracketing of instrumental production and the readiness to undergo a transformation or turning *[Kehre]*—which is both a philosophical and a practical-political turning or *periagoge*. In this change, humans turn from oblivion to the recollection of being, whereas the latter returns to display its nurturing care or *Brauch*. As Heidegger concludes, paraphrasing Hölderlin, ours is an age of danger. But danger "is" most genuinely when "being itself takes a final stand (in withdrawal), thus turning about the oblivion it had sponsored."[27]

Beyond the stark issue of planetary control, Heidegger's argument is relevant more broadly to questions of social control and hence of social and political equity. In contemporary (Western) society, questions of equity are typically articulated in terms of "rights," which usually means resort to legal processes of adjudication. Legal theory and jurisprudence, in fact, are replete with "rights talk" and admonitions to "take rights seriously," coupled with acceptance of the "legalization" of social bonds. Although valuable in the face of totalitarian abuses, however, rights language is elusive unless attention is paid to the carriers of rights and to the entanglement of rights with power or domination. For can one really treat as equivalent the rights of the rich and the poor, the powerful and the powerless, the victimizer and the victims? This question points to the power structure of society and to its equity or inequity. Typically, rights are initially acquired through struggle; yet, once social conditions stabilize or solidify, there is a subtle transition from rights to "vested rights"—commonly to the detriment of the underprivileged or the outcasts of society. It is at this point that Heidegger's discussion of equity or justice comes into play, with its emphasis on "presencing" and on the "passing while" enjoyed by presentness between a twofold absence: that of arrival and departure, past and future. Unless mindful of their passing while, present rights claims are liable to deteriorate into privileges, into the attempt to monopolize social control and to shuffle aside both past and future generations or social groupings. As it happens, vested rights tend to enjoy the blessing of law or the legal system, with the result that challenges to control are castigated as unlawful or iniquitous. Although a major acquisition of modern constitutional government, the "rule of law" cannot operate abstractly on the level of equivalence (of rights), but must be constantly open to interpretation and reinterpretation in the light of changing social conditions and demands for social equity.[28]

From the vantage of Heidegger's writings, the latter demands are not simply willful assertions, but an outgrowth of *Seinsfuge* and its linkage of presence and absence. Correspondingly, lawfulness means not only legality in the sense of obedience to given rules, but also attentiveness to equity or mindfulness of juncture and disjuncture. As he writes in the *Letter on Humanism,* only being can yield or dispense guideposts that might become rules of human conduct. In Greek, such yielding is termed *nemein*. Hence, he adds, "*nomos* is not merely 'law', but more originally the dispensation latent in the happening of being. Only this dispensation is capable of 'joining' humans into being, and only such 'juncture' is able to bind and to sustain. Otherwise all law or legality remains a machination of human rationality." In these comments on law, the *Letter* thus invokes and pays tribute to *Seinsfuge,* though without explicitly developing this theme. The theme also surfaces in the *Letter*'s observations on being and non-being, on goodness (or the hale) and evil, and particularly on the "difference" (or conflictual juncture) of being itself. "Together with the hale," we read, "evil too appears in the clearing of being. The latter's nature does not consist in the mere baseness of human action but rather in the malice of rage *[Grimm].* Both of them, however, the hale and the rage, can occur in being only because being itself is contestable—by harboring the origin of non-being." In light of these passages, I believe, one has to see Heidegger's noted reservations or reticence regarding ethics. The target of this reticence is formalized ethical theory, but not ethics seen as reflection on juncture and disjuncture, justice and injustice, good and evil. This conclusion is warranted, I think, by a passage in the *Letter* in which Heidegger expresses his view forthrightly, saying, "If, in keeping with the basic meaning of *ethos,* the term 'ethics' should designate a reflection on *Dasein's* mode of dwelling, then that type of thinking which ponders the truth of being as primordial abode of eksisting-ekstatic *Dasein* is in itself the original ethics."[29]

15

Stories of Being

JOHN VAN BUREN

There has been much talk recently about deconstructing and demythologizing Heidegger—this twentieth-century father Parmenides in the
postmodern *gigantomachia peri tes ousias*.[1] Different strategies have been
pointed out for displacing the post-metaphysical topic *[Sache]* of
Heideggerian thought from its covert residual metaphysics of inter alia
Greco-Germanic ethnocentrism, religious world-view, mythopoetic speculation, political ideology, gender bias, anthropocentrism, and philosophical authoritarianism. Thomas Sheehan, John Caputo, Theodore Kisiel,
Victor Farias, Hugo Ott, Jacques Derrida, Jürgen Habermas, Richard Rorty,
and others have argued, each in his own way, that such residues ambigu-
ously permeate Heidegger's very postmetaphysical formulations of the
question concerning being. His thought is an ambiguous and irksome
play of tendency and countertendency. The initial Heidegger receptions
that performed valuable services by translating and explaining his texts
thus no longer suffice, at least as ends in themselves. Appropriation without critique is blind, just as critique without appropriation is empty. The
philosophical love affair with Heidegger's philosophy is not at an end
because it is only just beginning in the sense of the creative love-hate
relationship of dispute *[Auseinandersetzung]* that is supposed to be motivated by the very self-differentiating character of his topic of the *Ereignis*
of being.

Heidegger himself had already worked out a merciless project of
deconstructing and demythologizing metaphysics in the lecture courses
and essays of his youthful Freiburg period between 1919 and 1923. Can
this project be turned on his own later metaphysical residues, thus providing another strategy for coping with the ambiguity of his thought? In
pursuing this question, I sketch out the young Heidegger's understanding

of metaphysics as myth, his project of demythologizing it, the later Heidegger's partial remythologizing of the question concerning being, and how the young and the later Heidegger can be played off against each other.

The young Heidegger referred to the various attempts of metaphysicians to secure "absolute knowledge" of an unchanging "present" in the following terms: "this fantastic path to the transhistorical," "mythical and theosophical metaphysics," "religious ideology and fantasy," "the swindle of an aestheticizing intoxication," "masking," "a dream of ideal possibilities of absolute knowledge," "a soporific opiate," a "dream-state," sleep-walking through "the land of the blessed and absolute." "Philosophy," he said to his students (here quoting Kierkegaard), "has created the illusion that human beings could, as one soberly says, speculate themselves out of their own good skin and into pure light." He told them in a rare moment of humor that the neo-Kantian concept of a pure consciousness is really *ein pures Gespenst,* a pure ghost around which ideal truths and values "flutter about like phantoms." At another time, he read out Plato's criticism in the *Sophist* (242c) of the mythopoetic thinking of the pre-Socratic *gigantomachia peri tes ousias:* "It seems to me," his translation ran, "that each of them (the old philosophers of being) tells a *mython,* a myth, a story, as though we were children." This quotation was echoed in Heidegger's 1927 *Being and Time:* "If we are to understand the problem of being, our first philosophical step consists in not *mython tina diegeisthai,* in not 'telling a myth, a story'." Taking up Plato's related theme of the philosopher-cum-parricide who wounds the pre-Socratic fathers, the young Heidegger even demanded that "the philosopher must dare to become a father-killer"![2]

Heidegger's own postmythic sense of philosophy was what he called the *hermeneutics of facticity,* where the question about being is to be pursued as it comes interpretively to language in the form of sense *[Sinn]* within factical life. As he formulated it, "life = Dasein, there-being, 'be-ing' in and and through life." Using Husserl's notion of intentionality, he configured this being-sense *[Seinssinn]* into four intentional moments. First, there is the noemetic content-sense *[Gehaltssinn],* that is, being as the intentional object of the world that includes the technical environing world *[Umwelt],* the interpersonal with-world *[Mitwelt],* and the personal self-world *[Selbstwelt].* Second, relational-sense *[Bezugssinn]* is the sense of the intentional relating to world that takes the forms of care, mood, understanding, and language. Finally, there is the sense of the temporalizing *[Zeitigungssinn]* and the enactment *[Vollzugssinn]* of be-ing, that is, the depth-dimension of the temporal unfolding of the intentional person-world doublet and its concrete enactment on the part of the individual person. In his early Freiburg period, Heidegger called this radical depth-dimension there is—it gives *[es gibt]*, it worlds *[es weltet]*, event *[Ereignis]*, and *kinesis*, movement.[3]

For the young Heidegger, this intentional content-relation-temporalizing configuration of the *Ereignis* of being spelled the end of philosophy. "This so understood skepticism," he announced to his students, "is a beginning, and as a genuine beginning it is also the end of philosophy." The new postmetaphysical beginning was supposed to be a type of skepticism about all claims that being has a fixed sense. But it also meant skepticism in the sense of an endless questioning after *[skepsis]* the *Ereignis* of being in historical situations. Since no ruling *arche* controlled this *Ereignis* from above, there is only the situationally un-archic happening of different principles and philosophies. "There is no such thing as *the* philosophy," Heidegger stated. The sense of being is thus characterized by a constant questionableness *[Fraglichkeit]*. "This situation," he explained, "is hardly the saving coast, but rather the leap into the speeding boat, and now everything depends on getting the rope for the sail into one's hand and looking towards the wind. . . . To steer into absolute questionableness and to have it in sight, this means taking hold of philosophy authentically."[4]

The young Heidegger's kinetics of being was at the same time a *personalist* kinetics. Prior to 1923 his predominant term for human life was not *Dasein*, but *person*. Therefore we find him speaking of "personal life," the "historical I," "personal Dasein," the "Dasein of personal life," "*my* Dasein." His 1919 term *Ereignis* means not only a historical and epochal happening in which the individual is caught up and swept away, but also a personal *Er-eignen*, a personal ap-propriating, en-owning, or coming-into-one's-own. As he put it, "*ich selbst er-eigne es mir, und es er-eignet sich seinem Wesen nach*, I myself e-vent—en-own [lived experience] to myself, and it e-vents—en-owns itself according to its essence. . . . 'outer' and 'inner' have as little sense here as 'physical' or 'psychical.' Lived experiences are *Er-eignisse*, en-ownments, insofar as they live out of *dem Eigenen*, what is own."[5]

Given the situational and personal character of *Ereignis*, there can be only an an-archic community of persons in the world. *Ereignis* is a pluralist concept that contains radical difference in itself. Heidegger writes: "If the lived experiences of other subjects have any reality at all, then indeed only as *Er-eignisse*, and they are such and can be evident only as *Er-eignisse*, as own-ed *[ge-eignet]* by a historical I. For me they are not *Ereignisse*, for at any time they essentially are precisely as only for an Other." And "I *am* never the Other." "Insofar as time is in each case mine, there are many times. *Time, the* time is meaningless. . . . time is the proper *principium individuationis*." "*Individuum est ineffabile*," the individual is ineffable. Philosophy must never attempt to take away the personal and unique character of *Ereignis* by dissolving it in abstract universals and absolute truths; rather, it should strive to achieve a "noninterference in personal decision-making and so set the individual free for self-reflection." As a hermeneutics of facticity, ontology must preserve the personal relational-sense and enactment-sense of being, since being is always " *'being'* in and through [my personal] life."[6] Such is Heidegger's early personalist-phenomenological *Denkweg* of the *Ereignis* of being, which has to be distinguished from the ambiguous transcendental subjectivizing of being in his later *Being and Time*.

The young Heidegger stressed that living in the face of the personal kinetic predicament of being means "difficulty" and "unrest." He called the tendency to flee from this difficulty *the hyperbolic,* that is, projecting oneself into a beyond *[hyper]*. In everyday life, this beyond takes the form of the public abstractions of *das Man,* the they, what the others are saying and doing. Heidegger also called this *masking,* hiding oneself, disguising the personal kinetic face of being. In this way, one seeks *Erleichterung,* making things easy and comfortable. Metaphysics, he thought, is only a more refined expression of this hyperbolic masking and this taking a vacation from life. Here the beyond, the mask, is the "illusion" of an "absolute philosophy," the fantasy of a "pure present," the "dream" of unchanging and universal truth, which is a rarified form of the "publicness" of *das Man.*[7] This lack of nerve on the part of metaphysics, its failure to look squarely into the face of being, its attempt to sneak away into static impersonal abstractions is what the young Heidegger meant by the *mythical, fantasy, illusion, dream, opiate, aestheticizing intoxication, telling stories.* Metaphysicians hide the personal kinetic physiognomy of being with the masks of philosophical myths.

Metaphysics is a mythologizing abstraction from all three intentional senses of being (G56/57 89–90). Its various notions of a world of universal meaning and values abstract from the concrete content-sense of environing world, social world, and self-world. Heidegger called this a *designifying [Entdeutung]* and *deworlding [Entweltlichung]* of the world. On the other hand, the representation of persons as pure reason, soul, transcendental consciousness, or pure spirit performs a deliving *[Entleben]* or depersonalizing of the personal relational-sense of being. And, finally, metaphysics dehistoricizes *[entgeschichtlicht]* the *Ereignis* of the person-world relation by dissolving its personal and temporal character either into the notions of eternity and logical atemporality or into the extended present of objective physical and historical processes. Heidegger refers to all three types of abstraction as *Ent-lebnis,* un-life or de-life, because they place life away *[ent-]* from itself into the beyond of alienating metaphysical constructions. Metaphysics actually defaces the personal kinetic physiognomy of being.

The young Heidegger thus proposed a deconstruction *[Abbauen]* of metaphysics, an unmasking of "mythical and theosophical metaphysics," that amounted to a project of demythologizing it. "Philosophy," he wrote, "has to start thinking about . . . giving up the swindle of its aestheticizing intoxication of itself and its contemporaries." "Absolute knowledge: . . . at bottom a dream. . . . one should be on guard against the use of the idea of absolute truth as a soporific opiate." To deconstruct in the sense of demythologizing meant to loosen up the deworlding, deliving, and dehistoricizing abstractions of traditional philosophy and to repeat them from within and for the worldly content-sense, the personal relational-sense, and the temporalizing-sense of "one's time," of one's *kairos* "here and now . . . at this place. . . . You before me, I before you, we with each other." Heidegger called this deconstructive and demythologizing repetition of the question concerning being a "working out of the hermeneutical situation," a "kairological-critical questioning 'in one's time'."[8]

It was this type of thinking that the theologian Rudolf Bultmann learned from Heidegger during their collaboration in Marburg in the early 1920s and came explicitly to call *demythologizing*.[9] Bultmann took what Heidegger was doing on an ontological level and applied it to the specific domain of Christian experience, a project that was facilitated by the fact that Heidegger's ontology actually came out of his appropriation of the Christian notion of *kairos* from the New Testament to Kierkegaard. Myth in Bultmann's sense means any representation of the believer-God relation in terms of outdated imaginative forms that abstract from and are alien to the "now" character of this relation in one's own *kairos*. For example, the content-sense of eternal life with God could be imaginatively represented and deworlded as a "heaven" in a distant part of the cosmos. Or the lordship of the risen Christ could be depicted in the story of the Ascension, which is premised on the Babylonian mythopoetic cosmology of a flat earth under the vault of the firmament. The relational-sense of the anxious believing self might be represented and delived as pure spirit having only an accidental relation to the body. The enactment-sense belonging to personal choice of the God relationship might be dehistoricized into the Gnostic vision of the world as a theater of conflict between supernatural powers. The mysterious depth dimension of the temporalizing-sense of the *viva vox* that always speaks *pro nobis* could be dehistoricized into the distance of a static and mute eternity. In these examples, all three intentional moments of the God-believer-history configuration tend to be externalized and distanced into the ubiquitous, impersonal, and static content-sense of a mythic otherworldly dimension. To demythologize all this means to kairologize it by stripping away its alien imaginative forms and relating it as a message within one's own historical situation. Demythologizing means worlding, personalizing, and temporalizing the sense of being in the realm of Christian experience. Neither in Bultmann's theological sense nor in the young Heidegger's ontological sense does it mean the disenchantment of the world, that is, the banishment of mystery, the poetic, and the religious; rather, it would involve bringing their worldly, personal, and historical dimensions into play.

Heidegger's ontological demythologizing of metaphysics sought to erase the traditional mythic inscriptions of the intentional configuration of being-sense in Greek, medieval, and modern metaphysics and sought further to reinscribe the original personal kinetic physiognomy of this configuration in his own new beginning. In the following, I present some rough sketches of this demythologizing of the history of metaphysics. A precedent for my sketches is the later Heidegger's own very rough and fragmentary "Sketches for a History of Being as Metaphysics."[10]

In the young Heidegger's reading of the Greek epoch, the deworlding of content-sense showed up as idea in Plato and substance in Aristotle. Heidegger's demythologizing went back to the worldly realities that Aristotle especially had described in his practical writings, that is, the environing world of the household *[oikos]*, the social with-world of the *polis,* and the self-world of one's *ethos.* The Greek deliving of relational-sense expressed itself as theory, reason *[nous],* and assertoric *logos.* Again, Heidegger cut beneath this to the level of Aristotle's and Plato's analyses of praxis, striving *[orexis], phronesis,* passion, and *logos* as social discourse. The Greek dehistoricizing of temporalizing-sense was expressed as eternal being *[aei on].* But Heidegger's demythologizing attempted to return to Aristotle's theme of human *kinesis* toward practical ends interpretively fulfilled in the *kairos,* the present situation.[11]

The deworlding of content-sense in medieval scholasticism took the form of God as uncreated substance and first cause. In his lecture courses on St. Paul, Augustine, Luther, and Kierkegaard, Heidegger demythologized this abstract scholastic view of God by showing how it had lost sight of "the theology of the cross," that is, the concrete reality of the crucified God in the original Christianity of the New Testament. The scholastic deliving of personal relational-sense centered on contemplation and doctrine. Heidegger's deconstruction looked beneath this founded level to the anxious faith of the whole person. And his demythologizing of the scholastic dehistoricizing of temporalizing-sense as the *nunc stans* of eternity cut beneath this to the New Testament reality of the futural *parousia* or coming-to-presence of God within the *kairos* or moment.[12]

Finally, the modern deworlding of worldly content-sense especially took the form of the validity of logical meaning and values in neo-Kantianism and early phenomenology.[13] Heidegger undercut this to get at the immediate it-worlds and there is–it gives of the life-world. The neo-

Kantian deliving of relational-sense focused on the problem of judgments, whereas Heidegger's demythologizing went back to the more primordial dimension of personal Dasein. The neo-Kantian dehistoricizing of temporalizing-sense took the form of the atemporality of the validity of logical meaning and values. Heidegger's demythologizing showed how this was founded on the *Ereignis* of the intentional person-world doublet.

At the same time that the young Heidegger demythologized the three epochal inscriptions of the sense of being in the history of metaphysics by deconstructing them back to their historical foundations (the end of philosophy), he reinscribed in them the various formulations of his personalist-phenomenological configuration of being-sense (the new beginning); for example, in the world-person-*Ereignis* configuration of his 1919 lecture courses on neo-Kantianism (G56/57), in the world-care-kairological time configuration of his 1920–21 lecture course on Paul's letters and Luther's *theologia crucis,* and in the world-life-*kinesis* configuration of his 1921–22 lecture course on Aristotle (G61). Many years later, the old Heidegger maintained that after these "youthful leaps" he went on to pursue three predominant thought paths; namely, the "sense" of being in his *Being and Time* and then the "truth" and "topos" of being in his later writings (G15 344). In effect, each of these later paths took up the young Heidegger's question of " '*being*' in and through life" and reinscribed its intentional configuration of content-sense, relational-sense, and temporalizing-sense in a unique way. In fact, one finds this youthful terminology of *Gehalt, Bezug, Vollzug,* and *Zeitigung* recurring in different forms throughout the subsequent development of his thought.[14]

His later paths certainly amounted to filling out, deepening, and introducing novel elements into his original breakthroughs to his lifelong topic. I want to argue, however, that these paths also inscribed into his original postmythic formulations of his question certain tendencies of deworlding, deliving, and dehistoricizing that partially masked, defaced, mythologized, and erased the personal kinetic physiognomy of being that he had drawn earlier. Even if some of these tendencies were already latently and peripherally present in his thought from the very beginning, they became more and more aggravated as his thought developed. I also want to argue that these tendencies to a great extent make up the metaphysical residues targeted by recent trends toward deconstructing and demythologizing Heidegger. In what follows I thus present sketches of how these tendencies effected residual metaphysical reconstructions and mythologizings of his original postmetaphysical and postmythic question concerning being. Of course, I am not foolishly attempting to reduce Heidegger's later thought to these tendencies. Because they are usually accompanied by equally strong countertendencies, one can always use Heidegger to deconstruct and demythologize Heidegger. I am suggesting

that one of the best Heideggers that one can use for this is the young
Heidegger!

The Transcendental Configuration

In this configuration of the sense of being that Heidegger worked
out in his *Being and Time* under the influence of his turn to Kant around
1925–26, his earlier it-worlds of content-sense was rewritten as the existential-transcendental structures of the worldhood of the world. The
"Dasein of personal life" belonging to relational-sense now became the
existential-transcendental structures of Dasein. And the freewheeling
Ereignis and *kinesis* of temporalizing-sense was reinscribed in the form
of the existential-transcendental schemata of temporality. Can we not see
in this neo-neo-Kantian redrafting into the configuration of worldhood-
Dasein-temporal schemata especially a certain deliving (depersonalizing)
and dehistoricizing of Heidegger's earlier question concerning the *Ereignis*
of " '*being*' in and through [personal] life"? Was it not his eventual insight into the inadequacies of this ambiguous gesture toward a language
of the quasi-atemporal structures of an existentialized transcendental subjectivity that drove him to the so-called turn in his thought around 1930—
a turn in which he creatively returned to his pre-*Being and Time* thought
paths of *Ereignis* and the worlding of the world that had so radically
called for the end of philosophy and a new beginning?

The Poetic Configuration

In Heidegger's later poetic configuration of being-sense that was
worked out in his thought paths of the truth and the topos of being under
the influence of the pre-Socratics, the poet Hölderlin, and Nietzsche, his
youthful theme of the it-worlds of content-sense was reinscribed as the
worlding of the fourfold of earth and sky, mortals and gods. The "Dasein
of personal life" belonging to relational-sense was redrafted into the poetic dwelling of mortals. And the *Ereignis* of temporalizing-sense was
rewritten as *a-letheia* and *Ereignis* in the sense of an an-archic play of
epochal destining. This poetic fourfold-dwelling-*Ereignis* configuration
per se may express little or nothing that is metaphysical and mythic. But
at the same time clearly written into it were a number of residually
metaphysical and mythopoetic configurations that effected a dehistoricizing
and depersonalizing both of Heidegger's original question and of the
virtual sense of the later fourfold-dwelling-*Ereignis* configuration. I now
turn to some rough sketches of these residually metaphysical and mythic

configurations. The first group concerns especially the deliving of the personal relational-sense of being.

The Speculative Configuration

Temporalizing-sense tended to be rewritten here as a quasi-hypostatized and quasi-absolute *Ereignis* or there-is–it-gives that, as destiny, sends the epochal worlds of being (content-sense), which provide an *ethos* for mortals (relational-sense). What became obscured here was the young Heidegger's theme of our cotemporalizing and fulfilling enactment of this *Ereignis* in the sense of *Sich-Ereignen,* that is, a personal appropriating of this epochal happening within our particular situations. Suddenly *Ereignis* no longer included the *Ereignis* of persons, of the "Dasein of personal life." "In [the essay] 'Time and Being', however," Heidegger wrote, "the *relation* of the Appropriation *[Ereignis]* and the human being of mortals is consciously excluded" (my italics). When he did deal with the receptive role of human existence in the sending of the epochs, the essence of this was often supposed to be not something personal, not a "who," but rather a kind of transcendental-poetic ek-sistence (standing out) into the epochal truth of being. "The personal no less than the objective misses and misconstrues the essential presencing of ek-sistence in the history of being." Likewise, he suggested that considerations of both worldly content-sense (that is, of our historical worlds) and our personal relational-sense to these worlds were to be dimmed down and left in limbo until the deep speculative hermeneutics of *Ereignis* had been tuned into its saving truth, which was not supposed to happen until the very distant future of a new beginning. "In glancing through authentic time," explained Heidegger in his essay "Time and Being," "it has been our task to think being in what is its own—out of *Ereignis*—without a view to the *relation* of being to beings" (my italics).[15]

The Antihumanistic Configuration

Another rough sketch for further investigation can be made of Heidegger's tendencies toward an antihumanistic configuration of the sense of being. Temporalizing-sense shows up here as an *Ereignis* of the worldly epochs of being that possesses the following table of virtues: *freedom* (nonlimitation by historical laws); *uniqueness* (each epoch is unique); *dignity* (the ultimate for-the-sake-of-which); *integrity* or wholeness (affirmation of all epochal sendings); and *development* or *perficere* (the anarchic unfolding and self-accomplishing of epochal sending). The young

Heidegger's radically individual and personalized relational-sense, on the other hand, gets reinscribed here in the form of the "essence of humanity" that is sent through epochal *Ereignis;* as Heidegger suggested, each person is or wears the epochal essential *"persona,* the mask, of being" through which being speaks. Consequently, the preceding list of qualities is either only ascribed hierarchico-teleologically to the *Ereignis* of persons in a secondary sense or even looks like it is in fact withheld from persons, who seem to lack *uniqueness* (because reduced to a homogeneous epochal essence); *dignity* or being an end-in-itself (because for-the-sake-of the dignity of being); *freedom* and responsibility (because determined by destiny); *integrity* or wholeness (because the whole embodied person is modeled on a quasi-contemplative "thinking" and "poetizing"); and *development* and cultivation of *humanitas* (because the first task of persons is rather "waiting" upon the development of the truth of being, even though it withholds itself and abandons us to the dark ages of the epochal "world night" and "destitution" of modern technology, such that "only a god can save us" from all this). "Even this [attending to the dimension of the truth of being]," Heidegger wrote in his "Letter on Humanism," "could take place only for the dignity of being and for the benefit of the there-being *[Da-sein]* that the human being eksistingly sustains, not for the sake of the human being, so that through its creativity civilization and culture might assert their validity."[16] But can you really overcome technological anthropocentrism simply by reversing it into ontocentrism, that is, transcend the abstract exaggeration of the temporality of relational-sense (enactment-sense) by replacing it with an equally abstract elephantiasis of the deep temporality of content-sense? Is it not the same master-slave structure whether in the form of humanity the technological lord–being the slave ("standing reserve") or in the form of being the master–humanity the lowly servant ("the shepherd of being")? What happened to the young Heidegger's insistence upon the equiprimordiality of the different moments of the sense of being?

The Primitivist Configuration

The worldly content-sense of being was here written in the form of the fourfold of earth and sky, mortals and gods along with technological enframing *[Gestell]* as its inverted "photographic negative." The *Ereignis* of temporalizing-sense was inscribed as a dark, primitive, and arbitrary force that, in fatefully sending the epochs, oscillates between *lethe* (errancy) and *aletheia* (truth), darkness and light, earth and sky, nothingness and being, abyss and ground, malice and the hale, good and evil, horror and joy, violence and care, the daemonic power of technological enframing and the beauty of the fourfold. Relational-sense became the human being as a transcendental-poetic site and plaything of these neo-cosmic forces; our proper response to these was to be the passive and uncritical one of primitivist "awe" and fatalistic "corresponding."[17]

I turn now to another group of sketches of the later Heidegger's poetic fourfold-dwelling-*Ereignis* configuration that show him tending to obscure the an-archic character of the depth dimension of the *Ereignis* of temporalizing-sense, and thereby also tending to efface the personal-an-archic physiognomy of being, that is, the an-archic community of the *Ereignis* of persons. As John Caputo has argued so well in his *Radical Hermeneutics,* these tendencies show Heidegger hierarchico-teleologically privileging some specific and supposedly "proper" epochal sense, site, or reading of being, which leads to marginalizing those content-senses (worlds) and relational-senses (lives) that are Other. In these cases, we find Heidegger slipping into a philosophy of world-view and even ideology.

The Hellenic Configuration

In this configuration of the sense of being, relational-sense was inscribed as the model of the ancient Greeks, especially the pre-Socratics and the tragedians; content-sense was modeled on the early Greek experience of *aletheia* and the cosmological fourfold of earth and sky, gods and mortals. Temporalizing-sense was presented in the form of the circular eschatological destiny of *Ereignis* that effects both the end of the first Greek beginning of being and its apocalyptic return in a second neo-Greek beginning. Enactment-sense, the acting out of the temporalizing of this specific neo-Greek Dasein-world doublet, suggests a marginalizing of the epochal and cultural Other. What about Irish relational-sense, the Icelandic fourfold, or Persian temporalizing-sense?[19]

The Germano-Nazi Configuration

Here relational-sense was imprinted with the face of the German folk as the proper heir of the Greek ontological mission; in turn, the spirit of the folk was seen to be embodied in the state and its political Führer (Adolf Hitler) and its philosophical Führer (the aspirant Martin Heidegger). Content-sense was portrayed in the form of the culturally specific Greco-Germanic world of the fourfold that was modeled on the rustic country-side of the Black Forest. Temporalizing-sense was inscribed as the *Ereignis* of the destiny of the West in which the central site of the eschatological return of the first Greek beginning was supposed to be the country of Germany, this "land of poets and thinkers" possessing an exemplary relation to the truth of being. The enactment-sense of this destiny expressed itself as spiritual battle *[Kampf]*, danger, mobilization, militarism, and a general marginalizing of the non-Greco-Germanic Other (for example, see the list of Heidegger's unsavory and discriminatory actions before, during, and after his National Socialist rectorship at the University of Freiburg that has been compiled by Victor Farias and Hugo Ott).[19]

The Greco-Christian Religious Configuration

The worldly content-sense of being was here presented in the form of the religious as it appears in the Greco-Christian fourfold of the chthonic powers of earth and sky, mortals and gods, where Christ is only the last god to appear in the Greek pantheon. Here Heidegger took up the revivals of the Greek concept of the divine initiated by Nietzsche and especially Hölderlin. The relational-sense of religious experience was inscribed within the horizons of Greco-Christian religiosity (for example, piety, waiting, quasi-prayer, remembrance, thanking). Temporalizing-sense was portrayed as the destining of *Ereignis* in the form of a history of salvation *[Heilsgeschichte]* that promises the *parousia* and *kairos* of the eschatological rebirth of absent Greco-Christian divinity in the technological night of the world. The enactment-sense of this destiny suggests a marginalizing of the non-Greco-Christian religious Other. Would an Eskimo, a Christian, or a Hindu recognize himself or herself in this history of salvation?

The Gendered Configuration

Here the relational sense of being was sometimes inscribed in terms of white European male Dasein. Even though Heidegger opted in 1923 for the use of the neuter term *Dasein* (and even before that for the feminine noun *die Person,* the person) as opposed to the husky, masculine noun *der Mensch,* the human being, he often slipped back into the use of terms that have a gendered meaning or connotation—for example, his famous phrase *the shepherd/herdsman [der Hirt] of being* (n.b. not the shepherdess *[die Hirtin]* of being); and his later resuscitation of the phrase *das Wesen des Menschen.* Perhaps more serious is his burly philosophy of "hardness and severity" *[Härte und Schwere]* in the early 1930s; for example, he stated in "The Self-Assertion of the German University," his inaugural address as the National Socialist rector of the University of

Freiburg, that "young students, who at an early age have ventured into manhood *[Mannheit]* and who extend their willing to the future destiny of the nation, force themselves to serve this knowledge" and that "all faculties of will and thought, all strengths of the heart and all skills of the body must be unfolded *through* battle, heightened *in* battle, and preserved *as* battle." "We need a hard race/gender *[Geschlecht]*. . . . we fight heart to heart, man to man *[Mann bei Mann]*." In light of this, temporalizing-sense starts looking like a cosmic will issuing orders that are executed by a community of teutonic warrior-philosophers and the fourfold of content-sense like a nostalgic fatherland. Acting out this vision (enactment-sense) entails marginalizing the feminine Other.[20]

The Anthropocentric Configuration

The relational-sense of being always meant for Heidegger specifically *human* Dasein, because he believed that we are characterized by an "ontic priority," that is, we are the only being with an understanding of being (G2 sect. 4). Similar to the Christian theological view of the centrality of the human species *[imago Dei]* as the recipient of the revealed truth of God and as the custodian of creation, Heidegger's position is that we are the privileged site *[Da-sein,* there-being] of the truth of being and must take on the caring role of shepherds (who, by the way, usually eat the sheep). The so-called higher animals such as the family dog and anthropoids do not possess an understanding of being, of the sense of things. "I name the standing in the light of being the ek-sistence of human being. This way to be is proper only to human being." "Living beings are as they are without standing in the truth of being. . . . they are separated from our ek-sistent essence by an abyss." Thus the content-sense of the fourfold and the *Ereignis* of its temporalizing-sense mean the happening of earth and sky exclusively for human animals. Though involving the role of caretaker, the enactment-sense of this *Ereignis* suggests a marginalizing of the sentient Dasein of non-human Others, that is, a kind of friendly speciesism. Perhaps Heidegger was after all not antihumanistic enough![21]

The Authoritarian Configuration

Here the temporalizing-sense of being usually took the form of the claiming word *[Anspruch]* of *Ereignis* that addresses its truth to the author Martin Heidegger, who "corresponds" *[entspricht]* to this address. At times Heidegger wanted us to believe that in the entire tradition of

Western thought before him no one had raised "the question concerning being." The content-sense of being thus turns up as something inscribed primarily in the texts of his Collected Edition *[Gesamtausgabe]*, which, pushing the obvious religious analogy here to extremes, starts looking like a philosophical bible. Relational-sense shows up as the authority of Heidegger's self-interpretation of these texts that gets embodied in the Heidegger Inc. of official interpreters, literary executors, editors, and translators. Here authority means both the centrality of the *mens auctoris* and power. The acting out of the enactment-sense of this texts-authority-claiming word configuration has included such things as autobiographical distortion of Heidegger's youthful period and his involvement with National Socialism; the manipulation, suppression, and destruction of purportedly apocryphal manuscripts; the installment of his actual and his purported self-interpretations into the structure and contents of his "Last-Hand Edition" *[Ausgabe letzter Hand];* the emergence of a Heidegger-scholasticism with its doctrina and imprimatur of authorized interpretation, editing, and translating; and all in all the ideological intimidation of the hermeneutical Other, the heretic who has a different reading of Heidegger's texts.[22]

What makes these sketches so crude is that they are themselves abstractions from the corresponding countertendencies in Heidegger's later thought that radicalized his original question about the personal and an-archic physiognomy of the *Ereignis* of being.[23] Counter to the transcendental tendency of his *Being and Time* is his insistence on the radical "mineness" and historical facticity of being. Counter to his still later speculative, antihumanistic, and primitivist tendencies we find him insisting that there is no being without its enactment by human beings and that in some way being is supposed to make possible the *humanitas* of ethical life. And counter to his Hellenic, Germano-Nazi, Greco-Christian, gender-biased, anthropocentric, and authoritarian tendencies there is his insistence that *Ereignis* is an an-archic play of different and equally valid cultural epochs, sites, senses, and readings of being. Heidegger is an ambiguous mix of metaphysical apples and postmetaphysical oranges with which we are just going to have to live. If we want to get at the richness and greatness of the thought of this twentieth century father Parmenides, we need to deconstruct and demythologize his residual metaphysics and myths of ethnocentrism, religious world-view, gender-bias, anthropo-centrism, philosophical authoritarianism, speculation, antihumanism, and primitivism. "The philosopher," Heidegger himself said in 1924, "must dare to become a father-killer." To do this, that is, to loosen up Heidegger's dehistoricizing of *Ereignis* and his deliving of the "Dasein of personal life," we can use everything from Derridian deconstruction, radical hermeneutics, the later Heidegger himself, Levinas, the French poststructuralists, and neo-pragmatism to critical theory, hermeneutics, classical phenomenology, historical research, and whatever else works. Despite its own shortcomings,[24] we can also, as I have been suggesting, use the recently rediscovered writings of the young Heidegger. They alert us to what he always affirmed in his best moments; namely, that there is no being without personal being and that there really is no answer to the question concerning being. This is why I think we need to turn the young Heidegger's demythologizing loose on the later Heidegger's stories of being.

16

Sartre's First Two Ethics

THOMAS C. ANDERSON

Scholars generally are aware that Jean-Paul Sartre's thought evolved from an abstract individualistic conception of human reality, human freedom, and social relations to a more concrete and richer understanding of the human being, the power of circumstances, and the social-political character of human existence. Less well known is the parallel development of Sartre's ethical thought from an early abstract idealistic form, grounded in the ontology of *Being and Nothingness,* to a realistic materialistic ethics, which involved significant modifications of that early ontology. Of course, one could expect that different conceptions of human reality would give rise to different ethical theories by Sartre, because ethics for him was fundamentally humanistic; that is, he sought to develop a morality that was appropriate to the human condition; human reality provided the measure for human morality.[1]

Given the development of his thought, it is not surprising to find that, at the end of his life, Sartre stated that he had worked on a number of different moralities (three to be exact) over the years.[2] Until recently, however, little was known for certain about them because none of his writings devoted specifically to ethics were published in his lifetime. Fortunately, three years after his death, Sartre's adopted daughter published the only extant pages of his first ethics, written in the late 1940s, under the title *Cahiers pour une morale.* This is the ethics, or part of it, that Sartre promised at the end of *Being and Nothingness* and that was based on its ontology. More recently, thanks particularly to the efforts of Elizabeth Bowman and Robert Stone, the complete manuscript has surfaced of a lecture Sartre gave in 1964, in Rome, which contains valuable information about his second ethics. (Unfortunately, Sartre's third ethics, consisting of taped interviews, remains almost totally unavailable to this day.)

Using these materials, along with various works that Sartre himself saw published, this chapter will discuss his first two moralities and indicate the progress the second makes over the first. I will argue that the advances of the second ethics are due to the evolution of Sartre's thought from a very abstract, incomplete understanding of human reality and human freedom to a richer, more concrete one.

Sartre's First Ethics

In his first published work, Sartre divides all reality into two realms, that of spontaneous, nonsubstantial consciousness and that of inert, dense, nonconscious things. After a phenomenological analysis of consciousness and its object, he concludes "that there are only two types of existence, as thing in the world and as consciousness, is an ontological law."[3] This sharp division is repeated in his introduction to *Being and Nothingness* and maintained throughout that phenomenological ontology. Consciousness, or being-for-itself, is described as spontaneous activity, total emptiness, totally self-activated, and self-determined (i.e., totally free); all else, being-in-itself, is inert, passive, full positivity. From the perspective of a humanistic ethics, what is most significant is that throughout *Being and Nothingness* Sartre frequently identifies man, human reality, with being-for-itself, that is, with totally free, spontaneous consciousness. Sometimes in a particular discussion he will, without hesitation, refer indiscriminately to man, human reality, consciousness, being-for-itself, and freedom as if they were perfectly equivalent. On occasion he explicitly asserts such equivalence: "there is no difference between the being of man and his being free," he writes. And, after stating that "freedom is the being of consciousness" and that this means that being-for-itself is "an emptiness, a nothingness *[neant]* which is distinguished from the thing only by a pure negation," he asserts that I myself "am that nothingness." "This nothingness is human reality itself . . . this nothingness *is not* anything but human reality apprehending itself as excluded from being and perpetually beyond being."[4]

Now, of course, human reality is not literally nothing for Sartre. There are other passages in *Being and Nothingness* where he recognizes that it is both free, transcending consciousness and facticity, and even that consciousness itself exists in its body as its contingent facticity and dimension of being-in-itself. For example, he defines bad faith precisely as the refusal to accept *both* aspects of human reality. Nevertheless, I believe that Sartre's overall tendency in *Being and Nothingness* is to minimize severely the force and significance of the factical side of human existence while emphasizing, even exaggerating, the aspect of free consciousness. The extended discussion of the relation between human freedom and facticity that he undertakes in the last large section of the book, Part IV, amply supports this contention.

There, after repeating his usual argument that human reality is free because it detaches itself, negates, and transcends what-is in order to grasp goals that are not, he adds that its freedom "forces human reality to make itself instead of to be. . . . [Thus] *nothing* comes to it either from outside or from within . . . it is entirely abandoned to the intolerable necessity for making itself be—*down to the slightest detail*" (my emphasis). And he adds, "Man cannot be sometimes slave and sometimes free; he is wholly and forever free or he is not free at all."[5] He rejects any attempt to make a human being partly free and partly not simply by identifying *man* with spontaneous consciousness. He writes, "it is impossible for a determined process to act upon a spontaneity, exactly as it is impossible for a determined process to act on consciousness." Applying this to man he repeats, "either man is wholly determined (which is inadmissible because a determined consciousness . . . ceases to be consciousness) or else man is wholly free."[6]

But if human reality is wholly free, if it is what it makes of itself down to the slightest detail, what has become of human facticity, especially the body? Sometimes Sartre simply ignores it, as when he says "human reality is act" or is "wholly choice and act."[7] We are only by choosing ourselves, he asserts, and even our emotions and passions (including sexual passion) are freely chosen, just as are all our psychological characteristics (such as an inferiority complex).[8] Other times he does admit the reality of our facticity, for example, our biological and psychological makeup, our race, sex, past experience, habits, as well as our concrete situation in the world, including determinations that others impose on us. Yet in the final analysis, Sartre insists that our freedom always "nihilates," "negates," "denies," "escapes from," all these features insofar as it transcends them by grasping nonexistent goals, and this "is enough to assure its total independence in relation to the structures which it surpasses."[9] Furthermore, our transcendence, our free projects, and our free choices, even if they are not the sole source of the objects in our situation, are the unique source of *all* the meaning and value these things possess. Our freely chosen goals create the coefficient of adversity of things. Even if we encounter obstacles, "our freedom itself creates the obstacles from which we suffer," for "resistance and obstacles have meaning only in and through the free choice which human reality is."[10] Thus, Sartre concludes that each person's freedom is "absolute," "total," "infinite," "without limits."[11] "It follows," he says, that "there is no privileged situation . . . in which the for-itself would be *more free* than in others." Each situation offers "infinite possibilities of choice," and "choice is always unconditioned." Thus "the slave in chains is as free as his master."[12]

The ramifications of this view of human reality and freedom for ethics are made plain in numerous works written right after *Being and Nothingness* in which Sartre makes freedom the primary value of his (first) ethics. In the *Cahiers,* he states that the goal or end of his morality is "a reign of concrete freedom," a society where "freedom is valued and willed as such."[13] In *Existentialism and Humanism,* he says that our ultimate moral goal should be "the quest of freedom itself as such."[14] Because he identifies the human being with freedom, it makes perfect sense to propose it as our highest moral value. Obviously, such a goal is most consistent with the nature of human reality, and in fact, in *Existentialism and Humanism,* Sartre explicitly appeals to consistency in order to support his choice of freedom as the primary moral end. His argument rests on his ontological position that human freedom is the sole source of meaning and value in the universe. Because human beings alone, through their freedom, can supply meaning and justification for their existence, "strict consistency" requires that they choose freedom as their primary value. For if we do confer value on our freedom and then choose to value our existence, our lives will thereby possess meaning and be justified, Sartre says. Persons who reflectively choose to accept and to value their freedom as the source of all values are called *authentic.*[15]

Thus Sartre's first ethics, an ethics of freedom (or authenticity), appears perfectly consistent with his early ontology. Precisely this consistency, however, caused him to become dissatisfied with it and finally to give it up and attempt a second ethics. One problem with the first ethics is that Sartre's very appeal to consistency is itself unjustified. His argument for choosing freedom as man's supreme moral value seems to presuppose that there is some inherent value in being consistent with human reality. Yet in his early ontology, as we have noted, things have value only if one freely chooses them to be of value. Nothing, not consistency nor authenticity, has any intrinsic or objective value. Another problem, as Sartre himself admitted later, is that this early ethics is terribly abstract or idealistic insofar as it rests on an extremely one-sided understanding of human reality and its situation in the world. To identify the human being with freedom and choice; to claim that all conscious acts are totally spontaneous or free; to assert that human freedom is absolute, unlimited, and the sole source of all meaning and value; to maintain that all situations are equivalent in their freedom, that "the slave in chains is as free as his master," shows, even by the most sympathetic reading, a grossly exaggerated and incomplete understanding of human being and its relation to the world.

Such notations could, in fact, result in a quietistic or Stoical ethics. If human freedom is unlimited, absolute, and total inasmuch as we consciously negate and transcend every given situation; if, therefore, all situations are equivalent in freedom; if we always have infinite possibilities of choice, then there is no need to attempt to change the concrete conditions in which humans live, no matter how oppressive they may appear to be. Note, however, that this freedom is the freedom of consciousness, of being-for-itself, not of a flesh and blood human organism in the world. Similarly, if a human being's freely chosen project alone is responsible for the coefficient of adversity of things, then if one wishes to make things less adverse, one should simply change one's project. For example, if my poverty is an obstacle to my living the life-style of the rich and famous, all I need to do is to choose to live an ascetic life and my poverty will cease to be an obstacle to me. No need to attempt the more difficult, and perhaps unsuccessful, task of removing my poverty. "Conquer yourself, rather than the world," the Stoics advised.[16] Here again *self* refers only to one's consciousness, not to one's material being entangled with and subject to others and the physical world.

Recall that, in his early ontology, even human relations are described by Sartre primarily as relations between consciousnesses. It is not concrete social-political relationships between human organisms that he discusses in *Being and Nothingness*. Instead, he analyzes in detail psychological relations (love, indifference, hatred, etc.) between free consciousnesses who react in various ways to being objectified, and thus alienated and degraded, by other consciousnesses. The solution to such alienation is also psychological rather than social-political. A consciousness needs to objectify the other consciousness so that it is not objectified by it.[17] Indeed, in this early ethics, authenticity itself often seems to be primarily a matter of an individual's conscious choice to accept his or her freedom and situation whatever it is. It does not in and of itself involve changing social-political structures.[18]

I hasten to add that I do not mean to imply that Sartre himself, even at this early stage, would be completely comfortable with the kind of passive, Stoical, individualistic ethics that I have just outlined. Nevertheless, I believe that his exaggerated conception of human freedom, his overly abstract understanding of human reality, and his minimization of the power of circumstances lead in that direction. In addition, it remains extremely vague just what it could mean *concretely* to choose freedom as one's moral goal, because in Sartre's early ontology human beings are totally free in the first place.

Sartre makes a move in the right direction just a few years after the publication of *Being and Nothingness* when he broadens his notion of authenticity to include others. In *Existentialism and Humanism* he states that the authentic person "is obliged to will the freedom of others at the same time as his own."[19] The *Cahiers* also state that the authentic individual exercises authentic love by generously assisting others in accomplishing their freely chosen projects. Also, in the *Cahiers* and in other works of this period, Sartre proposes the city of ends, the reign of freedom for *all,* as his moral ideal. Because I have elsewhere analyzed Sartre's arguments in detail,[20] I will only briefly indicate here why he claims in his early ethics that we should will the freedom of others as well as our own. His strongest argument rests on the political and psychological interdependency of human freedoms. Politically, each of us needs others if we are to enhance effectively our freedom; psychologically, each of us wants others to value freely and positively his or her freedom. The best way for us to obtain the free affirmation and support we desire from others is for us to value their freedom and to assist them in achieving their freely chosen goals.

This is a solid argument, I believe, but it remains very abstract. What does it mean concretely to say one should value and assist the freedom of others, especially if according to *Being and Nothingness* human freedom is so total and absolute that no situation involves any more or less freedom than any other? Actually, by the time of the *Cahiers,* Sartre had come to recognize that one's situation does condition one's freedom by limiting or enhancing the number of possibilities available for choice. People in oppressive or impoverished circumstances have fewer opportunities and possibilities, and thus less freedom, than those in more favorable situations. Yet even this admission leaves it unclear just which possibilities the authentic person should try to provide to others and which he or she should not. Surely Sartre does not mean that the authentic individual should generously support every freely chosen project of every person, no matter what it may be. But no details are offered; and so, the ideal of his first ethics, freedom for all, remains vague.[21] To say this is simply to repeat Sartre's own later criticism, for he eventually labeled his early morality an *irreal idealism.*[22]

Sartre's Second Ethics

Sartre's second morality, begun in the 1960s and called *materialistic* and *realistic,* can be viewed as an attempt to remedy the abstract, formal character of the first. The Sartre of the 1960s and 1970s has a far richer understanding of human reality and human relations, as well as a more concrete grasp of their immersion in history, and his morality reflects this. Human beings are no longer identified with spontaneous consciousness or freedom; human facticity and the power of the situation are given their due. In the *Critique of Dialectical Reason,* the human being is defined as a material organism, a synthetic unity of the same molecules that make up all physical things. Of course, humans are conscious organisms, but consciousness itself is not defined as a purely spontaneous nonsubstantial being (or nonbeing) radically different from matter (or inert being). Rather, man is "wholly matter,"[23] Sartre insists, even though humans are the kind of organisms that are able to transcend and to organize (totalize) every situation into a unity in terms of their chosen goals. Because we are material bodies, we can act on other bodies to achieve our goals, but we are also subject to physical forces like other material things, and this passive dimension of our being is not totally under the control of our freedom. Although Sartre still holds that as project (or praxis) a human is free, insofar as he or she transcends every situation, he now acknowledges that this freedom is limited, sometimes severely, by the body.[24] Also, like every physical organism, human beings have needs that must be satisfied if they are to live and prosper; it is these needs, not human choices, that are the ultimate source of all human praxis, that is, of all actions on the physical and social environment.[25]

For the Sartre of the *Critique,* the relation of the human organism to the environment on which it acts, and thus of freedom to its situation, can be summed up in one word: dialectical. That is, human praxis acts upon and structures the world that, in turn, acts upon and structures human existence. Humans act on matter, worked matter reacts on them; human beings create a social environment that then conditions the humans within it.[26] Sartre contrasts this dialectical approach, which recognizes the power of circumstances to shape one's very being, with an analytic one, which views human nature as integral in itself and as intrinsically unaffected by historical circumstances.[27] Even our free projects, Sartre now concedes, do not totally negate or escape from the given situation, as *Being and Nothingness* claimed. They are always conditioned or "colored" by it for the very goals that one can realistically seek are delineated by the given situation.[28] Certain environments, he now admits, allow little or no freedom to those within them. Therefore in the *Critique* Sartre writes: "it is very important not to conclude that one can be free in chains," and in another passage, "It would be quite wrong to interpret me as saying that man is free in all situations, as the Stoics claimed."[29] Such statements seem deliberately worded to reject positions adopted in *Being and Nothingness.*

Sartre's second ethics is realistic, then, insofar as it embodies his realization of the many concrete factors that condition and limit human freedom, factors that must be confronted by specific moral choices and actions in the socio-political arena if freedom for all is to be achieved to any extent in human history. In his 1964 Rome lecture, for example, he is highly critical of what he calls the alienated morality of "private life." This is the view that one can be free and moral abstractly, "without passing through history," and without overthrowing oppressive systems.[30] Another mark of its realism is that the second ethics is based not on an abstract phenomenological investigation of human consciousness and its objects, but on a phenomenological analysis of the concrete moral experience of human beings dialectically related to each other and to the physical world.[31] Let us follow Sartre's analysis in his Rome lecture.

When we investigate concrete moral experience, namely, the experience of moral norms, values, and obligations, we find, Sartre says, a paradox. On the one hand, all existing moralities and moral norms are, like every human product, dialectically conditioned by the particular social systems in which they exist. On the other hand, every existing morality also has an unconditioned character, for every morality proposes norms that are to be followed no matter what the situation. Another feature of this paradox is that although all existing moralities and their norms are alienated by the social-political systems in which they are embodied, true morality and its norms is present in all of these alienated ones as their real foundation. In fact, alienated moralities and their imperatives and values are only the limitations and perversions of true morality and its pure norms, he claims.[32] Explicating this paradox will enable us to grasp the core of Sartre's second ethics.

The conditioned, alienated character of existing moralities, according to Sartre, comes from the fact that the particular imperatives and values of a given moral system are maintained by the socially dominant class in its self-interest. As a result, the concrete moral norms of that society involve the obligation to maintain the status quo with its hierarchies of power and its identification of humanity with those humans who have power. Nevertheless, true or unalienated morality is present in these alienated moralities inasmuch as all their values, imperatives, and norms, no matter how alienated their content, have a common "ontological structure," namely, their specific normative character. All moral experience, Sartre points out, is an experience of something unconditionally having-to-be-done, of "a future which *must* be created" *no matter what the circumstances.*[33] To experience this normative feature, then, is to experience that which is common to all moral systems and thus that which transcends the particular content of all particular systems. Every moral norm, Sartre argues, no matter what its specific content, insofar as it obliges us unconditionally, calls us to an unconditional future, "beyond all systems."[34] This pure future that we have-to-be is human reality's ultimate norm and end, Sartre claims, and he identifies it as "integral humanity," "human plenitude," and "man as an organism fully alive."[35] This identification is accomplished by means of his notion of needs, for "The root of morality is *in need*."[36]

Needs are not blind forces propelling us from behind, nor are they simply a lack of some object. They are felt exigencies, Sartre says, felt demands for their satisfaction. Needs transcend or surpass every situation toward their future fulfillment. As felt exigencies that demand to be satisfied no matter what the situation, needs are the source of the unconditional character of all moral norms. In other words, Sartre believes that the moral norms found in ordinary human experience have an unconditional character because these norms are rooted in human needs that demand satisfaction in every situation in which human beings exist. However variable its particular content, every morality has an unconditional normative character, according to Sartre, not because it is absolute or superhuman, nor because it is purely formal, but because it is concretely rooted in human beings who are present in all kinds of conditions in different societies. Human organisms share the universal human condition as members of the same species with generally the same basic needs.[37] Thus, no matter how different their historical situations, human beings have in common the ultimate moral norm and goal to fulfill these needs and so become fully human. This explains why Sartre maintains that true or pure morality is the basis of, and present in, all alienated moralities. Because all praxes, including the production of morality, issue from human needs, and human needs are, at bottom, demands for human fulfillment, it is plausible to claim that the alienated moralities and norms found in oppressive systems are just limited, truncated versions of that radical morality that has true integral humanity or human plenitude as its ultimate norm and goal.

This primary moral goal or norm of Sartre's realistic morality is much richer in content than the goal of his first ethics. We noted earlier how vague and abstract that goal of freedom is. Whereas integral humanity includes freedom or autonomy as its most important element, the human organism has more needs than just the need for freedom. Sartre also mentions very physical needs, for example, for protein and oxygen, and refers to human needs for other people, equality and fraternity, as well as, in general, our need for culture. All of these needs must be fulfilled if we are to become fully human.[38]

Sartre's two moralities also differ radically in what each one identifies as the source of moral values or norms. In the first ethics, human freedom was said to be the source of all values; in the second, human needs. This difference is significant for it means that in his realistic ethics Sartre believes, to some extent, that moral norms are "given," "assigned," even "imposed," on human beings rather than being the creation of free choice. Because humans are a specific kind of organism with specific needs, certain kinds of objects are necessary for them to fulfill these needs. Inasmuch as human beings do not freely choose their needs, they do not freely choose the general kind of thing that fulfills these needs.[39] Those kinds of things that would fulfill our human needs are precisely what we experience as *having-to-be-attained,* and therefore, as norms and values. Integral humanity itself is our ultimate moral norm, according to Sartre, not because we freely decide that it is but because it is given as the fulfillment of our needs. This end, he says "is *imposed* on each as his sole possible end, unsurpassable, and the real meaning of all his ends."[40]

Another significant difference between the two moralities lies in the justification each one offers to support its primary moral goal. In his first ethics, Sartre argued that freedom should be chosen as man's ultimate value because such a choice was most consistent with the human condition. Because nothing had any inherent value in Sartre's early ontology, however, there was no objective moral norm obliging one to choose to be consistent in the first place. The choice to value or not to value consistency was itself, in the final analysis, arbitrary and, in principle, unjustifiable.

As for the goal of the second ethics, integral humanity or human plenitude, Sartre states that, strictly speaking, it needs no justification, for "need dispenses with all justification."[41] Yet this goal is not arbitrary. It is not as if we are free to decide what our ultimate end or norm is, and so have to find reasons justifying this or that choice. Rather, our ultimate end is already decided by our ontological structure as practical organisms whose every act and goal is rooted in its needs and seeks their fulfillment. No reason has to be given to justify our seeking human fulfillment, for, like it or not, our needs demand it and all of our praxis is born of this exigency. Sartre calls integral humanity the "unsurpassable" goal of all human praxis. I understand this to mean that no other goal is more fundamental to human existence and, therefore, that there is no more basic norm or value to which one has to appeal to justify seeking it. Of course, we are free as regards the ways we choose to seek human fulfillment; we may even choose self-destruction. Nevertheless, integral humanity remains the primary goal of the needy human organism that we are.

A final difference between Sartre's first two moralities has to do with their social dimension, specifically the importance of, and the obligation to, others. On the one hand, the first ethics does offer a succinct argument, based on the interdependency of human beings, for one's obligation to will the freedom of others (see earlier, page 232). Neither in the Rome lecture nor in any other work of that period does Sartre explicitly formulate a comparable argument to demonstrate that we should seek the human fulfillment of others as well as our own. On the other hand, works pertaining to the second ethics offer far more detail about our need for others than do works of the first ethics. In the Rome lecture and elsewhere, for example, Sartre frequently describes the need for all humans to unite in order to control effectively the products and structures they create so that they can use them for the satisfaction of their needs.[42] Also, in his mammouth study of Flaubert, Sartre provides an extensive analysis of our radical dependency on others for self-knowledge and self-love. He maintains that, for human beings to love themselves and even to love life itself, they must be loved by others, especially by their parents. Sartre also shows that one's own self-knowledge, including one's awareness that one is free, is thoroughly dependent on one's relations with others.[43] Thus, although he does not explicitly formulate an argument obliging one to promote the well being of others, Sartre presents in detail his view that the fulfillment that all human beings seek demands their being acknowledged, respected, known, and loved by others. If this is correct, it would seem reasonable to argue that, for their fulfillment, human beings should love, respect, and, in general, promote the well being of all. Certainly, Sartre himself made it clear that this was the kind of humanism that animated his own life and work.

17 Cognition and Morality: Lyotard on Addressors, Addressees, and Ethics

BRIAN CATERINO

The recent writings of Jean-François Lyotard have been concerned with the formulation of a postmodern approach to ethics and politics. Central to the project of redefining morality are two aims: (1) to establish the limits of theoretical reason in relation to practical life, and (2) to reject the model of the autonomous subject as the bearer of a moral-practical reason based on free will. I want to consider these aims as an attempt to redefine the relation of theory to practical life. In place of this model, which in his view characterizes philosophical discourse in modernity, Lyotard wants to substitute a model based on the pragmatics of language that dethrones the autonomous subject and deflates the pretensions of philosophy in order to find a secure foundation for practical life.

Lyotard rejects what he sees as the traditional conception of theory. The traditional conception of *theoria,* according to Lyotard, presents the relation of theory to practical life as one in which practice is molded from above and subsumed by theory. Theory presents a uniform rule under which all practice can be uniformly subordinated. In Lyotard's view this is both illegitimate and politically calamitous. Theory usurps the practical task of creating a political community: it employs an ideal of cognitive validity that is inappropriate to the objects of practical life. In doing so theory inaugurates a project of domination that culminates in political totalitarianism. Against the speculative attempt to discover a theoretical discourse that unifies all others from above, Lyotard finds fundamental differences between discourses. He wants to redraw the boundaries of cognitive reason and give back to practical life its autonomy from theoretical imperialism. This is not simply a philosophical project. Lyotard aims to open up the space for an autonomous practice that is the basis for a genuine politics.

In undertaking this critique, Lyotard seeks to recover a notion of practical judgment first formulated by Aristotle. He accepts Aristotle's dictum that the objects of practical reason are not identical to those of theory. Wise judgment or *phronesis* judges particulars without reference to or subsumption under universals. It requires the experience of a participant who can judge each situation on the basis of its requirements, rather than the gaze of the theorist who applies a universal rule or timeless principle to evaluate actions. Lyotard, however, does not advocate a recovery of ancient traditions. He wants to reclaim this capacity by detecting its hidden traces in the archetypical philosopher of modernity: Kant. Lyotard accepts the Kantian notion of the Ideas and with it a conception of morality rooted in the Idea of freedom.

To provide a conception of judgment that is compatible with Kantian Ideas, Lyotard looks to the discussion of judgment formulated in the Third Critique. The philosopher is not a judge who applies a determinate ruler under which particulars stand. He or she is looking to find the rule that applies to or makes sense of a domain of thought. In Lyotard's words, "philosophical discourse obeys a fundamental rule, namely that it must be in search of its rule. Or, if you prefer: its rule is that what is at stake is its rule."[1] Philosophy discovers its discourse in order to "find out how it has the right to take place."[2] It judges without having present already existing criteria. This is Lyotard's interpretation of Kant's notion of critical reflection.

Lyotard also interprets the Kantian separation of the spheres of reason as being sympathetic to his postmodern project. The universes of cognitive, moral, and aesthetic discourse are not part of a unified totality rooted in speculative reason. They are heterogenous: the rules of one discourse are incompatible with another. This implies a second function of judgment. The task of political judgment is the communication between the universes of discourse. It has no object, but rather it has a field, the space in which the universes exist. The object of political judgment does not exist; like aesthetic judgment, it can be understood only analogically.

Although Lyotard endorses the Aristotelian separation of judgment from theory, his use of Kant requires a significant modification of Aristotle's notion of practice as exemplified in Aristotle's interpretation of the *sensus communis*. Aristotelians interpret the *sensus communis* as a form of ethical cognitivism. It is that fund of good judgments that can be explicitly stated and taught and that members of a community can draw upon and agree with. Although Aristotle considered these judgments to be consigned to a realm of practical reason differentiated from *theoria* because of the epistemic imperfection of the object, Lyotard holds that it is a form of knowledge just the same: a set of judgments that can be validated through experience and agreed upon by members of a community. Ethical-political judgment still has a cognitive object. It remains an attempt to interpret the community in a way the philosopher can comprehend and subsume.[3]

In contrast, Lyotard views the political *sensus communis* as a modality of the sublime. The enthusiasm that spectators feel for the French revolution is an example of this feeling. This *sensus communis,* however, is not a cognitive object, but a feeling that can be shared. Whereas for the aesthetic *sensus communis* the object is not sublime, for the political community the feeling is sublime. It results from the paradoxical attempt of the imagination to produce a presentation of an Idea of reason. The vocation of the imagination is to provide such a presentation, but it must always fall short of its task. The unpresentable can never be presented.

Although a good deal of attention has been paid to Lyotard's reading of Kant's Third Critique, less attention has been paid to his discussion of ethics and to his reading of the Second Critique. Here too, however, the question of the unpresentability of the object of morality plays a crucial role. I want to focus in this chapter on the way in which Lyotard develops the unpresentable nature of moral objects into a conception of morality that stresses the dissymmetry of participants and observers, a dissymmetry rooted in the incommensurability of cognition and obligation. Moral obligation differs from political judgment because it can never be put in the context of a finality or aim. It presents most clearly the dilemma Lyotard sees in representing the sublime feeling of awe and respect in the domain of the cognitive.

I agree with Lyotard's attempt to separate the cognitive and the moral and his attempt to rein in the pretensions of theory, however, I will argue in this chapter that his attempt to interpret moral life in terms of the impossibility of making moral judgment explicit is flawed. Through a critical reading of Lyotard's view of morality, I will develop the position that the realm of morality has an autonomous "rationality" in which we can make judgments about the rightness of moral norms. This rationality is rooted in the intersubjectivity of participants in social life. This perspective provides an alternative way of interpreting the preunderstanding that Lyotard cites in his notion of the political *sensus communis.* According to the interpretation that I want to advance, the *sensus communis* would have to be that group of preunderstandings that participants in a social world have. Although these can never be made explicit as a whole, moral judgments can be made explicit and can be critically assessed.

From Traditional Philosophy to a Pragmatics of Language

The dominant philosophical tradition from Plato to Marx has, in Lyotard's view, followed a consistent argumentative strategy. It has built a theory of justice on the basis of a theory of true being. The discovery of a pattern in reality by the theorist provides the basic model for structuring practical life. The theorist's authority derives from his or her privileged insight into what is.[4] The disinterest and supposed neutrality of the theorist is, however, an illusion. It masks a will to domination that is inherent in the totalizing extension of theoretical reason to the domain of the nontheoretical.

In his earlier work, Lyotard attempted to construct a critique of theoretical reason on the basis of positions drawn from Nietzsche and Freud. There he undermined the priority of consciousness from the standpoint of the unconscious.[5] This strategy proved unsatisfactory. Lyotard's own rejection of this anarchic stance was based on his encounter with the ineliminable character of the ethical.[6] The transition in Lyotard's work from Nietzsche to Kant required the rejection of a conception of ethics and politics derived from the intensities of a will to power. In that conception, reason and justice are simply effects of intensities of desire, but Lyotard is now willing to grant them an independent, if bounded, status. Lyotard tries to retrace the path of Kantian critical philosophy by defining the limits and boundaries of different genres of discourse, without, he hopes, re-creating the dilemmas of the philosophy of the subject that is part and parcel of a philosophical project of domination. Lyotard believes that he can overcome the subjectivism of modern philosophy through a movement from traditional ontology to a philosophy of language.

Lyotard thus looks to a pragmatics of language to do the work of traditional philosophy. In the philosophy of the subject, the force of communication lies in the will of the subject, that is, in its communicative intent. Subjective thought looks to the sincerity or insincerity of an utterance or to a consensus of wills. In contrast, Lyotard centers communicative force in the pragmatic organization of language, that is, in the specific uses of language that position addressors and addressees in universes of discourse. This pragmatic organization makes communication possible.

The transposition of philosophy into a pragmatics of language undermines the claims of traditional theory to a notion of truth or a conception of justice based on a correspondence or adequation with an external standard of being. Instead, the language-theoretical approach stresses the world-disclosing character of language. Language discloses and constitutes a world because only through the medium of language are addressors and addressees situated in a universe of discourse. Language as medium cannot be conceived of as the product of an independent subject or consciousness. Not simply a channel for messages or codes from independently existing subjects, language opens up modes of existence or ways of life. But the event-character of the world is opened up in incommensurable ways by different regimes of phrases such as descriptives, prescriptives, and narratives. These are distinct modes of disclosing events that cannot be unified in an overall discourse, such as the one proposed in the model of speculative discourse.

In *The Post-Modern Condition,* Lyotard develops his perspective through a theory of language games derived from Wittgenstein. In *The Differend,* however, this conception is modified, perhaps because the notion of a language game is considered too intentionalisitic.[7] In *The Differend,* Lyotard takes a structural, not a structuralist, approach that makes its basic unit the phrase or sentence. Each type of sentence presents a "universe" that consists of four basic poles, the addressor or sender, the addressee or recipient, the sense or meaning, and the referent:

> It should be said that the addressor and addressee are instances, either marked or unmarked, presented by a phrase. The latter is not a message passing from an addressor to an addressee both of whom are independent of it. . . . They are situated in the universe the phrase presents, as are its referent and sense . . . a phrase presents what it is about, the case, *ta pragmata,* which is its referent; what is signified about the case, the sense, *der Sinn;* that to which or addressed to which this is signified about the case, the addressee; that "through" which or in the name of which this is signified about the case, the addressor. The disposition of a phrase universe consists in the situating of these instances in relation to each other.[8]

The universes of sentences are regimes that can be organized as genres. Although a regime of sentences consists of an organization of the four poles just given, genres are ways of linking these heterogenous sentence regimes under a single aim or finality. Examples of genres would include science, philosophy, or tragedy.

Lyotard's attempt to resituate the questions of truth and justice within the framework of a pragmatics of language requires a closer examination than I can provide here. I want to point out, however, one problem in his position to which I will return later. In attempting to overcome the philosophy of the subject, Lyotard overemphasizes the world-disclosing character of language, while deemphasizing the necessity and the ability of participants to sustain and re-create meaning through their interaction. It may be true that language situates us, but we still are not simply passive recipients of it. Language is the medium of our interpretations. It requires an ongoing interpretive performance of members to be a language at all.

Obligation and Cognition: Prescription and Description

In his essay, "Levinas' Logic," Lyotard presents what is at stake in his analysis of the ethical: "The pragmatic reason for hating the neutral is that its assumption implies that the philosopher, the addressee of the message from the unnameable, comes and places himself in the position of the addresser, in order to proffer his commentary from the same place as the assumed first addresser, the unnameable itself. In this replacement, ethics necessarily dissolves."[9]

Central to Lyotard's project is the rejection of any attempt to use a neutral third person perspective to build a theory of ethics or justice. The recourse to a third person perspective confounds cognitive and ethical discourse. It implies taking the position of an expert toward the ethical. Obligations, however, cannot be an object of knowledge in the same way that statements about the world can be. The meaning of an obligation cannot be made the subject of an authoritative agreement. In showing this type of consensus to be impossible, Lyotard argues that ethical cognitivism is mistaken in its pursuit of certainty.

Lyotard attempts to demonstrate this point through the reinterpretation of arguments drawn from Levinas and Kant into the linguistic framework that was developed in *The Differend*. He must first of all distinguish between two types of sentence regimes: descriptives and prescriptives.

Descriptive sentences assume a symmetrical relation between addressors and addressees. Because they are concerned with the truth of a description, subjects in cognitive discourse can address each other with arguments about the truth of statements made in descriptions. Each participant is capable of answering the claims of others with arguments aimed at establishing what is the case about some event, object, or state of affairs. In this discourse, participants take the role of observers or neutral arbiters. They take a reasoned yes or no position on the claims put forward by others and decide what is rationally warranted by the evidence presented.

The symmetry that holds for cognitive discourse does not hold for the realm of ethics. The relationship between addressor and addressee no longer takes a symmetrical form. A prescriptive phrase or sentence does not present, in the manner of descriptions, a world of facts or states of affairs. Rather it is literally an imperative or an incitement to act. For Lyotard, the paradigmatic case of an obligation is the order given by God to Abraham to sacrifice his son. Abraham obeys because he believes that he is obligated to obey God's commands, whether he understands them or not. In Levinas's interpretation, which Lyotard is following here, we are compelled to do before understanding. The ethical obligation is a request or a command that takes the form of the imperative "do X." This imperative is addressed to us from an external perspective. It calls for a response, to obey or disobey, that we cannot fully understand or justify.

Lyotard contends that any attempt to justify or to legitimate our obligations from inside the ethical is impossible for two reasons: (1) each attempt to justify an obligation is caught up in a performative contradiction, and (2) the object of an obligation is indeterminate; its meaning cannot be fixed by any discursive process. I want to consider these points in turn.

The addressee who attempts to justify a particular obligation must relinquish the position of a participant to whom a request to act is addressed and must instead take the standpoint of an observer who is a commentator on this obligation. In taking up the position of the commentator, however, that participant steps out of the framework within which obligations have meaning, that is, the regime of prescriptive phrases, and must employ descriptive phrases. Therefore Lyotard asserts: "A phrase is obligatory if its addressee is obligated. Why he or she is obligated is something he or she can perhaps think to explain. In any case, the explanation requires further phrases, in which he or she is no longer situated as the addressee, but as the addressor, and whose stakes are no longer those of obeying, but those of convincing a third party of the reasons one has for obeying."[10] The speaker in a commentary has to perform a contradictory role. If one gives a commentary, an account or a justification, one cannot understand the obligation; if one is obliged, then one cannot understand.[11] There is an incommensurability between obligation and cognition. In cognitive discourse, the addressor and the addressee are both named and are both specific individuals. In the ethical genre, the other can have no name. The moral law is anonymous. No named addressor (you or I, the philosopher, the experts, the state) can ever claim the authority of the law without violating the conditions of ethics as such.

Lyotard also claims that the object of obligation is not a cognitive object. He draws on arguments from both Kant and Levinas to support this claim. From Kant, Lyotard draws the argument that distinct relationships of objects in the world to transcendental frameworks exist in cognition and obligation. Translated into Lyotard's linguistic framework this is the relation of object language to metalanguage.

In the *Critique of Pure Reason*, the relation between the objects of experience and the transcendental categories is isomorphic. The properties of objects in the world are subsumable under the categories of time, space, and causality, and objects can be identified through appeal to evidence. This is not the case for the world of practical reason as it is analyzed in the Second Critique. The moral freedom that is presupposed as the basis of our obligation has no empirical correlate. It is not in space and time as are physical objects. Events in the empirical world are implicated in causal chains. The effects of one set of causes are part of the set of causes that produces further effects. Moral freedom, in contrast, presupposes autonomy, the ability to determine one's own will.

Lyotard draws three implications from this analysis. First of all, Kant's position entails that the relation between categories of pure practical reason and the empirical world are reversed. Whereas the categories of pure reason stand at the conclusion of a deduction that is intended to establish their existence, the categories of pure practical reason have to be supposed at the beginning. But this means that the categories of pure practical reason do not subsume the objects in the moral world in the manner of the categories of pure reason. No one can prove or confirm moral obligation by a third person observation. Rather, moral freedom is to be discerned in action, as what is always already there.

Second, the object of morality is not an object of theoretical knowledge, nor is it an empirical event. But here Lyotard argues against Kant and claims that morality cannot be explicated in determinate rule. When Kant attempts to take up the principle of universalization as the primary moral norm, he falls prey to the illusion that we can transcribe prescription onto description. According to Lyotard, all normative phrases are descriptives; they neutralize the executive force of imperatives. Ethical obligations have no consensually agreed upon meanings.

Finally, Lyotard claims that prescriptive sentences, although they create a universe of discourse, do not implicate a world. The ethical obligation is, as Kant noted, not concerned with the consequences of action. An obligation is not addressed to past events or to future consequences. It measures each moment according to a demand to obey unconditionally. Thus in the biblical parable of Hagar, who gives her dying son a drink, the angels ask whether God should allow Hagar to give water to Ishmael who will later cause Israel great harm. The angels take the Hegelian view of the end of history, of a future development. Hence Hagar should not give Ishmael a drink.[12] But God judges each person by his or her present state, not by what that person will become. Ethics has no necessary connection with a philosophy of history; to imply otherwise is to interpret ethics through the discourse of speculative reason. Following Hegel, it measures everything by the *Resultat,* that is, by a claim of finality that claims to know the course of history.

Obligation and the Question of Otherness: Autonomy and Heteronomy

For all his sympathy with Kant's project, Lyotard must ultimately reject Kant's conception of a transcendental subject. He cannot accept the notion of moral autonomy that lies at the heart of Kant's thought. As an alternative, Lyotard reformulates insights from Emmanuel Levinas's ethics in his own linguistic framework to provide a notion of the otherness of obligation that is lacking in Kant. Levinas employs the notion of otherness to avoid what he sees as the pitfalls of identity theory inherent in the philosophy of the subject (most notably in Husserl's phenomenology). He also rejects the model of intersubjectivity based on the I-Thou model found in Buber, as well as the speculative philosophy of Hegel.[13]

Levinas criticizes both transcendental philosophy and the I-Thou relationship because both are based on the model of assimilation. The transcendental philosopher employs a notion of essence that claims to capture all that is under concepts. Transcendental philosophy holds that every object of thought can be established through adequate evidence. It assimilates the infinite to the finite. Hence it neglects the problem of *transcendence*. The I-Thou relationship, in a similar fashion, assimilates the other to the familiar, to someone who is like myself. In contrast, Levinas claims that the other signifies that which escapes assimilation. It exceeds the grasp of a speculative totality and the egocentrism of the self. I will not pursue Levinas's critique of the philosophy of identity here. Instead, I want to focus on his analysis of the role of otherness in intersubjectivity.

Consistent with the model of assimilation, Levinas considers the ego to be caught up in a web of narcissistic relationships with the world. Originally, the ego sees the world as nourishment. It does not view the world instrumentally as a means to an end or as an object of manipulation (as Levinas thinks that Heidegger does). Instead Levinas focuses on the pleasure involved in living in a world that is a context for enjoyment. Levinas describes this condition as a state of at-homeness, a sense of familiarity with the world. But this familiarity with the world is, for Levinas, the rule of the same or identity. Even when we experience our own separation, Levinas argues, we experience it in a context of the same, the familiar, and the assimilable. Our intersubjective relations do not break with this principle. Levinas interprets the I-Thou relationship along the model of intimate relationships. The I-Thou relationship is feminine: it takes the other to be one like myself, one for whom I care. Thus they stay within the orbit of familiarity.

According to Levinas, the encounter with the other introduces an I-you relationship rather than an I-thou relationship. The *you* in this relationship, however, comes from without. It fractures the interiority of the ego with a demand that it step beyond its egocentric framework to encounter something absolutely different: the alien. The call from without is the request of the suffering other, the poor, or the victims of injustice and exploitation. In Lyotard's interpretation of Levinas's position, this means that the victim is defined by his or her inability to make a claim within an established moral discourse.[14] He or she can only cry for help. The other calls on us to act, to help the poor or the exploited without the assurance of reciprocity—the violated may not wish to reciprocate. Otherness is manifest in the face-to-face encounter. "The face is present in its refusal to be contained. In this sense it cannot be comprehended, that is, encompassed. It is neither seen nor touched—for in visual or tactile sensation the identity of the I envelops the alterity of the object, which becomes precisely a content."[15]

The face-to-face encounter presents a sign of the infinite that can never be fully present and that is never affirmed by evidence. It transports the individual beyond his or her at-homeness and toward a true vocation: to leave home in order to encounter the infinite. Levinas conceives of the encounter with the other in terms of the stranger or the alien. It is this encounter with the unfamiliar that provokes us to recognize our ethical destiny. For in the encounter with the stranger, we cannot rely on bonds of social solidarity gained through mutual interest or recognition of any sort. We are forced to consider obligation without reference to our attachments or to the conditions of our existence. Levinas's notion of the unconditioned is not based on the model of neutrality or impersonality. It is an originary mode of Being that we have to encounter or that is provided to us. This mode of Being is the manner of disclosure of the ethical to the participant. As Lyotard notes, however, this position is not to be equated with the one held by Heidegger. In addition to Levinas's aforementioned preference for homelessness, his notion of obligation does not claim that Being needs humanity. Rather, humanity and the Other are simply given as the conditions of the ethical.[16]

Using Levinas's discussion of the alterity of the ethical as a background, we can clarify the reasons why Lyotard rejects the Kantian principle of universalization. Lyotard wants to separate the normative from the obligatory. According to Lyotard, the normative phrase, "Someone says 'N is a valid norm' when linked with the obligatory phrase 'do X' to make the phrase 'Someone says "N is a valid norm" therefore "do X" ', " introduces a descriptive phrase into an ethical discourse. It also, however, ignores the alterity of the ethical, concealing its genuine principle. The normative phrase that obliges everyone to do *X*, introduces the rule of the same. It reduces all participants to observers who legislate for others.

> If the maxim of your will ought to be able to set up as "a universal law of nature," to constitute "a universal legislation," it is apparently because the dyssmetry between *I* and *you* ought to be disregarded for the benefit of some universal, "humanity," the we of exchangeable I's and you's. . . . They are thus exchangeable not only upon the instance of the obligated one, the you of *You ought to,* in order to form a community of hostages, but also upon the instance of a legislator, the I of the *I am able to,* in order to form a community of constituents.
>
> Isn't an abyss filled in here, from the fact of this perfect symmetry? And isn't the regimen of obligation annexed right down to the form of its phrases by the regimen of cognition? . . Haven't they become referents for this third party?[17]

Lyotard separates what he thinks Kant conflates, the "you ought to" of the ethical universe and the "I can" of the empirical world. To speak from the position of the "I am able to," is to speak the language of the legislator who creates a community. But ethics is not a community in this sense. It is not an empirical world. It never fits into that world without remainder. It exceeds the bounds of narratives with which communities are woven together.

The conception of the ethical as an address from the other undermines the Kantian conception of autonomy. For Kant, the moral subject has free will. One is not compelled to act by the chain of empirical causes, but determines one's will in accordance with a moral law inherent in each individual. Ethical obligation is in the nature of individual human agency. I have obligations because I have freedom and because my moral personality implies a relation to my own self. My duties are really duties to myself. Kant gives priority to the pole of autonomy.

Lyotard employs Levinas to reverse this polarity. It is neither our capacities as agents, persons, or speakers, which are active, but our capacity as hearers that provide obligations.[18] Obligation is first of all heteronomous; it is a determination that comes from outside the ego. The address of an obligation implicates the ego in a relationship that it did not author or choose. It is prior to freedom of the will. As Lyotard notes in an early formulation of this issue:

> I know that it is the question of prescription in the sense that there is a kind of imperative in which, as soon as I have been spoken to as well as spoken of (in the sense that I have a name, etc.) I have to speak. And in

this sense, the will is never free, and freedom does not come first. That I may say something else later, granted; that then there is will, granted. But this will can be exercised only against the backdrop of an obligation that comes first and is much older, much more archaic, and it is not subject to legislations; it has not been the object of a decree; and it is literally anonymous.[19]

Lyotard argues that we need to privilege the pole of heteronomy, the passivity or receptivity that precedes freedom in order to provide a notion of the social—a notion that cannot be produced from the concatenation of autonomous egos. "The absolute privileging of the pole of the addressee," Lyotard claims, is "the only site in which the social body can hold."[20] But the social body is disclosed in the act of obligation; it can never be fully articulated in any normative claim. It can never be an object that can be made fully explicit. It is, rather, concealed by every normative or descriptive claim.

Nonidentity opens up the possibility of individual refusal without recourse to the standards of a community that must always to some extent homogenize. The acceptance of an obligation that other members of a community do not recognize or the refusal to acknowledge a norm in general recognition cannot be fully justified. It represents the orientation to a different destiny that may not at first be understood by others and can exhibit its binding power only in the course of action.

Because our sense of obligation can never be explicated in advance or known fully, Lyotard argues, acts of conscience, the address to our sense of obligation, should never be suppressed or contained by any normative or political directives. He wants to protect our independent access to moral sense from totalitarian or even mass democratic interference. As well, however, Lyotard wants to avoid falling back on a type of liberal individualism based upon the conception of an autonomous subject. Whether this strategy can succeed is the subject of the rest of this chapter.

Some Questions on Morality: Toward a Critique of Lyotard

Self and Other

Lyotard proposes a conception of the asymmetry of ego and other, taken from Levinas, to develop an ethical theory that avoids the assumptions of the philosophy of the subject. He grounds the ethical in the passive and receptive capacities of the ego; in this way he hopes to recover the social bond hidden in Kant's position. Lyotard's position, however, does not entirely overcome the problems inherent in Kant's formulation. He reintroduces a conception of identity that his argument is meant to overcome. The asymmetry of self and other conceals the violence between human beings. The social world does not, on its own terms, create its own moral norms or create its own conditions for moral order. It is saved from falling into violent conflict only by recourse to the postulate of a positive infinity, a tacit postulate of identity: God.[21]

Levinas does not conceive of the mundane social world as an ethical universe. Like Kant, he views the actions of associated subjects to be part of an empirical world in which the ethical demand does not appear. Whereas Kant locates moral sense in the autonomous subject, Levinas, in contrast, circumvents the priority of the cognitive subject by transforming this agent from a calculating, instrumentally rational subject to an expressive subject of pleasure. The world is an object for our playful enjoyment and creative self-expression. In Levinas's interpretation, alter is always reduced to the same. Mundane intersubjectivity is thus conceived of as the relation of same to same. In contrast, the notion of alterity or otherness must stand outside of this mundane relationship. It has to indicate a relationship to the infinite. Levinas's recourse to the infinity of God makes mundane ethical discourse an impossibility. Language is not necessary between the identical and not possible between the ego and the wholly other. When Levinas argues that the self-enclosed interiority of the subject of pleasure is shattered by the encounter with the other, he has already introduced a dilemma that undermines his ontology: the other cannot be wholly exterior nor the ego wholly interior.[22] If the request of one, the suffering other, can be recognized as a request by the ego, then it must already share a bond with the ego. Its receptive character alone seems to guarantee its openness to the world. Hearing the call means the other is not absolutely other.

The assumption of Levinas's argument is that the social world is essentially a closed order. Without the intervention of the infinite, it remains closed to the call of otherness. I contend, however, that ordinary intersubjectivity has an open character that allows it to respond to this call within the social world. To view intersubjectivity as the rule of the same is to make a fundamental error. The suffering other is already implicated in the social world that it claims to disclose. The distress of the suffering other, or the request of the stranger, always occurs within an already interpreted social context. We must *recognize* the distress as distress; it is not an uninterpreted or uninterpretable command. The other's call can be understood as a call only within a social context in which its request can be understood as meaningful and to which it is appropriate to respond. It must already rest on a prior disclosure in which ego and alter are understood to belong to a common world; in Hegelian terms, it requires mutual recognition. But we must be careful not to interpret mutual recognition as an identity between subjects. Mutual recognition does not require an achieved consensus; it does, however, require a consensual social order. I will develop this further.

If this world is marred by violence and domination, as the example of the suffering other seems to indicate, what does the disclosure of the infinite achieve? The ethical demand requires an awareness of historical conditions and consequences rather than their suppression. We have a responsibility toward the conditions of existence that we cannot defer to God.

Lyotard is aware of the problem with an ontology of the infinite. He believes, however, that he has avoided the problem through his linguistic reformulation of Levinas. He contends that the transcription of the hearer of the request from God into the hearer of an imperative transposes the point of view of the addressor from the infinite (God) into the Kantian Idea of Reason. For Lyotard, the Kantian Idea is the addressor of the ethical demand; it is the idea of a free, reasonable community of beings. The Kantian community is not the beyond, however, it is simply a necessary postulate of reason. It is an expression of the social body that has no final interpretation, but that states a goal. The return to the Kantian Idea of Reason, however, does not solve the basic problem posed by the asymmetrical distribution of ethical positions. It just transfers the problem to another level.

Lyotard still maintains the priority of the hearer over the speaker in the ethical realm. He maintains that this avoids the closure implied by the priority of the cognitive subject. The problem of the interpretive context in which hearing can occur, however, still remains at issue. Although Lyotard is surely correct in claiming that no social world can appear from the concatenation of thinking egos, it does not follow from this assumption that we must give priority to the pole of the hearer. Nor does it follow that avoiding a cognitive closure requires deemphasizing the acting subject. Every hearer who can receive a call is also an interpreter who knows how to achieve that call. Both poles of the relationship have to be symmetrically distributed for ethical obligation to exist. Without reciprocity, our mutual orientation to the wordless Idea that creates the ethical bond would be little more than the speechless appeal to the sacred transposed to the secular; our relationship to our fellow humans in which we can be both ego and alter, however, creates the space within which an ethical bond can be disclosed.

Lyotard's use of the Idea of Freedom here parallels Levinas's address of the Infinite. If the address of the law in the face of suffering is the idea of a universal humanity, then that call asks us to assume responsibility for that suffering. The Kantian "act so that" then implicates us in the world. We cannot, as Kant advises, judge each obligation according to its binding character for a transcendental subject. Such a position in any case would be unavailable for Lyotard. The suffering of the other is rooted in the conditions of existence. To answer this call of the ethical world would require not just the right intentions, it would require an ethic of responsibility that takes account of the consequences of action. We are not simply passive recipients of the call, we are its agents and interpreters. We have to address the conditions of suffering and inequality, not simply hear the call.

Lyotard may well be receptive to the ethic of responsibility that I have outlined. This ethic, however, would require assumptions about the reciprocity of self and other that do not fit Lyotard's position. If hearers are simultaneously interpreters, then to be a hearer is already to be situated in a world of interpretations in which one can recognize an obligation. Lyotard's notion that one does before understanding is not a proper characterization of the ethical, but only of the religious leap of faith that trusts in God's will without making a judgment. This is meant to maintain openness to the other and to protect freedom of conscience, however, it ends up being a blind trust. This, I claim, can account for neither the binding force of ethical prescription nor the appeal to conscience that Lyotard wants to maintain.

We require a different conception of the basis of prescriptive force. I would agree with the claim of Anthony Giddens that "Human agents or actors . . . have as an inherent aspect of what they do, the capacity to understand what they do while they do it."[23] Giddens's characterization stresses the reflective self-understanding that is necessary for all social action. The meaningful character of human action rests not simply on interpreting self and other, but on the reflective understanding of the grounds of our action. What Giddens terms the *reflexive monitoring of action* refers to the fact that human beings "keep in touch" with the grounds of their action while they are doing it.[24] This does not require an understanding of causal chains, but takes place against a background of reciprocal expectations. As Giddens also points out, the reflexive monitoring of action implies that we are always in the process of checking and modifying our understanding. Our self-understanding is not rooted in a speculative activity in which the mutual recognition is subordinated to the self-identity of an absolute subject, it is rooted in the ongoing practical acts of mutual understanding. There is no final interpretation in this practical realm; the achievement of understanding must be constantly maintained and reachieved. Ethical prescription is not based on the idea of freedom that acts as a regulative idea, but on a domain of action: the domain of reciprocal expectations. Our mutual accountability is the basis for our self-reflective capacities and our capacities as participants in social interaction. To be a self at all requires that we can recognize selves and others as belonging to a common social world. This forms the background condition of human action, and it is the basis of morality.

The recourse to the suffering other does not disclose the ethical as such. The suffering other or the outsider challenges us to reconsider and expand our preexisting interpretations and expectations of responsibility. Because our understanding is reflexive, we have the capacity to respond to a challenge to our existing understandings. Even when an individual does not respond or cannot articulate the basis of his or her own suffering, we already have a generalized understanding of intersubjective expectations upon which we can draw. That is, we already live in a moral universe within which we have to make sense of this claim. Within this context we can be challenged to understand the cry of the outsider as an indication that we may have to revise or even radically overthrow our received understanding. The social world, then, is not built up from the commonality of hearers, but is the world of legitimate, reciprocal expectations. The moral law, in these reformulated terms, should be seen as the regulative principle of a world of reciprocal expectations. This conception, however, requires that we modify our notion of the disclosing character of the ethical. What the ethical has to disclose is not just an originary encounter with obligation, but a social world that is sustained through an ongoing interpretive process among participants.

Lyotard and Levinas both reject this solution. They would view my suggestions as a tacit appeal to principles of identity. They would argue that taking the role of the other, as a theory of intersubjectivity dictates, means imposing an identity onto the other. It makes the other one identical to me. I believe that this view of the intersubjective relationship mistakenly assimilates intersubjectivity to the subject-object model. In the subject-object model the subject confronts a world external to the self. This subject can only assimilate the other to the self or exclude it. The model of intersubjectivity presented here, however, does not rest on isolated individuals. Like Lyotard's notion, it sees subjects as implicated in a web of communicative relationships. Unlike Lyotard's conception, however, it views the self-understanding of subjects as constitutive of the linguistic web. This notion of intersubjectivity does not require the reduction of difference to the same. Alterity is built into our processes of mutual recognition. To recognize you as another to whom I speak or as one who speaks to me does not imply that I consider you to be a reflection of my own self. Rather, it requires the recognition that you are a fellow participant in a language who can respond to my questions, assertions, or imperatives with reasons of your own and from another standpoint within a language. Agreement does not mean assimilation. It can mean that, from different perspectives within language, we can agree on reasons for acting. Reaching an accord does not require identity, it creates a common context for action.

The social universe is a world just as the empirical world is. It is the world of legitimate reciprocal expectations. Lyotard and Levinas take refuge in the other because they themselves have not overcome the bias of the cognitive that they have identified in other ethical theories. They privilege the cognitive world in relation to the ethical world, for only it can have objects of knowledge in the context of an empirical world.

The Cognitive Status of Prescriptives

Thus far I have concentrated on Lyotard's reliance on otherness as the basis for his ethical theory. In this section, I want to focus on a second problem: Lyotard's separation of prescriptives and descriptives. Although it is correct to argue that the normative and the empirical can be separated, I will argue in this section that Lyotard's claim that all knowledge requires the descriptive attitude is unwarranted.

That Kant's philosophy privileges the empirical world over what I have termed the social world is clear. Kant's notion of the monological subject generates a theory of agency that applies only to the isolated subject. The notion of the social world as a web of meanings and reciprocal expectations is not available to him. The world is the empirical world, and only those objects that can be grasped under its categories can be objects of knowledge. The category of the person is not an empirical one, but belongs to the noumenal world. No evidence can confirm it. We can never know whether an individual is acting out of self-interest or good will. We can know only that the notion of moral will is a transcendental requirement. Note, however, that the standard of evidence here is the traditional empirical one, namely, that of behavioral observation of the external world.

Levinas's target is Husserl as much as Kant, but he faces a similar problem in regard to evidence of the social world. The problem of intersubjectivity in Husserl is well known.[25] From the standpoint of the intentional acts of a solitary ego, no evidence can be given of a world of legitimate interpersonal expectations. Levinas is critical of Husserl, but in one respect he stays within the ambit of his thought. Instead of looking to the social world as a different type of "world," he takes the empirical world as the sole criteria of possible evidence. He contends that the encounter with the other is that which exceeds evidence and, therefore, cannot be represented.

Lyotard's target is the consensus theory of truth of Habermas and Apel. In the consensus theory, sufficient evidence can never be gained from the standpoint of the solitary observer, but can be determined only discursively.[26] The truth of a proposition can be established only when inquirers convince each other of the truth or falsity of assertions or of the validity of norms under the conditions of discourse. It presumes that each inquirer can address others and be addressed by them and that one inquirer can take both roles.

Lyotard argues that this reciprocity of perspectives is precisely what is denied in the prescriptive phrase. He argues that the consensus theory, like all theories, requires a third-person perspective that denies the standpoint of the participant. The third-person perspective is the model of the objective (seemingly neutral) observer. That is, evidence can be given only in an attitude of description. But because the ethical cannot be disclosed in the descriptive regime of phrases, there is, in Lyotard's view, an abyss between description and participation. There is a *differend* or constitutive dispute that can never be resolved.

In taking the model of pure description to be the standard for all types of explicit knowledge, however, Lyotard employs a conception of knowing that is, at best, suitable for an objective world. Lyotard does not take into account the access to the participant's meaning required of our knowledge of the social world. He postulates a world of objects to which access is not mediated by meaning.

Anthony Giddens, among others, has explicated the notion of a double hermeneutic involved in all social inquiry (and, in a broader sense, in our interpretation of our social world).[27] Whereas all knowledge is discursive and mediated through meaning, there is a difference between the access we have to an objective world and the access we have to the social world. In the first instance, our access to objects or things is not based on their ability to respond to us. The objects of the social world have a different character; they are fellow participants with which we inhabit a common world. Thus social inquiry has to concern itself not only with the interpretive framework through which it gains knowledge of the world, but also with the preexisting interpretive frame of subjects.

We have access to the social world not as observers, but because we too are participants in that world, that is, through our preexisting practical frame of knowledge. We can never, however, bracket our participant's knowledge to take the standpoint of things in an objective world and continue to understand others as others. We fail then to understand ourselves in the very ways that we make sense to each other.

The confusion in Lyotard's formulation of the problem is centered around his use of the notion of neutrality. A pure description, the true third-person perspective, has to neutralize the executive force of the command as well as neutralize its character as command. Strictly speaking, the third-person perspective is a behavioral one. It reduces meaningful actions to observable behaviors. Therefore, it has to stand outside the perspective of a participant's meaning that constitutes the social world. Pure description has to reinterpret meanings as behaviors.

Following the suggestions of Giddens and Habermas, I propose a different way of interpreting the possibility of a normative discourse. We reconsider our moral notions when they become problematic. This may occur because, in the course of our participation in social life, our accepted moral notions and our experience become dissonant or because someone may challenge our moral judgments or our integrity in a way that we cannot adequately answer although we are yet compelled to respond. When this occurs we have to reexamine the linkages between our actions and the norms and principles we use to explain them to ourselves and to others. These are not, however, simply questions of theory. If norms and principles are part of the reflexive monitoring of action, then they affect a major aspect of our sense of identity. We reflectively examine our own reasons for action in the light of these challenges in order to understand more fully why we do what we do.[28]

This form of reflection, however, does not require a neutralization of the normative force of action, but its virtualization. By this term I mean that in the reflective examination of our actions, we must suspend the relation between meaning and action. We may engage in examining different alternatives, or different justifications, without committing ourselves to them. But we never bracket the fact that at some point we must be committed to act on the basis of some rationale for action. We do not bracket our capacities as moral actors. If we were to bracket this capacity, then we could not, in the process of reexamining our reason for acting, morally assess them at all. Lyotard's conception of the third-person perspective requires that we do precisely this, that we bracket our capacity as moral judges of our own actions.

Even the standpoint of the social scientist, which is seemingly the most distant from practical life and the most "objectified," cannot completely suspend the participant's perspective. The social scientist must maintain his or her position as a participant in order to understand the social subjects under inquiry. He or she must view others from the standpoint of their ability to act with reasons, that is, to have beliefs that have rationales. This implies that inquirers do not suspend their own ability to understand others as sense-making beings. If this is so, however, then the abyss that Lyotard posits cannot be maintained in the way in which he formulates it. There can be knowledge of social life that can be compatible with a participant's perspective.

Lyotard does not grant that our participant's perspective requires both that we hear obligations and that we address them. If, however, understanding an obligation means knowing what is meant by the addressor and knowing under what conditions such an address is appropriate, then it seems that understanding an obligation requires maintaining the standpoint of a participant. We can be accountable and responsible to one another within a web of reciprocal expectations. But then reasons for action are internal to obligation. They are not addressed from the standpoint of the theorist, they are a part of our practical life. They become the medium through which the reciprocal expectations of participants are reproduced or modified.

If reasons for action are part of the medium of reproduction of social life, then it does not seem to be true that they are simply a neutralization of the force of prescriptives or norms, but rather that they are the medium of prescriptive force. We do not, and we should not, obey before understanding (although sometimes we may be put in a position to act without knowing what is best) or act without reasons. Rather, we need to consider the reasons for action that we can provide when we are called to justify our actions or come to a decision in a practical situation.

An analysis that followed the line of thought outlined here would provide a different conception of the relation of practical reason and judgment than the one presented by Lyotard. Where Lyotard views the moral law and judgment as applying to different regimes, a communicative conception of social life views these two notions as complementary features of our moral life. Moral norms and principles do not subsume particular judgments under universal rules in the same way that things can be classified under the concepts of an objective world. In line with the double hermeneutic of social life, moral norms are not only interpretive explications of the requirements of moral life, they always require a second level of interpretation. By this I mean something more than the mere application of a rule. The meaning of moral principles is not invariant in all circumstances nor is their relevance the same in all contexts. Interpretation also has the aim of understanding how a moral principle is relevant to the context of social life, not just in a particular case, but in general.

Perhaps this is not far from the ideas that Lyotard develops in his conception of judgment.[29] His notion that the moral law is unnameable, that is, that it is rooted in a sublime that can never be made explicit, does not, however, hold up to an investigation of the relation of meaning to social life.

18 Deconstruction and Suffering: The Way to the Ethical

JEROME A. MILLER

In this chapter I would like to address the much discussed question of whether ethics is possible in our postmodern, deconstructionist situation, and if so, what kind of ethics this might be. If this topic is now under intense and even urgent discussion by thinkers in the phenomenological tradition, it is not because their interest in one of the traditional fields of philosophy has been reawakened, but because they are trying to explore the ethical implications of calling into question the entire philosophical project as it has typically been conceived and practiced within the tradition. As Drucilla Cornell poses it, "the issue is . . . what figure the Good can take on after the deconstruction of foundationalist philosophy."[1] If one dismantles the foundationalist project, does anything of ethics remain? Does the deconstruction of philosophy unloose an ethical an-archy upon the world, as those who continue the traditional search for an immovable arche suspect and dread? Or is there another possibility? Might the very destabilizing of foundations create an opening for the ethical that cannot occur in any other way? This is the striking possibility that is being explored, under Levinas's inspiration, by thinkers such as Cornell and John Caputo.[2] Indeed, Cornell claims that "the entire project of deconstruction . . . is driven by an ethical desire to enact the ethical relation."[3] It would be difficult to find a more positive, hopeful way of reading our deconstructionist situation. The pressing question is whether it makes any sense to place our hope in this possibility, given the fact that it would be a hope without foundation—a hope without any of the security that foundationalism has traditionally tried to provide.[4]

Ever since the foundations on which the ethical life traditionally depended were jeopardized by Nietzsche's deconstructionist critique, hope

259

has meant hoping that there might be some way of shoring up their ruins; the only alternative to that hope has been to despair over the loss of foundations and so, it seemed, to despair of the ethical itself. The more seriously one took the deconstructionist critique of traditional metaphysics and the epistemologies inseparable from it, the more carefully one had to guard against hope of any sort because hope seemed of its very nature to require clinging to some illusion and refusing to let it be undermined. But when we despair of the ethical because it has no epistemologically or metaphysically secure basis, perhaps this is not because deconstruction has succeeded so well in disillusioning us, but because it has not yet done its deepest work. To despair because the foundationalist presumptions underlying much of the traditional ethical thinking have been undermined means that one is still so attached to them that one cannot conceive of the ethical without them.[5]

Perhaps if we allow it to do so, deconstruction can lead us beyond both the false hope of securing a foundation and the despair of being without one, to the possibility of an ethics without foundations that is for that very reason in some sense beyond deconstruction. When deconstruction pulls our foundations out from under us, it may put us in a position to appreciate the ethical in a way that we could not have done without it. It would be a mistake to say that our hopes "rest" on this possibility because this way of speaking would imply that our hopes still depend on our having solid ground under us. Better to say that hope is "set in motion" by this possibility, even if, as a result of it, the ground is pulled out from under us and we are left with nothing on which to stand. The situation into which we are put by deconstruction—one in which we have nothing to stand on or to hold onto and nothing to brace us or to break our fall—perhaps this is *the* ethical "position" par excellence.

It is this possibility I would like to explore here. Before I do so let me proffer one important caveat. Deconstruction itself cannot be one if it is disruptive of the one and provocative of difference. There can be only many deconstructions. If I speak of it in the singular in this chapter, it is only because I am trying to concentrate on the event of disruption itself that makes the emergence of difference (and different deconstructions) possible.

The Ethos of Foundationalism

I would like to begin with the metaphor on which foundationalism is founded. The purpose of a foundation is to provide a secure basis for whatever edifice is to be erected upon it. Those who build foundations are not necessarily foundationalists; they become so only when they concentrate on making their foundation so firm that there is no reason to doubt or to question it. Those who are to live within the edifice raised on the foundation typically tend to encourage this attempt because they would like to be able to take the foundation of their lives for granted. The ground on which any foundation has to be laid, however, has fault lines and is not wholly hospitable to us. Because of its inevitable dependence on the faulty ground under it, even the most expertly constructed foundation is liable to deconstruction. The only way to provide perfect security for an edifice would be to erect it on an immovable, irrefragable foundation, one that could not be dislodged or unsettled, a foundation exempt from even the possibility of deconstruction. Such a foundation, however, could not be dependent on anything beneath itself because such dependency would make it vulnerable to being undermined. It would, therefore, have to be either self-grounding or in no need of a ground at all. It would have to be immune to disruption from below and not in any way earthbound. In short, the only way for a foundation to be perfectly safe from the possibility of being undermined would be for it to be wholly off the ground and disconnected from it.

The quest for an absolutely secure ground cannot lead in any other direction except *away* from the ground, even though our whole purpose in seeking it is to have something immovable under our feet. What is frail, fallible, or liable to fault is not unconditionally reliable; surety can be achieved only by resting on an absolute that is not earthbound, that has no conditions or dependencies, no faults or frailties, and, therefore, no possibility of being pulled out from under us. We would like the ground on which we rest to be eternity itself, conceived of as a place that is as impenetrable, as inviolable, as immune to rupture as the womb would be if it had no opening to the world.

This suggests, however, that there is something oxymoronic about the very concept of an absolutely secure foundation, because to be secure absolutely it must transcend everything earthly and to be a foundation it must provide us with firm ground on which to stand. The absolute on which the foundationalist hopes to secure his edifice must at the same time be above and beneath him, superior to and subordinate to him. On the one hand, it must transcend everything earthly if it is to be invulnerable to disruption and free of any of the fallibilities that might set in motion its deconstruction. On the other hand, the purpose of the foundation is to provide the foundationalist himself with an absolute position; to do this it must be positioned *beneath* him, in a subordinate relationship to him. For foundationalism to work, the foundationalist has to have it both ways at once. But if the principle on which the foundationalist wishes to depend is an absolute that radically transcends him, it is difficult to see how he can be justified in placing it beneath him; and if the principle is placed beneath him, it is difficult to see how it can have the transcendent stature it must have to be unassailable. Either way, the foundationalist cannot have what he needs: an earth beneath him that is as immune to change as eternity is purported to be.

This dilemma exists regardless of whether the foundation in question is meant to provide the basis for an epistemological or a metaphysical theory or for a normative ethics. Normative ethics is certainly one area in which the foundationalist impulse has often been at work, and one way to deconstruct it might be to apply the preceding diagnosis to it. But a normative principle is also implicitly operative in *all* foundationalist thinking, irrespective of its field. For foundationalism always works on the normative presumption that nothing is more important than to find an unassailable position and to take possession of it. Insofar as it occurs within a foundationalist framework, all our thinking is under the sway of an ethos that prizes unassailability and that tries to repress the possibility of being wrong. In our lives as theorists, the possibility of being wrong is the most mortifying kind of vulnerability.

It is precisely this vulnerability that the deconstructionist critic seeks to expose. Her purpose is not so much to find faults in the structure that the foundationalist erects, as it is to help us to understand how the desire to eliminate the very possibility of fault has influenced the logic of its construction. The deconstructionist is not out to prove that all such attempts are bound to fail, but to suggest that foundationalism is mistaken in its very effort to succeed in this way. Foundationalism errs in its very effort to repress the possibility of erring. The foundationalist's need for an immovable arche derives from an awareness of his own frailty and from a desire to compensate for it. By using the truth that he affirms to be transcendent as a ground to secure his own position, however, he puts that very truth in the service of an avoidance. He uses it as a foundation to cover up his own vulnerability to error. The more secure such a foundation seems to be, the more of an error it is, because whatever truth it contains is being used to sustain a self-deception. In his very quest for an unassailable truth, the foundationalist subordinates truth to his desire to possess it and thereby overcome his own fallibility. The quest for an absolute position is itself governed by the will to untruth.

Suffering Deconstruction

Deconstruction, on the other hand, is something like the opposite of such a quest. It has rightly been perceived as an attempt to jeopardize not this particular theory or that one, but the entire foundationalist project of trying to make theory unassailable. This raises the perplexing question of where the deconstructionist herself is positioned when she puts her critique into practice. *For* what position, *in* what position, does the deconstructionist stand? If the deconstructionist does not answer this question in a straightforward way, it is not because she is confused about her position, but because she is calling into question the entire project that equates thinking with the effort to secure a position for oneself.[6] Deconstruction is not a counterposition, but a counter to the very project of positioning. In a real sense, then, it does not intend to take a stand. A critic may understandably conclude from this that it has nothing positive to say and that it offers no affirmative alternative to the theories it purports to dismantle. Interpreted in this way, deconstruction is nothing but a frivolous play (and display) of critical facility.

A profound insight is imbedded within such a critique of deconstruction that the deconstructionist herself is especially qualified to appreciate. Refusing to assume a position, or ever to take a stand, can itself be a very effective way of rendering oneself unassailable. Because one's position cannot possibly be undermined if one does not have any, standing above the fray of contending positions is a better strategy than any other for making sure one cannot possibly lose face. Only someone who claimed to occupy this superior vantage point would think of himself as being in a position to survey all possible positions and to know them to be relative. The relativist who has no principles, unlike the foundationalist who is wedded to them, thinks that he is in a position to know that principles are indistinguishable from arbitrary postulates. Free of the hope that a foundational truth may be found, the relativist has no reason to suspect that he himself may be in danger of being wrong. Indeed, once truth is abandoned, it is actually *impossible* to be wrong. Relativism is, for this reason, the metaposition par excellence. The more sophisticated the relativist is, the more adept he is at devising one metalanguage after another so that he is always one level above the foundationalist who tries to capture him at the moment he is defending a position. The relativist always manages to absent himself from the position he seemed to occupy just a moment ago. But in eluding the foundationalist, he is simply trying to beat him at his own game. The relativist is playing the part of absence in an epistemology of presence; he is neither this nor that; he never allows us to meet him Face to Face.

Now some readers may find in deconstruction simply a new, more subtle relativism, that is, a sophisticated metaversion of the very quest for unassailability that all of its efforts are devoted to disrupting. But those disruptive interventions themselves, if taken seriously, suggest that deconstruction is trying to lead us in exactly the opposite direction: they upset us so that we may acknowledge our deepest vulnerabilities and cease repressing them. If this painful invitation is not always heard, perhaps it is because we have developed the habit of thinking that deconstruction is an operation performed by the deconstructionist on the foundationalist; we have come to think of it as something to be done to others, rather than as something to be suffered oneself. But how can one be a deconstructionist without becoming one or become one without being deconstructed? Are there born deconstructionists who have never made the mistake of foundationalism, who have never experienced the need to secure an unassailable position? Or is birth itself the original deconstruction from which we all try to save ourselves by finding a more perfect womb that will not expose us to the possibility of not-being in any way? To be anything and not have to become it, to be already what otherwise one would have to become through time and in time, would mean being in the ultimate foundationalist position. But being born involves precisely the irretrievable loss of such a position.[7]

What, then, does deconstruction entail when it is understood not as an operation performed on another, but as a process that one undergoes oneself? First of all, because deconstruction is not simply another theory, becoming a deconstructionist cannot simply be a matter of changing positions, as the debate between foundationalism and deconstruction may have led us to believe. It is, rather, a matter of giving up the quest for an unassailable position and plunging into the abyss that opens before us when we do not try to avoid our deepest vulnerabilities. To let deconstruction do its work means to let it deprive one of the superior position that one has sought to occupy and to do nothing to escape the gravity of the fall this loss causes.

To suffer that loss, to experience that deconstruction, does not mean being a passive victim of it. The deconstruction of the self requires my own active letting-go; it requires that I voluntarily relinquish the position that I have tried to make unassailable. Cornell says that "the ultimate embarrassment to the sovereign subject [occurs when] he finds that he's not as in control as he likes to think."[8] But *freely choosing* to abandon one's superior position and to relinquish the control it enabled one to exercise transforms this embarrassment from a passive passion into an active one. We ordinarily think suffering can be only passive because we ordinarily identify action with the effort to control. If deconstruction is undergone only passively, however, if the person to whom it happens is unreceptive to it, the loss remains external to her and leaves her will to retain control unaffected. Without the letting-be of the loss, there can be no letting-go; if there is no letting-go, no deconstruction of the self in its very determination to be in control occurs. Suffering, understood as the opening of oneself to loss, is the only way to be deconstructed, for only in and through suffering, as so defined, does the will to occupy an unassailable position turn into the willingness to relinquish it.[9]

At first glance, this description of deconstruction may seem to be in accord with the one advanced by John Caputo when he says that, to take deconstruction seriously, we must

> face the worst, the play of epochs, of the temporary constellations within which we live out our historical lives, [we must] wade into the flux and try not to drown. . . . We ought to produce our schemes and our programs for *dealing with* the flux—and we shall certainly continue to do that, we cannot avoid it, we have to act and plan and direct and teach. (Italics added.)[10]

But if we find ways to "deal with" the loss of an unassailable position, or ways to "handle" and "manage" it so as not to "go under," we are still trying to remain in control in order to avoid the suffering involved in being wholly and radically vulnerable.[11] *Coping* has become the paradigmatic verb in our postmodern vocabulary. Through our ubiquitous use of it, we acknowledge that deconstructions are bound to occur in our lives, that we cannot achieve the kind of mastery we would have if we stood at the Archimedean point of an all-inclusive and undeconstructible system. Insofar as we realize that we cannot exclude the very possibility of flaw or fault from the frameworks we use to structure our lives, we tend to think that all we can do is repair the breakdowns that are bound to happen and postpone for as long as possible the inevitable collapse of our world. But such postponements and repairs are themselves motivated by the desire to avoid deconstruction. We "deal with" interruptions in the hope of preventing them from becoming ruptures that would devastate us. The shift from foundationalism to pragmatic coping may seem revolutionary at first blush, but it occurs within the context of an unchanging will to be in control. For in dealing with things, even in coping with them, we still work to deprive them of their power to unsettle us, to get the better of us, to destroy the equilibrium that we enjoy when we keep them subordinate to us. To cope with something means precisely to succeed in repulsing its threat to one's composure. To be deconstructed, on the other hand, means precisely to lose one's composure and, with it, the hope of being able to recover it.

Such a loss of composure is not devastating when it involves losing control over only this or that particular area of one's life. It becomes unmanageable and overwhelming, however, when it involves relinquishing control over one's life as a whole. Heidegger called this the most upsetting of all experiences because it dislodges the self as controller from its Archimedean position.[12] Whoever lets such a loss be, not in the negative and passive sense of allowing one's privileged position to be taken away, but in the positive and active sense of voluntarily relinquishing it, undergoes a kind of death. No matter what structure I have given to my life, the experience of its deconstruction plunges me into that "abyss from which all menaces announce themselves."[13] Deconstruction does not merely expose the vulnerabilities of my position, it requires that I give up my position entirely and embrace vulnerability itself. It means relinquishing my possessive hold on life and becoming both defenseless and destitute. The one who accepts such a condition of poverty and self-exposure has nothing to stand on, has lost all stature, has become, in a real sense, nothing itself.

As *Being and Time* helped us to realize, the mortifying possibility of such a mortal loss lies concealed within every kind of fault or failure; the reason we seek an unassailable position in the first place is precisely to protect ourselves from it. The underlying purpose of all of our securely founded edifices is to provide us with a refuge from our own deconstruction. This purpose could be achieved, however, only if we could build on a foundation that was as invulnerable, as impervious to rupture, as absolute and undeconstructible as the absolute itself. The longing for such an absolute and our effort to ground our lives in it together constitute an economy of avoidance. The ethical itself, insofar as it tries to anchor our lives in something absolute, is part of this effort to avoid our deaths. Ethics, as so conceived, is not merely secondary to the ontological because of its ontic character, it is actually repressive of the ontological insofar as it plays a role in an economy designed to hide our ontological vulnerabilities. Our uplifting beliefs, by virtue of the very fact that they uplift us, are in the service of a resentment that we harbor against mortality and are part of our effort to escape the gravity of our deconstruction.

If this diagnosis is right, however, the entire economy of avoidance that underlies and governs the foundationalist project is itself governed by an unspoken normative injunction. This injunction enjoins us to find an unassailable position and avoid being vulnerable, to secure a foundation and avoid being deconstructed, to strive for control and avoid suffering, and to hold onto life and deal with death, even when it happens to be our own. *This* principle of good and evil, unlike any of the traditional normative principles that the foundationalist may use to secure his edifice, is already operative in his very effort to construct it; it is what sets the whole foundationalist project in motion. The evil that the foundationalist is working to avoid is more fundamental, in his eyes, than any of those proscribed by the rules he may come to adopt; his adoption of those rules is itself motivated by the desire to avoid this evil. The worst thing that can happen, from his point of view, is not a violation of the ethical, but the deconstruction of his world. Foundationalism always operates on the presumption that mortality is the supreme horror and on the injunction that we ought to avoid it.

That it is possible for us to be open to our deaths, instead of avoiding them, is confirmed by the practice of deconstruction itself insofar as it is actively suffered, not passively undergone. But one has not got the point of that mortal and mortifying process if one thinks it might be possible to start over again on fresh ground after one has completed it. No matter what kind of foundation one designs, one's very use of it as a foundation will activate the same subversive, deconstructive irony by which one has already been undermined. To get to the bottom of deconstruction, one must not just relinquish one's whole world, completely and irrevocably, but give up the hope of building another in its place. To stay on the path of deconstruction all the way to that terminal point may seem, must seem, like following it to a dead end. But such a death may make it possible not to begin again on fresh ground, but to live in a completely different way—without a ground at all.

The Breakthrough to the Other

What, then, is this other way? What possibility is opened up to us when we embrace, instead of avoid or delay, the destitute condition to which deconstruction leads?

Only an acceptance of our destitution, our nothingness, puts us in a position (radically exposed and defenseless, and in that sense not a position at all but an open, vulnerable site) to appreciate what-is without being preoccupied by the threat it might pose to our privileged stature. Prior to such an acceptance of our destitution, our ontological insecurities cause us to subordinate *everything* to the priority of keeping the structure of our lives intact. Only by letting go of all protective structures and accepting our nothingness—only by embracing our impotence instead of trying to find some weapon that will compensate for it—can thought and action be liberated from the economy of avoidance.

How would we act and think if we lived out of our very impotence? We would not seek to secure a position, to build a foundation, to deal with or manage or in any other way control what-is in the hope of mitigating our destitute condition. The verbs in our ordinary vocabulary, as they are ordinarily understood, are part of the economy of avoidance and have connotations that prevent them from saying what this other way of being might be. But that does not mean that language itself cannot be freed from its foundationalist register to describe a kind of action that is not an exercise in control. The first act is to say, "I think I have been wrong."

In fact, we would have to say, "I have been wrong about every-thing," because prior to this point, we have viewed everything either as a threat to our foundation or as a reinforcement of it.[14] From the foundationalist perspective, every Other, precisely by virtue of her Other-ness, jeopardizes our otherwise unassailable position; for the very fact that she is Other means that she is not naturally subordinate to us. The project of securing an unassailable position always requires effacing the Otherness of the Other to disarm the threat to one's ontological security that the very fact of her Otherness poses. On the other hand, by abandon-ing completely the hope of ever having such security, by relinquishing the grip one has tried to keep on everything, one liberates the Other from one's grasp and thus makes it possible for her very Otherness to pro-nounce itself. The desire for ontological security undermines every rela-tionship with every Other because security can be secured only by repressing Otherness. Thus, we can become receptive to the Other only by first relinquishing the hold we would like to have on being. Only by dying, only by actually entering into the mortifying ordeal that the pro-cess of being deconstructed sets in motion, do we reach the dead end of our desire to be unassailable and so allow the Other to come alive for us.

In this death of the desire to be unassailable, and this awakening to the Other as Other that it makes possible, occurs the turn, the reversal, the conversion that institutes the ethical relationship. By relinquishing the attempt to secure an unassailable position for oneself, one ceases living as if one's own ontological preservation were the primary good to which all Others are subordinate. One becomes open to the Other in her very being as the good Other than one's own being. The ethical relation-ship with the Other is born with one's acknowledgment that her existence is the good that takes precedence over one's desire to avoid deconstruction. And this acknowledgment does not occur except in and through that death by virtue of which one actively relinquishes the privileged position that one has spent one's life tying to secure.

It should be noted here that saying that the Other takes precedence over one's ontological self-preservation is not the same as saying that the Other takes precedence over one's self. The foundationalist project, which the ethical requires us to abandon, is not centered on the self, but on the desire to protect the self from its own vulnerabilities and to cover up its own destitution. Abandoning this project, therefore, can have just as lib-erating an effect on the self as it has on the Other, for it releases the self that I am from my possessive attitude toward it. Deconstruction does not deconstruct the self, but the project of securing a privileged position for it.[15] Abandoning this project entails a radical and irreparable disruption of the economy of self-interest; but this makes it possible for one to institute an ethical relation with one's self analogous to the one instituted with the Other.[16]

Thus the irreconcilable difference, which can never be diluted or effaced, is not between the self and the Other, but between the desire to subordinate everything that is to my self-interest and the willingness to reverence everything that is, including my self, as a good Other than self-interest.[17] Indeed, the difference between being possessive toward what-is and reverencing it, between subordinating it to my interests and liberating it to be itself, between enclosing it in an economy of self-preservation and assenting to it as Other than my tool or obstacle, is the difference from which all other differences emerge. To be ethical means precisely to live in the crux of that difference and to undergo actively the mortifying process of dispossession and relinquishment that allows it to emerge. It takes a whole lifetime to practice this death. The point is not to get beyond it, because all that is beyond it is accessible only in and through it. By entering the throe of this rupture we lose ground, relinquish privilege, become destitute. But in accepting that destitution we cease dominating the Other and open ourselves to the possibility of openness itself. This possibility is not realized by finding a new way to organize one's life, a new arche on which to found a new, more securely structured world, but only by recognizing the Other, from the perspective of one's own destitution, as a good that is wholly, irreconcilably Other than self-interest.

Insofar as this difference between self-interest and the ethical is irreconcilable, I am led to suggest that it is absolute and that this absolute is constitutive of the ethical itself. We usually think that it would be possible to speak of an absolute only if it were possible to achieve and to speak from an absolute standpoint.[18] But the logic of deconstruction, as I have read it, does not justify this presumption. In fact, quite the contrary. Deconstruction enables us to understand that, in our quest for an absolute standpoint, for a foundation immune to deconstruction, we *use* the absolute as a ground and thus *subordinate* it to our project of acquiring an unassailable position for ourselves. The abandonment of that project *does* mean losing the hold we presume to have on the absolute. Far from rendering the absolute irrelevant to us, however, this actually releases it from its subordinate position and permits it, for the first time, to emerge as an Other, indeed, as the very Otherness of the ethical from self-interest. The absolute is Otherness itself in its irreducibility to the economy of the Same. The absolute as Other than self-interest, far from being accessible to us only if we are able to secure an absolute standpoint, becomes accessible to us only when we irrevocably abandon our quest for such a standpoint and open ourselves to the destitution from which we would have liked it to protect us.

What is ultimately Other than us, in our destitution, is being itself. We are in no position to appreciate this fundamental fact, that being itself is not us but rather our radical Other, as long as we are governed by our ontological insecurities and driven by them to make unassailable our hold on being. Insofar as it requires us to let go of being, instead of holding onto it, the process of being deconstructed releases being from our grasp and makes it possible for us to institute an ethical relationship with it. This ethical relationship, far from signifying the demise of the ontological, liberates our thought about being from the influence of our insecurities. The ethical, and the ethical alone, institutes the kind of relationship with being that allows being to be itself. Ethics is not founded on or derived from ontology; ontology is a derivative of the ethical.[19] But the ethical, on which ontology is grounded, is not a ground at all: it is our radical vulnerability to Otherness.

From the perspective of the ethical as thus understood, the possibility of our own nothingness is not, as Heidegger tried to convince us,[20] the greatest of all horrors. Indeed, we are ethical only to the degree that we embrace this possibility, only to the degree that we open ourselves to our deaths. For the person who is in the process of making this mortal and mortifying breakthrough, the experience of nothingness is not the worst thing that can ever happen. What is far worse is not to experience it, not to suffer radical disruption, not to be deconstructed. For if we are never deconstructed, we will never abandon our superior position, never be mortified, and so never come to realize the existence of the Other and the reality of the ethical. The absolutely worst thing that can happen is not death, but the violation of the Other, for that is a violation of the absolute itself. For us here, in these theoretical conversations, the most dreadful scenario is not to be wrong, but to be wrong and not acknowledge it; that is, to succeed in avoiding deconstruction.[21] Far more horrifying than death is repressing the call of the ethical.

Since Nietzsche, philosophy has developed a hermeneutic of suspicion for the purpose of undoing our avoidances of death. Under his influence, the affirmation of the ethical was itself suspected of being an effort to create an uplifting belief for the purpose of quieting the terror of the abyss. Relinquishing such beliefs sets in motion the process of deconstruction that culminates in an acceptance of our destitution and a loss of control over our lives as a whole. But that loss, though it must seem like the end of the world, is really the end of the world founded on the arche of self-interest and the emergence of all Others in their Otherness: it is something like the beginning of a million different universes, none of which is, or ever will be, under our control. From each of them there issues a call to justice that we are capable of hearing only if we remain in that condition of destitution to which deconstruction brings us. Deconstruction does not destroy the ethical; it releases the ethical from the subordinate position in which we keep it when we use it as a foundation. It allows it to become an unconditional claim, an absolute call over which we have no say because it is said to us by the Other.

Deconstruction means the end of philosophy as the effort to secure an invulnerable position. But if philosophy is the practice of dying and the cultivation of a wisdom that is not accessible to us except in and through a mortifying acknowledgment of the Other, deconstruction makes it possible and sets it in motion. It is the way we actively suffer the emergence of the ethical.

19

Emmanuel Levinas:
Ethics as Domination or Desire

WENDY FARLEY

Introduction

For Emmanuel Levinas, ethics is the condemnation of the violence of egocentricity together with the transformation of the ego into existence for the Other. Within the logic of totality, the Same and the Other exist in mutual antagonism. Ethical existence is a fundamental alternative to totality that purges the Same of its violence. Ethics permits the Other to be encountered as the object of desire and of obligation. Ethical existence is the domain of the Good: it is the goodness glimpsed in the face of the Other; it is the goodness of the ego as it is emptied of its violent autonomy and begins to exist for the Other.

Levinas, in *Totality and Infinity,* combines two different metaphors to express the distinctiveness of ethical existence. Ethics is both a command issued by alterity and a desire for the Other. Command expresses the imperative of obligation that judges the illusion of autonomy characteristic of totality. Desire is the longing for alterity that drives the ego toward the Other. These two motifs, command and desire, express different dimensions of ethical existence. In pressing the logic of each metaphor, however, quite different ethical visions emerge. My thesis is that command bears too close a resemblance to the logic of totality and domination and is therefore insufficient as a phenomenology of ethical existence. Desire is a more adequate description of the genesis of ethics; it effects a self-emptying of the Same without resorting to the violence of domination.[1]

This argument will be developed in three steps. The first step shows how command functions to criticize philosophies of totality. The second

273

step displays the nostalgia for domination implicit in this way of describing ethical existence. The final section argues that it is primarily through desire for the Other, rather than through submission to command, that the subject begins to exist ethically.

Ethics as the Command of the Master

Despite apparent similarities between Levinas and Martin Buber, Levinas labors long and hard to differentiate himself from Buber's dialogical philosophy.[2] Levinas does not think that Buber's model of mutuality is sufficient to effect a rupture with totality. Totality can be challenged adequately only by a *judgment* that condemns the autonomy of the Same. Judgment requires not mutuality, but an irreversible or assymetrical relationship.

Prior to a recognition of the radical alterity of the Other, my freedom is gloriously unhindered, but also blindly destructive. The transformation to ethical existence requires that both the violence and the arbitrariness of my freedom be called into question. The Other as a victim of totality reveals that "I am not innocent spontaneity but usurper and murderer."[3] The Other forces the ego to face the consequences of her freedom, to see the corpses that her "innocent" freedom and "disinterested" love of knowledge have produced. Mutuality presupposes equality and cannot undo the violence of totality; judgment of the ego requires not an equal, but a Master.

When I recognize in the face of the Other the destruction that I have caused, I am ashamed. I measure myself against the infinity I have tried to tame or thwart and see that my freedom is "murderous in its very exercise" (TI 84). By forcing the Other to fit my ideas and needs, I have subjected her to myself and destroyed her alterity. I have imagined a world in which I am autonomous and the Other is real only in relationship to me. I believe my freedom is primordial and absolute. The Other teaches me that all of this is an illusion. The ethical encounter with the Other forces me to realize that my freedom is not self-justifying: freedom is founded upon something prior to it. I do not constitute the world, but participate in a world that precedes me, in which and for which I am responsible. The Other judges my naive spontaneity and in this way reveals the purpose of my freedom. "Existence is not in reality condemned to freedom, but is *invested* as freedom. Freedom is not bare. To philosophize is to trace freedom back to what lies before it, to disclose the investiture that liberates freedom from the arbitrary" (TI 84–85). I become ashamed of my destructive autonomy at the moment that I see that my freedom is not for me at all; it is *for* the Other. My freedom is then no longer trivial and violent, but becomes purposive. The Other is the Master who condemns my autonomy; the Other is also the Master who invests my freedom by showing that responsibility, rather than aimless curiosity or violent self-assertion, is the purpose of my freedom. Freedom is not a gift that privileges the ego; it is what enables the ego to exist for the Other.

The purgation of the ego of its *aseity* is the condition of the possibility of entering into ethical existence. But ethical existence itself is responsibility to the Other. Just as the command of the Master judged my freedom, this command also issues the unconditional imperative of obligation. Morality is submission to this command. The foundation of freedom does not consist in knowing oneself, "but rather in submitting oneself to an exigency, to a morality" (TI 86). According to Levinas, this submission is not to law, to an impersonal reason, or even to a divine revelation. One submits oneself to the Other. When I see the glimmering of infinity in the face of the Other, I am pierced by the knowledge that I have violated another *person*. In the humiliated knowledge of my own violence, I am subjected to the Other and submit myself to the authority I see in her face. Ethics is issued as a command, an order: it comes from above me and demands my obedience. The Other, as the locus of obligation, appears to me from the dimension of height and authority (TI 75, 86).

The peculiarity of Levinas's ethics is that the unequivocal Master to whom I am subjected is the very one who is destitute in body and in soul.

> This gaze [of the Other] that supplicates and demands, that can supplicate only because it demands, deprived of everything because entitled to everything, and which one recognizes in giving—this gaze is precisely the epiphany of the face as a face. The nakedness of the face is destituteness. To recognize the Other is to recognize a hunger. To recognize the Other is to give. But it is to give to the master, to the lord, to him whom one approaches as 'You' [Vous] in a dimension of height. (TI 75)

At the same time that the Other is my Master, the Other is also the one who is radically vulnerable. Levinas is unusual among philosophers in recognizing the extreme vulnerability to which human beings are subject.[4] Murder is not the only or even the worst violence. Socrates died an unjust but still a noble death. "Yet we know the the possibilities of tyranny are much more extensive. It has unlimited resources at its disposal, those of love and wealth, torture and hunger, silence and rhetoric. It can exterminate in the tyrannized soul even the very capacity to be struck, that is, even the ability to obey on command."[5] The human being is not only subject to murder, he can first be stripped of his infinity; she can be denuded of her personhood. The intensity of obligation arises from the extremity of victimization. The Other is all of my sisters and brothers who are tortured, maimed, murdered, starved, and enslaved. The Other is the child who is destroyed by abuse; the Other is the mother who watches her baby disappear into the living fires of the ovens of Auschwitz. These victims impose on me an unutterable but absolute command. Their very helplessness and suffering before the villainy of force impales my freedom. I do not exist prior to their suffering. I come into a world already constituted by tyranny. In this world, my freedom belongs to the victim.

The Other has no power over me; she cannot force me to obey. But when I recognize the Other, I know that my freedom is dominated by her very vulnerability. I now know, for the first time, beyond all laws or commandments, the ethical impossibility of murder. When I see in her face this unconditional command, I know her to be my Master. I have no power over her any more, but, on the contrary, she, in her complete nakedness and vulnerability, now commands me.

"The Other, whose exceptional presence is inscribed in the ethical impossibility of killing him in which I stand, marks the end of powers" (TI 87). The transition from the violence of totality to ethical existence occurs through this subjection of my freedom in which its egocentric power is stripped away; I serve the Master rather than usurp her alterity. The hegemony and dominance of the Same is shamed, humiliated, and emptied of its own power when it is faced with another. In this inversion of totality the absolute imperative of ethics is finally encountered. Murder, which for totality is the essential modus operandi, becomes for ethics *impossible*.

The Other as Master: A Return to Totality

Levinas accomplishes a startling reversal of the logic of domination by attributing to the destitute one the authority of the Master. Ethics inverts the ordinary understanding of power and authority, but it does so by maintaining the language and structures of totality. I suspect that there is a danger in configuring ethics through totality's language of domination. In this section of the chapter, I will suggest why the logic of domination is inappropriate and the sense in which Levinas's analysis begins to look uncomfortably close to this very logic.[6]

Levinas uses the assymetry of command and submission to describe the dignity of the Other and the absoluteness of responsibility. But there is another side of this hierarchical assymetry. In a hierarchy, the human person is reduced to her role in the system; her value and dignity are merely a function of the hierarchy itself. This hierarchical ordering of human beings denudes them of their infinity. The violence of this formal ordering of the human being according to a preestablished system is intensified when one is placed in the hierarchy in a subservient position. The human being is circumscribed both by its reduction to participation in a system and by its humiliated role in the system. Hierarchy is, therefore, characteristic of the logic of domination.

Domination requires a passive object, one whose will has become inert. Domination is indifferent to the freedom of the commanded. The person is simply an extension of the will of the tyrant, a passive tool, a mindless obedience. This indifference is not neutral, but efficacious: domination creates a servile soul. The servile soul may respond to command, but it lacks the ability to experience obligation. Domination does not invest freedom, but destroys it. The violence of tyranny makes people "betray not only commitments but their own substance, making them carry out actions that will destroy every possibility of action" (TI 21). The structure and power of domination makes the human being into an object that can carry out commands. As such, it is the very antithesis of ethics and of infinity. Domination is intolerant of alterity: it can exist only by eroding the infinity and humanity of the Other.

It is against this power of tyranny that Levinas writes with such genius and passion. But by using precisely the categories that so completely strip people of their humanity to describe ethical existence, the assymetry of ethics looks unnervingly similar to the domination that creates a servile soul. Ethics consists of "submitting oneself" to the Other (TI 86). "The relationship with the Other does not move (as does cognition) into enjoyment and possession, into freedom; the Other imposes himself as an exigency that dominates this freedom, and hence as more primordial than everything that takes place in me" (TI 87). Levinas's description of the "investiture" of freedom as submission, domination, and shame presupposes an essential "allergy" between myself and the Other (see TI 47, 51). The naive violence of the ego is tamed by being forced into obedience. Within the logic of domination I can only be obedient to command. That is, the *only* configuration of the ego and the Other is one of domination: either the Other is subjected to my tyranny, or I am subjected to her command. Levinas uses the logic of domination to preserve the dignity of the Other and the imperative of obligation, but at the expense of defrauding the subject of its own alterity. The hierarchy that makes the ego superior to the Other is inverted; the ego has value *only* in relation to its subjection to the command of the Other. Ethics becomes the servility of obedience. The ego is condemned for its intolerance of the Other and then sentenced to a life of subservience. Passive obedience replaces active domination. This does not displace the destructive power of domination, it merely rearranges its parts.

Obedience is not sufficient for authentic ethical existence. If ethics entails the ability to recognize the victim's abased vulnerability, it also entails an Other to see and respond. Levinas himself writes: "If the Other can invest me and invest my freedom, of itself arbitrary, this is in the last analysis because I myself can feel myself to be the Other of the Other" (TI 84). But domination—even in the service of ethical existence—destroys alterity. I can be forced to obey the imperative issued from my Master, but I cannot be forced to desire the good of the Other. I cannot be commanded to care that he or she is suffering. Subjection to command does not adequately describe the transformation of the violence of domination into existence for the good of the Other. The very possibility of a real response to the Other's destitution is undermined when ethics is configured through the conceptuality of domination. Even the subject's murmers of sorrow, compassion, or comfort are excluded, because they could never arise from command and obedience.

An ethic of command or mastery begins to cleave the logic of totality. It teaches the ego that its freedom is murderous of the Other and that the powerlessness of the widow, orphan, and stranger does not issue an appeal for pity, but rather the imperative of obligation. By framing the attack on totality in its own most violent language, however, an ethic of command betrays the logic of infinity. Relation to a Master produces the violence of war or the docility of the slave. Domination, even by an ethical command, curtails the capacity to experience a desire for the good of another. It can produce obedience in the ego, but only by demanding its suicide.

Beyond Totality: An Ethic of Desire

Totality is like a magnificent despot that possesses and controls everything: food, sex, power, knowledge, houses, forests, and fields. "I can 'feed' on these realities and to a very great extent satisfy myself, as though I had simply been lacking them. Their *alterity* is thereby reabsorbed into my own identity as a thinker or possessor" (TI 33). But beyond the lust for possession emerges a desire for something altogether different, a desire for what is qualitatively different from anything that could be possessed or interiorized. "The metaphysical desire tends toward *something else entirely,* toward the *absolutely other*" (TI 33). As totality achieves its most complete success, metaphysical desire exposes a vista that extends far beyond the realm of possessable beings.

The frustration of totality is that its most perfect apprehension of the Other fails to satisfy the urgency of desire. A gap remains. Levinas describes this gap as the transcendence of infinity (CPP 56; TI 49). Desire enters into the hiatus between alterity and its presence in the ego and in this way reveals the essential and irredeemable failure of totality. Totality encounters alterity only as a part of itself. Desire longs for just the opposite. Desire yearns for that which *cannot* be made a part of itself, which *cannot* be "reabsorbed into my identity as thinker or possessor" (TI 33).

This analysis of desire is a clue to another route to ethical existence, different from that of command. In addition to the murderous hegemony of the ego, there is a yearning in the ego for the Other in her infinity and nonquiddity. Metaphysical desire suggests that the well-being of the Other is in some sense intrinsic to the well-being of the subject. The self-sufficiency of the ego finds itself restless in its very plenitude, frustrated in its very satisfaction. Its own good, its own desire, calls it outside of itself to that which is incradicably different from itself.

Desire empties the ego of its jaded sufficiency and opens it for the Other. In the ethics of desire, possession of the world is transformed into generosity. The lust for the world characteristic of totality becomes the enjoyment of having something to give (TI 75). Desire fundamentally reorders the ego by effecting an "erosion of the absoluteness of being by the presence of the Desirable" (TI 63). This "erosion" produces a new ethical situation. The ethical problem is no longer to tame and to humiliate the imperialism of the ego. The ego is dislodged from this imperialism by desire. Desire for alterity enables the subject to transcend its egocentrism, to see and respond to the face of the Other person.

The self-emptying of the ego by desire parallels the emptying of the ego by humiliation and command. Both command and desire refuse to leave totality intact. Command judges and condemns the ego; desire whispers that its happiness lies elsewhere: it promises a "plenitude and joy . . . [to] the being who experiences it" (CPP 57). Command and desire are two ways of accomplishing the first moment of ethical existence, the moment when the subject realizes that it exists in a world with others and these others qualify its freedom and aseity.

A second moment of ethical existence occurs as the imperative of obligation. Command and desire, again, represent alternative ways of conceiving of this imperative. In an ethic of command, the Master reveals to the ego that its freedom is not for its own self-indulgence, but is for responsibility to the Other. Desire also compels the ego to exist ethically, but in a different way. Metaphysical desire for the Other qua Other is not itself ethical, yet it makes ethics possible by making awareness of the reality of the Other possible. Although my knowledge of any particular person or group of people can never perfectly grasp or comprehend them, desire presents them as more than a projection of my totalizing ego. I can begin to know something true about the Other. I can see for the first time that her face bears the marks of suffering; this matters to me because she is the object of my desire. This is not the same thing as experiencing an alien command, nor is it being subjected to another. I see that the desired one suffers and this knowledge afflicts me. My pain arises from the fact that another's suffering has become real to me. Having been lured out of the security of my totalizing self by metaphysical desire, I am now exposed to her pain. Before, she was at most a vague shadow; now, through desire, I know the reality of her suffering and that reality burns me.

Because the Other is the object of desire, and therefore important to the subject's own well-being, knowledge of her suffering can be transformed into compassion. Compassion suffers for the suffering of the Other, but it is based on care and desire for the Other, rather than on duty towards her. Ethical existence emerges from totality when metaphysical desire effects a self-transcendence that permits the subject to see the suffering in the face of the Other and to be moved to compassion by this suffering.

Desire is what enables the subject not only to obey the imperative to responsibility, but to long for actively and spontaneously the Other's good. Ethics rooted in desire goes beyond obedience; through desire "being becomes goodness: at the apogee of its being, expanded into happiness, in egoism, positing itself as *ego,* here it is, beating its own record, preoccupied with another being!" (TI 22). Just as the ego is completely satiated with its own self-sufficiency, it pours itself out of itself and becomes preoccupied with another. This emptying of the ego for the Other is its transformation into goodness. "[B]eing-for-the Other is not a relationship between concepts . . . but my goodness. The fact that in existing for another I exist otherwise than in existing for me is morality itself" (TI 261, see also 63). Desire is the origin of the order of morality because it transforms existence for me into an existence for the Other. Relationship to the Other need no longer be subjected to the terrible logic of totality: dominate or be dominated. The Same and the Other are connected (not united, not totalized) by goodness rather than domination.[7]

Desire creates an ethical context between the ego and the Other constituted by goodness in which mastery and subjection have no place. The imperialism of freedom becomes the *desire* for the good of the Other. The imperative of obligation is the urgency that the destitution of the Other arouses in one who desires her good. The absoluteness of obligation remains, but it is cleansed of the degradation of domination. I do not simply obey the Master, I burn with compassion for her. This fire of compassion empowers me to resist the tyrant. Compassion, beyond all subjection to command, is the power to contest the right of the tyrant to its victims.

Conclusion

By uncovering two competing metaphors within Levinas's own work, I have tried to clarify the dangers of continuing to resort to the language of domination. Subjection to the mastery of the Other challenges the imperialism of the ego, but it does not overcome totality's allergy to alterity. The language of subjection to command reverses but does not abolish the violence of totality. Because of the destructive power of tyranny and domination, it is of the utmost importance to resist both domination itself and the logic and language of domination.

I have also suggested an alternative embedded in Levinas's own ethical vision. Only when the ego is cleansed both of its hegemony and violence *and* of its humiliated subserviance does it become capable of morality. Desire ruptures totality not only by dismantling the hegemony of the ego, but also by repudiating the logic of totality expressed in relationships of domination. Desire for alterity prevents this ethics from reinstituting hierarchical relationships but preserves the assymetry demanded by ethical experience. Ethics is existence for the Other, hence its assymetry. But it is desire that purges freedom of its violence and fills it with longing and compassion for the Other. Desire accomplishes what command cannot: it transforms the ego into a moral being.

20 Facing Figures: Levinas and the Claims of Figural Interpretation

JILL ROBBINS

What, after all, is a figure? What is in a figure? What does it mean to be or to happen *in a figure,* as when Paul, in 1 Corinthians, says of the Israelites in the desert, "Now all these things happened to them in a figure"?[1] And what would be the relationship between figure and what Emmanuel Levinas has called *ethics?* For Levinas, ethics denotes not a set of moral precepts, but a responsibility—at its most originary—that arises in the encounter with the face of the other *[le visage d'Autrui].* When the other is encountered *as* a face, the infinite alterity of the other is revealed. Yet the face escapes the very phenomenology of Levinas's descriptions. And it is largely in accordance with this antiphenomenological emphasis that Levinas asserts repeatedly that the face is by no means form and in no way figure.[2]

Still, to ask about figure in relation to ethics is necessarily to ask about figure in relation to face. To get at this question, I will consider an early text by Levinas, "Persons or Figures," where it will be a question, first of all, not just of figure, but of *figura.* Levinas's manifest concern in this text is with the figures of *figural* interpretation; namely, with those persons or events in the Hebrew Bible that are said to anticipate the New Testament proclamation. Now, as Erich Auerbach has shown, there is considerable distance between *figura,* in the anticipatory, typological sense used by the Church Fathers, and *figure,* in the rhetorical sense largely developed by Quintillian.[3] And there would be an even greater distance to the technical sense of rhetorical figure that, in recent years, has been taken up and inflected by literary critics such as Gerard Genette and Paul de Man. For Auerbach, the different senses of *figura* would be distinct, yet related. They would emerge in the history of the word, as it moves from its earliest sense of plastic form, to (nonplastic) rhetorical figure, to its eventual patristic usage as prefigural type, a history that is itself, in its very movement from sensory to nonsensory sense, figural.[4] Thus the link between all these senses, and any future senses, of *figure* is *itself* prefigured and, in this way, necessarily presupposed by Levinas's discussion. It should be of no surprise, then, that precisely when Levinas faces the claims of figural interpretation his discussion of the ethics of figural reading, or better, the ethics of figure, becomes most prominently and fully articulated.

Lacking in Figure

The essay "Persons or Figures" was first published in 1950 in the French Jewish periodical *Evidences*. It was later reprinted in Levinas's 1963 collection, *Difficult Freedom,* which appeared two years after the publication of *Totality and Infinity* and which was the first of his nonphilosophical or confessional works.[5] The overall project of *Difficult Freedom,* and this would extend to all the confessional writings (including the four volumes of talmudic readings), is to render explicit what Levinas calls *the hidden resources* of the Judaic tradition. These resources are hidden, if you will, because they have been for the most part covered up by the negative and privative determinations of the Judaic within the dominant (Greco-) Christian conceptuality. Levinas's hermeneutic of Judaism entails a double interpretive movement: he takes a negative term for the Judaic (invariably the subordinated term within a dyadic hierarchy, as in the Pauline tropes of blindness-sight, servitude-freedom, letter-spirit), radicalizes a possibility inherent in it, and reinscribes it to bring out its positive force, even the alternative intelligibility that it harbors. For example, the observance of the law in traditional Judaism is not a yoke, a legalism, but an originary ethical orientation, a fundamental awareness of the other. In the terms of *Difficult Freedom,* it is freedom, albeit a weighty freedom made up of obligations. Ethics itself is this difficult freedom.[6]

Here "Judaism," the meaning of which we can no longer take for granted, provides Levinas with a privileged precedent for his own thinking of the ethical. Yet, at the very same time, there is no immediate access to Judaism. To approach the Judaic in its specificity *requires* the detour through the Christian conceptuality. That is why the essay "Persons or Figures"—the only place in Levinas's work where he comments explicitly on the procedures of Christian interpretation—only hints at how the Judaic would appear over and against the Christian conceptuality (and in this chapter I will not get to the Judaic either, but will remain primarily within this detour).

The opening essay of *Difficult Freedom* exemplifies the double reading characteristic of Levinas's approach to Judaism. He writes:

> For a long time Jews have thought that all the situations in which humanity recognizes its religious direction find in ethical rapports their spiritual signification, that is, their meaning for adults. In consequence they have thought morality in a very vigorous manner. . . . And yet a long acquaintance with Christianity in the West has been able to create, even among Jews who are sincerely attached to Judaism . . . a state of uneasiness. Morality, social action, the concern for justice—all this would be excellent. But it would be only morals! An earthly propaedeutic! Too abstract to fill an inner life. Too poor in figures of style to recount the story of a soul.[7]

In other words: Judaism thinks the ethical. But precisely to the extent that it thinks the ethical, it finds itself lacking. Its very concern for earthly justice, however commendable, leaves it earthbound, stuck in immanence. The point will be echoed in one of Levinas's talmudic readings, where the ritual life of Judaism is characterized as not just "abstract," but "flat," lacking the spiritual heights and depths that make up what Levinas refers to as the Christian "drama" of personal salvation and the rich inner life it allows.[8] Judaism, on the other hand, is so oriented toward the exterior and the outside, it seems to lack even the possibility of such interiority. By lacking that which Levinas calls *temptation*—denoting at once sin and trial—it lacks the very means by which Christian experience (or, for Levinas, any experience) organizes itself. Lacking the turns of Christian experience—the aversions, peripeties, and conversions that figure and prefigure its way toward personal salvation—it lacks even the turns of phrase that would recount them. It is, as Levinas says, "too poor in figures of style to recount the story of a soul" (DF 4). Thus unable to narrativize itself (and without, in any case, a story to tell), Judaism would find neither the forms of biography (saints' lives) nor autobiography (narratives of personal conversion) available to it. It is too "poor in figure" or lacking in figure.

Of course, these lacks can and should be referred to the importance, within Judaism, of the second commandment, which prohibits the making of images and has had a decisive impact on the specific course of the Jewish imagination. As Geoffrey H. Hartman suggests, all the forms of expression of the Jewish imagination are marked by this antiiconic tendency. This accounts not only for Judaism's "text dependency," but also for its particular ambivalence about imagination. For example, the Talmud—its central achievement—is, in Hartman's words, at once "liberated" and "hemmed in" by its necessary relationship to text and to a tradition of commentary.[9] Moreover, Judaism's orientation toward the exterior—its being what Levinas calls "all ears and obedience" (DF 50), expressed in a single word, *shema*—and its turning away from the visible seem grounded specifically in the biblical account of the experience of Sinaitic revelation. In that experience, as it is retold in Deuteronomy: "The Lord spoke to you out of the fire; you heard the sound of words but perceived no figure *[temunah]*—nothing but a voice."[10] Would this be why Judaism is lacking in figure?

Too Many Figures

When it comes to the Christian interpretive imagination, it is a matter, if anything, of too many figures. The essay, "Persons or Figures," appearing in a part of *Difficult Freedom* entitled "Polemics," reviews a commentary on the Old Testament by the poet Paul Claudel. As a polemical target of Levinas's essay, Claudel's commentary represents not an authoritative tradition of Christian exegesis, but an aesthetic response to the Old Testament on the part of a giant of French letters. Claudel had, as a young man, converted to Catholicism; later in life, he wrote several biblical commentaries, including the 1949 *Emmaus*.

As a biblical commentary, *Emmaus* can be classified as an imaginative or poetic retelling. Levinas calls it a "personal exegesis" (DF 119). Suffice it to say that it abounds in figural readings, taking as its guiding principle the Pauline phrase, "now *all* these things happened to them in a figure": *omnia in figura*.[11] Claudel's figural reading discovers not just the Old Testament types that prefigure and announce events and persons of the New Testament. It also finds in the Old Testament, in a gesture that cites and echoes similar exegeses by Saint Paul, prefigurations of the (pre)figural relationship itself. Thus for Claudel, Joseph is "a prefiguration of the Savoir"; Esau and Jacob are "the intertwined conflict between Law and Grace." The Israelites stand at the foot of Mount Sinai, but, Claudel addresses them, "later, on another mountain, there will be Someone who will speak to you in something other than thunder and there will be no need for a Moses to interpret him." For "the commandments from Sinai are no longer merely external to me, that is, on the tablets of stone on which I find them written; they are—in a new sense—in my heart, in my most inward sensibility, my most secret communication." Claudel even has (his) Moses assert, as he descends Mount Sinai with a veil over his face, "I am only a figure."[12]

When Auerbach describes *figura,* he emphasizes the interpretive invention it encourages, the way in which it foregrounds the *ability* of the interpreter to discover resemblances in the biblical text. (This is at least as important as any actual accord between the two testaments.) But is he also correct to insist on the diversity of its productions? The fact is that, in the hands of Claudel at least, the Old Testament—read figurally—is a monotonous document indeed. Levinas asks: "If all the unsullied characters in the Old Testament announce the Messiah, and all the unworthy ones, his executioners, and all the women, his mother, does not the Book of Books—obsessed by a single theme and invariably repeating the same stereotypical gestures—lose its lifelike quality *[sa vie vivante]?*" (DF 121). When does a type become a stereotype? Is there not a price to pay for the discovery of Old Testament types, or in Levinas's terms, a loss? The loss, as Levinas formulates it, would be to the "lifelike" quality of the Old Testament, its sense of being rooted in concrete everyday situations, "material interests, crimes, jealousy, hatred, murder, that even fraternity does not resolve" (DF 101). Levinas's formulation further implies that what is lost is not just the lifelike *quality* of the Old Testament, but life itself, "its living life" *[sa vie vivante]*. The Old Testament is thus killed off by figural interpretation, is perhaps rendered truly (and for the first time) a dead letter.

One may well object that as a *representation* of life, rather than as life itself, the Old Testament never had any life to lose. But let us not take for granted that we know what Levinas means by *living*. In this usage, *living* does not necessarily refer to the presence of the present. It will have to do with the face and the distinctive way in which the face signifies. "The face is a living presence; it is expression," he says in *Totality and Infinity*.[13]

But there are other losses that figural interpretation incurs when it reads the Bible as a procession of types, a repertory of figures. Levinas intertwines his polemic against figural interpretation with his polemic against the mythological and the sacred, a realm of involuntary participation where events are played out "in spite of the self," thereby absolving the self of responsibility to the other. He asks, "does the spiritual dignity of these men come from their reference to a drama situated on a miraculous plane, in a mythological and sacred beyond, or rather from the meaning that this life—which is conscience—gives to itself?" (DF 121). The central assertion here is that the Christian emphasis on the otherworldly is at the expense of the Bible's reference to *this* life, which, says Levinas, "is conscience," that is, which is the space of the ethical. If the Christian religious imagination can be characterized by its movement from sensory to nonsensory sense both in its interpretive modes and in its understanding of the economy of personal salvation, Judaism, with its perpetual

recourse to the interhuman, can be understood as a refusal of this movement. Elsewhere in *Difficult Freedom,* Levinas writes: "Moses and the
prophets are not concerned with the immortality of the soul, but with the
poor one, the widow, the orphan, and the stranger" (DF 19–20). Or, "it is
on the earth, among men, that the adventure of spirit unfolds . . . in responsibility—whence comes the conception of a creature who has the
chance to save himself without falling into the egoism of salvation" (DF
26). And finally: "History is not a perpetual test with a diploma of eternal
life as its goal, but the very element in which the life of spirit moves"
(DF 100). In short, the reference to the interhuman, to *this* life, is precisely what is most specific to Judaism and to the Judaic reading of the
Bible. It is this distinctively Judaic reference that is lost in figural interpretation.

For even when figural interpretation does represent the interhuman,
a loss of historicity results. As Levinas puts it, "the relationships which
man holds with himself and with his neighbors appear frozen *[figes],*
unalterable, eternal" (DF 99). The problem seems to go even further than
figural interpretation's manner of representing the interhuman or, for that
matter, even further than its manner of representing the self's preoccupation with personal salvation. It has to do with the possibility of representing these things at all. To represent the rapport between persons is to
"freeze" it; it is to turn what ought to be an ethical relationship into a
theatrical pageant, into what is referred to earlier as "a drama situated on
a miraculous plane."[14] Similarly, to represent the self's relationship with
itself as a dramatic journey on the way toward personal salvation is to
fall into what Levinas calls *the egoism of salvation* (DF 26). In short, to
aestheticize and theatricalize these rapports is to cover up the ethical. The
very complicity between Christianity and the aesthetic turns the Bible
into "a world of figures instead of a world of faces" (DF 140). It is in this
way, according to Levinas, that Christianity *loses* face.

Losing Face

Levinas will, however, counter the figural claim and its feat of
double casting each and every Old Testament character as a figure within
a Passion that is always already a passion play. He writes:

> The holy history is not the interpretation of a thesis play *[une pièce à
> thèse],* even if it is a transcendent one, but the articulation, made by a
> human freedom, of a real life. Are we on stage or are we in the world?
> Is to obey God to receive from him a role, or a command? We distrust
> this theatre, this petrification of our faces, this character that our person

would embrace *[Nous nous méfions du théâtre, de la pétrification de nos visages, de la figure que notre personne épouse]*. We distrust the poetry which already scans and bewitches our gestures, and all that which, in our lucid life, plays *[se joue]* in spite of us. It is because of this that in the final analysis the Claudelian exegesis leads us totally astray. A man as a person, as an agent of history seems to him less real than a figure-man, a statue-man *[l'homme-figure, l'homme-statue]*. The freedom proper to conscious man is envelopped in a kind of sublime and sacramental fate in which instead of *being*, man *figures [au lieu d'être, l'homme figure]*. God the director effaces God the Creator. He commands actors rather than freedoms. (DF 121–122)

Here, figural interpretation does not merely freeze the rapport *between* persons; it freezes the persons themselves. In Levinas's words, it turns them into *figure-men* or *statue-men*; it *petrifies the face*. The charge could not be more serious. For in Levinas's work, the encounter with the other's *face* is the irreducible experience of what is called *ethics*. It is the central meditation of his work, the "figure," as it were, for the human and for the interhuman order as a whole. *Face* denotes the other (person) insofar as the other breaks out of the phenomenon, looks back, and speaks. *Face* denotes the infinite alterity of the other who, in his or her very poverty and distress, commands ethical responsibility or response.

To speak, then, of the petrification of the face is to announce an event that, within the terms of Levinas's ethical thought, is one of the worst things that could happen. It would be a violence directed *at* the face, the essential characteristic of which is mobility: "The face is a living presence; it is expression. The life of expression consists in undoing the form in which the existent exposed as a theme, is thereby dissimulated. The face speaks *[le visage parle]*."[15] If the face, in Levinas's descriptions, is not reducible to a plastic image, surface, or mask, that is in part because the face is always on the move, divesting itself of its form, confronting the self with its expression, speaking a primordial speech. Hence, at issue here is a violence directed not just at a face or at particular faces; the petrification of the face would do violence to the very possibility of the ethical's arising. It would put a stop to the ethical at the level of its condition of possibility. It is a violence that (because it would occur on this originary level) could serve as an alibi for all violent action.

The petrified face or the frozen face would also be, to an extent, an image or "figure" for the Holocaust, as it is marked in "Persons or Figures." It would denote at once the violence directed at the face of the other—the loss of the other's face—and also the loss of face on the part of the persecutors. Claudel's figural reading loses face in this double sense when the Old Testament is said to prefigure, and thus to charge itself with, deicide: "Cain represents a certain kind of prefiguration of the Jewish people, the assassin of God."[16] Such an anti-Judaic reading may be an occupational hazard of figural interpretation, especially in its patristic and late medieval form. But when such a reading is advanced in 1949, that is, "after Auschwitz," it is, says Levinas, discourteous of our troubles (DF 122).[17]

In Levinas's terms, the figural reading of the Old Testament covers up "freedom," that is, the heteronomous freedom in responsibility that a Judaic reading of the same testament could reveal. Moreover, to say that figural interpretation petrifies the face also is to reverse implicitly the Pauline reading of Moses descending Mount Sinai, tablets of stone in hand, a veil over his face to conceal its fading splendor, a reading in which the threat inherent in a literal, Judaic relation to the law, written on stone, is the petrification of the interpreter himself.[18]

Levinas's ethical objection to figural interpretation, however, seems to go beyond his general assertion that the force of a specifically Judaic reading of the Old Testament is covered up. And here it is necessary to attend to a whole other register of Levinas's antifigural discourse and to consider again the significance of his turning away from figure. For Levinas seems to object to the possibility of theatrical representation itself. The very fact that a person may assume a character or take on a role is said to threaten the ontological status of the real: "instead of being, man figures" (DF 122). To take on a character [une figure] is to risk becoming a figure, and thereby to lose what is human, to be turned into a statue, to be turned into stone. To take up a character is said to render one incapable of distinguishing illusion from reality, "stage" from "world," a directorial command from a divine one. In short, the way in which Levinas tropes these charges requires comment.[19] For it is not just the figures of figural interpretation that are said to cover up the ethical. It is as if figures themselves were unethical, as if anything that plays were ethically suspect.[20] Levinas says: "We distrust that which plays [se joue] in spite of us" (DF 121).

There is thus in Levinas's discourse an antitheatrical trope. It can be situated within a tradition that goes back to Plato, with his negative judgment on mimesis as ontologically derivative and debased, as well as to the Church Fathers, where the theater is viewed as too pagan and idolatrous, that is, as attached to what is visible and sensible. Levinas's formulations most resemble the antisacramental and antiliturgical strain within Protestant Christianity, in which, as one critic puts it, the theater that is in question claims to be an enactment of the central truths of religion, and "the very thing . . . that reveals [its] devotional purpose . . . is the thing that offends . . . most bitterly."[21]

In closing then, and in abbreviated form, some consequences of the antitheatrical trope of "figure" with which Levinas articulates his critique of figural interpretation can be indicated. It can be shown that when Levinas speaks of the "figure-man," the "statue-man," and the "petrified face," the sense of figure to which he objects goes beyond the figures or characters of theatrical mimesis; it is also rhetorical. Levinas's ethical objection to *figura* is also an objection to figure itself, to the figurative or rhetorical dimension of language. This attitude toward figure can and should be read with the suppression of rhetoric—always understood in the sense of intersubjective persuasion—in Levinas's work as a whole, and the description it receives in *Totality and Infinity* as "injustice." It should be read together with Levinas's gesture of first subsuming all rhetoric under the category of persuasion, then rejecting it as ruse and violence. What, one wonders, would an understanding of rhetoric not just as persuasion, but also as trope, that is, an emphasis on the cognitive dimension of rhetoric as Paul de Man describes it, do to Levinas's antifigural discourse?[22]

Suffice it to note that Levinas's condemnation of the figure of mimesis relies on a series of dyadic oppositions: stage-world, dramatic play—real life, character-person, and, the essay's central opposition, with the provocative either-or that its title reinforces, figure and person. These oppositions are not only metaphysical; they are continuous with and proper to the very concept of mimesis that he is purportedly criticizing. Similarly, when Levinas says that figures are unethical, is there such a thing as a nonfigural position from which to speak? And if mimesis were no longer *the* privileged trope for artistic making, but simply one trope among others, then it would be, as de Man suggests, like paronomasis or punning, where language imitates sound on an intralinguistic level, merely an example of language's choosing to imitate a nonverbal entity with which it does not necessarily have anything in common.[23] It might be necessary, then, not to turn *away* from figure, as Levinas does, but to face the figure otherwise, as language's ownmost figurative potential, as that which is most distinctive to language, that is, to face language *as* ethical possibility.

The resources for such a confrontation would come from Levinas's work itself, which describes the ethical relation to the other as a kind of language, as responsibility, that is, as language-response to the other who faces and who, "in turn," speaks. As one of Levinas's commentators puts it, "the face then faces in language."[24] And as Levinas himself has surely taught us, ethics is something that "happens" in language. This is what makes even the face, in the last analysis, a facing figure.

Notes

Chapter 1. Political Aspects of Husserl's Call for Renewal

1. Edmund Husserl, *Aufsätze und Vorträge (1922–1937)*, ed. T. Nenon und H. R. Sepp, Husserliana XXVII (Dordrecht: Kluwer Academic Publishers, 1989). After first citation, references to this and other volumes of *Husserliana: Edmund Husserl—Gesammelte Werke* use the abbreviation "Hua" and volume number.

2. This point is made by Husserl himself; see editor's introduction, Hua XXVII, p. xi.

3. This is the only *Kaizo* article that has been translated into English. See, "Renewal: Its Problem and Method," trans. J. Allen in *Husserl: Shorter Works*, ed. P. McCormick and F. Elliston (South Bend, Ind.: University of Notre Dame Press, 1981), pp. 326–331.

4. Hua XXVII, p. 6.

5. Hua XXVII, p. 95. For background on the turmoil of Weimar Germany, an excellent source is Hagen Schulze, *Weimar Deutschland: 1917–1933* (Berlin: Severin und Siedler, 1982). A standard work on political decay in Weimar is K. D. Bracher, *Die Auflösung der Weimarer Republik. Eine Studie zum Problem des Machtverfalls in der Demokratie* (Villingen: Ring Verlag, 1964).

6. From the election of June 6, 1920 to the fall of Weimar, the Reichstag never had a pro-republican majority. For the lack of political consensus, see Ullrich Scheuner, *"Grundrechte und Verfassungskonsens als Stützen der Verfassungsordnung"* in *Weimar als Erfahrung und Argument* (Bonn: n.p., 1977).

7. See Schulze, *Weimar Deutschland 1917–1933*, pp. 31–47.

8. Husserl-Archive signature R. I. Bell 13.XII.1922. I am grateful to Professor Samuel IJsseling, director of the Husserl-Archive, for permission to cite this letter and other material from Husserl's unpublished *Nachlass*.

9. Husserl's youngest son, Wolfgang, was killed in action at Verdun, France, on March 8, 1916.

10. Hua XXVII, p. 3.

11. "A vrai dire, si l'occasion de conférences qu'il fut à donner en 1935 à Vienne, puis à Prague, donna naissance au projet de la *Krisis* telle que nous la connaissons, Husserl avait commencé à méditer cette question dès que l'ébranlement décisif de la Première Guerre mondiale démontra, à l'évidence, une crise qui remettait en jeu les fondaments spirituels et rationnels d'une Europe où, depuis vingt-cinq siècles au moins, la poursuite de l'idéalité rationnelle avait été l'ultime finalité de l'humanité. La Première Guerre mondiale marque en effet une brizure dans l'élan spirituel de l'Europe." Pierre Trotignon, *Le coeur de la raison. Husserl et la crise du monde moderne* (N. p.: Fayard, 1986), p. 14.

12. Oswald Spengler, *Der Untergang des Abendlandes: Umriss einer Morphologie der Weltgeschichte* (Munich: Deutscher Taschenbuch Verlag, 1972), p. X. Preface to first edition, 1917.

13. Hua XXVII, p. 4.

14. Franco Volpi, "Aux racines du malaise contemporain: Husserl et la responsabilité du philosophe" in *Husserl,* ed. E. Escourbas and M. Richir (Grenoble: Editions Jérome Millon, 1989), pp. 158–159.

15. Hua XXVII, see especially pages 79–89.

16. Edmund Husserl, *Die Krisis der europäischen Wissenschaften und die transzendentale Phänomenologie,* ed. W. Biemel, Husserliana VI (The Hague: Martinus Nijhoff, 1954). English translation by David Carr, *The Crisis of European Sciences and Transcendental Phenomenology* (Evanston, Ill.: Northwestern University Press, 1970). For the mechanics of this forgetfulness by natural science, see especially section 9.

17. Hua XXVII, p. 94.

18. Hua XXVII, p. 3.

19. See my more extensive treatment of this problem in P. Buckley, *Husserl, Heidegger and the Crisis of Philosophical Responsibility* (Dordrecht: Kluwer Academic, 1992), Chapter 5, section 2.

20. As Karl Schuhmann has pointed out, the word *Politik* appears fewer than ten times in the first twenty volumes of Husserliana. See K. Schuhmann, *Husserls Staatsphilosophie* (Freiburg: Verlag Karl Alber, 1988), p. 18.

21. Hua XXVII, p. 5.

22. Hua XXVII, p. 6, "welche [die rationale Widssenschaft] eine Rationalität im sozialen, im politischen Handeln und eine rationale politische Technik begründen würde . . . "

23. Edmund Husserl, *Zur Phänomenologie der Intersubjektivität. Texte aus dem Nachlass,* ed. I. Kern, Husserliana XIII–XV (The Hague: Martinus Nijhoff, 1973). Here we cite Hua XIV, p. 357.

24. Hua XIV, p. 359.

25. This notion of a "personality of a higher order" is found already in *Ideen II* (Hua IV, section 51) and is worked out more fully in manuscripts dating from the same period as *Kaizo;* see, for example, Hua XIV, texts 9 and 10. It is not surprising that it plays a central role in *Kaizo* as well, see Hua XXVII, p. 22.

26. Hua XXVII, p. 22.

27. Hua XXVII, p. 6.

28. Hua XXVII, p. 49.

29. James Hart, "I, We, and God: Ingredients of Husserl's Theory of Community" in *Husserl-Ausgabe und Husserl-Forschung,* ed. S. IJsseling (Dordrecht: Kluwer Academic Publishers, 1990), pp. 137–138.

30. See, for example, the sarcastic treatment of the "liberale Einzelmenschenbewusstsein" in C. Schmitt, *Politische Theologie. Vier Kapitel zur Lehre von der Souveränität,* 2. Ausgabe (Munich und Leipzig, 1934), p. 74.

31. Hua XXVII, p. 53.

32. Hua VI, p. 348; *Crisis,* p. 299. See also Husserl's attack on "lazy reason," in Hua VI, p. 14, *Crisis,* p. 16.

33. Hua XXVII, p. 53.

34. Hart, p. 130.

35. Hua XXVII, pp. 28, 107.

36. Hua XXVII, p. 53.

37. "Die Philosophen sind die berufenen Repräsentanten des Geistes der Vernunft, das geistige Organ, in dem die Gemeinschaft ursprünglich und fortdauernd zum Bewusstsein ihrer wahren Bestimmung (ihres wahren Selbst) kommt, und das berufene Organ für die Fortpflanzung dieses Bewusstseins in die Kreise der 'Laien'." Hua XXVII, p. 54.

38. Husserl-Archive manuscript *K I 28/25a.* Sections of this manuscript are published in Husserliana XXI. This citation is found on Hua XXI, p. 231.

39. Hua XXVII, p. 52.

40. Hua XXVII, pp. 28–33, 98.

41. Hua XXVII, p. 58.

42. Hart, pp. 141–142.

43. Hua XV, p. 412. "Staat ist eine Einheit durch Macht, durch Herrschaft."

44. Hua XXVII, pp. 73–74.

45. Hua XXVII, p. 95.

Chapter 2. Arendt/Foucault: Power and the Law

1. Claude Lefort, "Hannah Arendt and the Political," in *Democracy and Political Theory,* trans. David Macey (Minneapolis: University of Minnesota Press, 1988), p. 54.

2. Jürgen Habermas, *The Philosophical Discourse of Modernity,* trans. Frederick G. Lawrence (Cambridge, Mass.: MIT Press, 1990), p. 284.

3. Michel Foucault, *Power/Knowledge* (New York: Pantheon Books, 1980), p. 123. Hereafter referred to in the text as P/K.

4. Habermas, *The Philosophical Discourse of Modernity,* p. 284.

5. Michel Foucault, "The Subject and Power," afterword to Hubert L. Dreyfus and Paul Rabinow, *Michel Foucault: Beyond Structuralism and Hermeneutics* (Chicago: University of Chicago Press, 1982), p. 221.

6. Augustine, *The Confessions,* trans. John Ryan (New York: Image Books, 1960), p. 196. For Arendt's discussion of freedom and the subjective will, see "What Is Freedom?" *Between Past and Future* (New York: Penguin Books, 1978), and *The Life of the Mind,* volume 2 (New York: Harcourt, Brace, Jovanovich, 1978). In *The Life of the Mind,* see especially the chapter "Augustine, the First Philosopher of the Will," pp. 84–110.

7. Hannah Arendt, *On Revolution* (New York: Penguin, 1977), p. 171; hereafter referred to in the text as OR.

8. Hannah Arendt, *The Origins of Totalitarianism* (New York: Harvest/ Harcourt, Brace, Jovanovich, 1979), p. 293; hereafter referred to in the text as OT.

9. Hannah Arendt, *On Violence* (New York: Harvest/Harcourt, Brace, Jovanovich, 1970), p. 44; hereafter referred to in the text as OV.

10. Montesquieu, *The Spirit of the Laws,* trans. Thomas Nugent (New York: Hafner Press, 1949), p. 115.

11. Claude Lefort, "Permanence of the Theologico-Political?" in *Democracy and Political Theory,* p. 226.

12. Of course, this is precisely Lefort's point. Indeed I would suggest that Lefort's reflection on the *mise en sens* and the *mise en scene* develops many of Arendt's insights concerning the necessary distinction between the social and the political.

13. Hannah Arendt, *The Human Condition* (Chicago: University of Chicago Press, 1958), p. 180.

14. I am indebted to Ignace Lecluyse for continuing to raise the question concerning Arendt's distinction between the public and the secret at the 1990 session of the Collegium Phaenomenologicum.

15. Hannah Arendt, *Lectures on Kant's Political Philosophy* (Chicago: University of Chicago Press, 1982), p. 75.

Chapter 3. Self-Overcoming in Foucault's *Discipline and Punish*

1. Michel Foucault, *Discipline and Punish,* trans. Alan Sheridan (New York: Random House, 1977), p. 255. All subsequent references to this volume will occur in the body of this text noted by DP and the page number.

2. See for elaboration of this point, Susan Griffin, *Rape: The Politics of the Unconscious* (San Francisco: Harper and Row, 1986).

Chapter 4. Resisting Subjects: Habermas On the Subject of Foucault

1. Jürgen Habermas, *The Philosophical Discourse of Modernity,* trans. Frederick Lawrence (Cambridge: Massachusetts Institute of Technology Press, 1987), p. 314.

2. Jürgen Habermas, "A Postscript to *Knowledge and Human Interests,*" trans. Christian Lenhardt, *Philosophy of the Social Sciences* 3 (1973), p. 167.

3. Ibid., p. 169.

4. Ibid., p. 168.

5. Ibid., p. 169.

6. Jürgen Habermas, *The Theory of Communicative Action,* vol. 1. *Reason and the Rationalization of Society,* trans. Thomas McCarthy (Boston: Beacon Press, 1984), p. 9.

7. Habermas, "Postscript," p. 179.

8. Jürgen Habermas, *Erkenntnis und Interesse* (Frankfurt: Surhkamp Verlag, 1981), p. 391. (The paragraph from which this quote has been taken does not seem to have been included in the English translation. The translation here is my own.)

9. Habermas, "Postscript," p. 171.

10. Mary Hesse raises the following question with regard to Habermas's notion of truth: "the implication is that *every* culture implicitly contains this very ideal of truth. Habermas wishes to describe this as neither an empirical description, since it is highly counter-factual, nor an option for arbitrary decision, but a transcendental implication of discourse as such. But what is his response to actual situations in which it is of the essence of the culture *not* to recognize such an ideal? These may be cases of totalitarian oppression in complex societies, or mythopoetic authority in archaic ones." Mary Hesse, "Habermas' Consensus Theory of Truth," in *Revolutions and Reconstructions in the Philosophy of Science* (Bloomington: Indiana University Press, 1980), p. 221.

11. Habermas, *Action,* p. 51.

12. For the implications this has for rationality—which is ultimately what Habermas seeks to secure by means of a consensus theory of truth—see Rodolphe Gasché, "Postmodernism and Rationality," *The Journal of Philosophy* 85 (1988): 528–538. There Gasché notes: "Yet, if rationality is the issue today, is it merely to conjure the alleged lack of philosophical argumentation and discursive consistency? Is it not, rather, because thinking has discovered a new sort of finitude which requires not the abandonment of the traditional forms and claims that constituted it, but their displacement within operations of thought whose calculated economy obeys a 'rationality' of its own?" (p. 538).

13. Habermas, *Modernity,* p. 246.

14. Ibid., p. 297.

15. I suspect that the notion of consensus outlined here could have occurred only to a tenured professor in Germany. To everyone else who must work from paycheck to paycheck the real constraints on the "free" participation in speech situations are much more evident.

16. The crux of Habermas's argument is that the media of consensus formation are innocent of power. This is itself an assumption informed by history. For it is part of the ideology of late (and state monopoly) captialism that the state is informed of the interests of the people via neutral means of communication. These media of communication, however, are specific political phenomena that will continue to exercise their own politics.

17. Michel Foucault, "The Subject and Power" in Hubert L. Dreyfus and Paul Rabinow, *Michel Foucault: Beyond Structuralism and Hermeneutics* (Chicago: University of Chicago Press, 1983), p. 208.

18. Ibid., p. 212.

19. Ibid., p. 220.

20. Ibid., p. 220.

21. Ibid., p. 208. Foucault also explains, with regard to the power that is thereby exerted: "This form of power applies itself to immediate everyday life which categorizes the individual, marks him by his own individuality, attaches him to his own identity, imposes a law of truth on him which he must recognize and which others have to recognize in him. It is a form of power which makes individuals subjects" (p. 212).

22. Michel Foucault, *Madness and Civilization*, trans. Richard Howard (New York: Random House, 1973), p. 264.

23. Ibid., pp. 264–265.

24. Foucault elaborates on this in *The History of Sexuality, Vol. 1: An Introduction*, trans. Robert Hurley (New York: Random House, 1980), p. 58: "Since the Middle Ages at least, Western societies have established the confession as one of the main rituals we rely on for the production of truth. . . . For a long time, the individual was vouched for by the reference of others and the demonstration of his ties to the commonweal (family, allegiance, protection); then he was authenticated by the discourse of truth he was able or obliged to pronounce concerning himself."

25. Ibid., p. 70.

26. "The essential features of this sexuality are not the expression of a representation that is more or less distorted by ideology, or of a misunderstanding caused by taboos; they correspond to the functional requirements of a discourse that must produce its truth." Ibid., p. 68.

27. Foucault explains the notion of confession as follows: "What I mean by 'confession', even though I can well see that the term may be a little annoying, is all those procedures by which the subject is incited to produce a discourse of truth about his sexuality which is capable of having effects on the subject himself." Michel Foucault, "The Confession of the Flesh," in *Power/Knowledge: Selected Interviews and Other Writings 1972–1977*, ed. Colin Gordon (New York: Random House, 1980), pp. 215–216.

28. Foucault, *Introduction*, pp. 61–62.

29. With regard to the study as a whole, Foucault takes pains to analyze and distinguish his work from what he terms "the repressive hypothesis." For the discourse of sexuality in modern Western societies operates on the assumption that it has been repressed up until very recently. In this way the necessity of confession only disseminates itself further. Indeed, Foucault raises the question: "Did the critical discourse that addresses itself to repression come to act as a

roadblock to a power mechanism that had operated unchallenged up to that point, or is it not in fact part of the same historical network as the thing it denounces (and doubtless misrepresents) by calling it 'repression'? Was there really a historical rupture between the age of repression, and the critical analysis of repression?" (ibid., p. 10). Foucault thereby emphasizes that his study is not aimed at identifying what the discourse of sexuality has repressed. *The History of Sexuality* seeks instead to identify how the discourse of sexuality functions to situate subjects in a self-regulating system of discursivity and behavior. These systems are organized roughly into three historical phases characterized by the following: the care of the self, the confession of the flesh, and the confession of repression.

30. As Foucault explains: "For them, reflection on sexual behavior as a moral domain was not a means of internalizing, justifying, or formalizing general interdictions imposed on everyone; rather, it was a means of developing—for the smallest minority of the population, made up of free, adult males—an aesthetics of existence, the purposeful art of freedom perceived as a power game. Their sexual ethics, from which our own derives in part, rested on a very harsh system of inequalities and constraints (particularly in connection with women and slaves); but it was problematized in thought as the relationship, for a free man, between the exercise of his freedom, the forms of his power, and his access to truth." Michel Foucault, *The History of Sexuality,* vol. 2. *The Use of Pleasure,* trans. Robert Hurley (New York: Random House, 1986), p. 253.

31. Ibid., p. 83.

32. One of the most difficult cases with regard to this was the love between men and boys. This is because the boy involved was to one day enjoy a social status equal to that of the man's. The assumption of a role that was potentially submissive posed therefore a threat to the social order and the nature of subject.

33. Foucault, *Pleasure,* p. 28.

34. Ibid., p. 63.

35. Michel Foucault, *The History of Sexuality,* vol. 3. *The Care of the Self,* trans. Robert Hurley (New York: Random House, 1986), p. 41.

36. Ibid., p. 53.

37. Ibid., p. 85.

38. Ibid., p. 143.

39. Dreyfus and Rabinow, *Michel Foucault,* p. 244.

40. Foucault, *Introduction,* p. 33.

41. Ibid., p. 24.

42. Ibid., p. 127.

43. Ibid., p. 124.

44. Ibid., p. 114.

45. Foucault comments on this in "The Political Technology of Individuals," *Technologies of the Self,* ed. Luther H. Martin, Huck Gutman, and Patrick II. Hutton (Amherst: University of Massachusetts Press, 1988): "In all history it would be hard to find such butchery as in World War II, and it is precisely this period, this moment, when the great welfare, public health, and medical assistance programs were instigated. The Beveridge program has been, if not conceived, at least published at this very moment. One could symbolize such a coincidence by a slogan: Go get slaughtered and we promise you a long and pleasant life. Life insurance is connected with a death command" (p. 147).

46. Foucault, *Introduction,* p. 93.

47. To explore this micro-politics in more detail, the relationship between Foucault and the work of Gilles Deleuze would have to be explored. See, for instance, "Intellectuals and Power. A Conversation Between Michel Foucault and Gilles Deleuze," in *Language, Counter-Memory, Practice,* ed. Donald F. Bouchard (Ithaca, N.Y.: Cornell University Press, 1977), pp. 205–217 as well as Gilles Deleuze, *Foucault,* trans. Seán Hand (Minneapolis: University of Minnesota Press, 1988).

48. Foucault, *Introduction,* p. 96.

49. Ibid., p. 96.

50. Foucault, *Pleasure,* p. 9.

Chapter 5. Mastering a Woman: The Imaginary Foundation of a Certain Metaphysical Order

The author would like to thank the American publishers of Simone de Beauvoir, Jonathan Cape, who kindly gave her their permission to have a new translation of quotations of Simone de Beauvoir done for her book *Hipparchia's Choice* (Oxford: Basil Blackwell, 1991). And she would also like to say how grateful she is to Robert Gallimard for his very kind support. In this chapter she has taken up some of these quotations. Because she was back in Paris when she revised her chapter for publication, she has taken the liberty to document all quotations by French authors to the French texts, and the quotations that are given here are according to the translation that has been discussed with and agreed to by Tamara Parker. In her mind, it does not imply any criticism of the standard English translations, but refers only to the fact that it is quite impossible to find an English translation of Rousseau in Paris.

This chapter is dedicated to Marie-Claire and Jean-Jacques Rosat, who did not accept my view of Sartre until I wrote it.

1. Jean-Jacques Rousseau, *L'Emile,* book 5, in *Oeuvres Complètes* (Paris: Éditions Gallimard, coll. Pléïade, vol. IV, 1969), p. 857.

2. Simone de Beauvoir, *Mémoires d'une jeune fille rangée* (Paris: Gallimard, 1958; paperback Paris: "Folio," 1975), p. 473.

3. Simone de Beauvoir, *La Force de L'Age* (Paris: Gallimard, 1960; paperback Paris: "Folio," 1976), p. 29.

4. Jean-Jacques Rousseau, *Contrat* 1, Chap. 7 in *Oeuvres Complètes,* vol. III, p. 362.

5. *L'Emile,* p. 332.

6. Jean-Paul Sartre, *L'Etre et le Néant* (Paris: Gallimard, 1943), p. 120; henceforth EN.

7. Simone de Beauvoir, *Lettres au Castor,* vol. 1 (Paris: Gallimard, 1983), p. 57.

8. Sometimes, it is appropriate to say *he or she,* sometimes one has to say just *she* and sometimes one must say only *he.*

9. Michèle Le Doeuff, *Hipparchia's Choice,* trans. Trista Selous (Oxford: Basil Blackwell, 1991).

10. *L'Etre et le Néant,* p. 93.

11. See note 8.

12. Jean-Paul Sartre, *L'Existentialisme est un humanisme* (Geneva: Nagel, 1970), p. 39.

13. *Mémoires d'une jeune fille rangée,* p. 479.

14. Jean-Paul Sartre, *Vérité and Existence.* Sartre drafted this text in 1948. He left it unfinished and unpublished. It was edited after his death by Arlette Elkaïm-Sartre (Paris: Gallimard, 1948); henceforth VE.

15. Diedre Bair, *Simone de Beauvoir: A Biography* (New York: Summit Books, 1990), p. 203 and index.

16. Compare the Heloïse's complex I described in "Long Hair, Short on Ideas," *The Philosophical Imaginary* (Palo Alto, Calif.: Stanford University Press, 1990).

17. Margery Collins and Christine Pierce, "Holes and Slime: Sexism in Sartre's Psychoanalysis," *Philosophical Forum* 5 (Fall–Winter 1973): 112–127.

18. Simone de Beauvoir, *Lettres à Sartre,* ed. Sylvie Le Bone de Beauvoir (Paris: Gallimard, 1990), vol. 2, p. 155; henceforth LS.

19. See my "Women, Reason, etc.," *Differences* (Fall 1990).

Chapter 6. Lacan and the Ethics of Desire: The Relation Between Desire and Action

1. Vicente Palomera, "The Ethics of Hysteria and of Psychoanalysis," *lacanian ink,* no. 3 (Spring 1991): 41–53.

2. Jacques Lacan, *Le Séminaire,* vol. 7 (1959–1960). *L'éthique de la psychanalyse,* ed. Jacques-Alain Miller (Paris: Seuil, 1986), p. 245.

3. Jacques Lacan, *Le Séminaire,* vol. 15 (1967–1968). *L'acte psychanalytique* (unpublished seminar).

4. Aristotle, *The Ethics of Aristotle: The Nicomachean Ethics,* trans. J. A. K. Thomson (New York: Penguin Books, 1976).

5. Ellie Ragland-Sullivan, *Jacques Lacan and the Philosophy of Psychoanalysis* (Urbana and Chicago: University of Illinois Press, 1987), pp. 166–167.

6. Sigmund Freud, *The Project for a Scientific Psychology* (1895), *Standard Edition* (London: Hogarth Press, 1964), vol. 1, pp. 283–397, see p. 300.

7. Sigmund Freud, *The Interpretation of Dreams* (1900), *Standard Edition,* vols. 4 and 5.

8. Jacques Lacan, *The Four Fundamental Concepts of Psycho-Analysis,* ed. Jacques-Alain Miller, trans. Alan Sheridan (New York: W. W. Norton & Co., 1981), p. 180. See the French text, *Le Séminaire,* vol. 11 (1964).

9. Jacques Lacan, "The Subversion of the Subject and the Dialectic of Desire in the Freudian Unconscious," in *Ecrits: A Selection,* trans. Alan Sheridan (New York: W. W. Norton & Co., 1977), pp. 314–315.

10. Jacques-Alain Miller, "To Interpret the Cause: From Freud to Lacan," *Newsletter of the Freudian Field* 3, nos. 1–2 (Spring–Fall 1989): 30–50, see p. 47.

11. Jacques-Alain Miller, "Extimité," *Prose Studies* 11, no. 3 (December 1988): 121–131.

12. Serge Cottet, *Freud et le désir du psychanalyste* (Paris: Navarin, 1983), p. 143.

13. Teresa Brennan, "The Construction of Imaginary Time," unpublished manuscript.

14. Jeanne Granon-Lafont, *La Topologie Ordinaire de Jacques Lacan* (Paris: Point Hors Ligne, 1985), p. 4.

15. Immanuel Kant, *Critique of Practical Reason,* trans. N. K. Smith (New York: St. Martin's Press, 1929).

16. Alphonse Donatien, the Marquis de Sade, *La philosophie dans le boudoir,* posthumous work of the author of *Justine,* 1795, 2 vols.

17. Sigmund Freud, *Civilization and Its Discontents,* in *Standard Edition,* vol. 21.

18. *The Holy Bible, The King James Version, The New Testament,* Romans 3:23.

19. Jacques-Alain Miller says conscious fantasies are essentially daydreams which a person enjoys. Unconscious fantasies are the basic constructions on which individuals build their subjective realities. The structure of all fantasies of a given subject depends on the fundamental fantasy, "the structure from which anything makes sense to a particular subject. This universal of his fantasy is, as a rule, unknown to him . . . because he is inside it." [from "Duty and Drives," in *Newsletter of the Freudian Field,* vol. 6, no. 1–2, forthcoming.]

Lacan's formula ($ \$ \lozenge a $) means that people imagine that things (that *a*) will fill up the lack-in-being ($\$$). But no one ever closes the gap in any final way because each of us is divided, as the lozenge ($\lozenge$) symbolizes, by alientation (language) and separation (the drives). Both of these are media in which individuals represent themselves in the world at one remove from the lack that is a permanent structure in being.

20. *The Holy Bible*, Matthew 22:39; see also Mark 12:31.

21. Sigmund Freud, "The New Introductory Lectures on Psychoanalysis," *Standard Edition,* vol. 22, p. 80.

22. Albert Camus, *The Myth of Sisyphus,* trans. Justin O'Brien (New York: Alfred A. Knopf, 1961), p. 138.

Chapter 7. Julia Kristeva's Speaking Body

1. *La Revolution du langage poetique* (Paris: Seuil, 1974), trans. as *Revolution in Poetic Language* by Margaret Waller (New York: Columbia University Press, 1984), p. 13; referred to as RPL from now on in the text.

2. Compare this to a passage in Lacan's 1953–1954 seminar, where he claims that the symbol opens up the world of negativity. *The Seminar of Jacques Lacan, Freud's Papers on Technique, 1953–54.* Book 1, trans. John Forrester (Cambridge, Mass.: Cambridge University Press, 1988), pp. 173–174; referred to as S1 from now on.

3. Lacan also identifies a negativation that is prior to the "no" (S1 173–174). Kristeva suggests that this is already a symbolic operation.

4. *Pouvoirs de l'horreur* (Paris: Éditions du Seuil, 1980), trans. Leon Roudiez as *Powers of Horror* (New York: Columbia University Press, 1982), p. 10; referred to from now on as PH in the text.

5. Kristeva, *Soleil Noir: Depression et Melancolie* (Paris: Gallimard, 1987), trans. as *Black Sun* by Leon Roudiez (New York: Columbia University Press, 1989); referred to as BS from now on.

6. Kristeva, *Etrangers à nous-mêmes* (Paris: Fayard, 1989), trans. as *Strangers to Ourselves* by Leon Roudiez (New York: Columbia University Press, 1991); referred to as SO from now on.

7. "Le Temps des femmes," originally published in *34/44: Cahiers de recherche de sciences des textes et documents,* no. 5, trans. A. Lardine and H. Blake as "Women's Time," in *Feminist Theory: A Critique of Ideology,* ed. N. Keohane, M. Z. Rosaldo, and B. C. Gelpi (Brighton: Harvester Press, 1982), p. 52.

8. Ewa Ziarek points out that maternity is the most troubling example of alterity within identity because this body exists within the heart of domestic stability and the continuation of the species. Ziarek, Ewa, "At the Limits of Discourse: Heterogeneity, Alterity, and the Maternal Body in Kristeva's Thought," *Hypatia, a Journal for Feminist Philosophy* 7, no. 1 (1992).

9. For Kristeva, within the Catholic discourse of maternity, the Virgin Mary contains this outlaw love. The virgin cuts this narcissistic identification between daughters and mothers and substitutes an identification with the symbolic. So, the mother is sacrificed to the virgin. And, it is no wonder that the virgin can no longer provide the necessary support against feminine paranoia. Although Kristeva argues that the cult of the virgin is crumbling and that it no longer provides a "solution or else provides one that is felt as too coercive by twentieth-century women," she does so with a kind of nostalgia for her lost paternal mother. "Stabat Mater," in *Tales of Love,* trans. Leon Roudiez (New York: Columbia University Press, 1987), p. 259; referred to as TL from now on.

10. "A New Type of Intellectual: The Dissident," in *The Kristeva Reader,* ed. Toril Moi (New York: Columbia University Press, 1986), p. 297. Kristeva's discussion of the pregnant maternal body is the central focus, around the time of her own pregnancy, which lead to the birth of her son in 1976, in two essays: "Stabat Mater" and "Motherhood According to Giovanni Bellini," trans. Thomas Gora, Alice Jardine, and Leon Roudiez, in Leon Roudiez, ed. *Desire in Language* (New York: Columbia University Press, 1980); referred to as MGB from now on.

11. Compare PH 37.

12. "Interview with Julia Kristeva," in *Women Analyze Women,* ed. Elaine Baruch and Lucienne Serrano (New York: New York University Press, 1988); referred to as WAW from now on.

13. Compare, Lacan, *Ecrits: A Selection,* trans. Alan Sheridan (London: Tavistock, 1977), p. 207; Kristeva, "Postmodernism?" in Harry Garvin, ed., *Romanticism, Modernism, Postmodernism* (Lewisburg: Bucknell University Press, 1980).

14. *Au commencement etait l'amour,* 1987, trans. Arthur Goldhammer as *In the Beginning Was Love: Psychoanalysis and Faith* (New York: Columbia University Press, 1988), p. 42; referred to IBWL from now on.

Chapter 8. Irigaray and Con(fusing) Body Boundaries: Chaotic Folly or Unanticipated Bliss?

My thanks goes to the audience at the SPEP conference at Villanova for their reactions and constructive criticism.

1. "Il me semble que si le patient risque de devenir idiot en psychanalyse, c'est par privation sensorielle et privation de l'adéquation de la parole à la sensation et la perception." This passage comes from *Sexes et Parentés* (Paris: Les Éditions de Minuit, 1987), p. 168; subsequent references to this book will be indicated by SP, followed by the page number.

2. "Ne pas entendre ce déséquilibre perceptif, c'est risquer de déraciner le patient de son corps, de son histoire. Cela revient alors à le situer dans une énergie abstraite, mécanique, neutre?, à en faire un automate avec une histoire artificielle" (SP, 169).

3. "Il convient de rendre ces résidus perceptibles au patient, de les fluidifier et de les remettre en perspective pour libérer la création. Cela signifie, par exemple, qu'il faut tenter de restituer, à chaque sens, les vitesses objective et subjective de ses perceptions actuelles et rendre possible l'harmonie entre eux et avec l'histoire passée, présente et future du sujet" (SP, 170–171).

4. This is my response to the current debate about Irigaray and her "essentialist" tendencies. It seems odd to me to label Irigaray an *essentialist,* given her critique of language and the inherently essentializing tendencies of its "masculine" logic. I take her emphasis on the feminine, the mother-daughter relationship, and a feminine genealogy as a strategic move appropriate to our particular situation. Because these are crucial areas of human experience that are currently underrepresented and devalued in our culture, it is to these areas she turns to open up new possibilities for understanding ourselves and our world. Opening up such possibilities, in her view, also entails radical stylistic innovations that open up new ways of using language more appropriate to alternative ways of conceiving truth, subjectivity, and rationality. For more on the debate on essentialism, see the issue of *Differences* (vol. 1, no. 2) on essentialism, Donna C. Stanton, "Difference on Trial: A Critique of the Maternal Metaphor in Cixous, Irigaray, and Kristeva" in *The Thinking Muse: Feminism and Modern French Philosophy,* ed. Jeffner Allen and Iris Young (Bloomington: Indiana University

Press, 1989); and Diane Fuss, *Essentially Speaking* (New York: Routledge, 1990). I am quite sympathetic to Margaret Whitford's approach in *Luce Irigaray: Philosophy in the Feminine* (New York: Routledge, 1991) and Elizabeth Grosz's approach in *Sexual Subversions: Three French Feminists* (Cambridge, Mass.: Unwin Hyman, 1989) to Irigaray with respect to this point. Also see Teresa Brennan's introduction to *Between Feminism and Psychoanalysis* (New York: Routledge, 1989).

5. Irigaray develops the theme of a kind of speaking (in her view, woman's speech) that subverts masculine logic by refusing fixed concepts in *Speculum of the Other Woman* (Ithaca, N.Y.: Cornell University Press, 1985) and *This Sex Which Is Not One* (Ithaca, N.Y.: Cornell University Press, 1985). See my book, *Gender, Identity, and the Production of Meaning* (Boulder, Colo.: Westview Press, 1990) for a discussion of "sensation-ideas" in Irigaray's reading of Plato's cave analogy in *Speculum*.

6. There are many excellent discussions of Lacanian theory and an increasing number of works on the relationship of Lacanian theory to feminism. Some more recent ones include Judith Butler, *Subjects of Desire* (New York: Columbia University Press, 1987) and *Gender Trouble: Feminism and the Subversion of Identity* (New York: Routledge, 1990); and Elizabeth Grosz, *Jacques Lacan: A Feminist Introduction* (New York: Routledge 1990). Ellie Ragland-Sullivan, *Jacques Lacan and the Philosophy of Psychoanalysis* (Urbana: University of Illinois Press, 1986); and J. Rose and J. Mitchell, *Feminine Sexuality* (New York: W. W. Norton, 1985) are also very useful.

7. "Cette dualité: lieu, d'une part, idées et nombres, de l'autre, n'est—elle un des symptômes du divorce entre masculin et féminin? Pour surmonter l'attraction pour le premier et unique lieu, l'homme, en ce qu'il a de mieux, s'exerce aux idées et aux nombres indépendants du lieu? Cette "ascension," non inscrite dans le lieu, y rend le retour impossible, sinon sous forme de déchéance, de chute dans l'abîme, etc." This passage comes from Luce Irigaray, *L'Éthique de la différence sexuelle* (Paris: Éditions de Minuit, 1984), p. 45; subsequent references to this book will be indicated by EDS, followed by a page number.

8. "Le maternel-féminin demeure le *lieu séparé de "son" lieu,* privé de "son" lieu. Elle est ou devient sans cesse le lieu pour l'autre qui ne peut s'en séparer" (EDS, 18).

9. "La fille est exilée de sa terre pour devenir femme, et la femme devient mère dans la généalogie de son mari. Ce devoir pour elle, ce droit pour l'homme, coupe la femme de ses racines en la réenracinant dans la famille de son mari où elle doit faire substance. Elle donne de la terre au nom de son mari et de ses ancêtres dans l'ordre patriarcal monogamique" (SP, 145).

10. I am using Carolyn Burke's translation of Irigaray's lecture on Levinas, "Fécondité de la caresse," published in *Face-to-Face with Levinas,* ed. R. A. Cohen (New York: State University of New York Press, 1986), pp. 173–199.

11. For a similar point see her discussion of eros in *Le Temps de la Différence: Pour une révolution pacifique* (Paris: Livre de Poche, 1989), pp. 110–111: "Le chemin de l'amour réciproque entre les personnes est perdu notamment en ce qui concerne l'érotisme. Et celui-ci, au lieu de servir à l'individuation, à la création ou recréation des formes humaines, sert à la destruction ou à la perte d'identité dans la fusion, et au retour à un niveau de tension toujours le même et le plus bas, sans devenir ni croissance." Subsequent references to this book will be indicated by TD, followed by a page number.

12. "Au contraire, *l'acte* sexuel serait ce par quoi l'autre me redonne forme, naissance, incarnation. Au lieu d'entraîner le déchéance du corps, il participe de sa renaissance. Et aucun autre acte ne l'équivaut, en ce sens. Acte le plus divin. L'homme fait ressentir à la femme son corps comme lieu. Non seulement son sexe et sa matrice mais son corps. Il la situe dans son corps et dans un macrocosme, la sortant de son éventuelle adhérence au cosmique par la participation à une microsociété" (EDS, 55).

13. Note that Irigaray does recognize a kind of mirroring activity that can be appropriate for affirming subjectivity. It is when one anticipates the shape one's reflection will take that one excludes responses from the other that could generate growth: "Nécessaire parfois pour séparer, le miroir—et le regard en temps que miroir—devrait demeurer moyen et non fin à laquelle je me plie. Le miroir devrait assister et non réduire mon incarnation. Il ne renvoie généralement d'images que superficielles, plates. Il en est d'autres, génératrices de volumes plus que le reflet spéculaire. . . . Nous avons été poissons. Nous aurions à devenir oiseaux. Cela ne peut se faire sans ouverture et mobilité dans l'air" (SP, 78).

14. Although women cannot objectify their mothers in the same way, Irigaray is very aware that it does not necessarily follow that women will have healthier relationships than men do with their mothers or with other women. Special problems arise for love between women due to the lack of representation of the mother-daughter relationship and a feminine genealogy. To take on some form of identity women cancel out their relationship with their mothers to become the maternal-feminine. In doing so, they destroy the possibility for love between them: "La place de la mère étant unique, devenir mère supposerait d'occuper ce lieu, sans relation avec elle en ce lieu. L'économie, ici, serait *ou l'une ou l'autre, ou elle ou je-moi.* Cette rivalité quant à la place et la fonction maternelles (les seules valorisées pour la femme en Occident) est commandeée par le relation de l'homme au maternel et le manque d'identité féminine. Pour se fair désirer, aimer de l'homme, il faut évincer la mère, se substituer à elle, l'anéantir pour devenir même. Ce qui détruit la possibilité d'un amour entre mère et fille" (EDS, 101). Also see "Le Corps-à-Corps Avec la Mère" in *Sexes et Parentés* and "And One Doesn't Stir Without the Other," *Signs* 7, no. 1 (1981) for more on this point.

15. This theme runs throughout Irigaray's work. In a talk given in Rome in 1988 she puts it this way: "Brutalement, des personnes réelles ne sont pas représentés ou sont représentées autrement que selon leur sexe. . . . La langue

laisse les hommes entre eux, et prive les femmes de l'entre-elles. L'ordre linguistique ne permet pas le dilemme. Il dévalorise génériquement le féminin. Il survalorise le masculin" (TD, 61).

16. In "Le Corps-à-Corps Avec la Mère" Irigaray says that we need to find words that speak of the archaic immediacy of the daughter's relationship to her mother's body and to her own. We need phrases that translate the tie between the mother's body and her daughter's body, and this daughter's body and her daughter's body, to constitute a feminine genealogy. A feminine symbolic would not provide substitutes for the body-to-body relationship of the feminine genealogy as the paternal language tries to do, but would accompany it. A feminine language would thus speak the body rather than attempt to bracket the corporeal aspect of our origins and our existence: "Nous avons aussi à trouver, retrouver, inventer les mots, les phrases, qui disent le rapport le plus archaïque et le plus actuel au corps de la mère, à notre corps, les phrases qui traduisent le lien entre son corps, le nôtre, celui de nos filles. Nous avons à découvrir un langage qui ne se substitute pas au corps-à-corps, ainsi que tente de le faire la langue paternelle mais qui l'accompagne, des paroles qui ne barrent pas le corporel mais qui parlent corporel" (SP, 31).

17. "Le lieu, l'intervalle" (EDS, 41–59).

18. "Par contre, se vit parfois dans le rapport des lieux, dans l'acte sexuel, la transgression de l'enveloppe, par porosité, perception de l'autre, fluidité. Si bien qu'il est possible d'imaginer qu'une génération d'un certain type se produirait par perméabilitié des membranes et participation aux humeurs de l'autre" (EDS, 51).

19. "Surmonter l'intervalle, tel est l'enjeu du désir, la cause du transport. L'intervalle tend vers zéro quand il y a passage au muqueux. Ou transgression du toucher à travers la peau. Le problème du désir étant de supprimer l'intervalle en ne supprimant pas l'autre. Car le désir peut dévorer du lieu et soit régresser en l'autre sur le mode intra-utérin, soit anéantir l'existence de l'autre de diverses manières. Pour que le désir subsiste, il faut un double lieu, une double enveloppe. Ou Dieu comme subsistance de l'intervalle, report de l'intervalle à et dans l'infini. Irréductible. Déployant l'univers et son au-delà. En ce sens, l'intervalle produirait le lieu" (EDS, 53).

20. "L'homme met l'infini dans un *transcendant* toujours reporté à l'au-delà, fût-il l'audelà du concept. La femme le met dans une *étendue* de jouissance ici maintenant tout de suite. Corps-étendue qui essaie de *se donner de l'extériorité, de se donner à l'extériorité,* de se donner dans un espace-temps non ponctuel, non orgastique au sens limité du terme. De se donner comme espace-temps sans fin. Ou très difficilement définissable" (EDS, 67).

21. In "L'Amour du Même, L'Amour de l'Autre," Irigaray comments on the masculine subject she is critiquing: "Il ne se souvient même plus du fait que son corps est le seuil, le portique de la construction de son, ses univers. Il existe

dans la nostalgie du retour au TOUT UN: son désir de retournement vers et dans la matrice originaire" (EDS, 99).

22. Although at times it may appear as if my reading is suggesting otherwise, I want to dispel any notion that attentiveness to the body and "body-based feelings" or "movement and life" in the present moment refers to some reservoir (contained, perhaps, in the unconscious?) of pure, "natural" sensation, untouched (and therefore untainted) by patriarchy and masculine logic. The body and its sensations are always already mediated through social meaning structures. These meaning structures can take different forms, however (e.g., body language that may reevoke memories of physical intimacy with one's mother), some of which are more subversive than others of more conventional linguistic structures. I am indebted to Gillian Gill for prompting me to articulate this point.

23. See *Speculum* and *This Sex Which Is Not One* for further elaboration on the breakdown of conventional categories in the "feminine" approach to language.

Chapter 9. Irigaray and the Divine

1. Published translations of which I am aware include the following: "Divine Women," Local Consumption Occaisonal Papers, No. 8, 1986; "Women, the Sacred and Money," *Paragraph* no. 8 (1986); "The Fecundity of the Caress" in *Face-to-Face with Levinas,* ed. R. Cohen (Albany: State University of New York Press, 1986); and "Equal to Whom?" *Differences,* no. 2 (1990). Among other, more general texts relevant to understanding her position, see "Women's Exile," *Ideology and Consciousness,* no. 1 (1977): "That Sex Which Is Not One," in *New French Feminisms,* ed. E. Marks and I. Courtivron (New York: Schocken Books, 1981); "When the Goods Get Together," ibid.; "When Our Lips Speak Together," *Signs*; "And One Doesn't Stir Without the Other," *Signs* 7, no. 1 (1981); (also in *Refactory Girl,* No. 23, 1982); "For Centuries We've Been Living in the Mother-Son Relation," *Hecate,* 9, nos. 1–2 (1983); "Any Theory of the 'Subject' Has Always Been Appropriated by the 'Masculine'," *Trivia* (Winter 1985). It appears as if, at long last, translations of many of her most recent texts will become available in English.

2. St. Teresa is Lacan's emblem of a *jouissance* or pleasure that women may experience—in sexual love or in religious devotion—that is 'beyond the phallus.' Yet for Lacan, although women can experience this pleasure, they cannot know or say anything about it. Compare Lacan, "God and the Jouissance of The Woman," *Feminine Sexuality,* J. Rose and J. Mitchell (New York: W. W. Norton, 1985); and Irigaray's response in "Cosi Fan Tutti" in *This Sex Which Is Not One* (Ithaca, N.Y.: Cornell University Press, 1985).

3. "Divine Women," p. 4.

4. *"Le Corps-à-Corps Avec la Mère,"* in *Sexes et Parentés* (Paris: Les Éditions de Minuit, 1987), p. 37.

5. "Divine Women," p. 3.

6. "Equal to Whom?" p. 64.

7. Ibid., p. 64.

8. Ibid., p. 65.

9. Ibid., p. 1.

10. See Lacan's comments on God, in *Feminine Sexuality*; and in *The Four Fundamental Principles of Psychoanalysis,* trans. Alan Sheridan (New York: W. W. Norton, 1981) where he discusses the Cartesian concept of God from the *Meditations*.

11. Merleau-Ponty, *The Visible and the Invisible,* trans. Alphonso Lingis (Evanston: Northwestern University Press, 1969), p. 139.

12. Her phrase in *L'Éthique de la différence sexuelle* (Paris: Éditions de Minuit, 1984).

13. "Divine Women," p. 12.

14. Ibid., p. 4.

15. Ibid., p. 5.

16. *L'Éthique,* pp. 22–23.

17. Ibid., p. 23.

18. In *Hecate* 9: 199.

19. "Ou et comment habiter?" *Les Cahiers du Grif* (March 1983).

20. "Divine Women," p. 10.

21. *L'Éthique,* p. 24.

Chapter 10. Irigaray's *Amante Marine* and the Divinity of Language

1. *Amante Marine de Friedrich Nietzsche* (Paris: Éditions de Minuit, 1980). *Marine Lover,* trans. Gillian Gill (New York: Columbia University Press, 1991). The feminine gender of *Amante Marine* is, unfortunately, lost in English.

2. *L'Éthique de la différence sexuelle* (Paris: Les Éditions de Minuit, 1984), my translation.

3. *Sexes et genres à travers les langues,* ed. Luce Irigaray (Paris: Grasset, 1990).

4. *Speculum de l'autre femme* (Paris: Éditions de Minuit, 1974). *Speculum of the Other Woman,* trans. Gillian Gill (Ithaca, N.Y.: Cornell University Press, 1985).

5. *Marine Lover,* p. 142; *Amante Marine,* p. 151.

6. *Marine Lover,* p. 153; *Amante Marine,* p. 164.

7. *Marine Lover,* p. 161; *Amante Marine,* p. 173.

8. *Marine Lover,* p. 178; *Amante Marine,* p. 191.

9. *Marine Lover,* pp. 181–182; *Amante Marine,* pp. 194–195.

10. *Marine Lover,* p. 185; *Amante Marine,* p. 198.

11. *Marine Lover,* p. 190; *Amante Marine,* p. 203.

12. "L'Ordre Sexuel du Discours," *Langages* 85 (1987): 81–123.

13. Ibid., p. 83.

14. Ibid., p. 89.

15. *Parler n'est jamais neutre* (Paris: Les Éditions de Minuit, 1985), pp. 26–31.

16. "L'Ordre Sexuel du Discours," p. 115.

17. Ibid., pp. 103, 115.

18. *Parler n'est jamais neutre,* p. 9: "dit ses sources."

19. *Je, tu, nous* (Paris: Grasset, 1990), p. 60.

20. *L'Éthique de la différence sexuelle,* p. 124.

21. *Je, tu, nous,* pp. 19, 30.

22. Katherine Stephenson, "L'Instance visuelle: analyse syntagmatique d'un corpus anglais," *Sexes et genres,* pp. 117–165; and Mark Calkins and Katy Swenson, "Discours sexué et intersexué," ibid., pp. 165–189.

23. Ibid., p. 13, my translation.

24. Luce Irigaray, "Conclusions," ibid., p. 393: "un chiasme partiel."

25. Irigaray, "Conclusions," ibid., p. 292.

Chapter 11. The Earth That Does Not Move

I would like to thank Michelle Frailey for her insight, her dedication, and her labor; Harvey Rabbin for his dazzling critique; and Peter Goodrich for more than his scholarship.

1. Edmund Husserl, *Ideen II*, p. 208, quoted in Ludwig Landgrebe, "The Phenomenology of Corporeality," *The Phenomenology of Edmund Husserl*, ed. Donn Welton (Ithaca, N.Y., and London: Cornell University Press, 1981), p. 42; hereafter referred to as PEH.

2. Martin Heidegger, *Being and Time*, trans. John Macquarrie and Edward Robinson (New York: Harper and Row, 1962), p. 417; hereafter referred to as BT.

3. Marianna Haraszti-Taka'cs, *Spanish Genre Painting in the Seventeenth Century* (Budapest: Ademlai Kiado, 1983), p. 83; hereafter referred to as SGP. Haraszti-Taka'cs gives a brief but interesting history of the *bodega*, from which the pictorial *bodegán* is derived: "the modern word 'bodega'—in Andalusian and in Latin America as well—imparts the meaning of a winc-tavern, a cellar or a small village-pub where some food and drinks are purchased or consumed. Even the Hungarian language has retained the word 'bodega'—now slowly becoming obsolete—with the meaning of a village shop, pub, possibly also a small milk-bar or snack-bar. In the Romanian language districts of Southern Transylvania the signboard 'bodega' is frequently encountered even in towns, for instance in the outskirts of Brasov: these are groceries or snack-bars where drinks may be obtained. According to the Historical Dictionary of the Hungarian Language, the first written occurrence of the word 'bodega' dates from 1879; referring to the Spanish origin, its first meaning is 'warehouse,' 'premises for goods.' A sentence by A. Agai from the turn of the century is quoted: 'Beside the Vienna cafe, the Munich beer-house and the Spanish bodega are gaining ground' sc., in Budapest. Our dictionary records also a second meaning, which is 'wine-cellar' or 'snack-bar' (the Austrian 'Imbissstube.') The Spanish word itself derives from the Greek *apodhtkh*, Latin *apotheca* (which also enriched the Hungarian vocabulary with the nouns 'butik' (any small shop) and 'patika' (chemist's shop))."

4. Oskar Hagen, *Patterns and Principles of Spanish Art* (Madison: University of Wisconsin Press, 1943), p. 78.

5. Fernand Braudel, *The Mediterranean and the Mediterranean World in the Age of Phillip II*, trans. Sian Reynolds (New York: Harper and Row, 1972), p. 104; hereafter referred to as MMW.

6. On "making room," see BT, sec. 24, pp. 145–148.

7. See SGP, p. 83.

8. In such a way each market thing determines the price of the next market thing; each time an orange is bought or sold there is some rippling across the surface of the marketplace, some fluctuation of price.

9. Fernand Braudel, *Civilization and Capitalism Fifteenth–Eighteenth Century, II, The Structures of Everyday Life: The Limits of the Possible,* trans. Sian Reynolds (New York: Harper and Row, 1984), p. 126; hereafter referred to as CCII.

10. See Edmund Husserl, *Ideas I* (New York: Collier Books, 1962, sec. 78, p. 202: "Every experience is in itself a flow of becoming, it is what it is within an original engendering *(Erzeugung)* of an essential type that never changes: a constant flow of retentions and protentions mediated by a primoridal phase which is itself in flux, in which the living now of the experience comes to consciousness contrasting with its 'before' and 'after'."

11. Edmund Husserl, *The Crisis of European Sciences and Transcendental Phenomenology,* trans. D. Carr (Evanston, Ill.: Northwestern University Press), sec. 45, p. 158; hereafter referred to as CES.

12. See Patrick Heelan, *Space-Perception and the Philosophy of Science* (Berkeley and Los Angeles: University of California Press, 1983).

13. Erwin Panofsky, *Renaissance and Renascences in Western Art* (New York: Icon Editions, Harper and Row, 1972), pp. 141–142. Such carpentry is manifest in those pictorial spaces of the fourteenth and fifteenth centuries, embedded with theological or symbolic prescriptions, in which all the perceptual data are reinterpreted from an iconographic point of view in order to depict an imaginary conjuncture of actual or possible structures and mythical events. One example is Ambrogio Lorenzetti's *Presentation in the Temple* (1342), in which a Christian church is cast in the role of the temple of Solomon. As Panofsky points out: "the temple of Solomon conceived or ornamented in such a way that its architectural features and even such decorative details as the statues of Moses or Joshua or the mosaic above the 'triumphal arch' allude to the omnipresent correlation between the Old Testament and the New—is . . . an imaginary building exemplifying that principle of 'disguised symbolism' which, once the pictorial space had been subjected to the rules that govern empirical space, compelled the artist to hide theological or symbolical concepts, openly revealed by his mediaeval predecessor, beneath the cloak of apparent verisimilitude."

14. Svetlana Alpers, *The Art of Describing: Dutch Art in the Seventeenth Century* (Chicago: University of Chicago Press, 1983), p. 133. It is interesting to note that, in the seventeenth century, the map and the microscope were epistemological twins. Each served to annihilate distance and thus enabled one to see something that was otherwise invisible: "Like lenses, maps were referred to as glasses to bring objects before the eye. To an artist like Jacques de Gheyn, who on occasion made both, the map was the obverse of the drawing of the fly."

15. Edmund Husserl, *Experience and Judgment: Investigations in a Genealogy of Logic,* ed. Ludwig Landgrebe, trans. James S. Churchill and Karl Ameriks (Evanston, Ill.: Northwestern University Press, 1973), pp. 201–202; hereafter referred to as EJ.

16. Jacques Berques, *French North Africa: The Maghrib Between Two World Wars* (New York: Praeger Books, 1962), p. 36.

17. Joshua Prawer, "Palestinian Agriculture and the Crusader Rural System," *Crusader Institutions* (Oxford: Clarendon Press, 1980), p. 159; hereafter referred to as PAC. As Prawer points out, the "objective size" of such a unit can be evaluated only approximately.

18. PAC, p. 159: "As the *faddan* represents the area ploughed during one day it is obviously smaller in rough mountain soil than in the plain." " . . . the *faddan* even today, does not have the same value everywhere. In mountainous regions like Jerusalem, for example, it is evaluated at 734 square metres; but, in the valleys and plains it is almost twice as large."

19. Jacques Le Goff, "Labor Time in the 'Crisis' of the Fourteenth Century," *Time, Work, and Culture in the Middle Ages,* trans. A. Goldhammer (Chicago: University of Chicago Press, 1980), p. 44; hereafter referred to as TWC.

20. Jacques Derrida, *Edmund Husserl's Origin of Geometry: An Introduction,* trans. John P. Leavey, Jr., ed. D. Allison (New York: Nicolas Hays, 1978), p. 81; hereafter referred to as EHG.

21. For Husserl on the earth as the basis body, see also his fragment "Fundamental Investigations on the Phenomenological Origin of the Spatiality of Nature," 1934, *Philosophical Essays in Memory of Edmund Husserl* (Westport, Conn.: Greenwood Press, 1968), pp. 307–325.

22. See Jacques Le Goff, "The Symbolic Ritual of Vassalage," TWC, pp. 243–248. It was after the second stage of the ritual of vassalage, the fealty, that the vassal became the "man of mouth and hands" of the lord. According to Le Goff, for Marc Bloch it is in a gesture of the hand that the essential act (of fealty) must be sought. "In 1110, for example, Bernard Atton IV, Viscount of Carcassonne, swore homage and faith in return for a number of fiefs to Leon, abbot of Notre-Dame-de-la-Grasse in the following terms: 'In the name of each and everyman, I do homage and faith by my hands and mouth to thee, my lord Leon, abbot and to thy successors'." And more explicitly, the expression can be found "in the *carta donationis* of 1109 of Dona Urraca, in which Alfonso the Battler uses it in addressing his wife: 'Let all the vassals *(homines)* who today hold this fief *(honor)* from you, or will hold it in the future swear fealty to you and become your vassals *(men)* of mouth and hands.' . . . This expression is manifestly important because it shows the essential place occupied by the symbolism of the body in the cultural and mental system of the Middle Ages. The body not only reveals the soul but is the symbolic site where man's fate—in all

its forms—is fulfilled. Even in the hereafter, at least until the last Judgement, it is in corporeal form that the soul meets its fate, for better or worse, or for purgation."

23. CES, p. 376: "Measuring belongs to every culture, varying only according to stages from primitive to higher perfections. We can always presuppose some measuring technique, whether of a lower or higher type, in the essential forward development of culture, (as well as) the growth of such a technique, thus also including the art of design for buildings, of surveying fields, pathways, etc.; such a technique is always already there, already abundantly developed and pregiven to the philosopher who did not yet know geometry but who should be conceivable as its inventor. As a philosopher proceeding from the practical finite surrounding world (of the room, the city, the landscape, etc., and temporally the world of periodical occurrences: day, month, etc.) to the theoretical world-view and world knowledge, *he has the finitely known and unknown spaces and times as finite elements within the horizon of an open infinity. But with this he does not yet have geometrical space, mathematical time, and whatever else is to become a novel spiritual product out of these finite elements which serve as material; and with his manifold finite shapes in their space time he does not yet have geometrical shapes, the phoronomic shapes; his shapes, as formations developed out of praxis and thought of in terms of gradual perfection,* clearly serve only as bases for a new sort of praxis out of which similarly named new constructions grow."

24. Pierre Legendre, *L'Amour du censeur: essai sur l'ordre dogmatique* (Paris: Editions du Seuil, 1974), p. 5. In other words, "the law in each system institutes its own science."

25. EHG, p. 178. The production of even surfaces and their perfection (polishing) ushers the cases where just distribution is intended. "Here the rough *estimate* of magnitudes is transformed into the *measurement* of magnitudes by counting the equal parts."

26. EHG, p. 78. An object in sedimented space—for Husserl, the sedimented space of the European sciences—is always and already a reconquered object, an object that is conquered by one law from another in the form of linguistic, juridical constraints. The problem of repetition, of the again and again of an ideality is thereby also a problem of sedimentation; what is repeated is not repeated again and again as the same object, but is preserved, communicated, and confirmed through its sedimentations. Such knowledge persists as habitual. See also EJ, p. 62.

27. See Fernand Braudel, *Civilization and Capitalism Fifteenth–Eighteenth Century, I, The Structures of Everyday Life: The Limits of the Possible* (New York: Harper and Row, 1981), p. 188; hereafter referred to as CCI: "Wherever it began, agriculture has been obliged to opt for one of the major food-plants; and had been built up around this initial choice of priority on which everything or almost everything would thereafter depend. . . . Three of these plants . . . wheat,

rice, and maize; . . . the 'plants of civilization,' . . . have profoundly organized man's material and sometimes his spiritual life, to the point where they have become almost ineradicable structures." Their history and the "determinism of civilization" they have exercised over the world's peasantry and human life (built up) "a complicated system of relationships and habits, . . . so firmly cemented together that no fissure was possible" (pp. 107–117).

28. PAC, p. 160. In everyday life the difference between the fiscal and the real *carruca* did not pose any great problems. Each village was evaluated at a given number of *carrucae,* which roughly corresponded to the totality of its arable. When a village was alienated in its entirety, the beneficiary received a quarter or a third of the harvest from its arable. Nor did the donation of part of a village, or of a number of *carrucae,* therein, pose difficult problems. We have seen this in the lordship of Tyre, where villages were divided between the Crown and the Venetians. The two parties divided the whole harvest in proportion to their respective rights, without any preliminary interference with the cultivation."

29. EJ, p. 42: "The world in which we live and in which we carry out activities of cognition and judgment, out of which every thing which becomes the substrate of a possible judgment affects us, is always already pregiven to us as impregnated by the precipitate *(Niederschlag)* of logical operations. The world is never given to us as other than the world in which we or others, whose store of experiences we take over by communication, education and tradition, have already been logically active, in judgment and cognition."

30. Justinian's *Digest,* XXII.4.1, "Documentary Evidence and Loss of Documents (De Fide Instrumentorum et Amissione Eorum)." Thus extending the domain of *de fide instrumentorum* from its original meaning in the *Digest,* where it designates any form of witnessing, a juridical account of an action, any faithful instrument of the law: " 'Instruments' include all the evidence relevant to a case. Hence, both oral evidence and witnesses are regarded as instruments."

Chapter 12. A Postmodern Musicological Approach to the Authentic Performance Debate

1. According to *The Music Index.*

2. Thomas Mace, *Musick's Monument* (Paris: Editions De Centre National De La Recherche Scientifique, 1958), p. 105.

3. J. S. Bach, *Clavier-Buchlein vor W. F. Bach,* ed. R. Kirkpatrick (New Haven, Conn.: Yale University Press, 1959), p. i.

4. These symbols are used throughout the following texts: Jacques Campion de Chambonnières, *Les Pieces de Clavessin* (New York: Broude Brothers, 1967); Matthew Locke, "Melothesia," *Musical Ornamentation, Part I,* ed. E. Dannreuther (London: Novello and Co., 1893); Etienne Louliè, *Elements or Principles of*

Music, trans. A. Cohen (New York: Institute of Mediaeval Music, 1965); Thomas Mace, *Musick's Monument;* Henry Purcell, "Lessons for Harpsichord or Spinnet," *Musical Ornamentation, Part I,* ed. E. Dannreuther; and Christopher Simpson, "Division-Violinist," *Musical Ornamentation, Part I,* ed. E. Dannreuther.

5. Edward Dannreuther, *Musical Ornamentation* (London: Novello and Co., 1893).

6. The major twentieth century works involved in this research include the following: Manfred F. Bukofzer, *Music in the Baroque Era* (New York: W. W. Norton and Co., 1947); Dannreuther, *Musical Ornamentation;* Thurston Dart, *The Interpretation of Music* (London: Hutchinson and Co., 1954); Arnold Dolmetsch, *The Interpretation of the Music of the XVII and XVIII Centuries* (London: Oxford University Press, 1916); and Robert Donington, *The Interpretation of Early Music* (New York: St. Martin's Press, 1974).

7. Examples of such facsimiles are Jean Henry d'Anglebert, *Pieces de Clavecin* (New York: Broude Brothers, 1965); Bach, *Clavier-Buchlein;* Francois Couperin, *L'Art de Toucher le Clavecin,* ed. A. Linde (Leipzig: Veb Breitkopf and Hartel Musikverlag, 1933); and Mace, *Musick's Monument.*

8. Brahms and Chrysander use the nineteenth century *pincé* throughout their edition of Francois Couperin, *Pieces de Clavecin,* ed. J. Brahms and F. Chrysander (London: Augener Ltd., 1888).

9. These symbols are used throughout the following texts: Charles Dieupart, *Six Suites Pour Clavecin,* ed. P. Brunold (Paris: Editions de l'Oiseau Lyre, 1934); Louliè, *Elements or Principles of Music;* Gottlieb Teofilo Muffat, *Componimenti Musicali,* ed. G. Adler (Graz: Akademische Druck, 1959); and Simpson, "Division-Violinist."

10. These symbols are used throughout the following texts: Couperin, *Pieces de Clavecin;* Jacques Hotteterre, "Principles of the Flute, Recorder and Oboe," *The Recorder: Its Traditions and Its Tasks,* ed. H. Peter (New York: C. F. Peters Corp., 1953); and Jean-Philippe Rameau, *Pieces de Clavecin,* ed. E. R. Jacobi (Basel: Barenreiter Kasel, 1958). Differences in these composers' symbols, however, may be due to the different instruments for which they were used. For example, Hotteterre composed primarily for the flute, whereas Couperin wrote for the keyboard. Difficulties arise when these pieces are transcribed for different (or modern) instruments, because the symbols may not match the capacities of those instruments.

11. These symbols are used throughout the following texts: Giulio Caccini, *Le Nuove Musiche,* ed. H. W. Hitchcock (Madison, Wisc.: A.-R. Editions, 1970); Chambonnières, *Les Pieces de Clavessin;* Girolamo Diruta, "The Transylvanian," *The Recorder,* ed. H. Peter (New York: C. F. Peters Corp., 1953); Simpson, "Division-Violinist"; Louliè, *Elements or Principles of Music;* and Purcell, "Lessons for Harpsichord or Spinnet."

12. Although all of these symbols reflect an elevation in tone, these symbols and realizations were not considered to be identical or transferable to the Baroque performer; this would have impeded the fluidity of expression, which helped contrast the Baroque period from the Classical or Romantic periods.

13. Saint-Lambert, *Principles of Harpsichord,* trans. R. Harris-Warrick (Cambridge: Cambridge University Press, 1984), p. 75.

14. Dolmetsch, *The Interpretation of the Music,* p. i.

15. James R. Anthony, *French Baroque Music* (New York: W. W. Norton and Co., 1974), pp. 366–367.

16. Peter Kivy, "On the Concept of the 'Historically Authentic' Performance," *The Monist* 71 (April 1988), p. 282.

17. Stan Godlovitch, "Authentic Performance," *The Monist* 71 (April 1988), p. 268.

18. Ibid., p. 259.

19. Ibid., p. 269.

20. James O. Young, "The Concept of Authentic Performance," *The British Journal of Aesthetics* 28 (Summer 1988), p. 233.

21. Ibid., p. 235.

22. Godlovitch, "Authentic Performance," p. 260.

23. This is what Young was referring to (in note 21) when he stated that the *beliefs* of the performer guide how the piece is played.

24. J. S. Bach, *Six Sonatas for Flute and Piano,* ed. J.-P. Rampal (New York: International Music Company, 1962).

25. Bruckner is a prime example of this; there are so many editions of his symphonies that nobody knows which one could possibly be established as definitive.

26. Georg Philip Telemann, *Sonata in F Major for F Recorder and Clavichord* (Melville, N.Y.: Belwin Mills Publishing Corp., 1962), p. 1.

27. Such may eventually be the case with Nicolas Bernier's 1765 treatise, *Principles of Composition,* trans. P. Nelson (New York: Institute of Mediaeval Music, 1964). For 150 years the manuscript was lost. When it appeared in a list of books sold from the library of French musicologist Jules Ecorcheville in 1920, the Biblioteque Nationale quickly purchased it. According to translator Philip Nelson, it is the only known copy (Bernier, *Principles,* p. 3). Bernier provides rules for the embellishment of compositions, with many examples of plain and ornamented lines.

28. Recall the Brahms and Chrysander (1888) edition of Couperin (1713).

29. This has been the case with Girolamo Frescobaldi's 1635 piece "Fiori musicali." Most performers ignore certain of Frescobaldi's score notes because they produce terrible sounds. Frescobaldi's comments indicate that performers must go beyond the score in their performances. For further discussion, see Young, "The Concept of Authentic Performance," p. 232.

30. For the professional performer, or advanced student, looking at a B♭ on a page does not necessitate a thought-process involving linguistic terms. Instead, the player plays the note automatically.

31. Even though Beethoven composed his final works while deaf, he had experienced how certain notes and combinations sounded before his loss of hearing.

32. Recall Godlovitch's remark (in note 26). He lists "scoring, key, interpretive directives." All of these are located in the notation of the score, or in accompanying ornament tables. Neither performance nor commentary has a place in this structure.

33. Since 1988, during any given week of major American symphony broadcasts and performances, one is much more likely to hear post-1950 American compostions than ever before. Here in the United States, world premiers of American pieces have become fashionable to an extent never previously experienced.

34. In other words, Baroque works not reflecting this type of fluidity of performance are questioned as to their authenticity.

Chapter 13. The Ethics of Reminiscence: Reading Autobiography

1. Christa Wolf, *Patterns of Childhood,* trans. Ursole Molinaro and Hedwig Rappolp. (New York: Farrar, Straus and Giroux, 1986); henceforth PC.

2. Barbara Johnson, *A World of Difference* (Baltimore: Johns Hopkins University Press, 1987), p. 146.

3. Jean-François Lyotard, *The Differend: Phrases in Dispute,* trans. Georges Van Den Abbelle (Minneapolis: University of Minnesota Press, 1988).

4. Jane Gallop, *Reading Lacan* (Ithaca, N.Y.: Cornell University Press, 1985), pp. 82–83.

5. For an insightful discussion of the relation between the task of mourning, or the recovery from melancholia, and the deconstructive rhetorics of bereave-

ment, see Eric L. Santner, *Stranded Objects: Mourning, Memory and Film in Postwar Germany* (Ithaca, N.Y.: Cornell University Press, 1990).

6. Hannah Arendt, *On Revolution* (New York: Viking Press, 1963), pp. 53–110.

7. Rita Felski, *Beyond Feminist Aesthetics: Feminist Literature and Social Change* (Cambridge, Mass.: Harvard University Press, 1989), p. 113.

8. The exception is the romanticist, who elevates the anecdote to the authoritative and essential. See Philippe Lacoue-Labarthe and Jean-Luc Nancy, *The Literary Absolute: The Theory of Literature in German Romanticism*, trans. Philip Barnard and Cheryl Lester (Albany: State University of New York Press, 1988).

9. Lyotard, *The Differend*, pp. xiv–xv.

10. Jacques Derrida, *Of Grammatology*, trans. Gayatri Chakravorty Spivak (Baltimore: Johns Hopkins University Press, 1976), p. 67.

11. Phillip Lejeune, "An Autobiography in the Third Person," *New Literary History* 9, no. 1 (Autumn 1977), p. 32.

12. I am inspired by Drucilla Cornell's reading of Derrida. In her reading, Cornell shows the ways in which deconstruction, especially Derrida's revisioning of Levinas's concept of the trace, is motivated by an ethical impulse. See Drucilla Cornell, *Beyond Accomodation: Ethical Feminism, Deconstruction, and the Law* (New York: Routledge, 1991).

13. For the deconstructive view of the "graphic" aspect of psyche, a hieroglyphics that exceeds logocentric closure, see Jacques Derrida, "Freud and the Scene of Writing," *Writing and Difference,* trans. Alan Bass (Chicago: University of Chicago Press, 1978), pp. 196–231.

14. I am quoting Barbara Hernstein Smith, in her presentation given at the conference "Is Violence Necessary for Justice?" Cardozo Law School, New York, October 1, 1990.

15. Johnson, *A World of Difference,* pp. 137–143.

16. Ibid., pp. 184–199.

17. Paul de Man, *The Rhetoric of Romanticism* (New York: Columbia University Press, 1984), pp. 75–76.

18. For an account of body-memory and place-memory, see Ed Casey, *Remembering: A Phenomenological Study* (Bloomington: Indiana University Press, 1987); "The World of Nostalgia," *Man and World* 20 (1987), p. 361–384.

19. Luce Irigaray, "And the One Doesn't Stir Without the Other," *Signs: Journal of Women in Culture and Society* 7, no. 1 (Autumn 1981), p. 63.

20. Luce Irigaray, *Speculum of the Other Woman,* trans. Gillian C. Gill, (Ithaca, NY: Cornell University Press, 1985); henceforth SO.

21. For an analysis of Irigaray's mimetic style, see Kate Mehuron, "An Ironic Mimesis," *The Question of the Other: Essays in Contemporary Continental Philosophy,* ed. Arleen B. Dallery and Charles E. Scott (Albany: State University of New York Press, 1989), pp. 89–101.

22. Irigaray, "And the One Doesn't Stir Without the Other," p. 65.

23. Ibid., p. 65.

24. Ibid., p. 60.

25. "Will there never be love between us other than this filling up of holes? To close up and seal off everything that could happen between us, indefinitely, is that your only desire? To reduce us to consuming and being consumed, is that your only need?" (ibid., p. 62).

26. Christa Wolf, *Cassandra: A Novel and Four Essays,* trans. Jan Van Heurck (New York: Farrar, Straus and Giroux, 1984); henceforth C.

27. Hannah Arendt, *The Origins of Totalitarianism* (Orlando, Fla.: Harcourt Brace Jovanovich, 1979), pp. 465–466.

28. Lyotard, *The Differend,* p. 6.

29. Martha C. Nussbaum, *Love's Knowledge: Essays on Philosophy and Literature* (New York: Oxford University Press, 1990), p. 182.

30. Ibid., p. 182.

31. Ibid., p. 180.

32. Christina Thürmer-Rohr, *Vagabonding: Feminist Thinking Cut Loose,* trans. Lise Weil (Boston: Beacon Press, 1991).

33. For a discussion of the way in which Nazi ideology perpetrated this inferiorization, see "The Second Sex in the Third Reich," by Claudia Koonz, *Mothers in the Fatherland: Women, the Family and Nazi Politics* (New York: St. Martin's Press, 1987), pp. 177–219.

34. Compare Wolf's reminiscence of the exemplary female figure coded by National Socialist ideology with Thürmer-Rohr's memory of the exemplarity of her sister in "Love and Lies: 'My Beloved Children'," *Vagabonding,* pp. 64–90.

35. For an insightful phenomenology of "feminine" shame, see Sandra Lee Bartky, *Femininity and Domination: Studies in the Phenomenology of Oppression* (New York: Routledge, 1990), pp. 83–98.

36. Ibid., p. 98.

37. Shoshana Felman and Dori Laub, M.D., *Testimony: Crises of Witnessing in Literature, Psychoanalysis, and History* (New York: Routledge, 1992), p. 123.

38. See the West German socialist-feminist collective project that has been accomplished in this regard, especially the chapter "Memory-work" in Frigga Haug, ed., *Female Sexualization: Questions/for/Feminism,* trans. Erica Carter (London: Verso, 1987), pp. 29–72.

39. Gallop, *Reading Lacan,* p. 90.

40. Santner, *Stranded Objects,* p. 151.

Chapter 14. Heidegger on Ethics and Justice

1. Major examples of a quasi-Kantian approach to ethics are John Rawls, *A Theory of Justice* (Cambridge, Mass.; Harvard University Press, 1971), Alan Gewirth, *Reason and Morality* (Chicago: University of Chicago Press, 1978); and Jürgen Habermas, *Moral Consciousness and Communicative Action* (Cambridge, Mass.: MIT Press, 1990). Regarding "virtue ethics," see especially Alasdair MacIntyre, *After Virtue,* 2d ed. (Notre Dame, Ind.: University of Notre Dame Press, 1984); and for a defense of a (quasi-Aristotelian) "naturalism" Michael Perry, *Morality, Politics, and Law* (New York: Oxford University Press, 1988). Concerning the Habermasian model of "discourse ethics," compare Seyla Benhabib and Fred Dallmayr, eds., *The Communicative Ethics Controversy* (Cambridge, Mass.: MIT Press, 1990). For a critical review of Gewirth (and Karl-Otto Apel), see my "Ordinary Language and Ideal Speech" in *Twilight of Subjectivity* (Amherst: University of Massachusetts Press, 1981), pp. 220–254; for an assessment of MacIntyre's study, my "Virtue and Tradition" in *Critical Encounters* (Notre Dame, Ind.: University of Notre Dame Press, 1987), pp. 183–208; and for a review of Perry's book, my "Nature and Community: Comments on Michael Perry," *Tulane Law Review* 63 (1989): 1405–1421.

2. See in this context especially Victor Farias, *Heidegger and Nazism,* ed. Joseph Margolis and Tom Rockmore, trans. Paul Burrell and Gabriel R. Picci (Philadelphia: Temple University Press, 1989); also Heinrich Ott, *Martin Heidegger: Unterwegs zu seiner Biographie* (Frankfurt-am-Main: Campus, 1988).

3. Compare in this context my "Rethinking the Political: Some Heideggerian Contributions," *Review of Politics* 52 (1990): 524–552.

4. Compare Martin Heidegger, *Interpretationen zu Aristoteles; Einführung in die phänemenologische Forschung* (1921–22), ed., Walter Bröcker and Käte Bröcker-Oltmanns, *Gesamtausgabe,* vol. 51 (Frankfurt-am-Main: Klostermann, 1985); *Ontologie (Hermeneutik der Faktizität)* (1923), ed. Käte Bröcker-Oltmanns, *Gesamtausgabe,* vol. 63 (Frankfurt-am-Main: Kostermann, 1988).

5. I am aware that Heidegger termed his analysis in *Being and Time* a "descriptive" (and not a normative) account; but clearly *description* here means not a positivist or empiricist description but a philosophical or ontological one (which transcends the fact-value split). For a critique of subjectivist readings of the text,

see Friedrich-Wilhelm von Hermann, *Subjekt und Dasein: Interpretation zu "Sein und Zeit"* (Frankfurt-am-Main: Klostermann, 1974).

6. Heidegger, *Beiträge zur Philosophie (Vom Ereignis)*, ed. Friedrich-Wilhelm von Herrmann, *Gesamtausgabe*, vol. 65 (Frankfurt-am-Main: Klostermann, 1989), pp. 14–16, 20–22, 33–36.

7. *Beiträge zur Philosophie*, pp. 9, 29, 65, 81–82, 282. On a strictly political level, the text actually contains numerous passages denouncing prevailing ideological beliefs, including the sway of "biologism," "racism," and "folkish" nationalism; see pp. 18–19, 61–62, 98–99, 143. (In the preceding I ignore peculiarities of German spelling, e.g., *Seynsfug* instead of *Seinsfuge*.)

8. Heidegger, *Schellings Abhandlung Über das Wesen der menschlichen Freiheit (1809)*, ed. Hildegard Feick (Tübingen: Niemeyer, 1971), pp. 130–132; for an English translation of that edition see *Schelling's Treatise on the Essence of Human Freedom*, trans. Joan Stambaugh (Athens: Ohio University Press, 1985). I have consulted the English translation; but I follow the text of the German edition and often substitute my own translation. For a brief summary of the lecture course, see my "Heidegger's Ontology of Freedom," in *Polis and Praxis* (Cambridge, Mass.: MIT Press, 1984), pp. 121–127. Compare also Parvis Emad, "Heidegger on Schelling's Conception of Freedom," *Man and World* 8 (1975): 152–174; and Michael G. Vater, "Heidegger and Schelling: The Finitude of Being," *Idealistic Studies* 5 (1975): 20–58.

9. *Schellings Abhandlung*, pp. 132, 135–136.

10. Ibid., pp. 142–144.

11. Ibid., pp. 169–171.

12. Ibid., pp. 172–173.

13. Ibid., pp. 176–182, 187.

14. Ibid., pp. 188–193.

15. Ibid., pp. 194–195. The difference from Schelling's position was spelled out more fully in seminars on Schelling held between 1941 and 1943; see especially pp. 208–210, 215, 218–219, 225–231.

16. Heidegger, "Der Spruch des Anaximander," in *Holzwege*, 4th ed. (Franksurt-am-Main: Klostermann, 1963), pp. 296, 299–301. For an English version, see "The Anaximander Fragment," in Heidegger, *Early Greek Thinking*, trans. David F. Krell and Frank A. Capuzzi (New York: Harper and Row, 1984), pp. 13, 16–18. As Heidegger adds (p. 18): "If we think from the vantage of the eschatology of being, then we must someday anticipate the distance of the dawn in the distant future and must learn to ponder temporal distance along these lines." (In this and subsequent citations I have slightly altered the English translation for purposes of clarity.)

17. *Early Greek Thinking,* pp. 19–22.

18. Ibid., pp. 24–26. As he adds (pp. 26–27): "We may call this revealing keeping in reserve of its truth the *epoché* of being. However, this term, borrowed from the Stoics, does not here have the Husserlian sense of objectification or methodical bracketing of acts of thetic consciousness. Rather, the *epoché* of being belongs to being itself; we are thinking it out of the experience of the oblivion of being *(Seinsvergessenheit)."* At a later point (pp. 50–51), oblivion of being is defined as "oblivion of the distinction of being and beings," an outlook that, in turn, is described as trademark of Western metaphysics.

19. Ibid., pp. 30–31, 34–37. Actually, Heidegger does not consider the entire first part of the fragment as authentic; but this fact does not significantly affect his interpretation.

20. Ibid., pp. 41–43.

21. Ibid., pp. 43–44.

22. Ibid., pp. 45–47

23. Ibid., pp. 48–54. At this point (pp. 55–56), Heidegger establishes a close linkage between the Greek term for *Brauch, to chreon,* and the notions of "hen" and "moira" as employed by Parmenides as well as the notion of "logos" as used by Heraclitus. Compare in this context his essays titled "Logos," "Moira," and "Aletheia" in *Early Greek Thinking,* pp. 59–78, 79–101, 102–123. For the German original of these essays see *Vorträge und Aufsätze,* 3rd ed. (Pfullingen: Neske, 1967), Part 3, pp. 3–78.

24. For an interpretation along these lines, see Jürgen Habermas, *The Philosophical Discourse of Modernity: Twelve Lectures,* trans. Frederick Lawrence (Cambridge, Mass.: MIT Press, 1987), pp. 150 155.

25. *Schellings Abhandlung,* pp. 177, 185, 193.

26. Ibid., p. 195. For the notion of undecidability compare, e.g., Jacques Derrida, *Spurs: Nietzsche's Styles,* trans. Barbara Harlow (Chicago: University of Chicago Press, 1979), pp. 59, 107, 117–121; and his "otobiographies," in Derrida, *The Ear of the Other,* ed. Christie V. McDonald, trans. Avital Ronell (New York: Schocken Books, 1985), pp. 3–38. The aspect of conflict and incommensurability (of life-words and language-games) has been strongly emphasized by Jean-François Lyotard, especially in *The Differend: Phrases in Dispute,* trans. Georges Van Den Abbeele (Minneapolis: University of Minnesota Press, 1988); justice or equity, from this vantage, is a kind of arbitration between incompatible games; see Lyotard and Jean-Loup Thébaud, *Just Gaming,* trans. Wald Godrich (Minneapolis: University of Minnesota Press, 1985). Compare also Stephen K. White, "Justice and the Postmodern Problematic," *Praxis International* 7 (1987–88): 306–319.

27. *Early Greek Thinking,* pp. 57–58.

28. See in this context my "Hermeneutics and the Rule of Law," in Gregory Leyh, ed., *Legal Hermeneutics: History, Theory, and Practice* (Berkeley: University of California Press, 1992), pp. 3–22. Regarding rights, compare especially Ronald Dworkin, *Taking Rights Seriously* (Cambridge, Mass.: Harvard University Press, 1978). Heidegger's position is more akin to the notion of "natural right" as articulated by Leo Strauss (minus the Platonic scaffolding); see Strauss, *Natural Right and History* (Chicago: University of Chicago Press, 1953), especially pp. 81–119.

29. Heidegger, "Letter on Humanism" (1947), in David F. Krell, ed., *Martin Heidegger: Basic Writings* (New York: Harper and Row, 1977), pp. 234–235, 237–239 (translation slightly altered for purposes of clarity). As one should note, Heidegger does not simply dismiss legality or moral rules in the ordinary sense. As he writes in the same *Letter* (pp. 231–232): "Great care must be given to moral rules at a time when *Dasein,* faced with technology and mass society, can maintain reliable steadiness only through an organization of planning and acting which matches technological demands. Who can disregard this predicament? Must we not safeguard and secure existing bonds—which sustain humans today ever so tenuously in sheer presentness? Certainly. But does this need relieve thinking of the task of being mindful of what still awaits to be thought: namely, being which grants to all beings initially their stay and truth?"

Chapter 15. Stories of Being

The following list of abbreviations will be used for references to Heidegger's writings in the original German and to the English translation, though I have usually altered the latter. *G* abbreviates Heidegger, *Gesamtausgabe* (Frankfurt: Klostermann, 1976–).

BZ   *Der Begriff der Zeit* (Tübingen: Niemeyer, 1989).

G2   *Gesamtausgabe,* vol. 2: *Sein und Zeit* (1977); *Being and Time,* trans. John Macquarrie and Edward Robinson (New York: Harper and Row, 1962).

G9   *Gesamtausgabe,* vol. 9: *Wegmarken* (1976).

G15   *Gesamtausgabe,* vol. 15: *Seminare* (1986).

G56/57 *Gesamtausgabe,* vols. 56–57: *Zur Bestimmung der Philosophie* (1987).

G61   *Gesamtausgabe,* vol. 61: *Phänomenologische Interpretationen zu Aristoteles. Einführung in die Phänomenologische Forschung* (1985).

G63   *Gesamtausgabe,* vol. 63: *Ontologie (Hermeneutik der Faktizität)* (1988); *Ontology (Hermeneutics of Facticity),* trans. John van Buren (Bloomington: Indiana University Press, forthcoming).

HW   *Holzwege,* 6th ed. (Frankfurt: Klostermann, 1980).

LH   "Letter on Humanism," trans. Frank A. Cappuzi in David Farrell Krell, ed., *Basic Writings* (New York: Harper and Row, 1977), pp. 193–242.

NG   "Nur ein Gott kann uns retten," *Der Spiegel*, no. 23 (May 31, 1976), pp. 193–219; "Only a God Can Save Us," trans. W. J. Richardson in Thomas Sheehan, ed., *Heidegger: The Man and the Thinker* (Chicago: Precedent Publishing, 1981), pp. 45–67.

PLT   *Poetry, Language, Thought*, trans. Albert Hofstadter (New York: Harper and Row, 1975).

SB   *Die Selbstbehauptung der deutschen Universität, Das Rektorat 1933–34* (Frankfurt: Vittorio Klostermann, 1983); "The Self-Assertion of the German University: Address, Delivered on the Solemn Assumption of the Rectorate of the University of Freiburg, The Rectorate 1933–34: Facts and Thoughts," trans. Karsten Harries, *Review of Metaphysics* 38 (1985): 467–502.

ZSD   *Zur Sache des Denkens* (Tübingen: Max Niemeyer, 1976); *Time and Being*, trans. Joan Stambaugh (New York: Harper and Row, 1972).

WHD   *Was Heisst Denken?* (Tübingen: Niemeyer, 1954); *What Is Called Thinking?*, trans. Fred D. Wieck and J. Glenn Gray (New York: Harper and Row, 1972).

WM   *Wegmarken*, 2d ed. (Frankfurt: Klostermann, 1978).

   1. See Thomas Sheehan, "Heidegger and the Nazis," *The New York Review of Books* (June 16, 1988): 47; John D. Caputo, *Radical Hermeneutics: Repetition, Deconstruction, and the Hermeneutic Project* (Bloomington: Indiana University Press, 1988), pp. 171–186, and his "Demythologizing Heidegger: Aletheia and the History of Being," *Review of Metaphysics* 41 (1987–88): 519–546; John van Buren, "Persons, *Kinesis*, Demythologizing," in Roy Martinez, ed., *The Difficulty of Life: Studies in Radical Hermeneutics* (forthcoming); Theodore Kisiel, "Heidegger's Apology: Biography as Philosophy and Ideology," *Graduate Faculty Philosophy Journal* 14–15 (1990–91): 363–404; Jacques Derrida, *Of Spirit: Heidegger and the Question*, trans. Geoffrey Bennington and Rachel Bowlby (Chicago: University of Chicago Press, 1989); Jürgen Habermas, "Work and Weltanschauung: The Heidegger Controversy from a German Perspective," trans. John McCumber, *Critical Inquiry* 15 (1989): 431–445; Richard Rorty, "Taking Philosophy Seriously," *The New Republic* (April 11, 1989): 31–34; Arnold I. Davidson, "Questions Concerning Heidegger: Opening the Debate," *Critical Inquiry* 15 (1989): 407–426; Richard Wolin, "The French Heidegger Debate," *New German Critique* (1988): 135–161; Luc Ferry and Alain Renaut, *Heidegger and Modernity*, trans. Franklin Philip (Chicago: University of Chicago Press, 1990); Victor Farias, *Heidegger and Nazism*, ed. Joseph Margolis and Tom Rockmore, trans. Paul Burrell and Bariel R. Ricci (Philadelphia: Temple University Press, 1989), especially the editors' foreword; Hugo Ott, *Martin Heidegger: Unterwegs zu seiner Biographie* (Frankfurt: Campus Verlag, 1988), pp. 7–16.

2. G63 65; BZ 25; G61 70, 81, 99, 111, 163–164, 182, 197; G56/57 19; G2 8/ 26; Hans-Georg Gadamer, "Auf dem Rückgang zum Anfang," in his *Neuere Philosophie, I; Hegel, Husserl, Heidegger, Gesammelte Werke,* vol. 3 (Tübingen: ⁻. ⌐. B. Mohr, 1987), p. 406.

3. G61 85, 52–53, 112; G56/57 63–117.

4. G61 35, 37, 66.

5. G56/57 4, 74–75; BZ 13, 17; Kisiel, "Why Students of Heidegger Will Have to Read Emil Lask," in Deborah G. Chaffin, ed., *Emil Lask and the Search for Concreteness* (Athens: Ohio University Press, forthcoming).

6. G56/57 78; BZ 16, 26; G9 39, 42; G61 85.

7. G61 104, 108–109; G63 48, 62–65, 103.

8. G61 3, 41, 63, 111, 163–164.

9. See Rudolf Bultmann, *New Testament and Mythology: and Other Basic Writings,* trans. Schubert M. Ogden (Philadelphia: Fortress Press, 1984).

10. Heidegger, *The End of Philosophy,* trans. Joan Stambaugh (New York: Harper and Row, 1973), pp. 55–74.

11. See my "Heidegger, Aristotle, Ethics," in Charles E. Scott and Arleen Dallery, eds., *Ethics and Danger: Currents in Continental Thought* (New York: State University of New York Press, 1992).

12. See Thomas Sheehan, "Heidegger's 'Introduction to the Phenomenology of Religion,' 1920–21," *Personalist* 60 (1979): 312–324.

13. See my "The Young Heidegger and Phenomenology," *Man and World* 23 (1990): 239–272.

14. See my "Heidegger's *Sache:* A Family Portrait," *Research in Phenomenology* (forthcoming).

15. Joan Stambaugh, "Introduction" to Heidegger, *The End of Philosophy,* p. xii; ZSD 25/24; WM 324/LH 207. Compare Thomas Sheehan, "Heidegger's Philosophy of Mind," in *Contemporary Philosophy: A New Survey,* Vol. 4 (Hague: Martinus Nijhoff, 1983), pp. 287, 305, 309; his "On Movement and the Destruction of Ontology," *Monist* 64 (1981): 535–536; and Caputo, *Radical Hermeneutics,* p. 266.

16. See WM 311–360/LH 193–242, especially 326/209; WHD 28/62; HW 265–316/PLT 91–142; NG 193–219/45–67. Compare Richard Bernstein, "Heidegger on Humanism," in his *Philosophical Profiles* (Philadelphia: University of Pennsylvania Press, 1986); Murray Miles, "Heidegger and the Question of Humanism," *Man and World* 22 (1989): 427–451; John D. Caputo, "Thinking, Poetry and Pain," *Southern Journal of Philosophy* 28 (1989): 155–181.

Heidegger's tendency to dissolve embodied human beings into an epochal "essence of humanity" and reduce their value and dignity to this essence was expressed clearly in a quasi-revisionist statement he made in 1949 that Jewish people did not really "die" in the Nazi death camps because their mechanized perishing was not in accord with the "essence" of death (while old peasants in the Black Forest around Todtnauberg, on the other hand, were presumably "dying" authentically). "Hundreds of thousands die en masse," he stated. "Do they *die?* They succumb. They are done in. Do they die? They become mere quanta, items in an inventory in the business of manufacturing corpses. Do they die? They are liquidated inconspicuously in extermination camps. And even apart from that, right now millions of impoverished people are perishing from hunger in China. *But to die is to endure death in its essence.* To be able to die means to be capable of this endurance. We are capable of this only if the essence of death makes our own essence possible" (translator's italics). In the same vein is his contention from the same year that, relative to the present epochal truth of being as technological enframing *[Gestell]*, there really was no "essential" difference between the mechanized killing of Jewish people in Nazi death camps and the mechanized farming of cabbages. "Agriculture is now a motorized food-industry—*in essence, the same as* the manufacturing of corpses in gas chambers and extermination camps, the same as the blockading and starving of nations [it was the year of the Berlin blockade], the same as the manufacture of hydrogen bombs" (my italics). Still in the same vein is Heidegger's earlier statement about the relation of individual Germans to the essence of German Dasein, that is, of the folk that was supposed to be embodied in the National Socialist state: "The individual, wherever he stands, counts for nothing. The fate of our people in their State is everything." See Sheehan, "Heidegger and the Nazis," pp. 38, 40–41.

17. G15 366; G9 359/LH 237. Compare Werner Marx, *Heidegger and the Tradition,* trans. Theodore Kisiel and Murray Greene (Evanston, Ill.: Northwestern University Press, 1971), pp. 243–256; his *Gibt es auf Erden ein Mass? Grundbestimmungen einer nichtmetaphysischen Ethik* (Hamburg: Felix Meiner, 1983), pp. 1–60; Caputo, *Radical Hermeneutics,* pp. 282–288; Jürgen Habermas, *The Philosophical Discourse of Modernity: Twelve Lectures,* trans. Frederick Lawrence (Cambridge, Mass.: MIT Press, 1987), pp. 131–160.

18. Compare Caputo, *Radical Hermeneutics,* Chapter 6.

19. NG 193–219/45–67; Farias, *Heidegger and Nazism;* Ott, *Martin Heidegger: Unterwegs zu seiner Biographie.* Compare Sheehan, "Heidegger and the Nazis," pp. 43–47.

20. WM 328/LH 210; SB 16/476, 18/479; Ott, *Martin Heidegger,* p. 231. Compare Winfried Franzen, "Die Sehnsucht nach Härte und Schwere," in A. Gethmann-Siefert and O. Pöggeler, eds., *Heidegger und die praktische Philosophie* (Frankfurt: Suhrkamp, 1988), pp. 78–92; John D. Caputo, "Heidegger's *Kampf:* The Difficulty of Life," *Graduate Faculty Philosophy Journal* 14–15 (1991): 72–77; and Jacques Derrida's *Spurs: Nietzsche's Styles,* trans. Barbara Harlow (Chicago and London: University of Chicago Press, 1978); "Geschlecht: sexual

difference, ontological difference," *Research in Phenomenology* 13 (1983): 65–83; "*Geschlecht* II: Heidegger's Hand," trans. John P. Leavey, in John Sallis, ed., *Deconstruction and Philosophy* (Chicago and London: University of Chicago Press, 1987), pp. 161–196.

21. WM 321/LH 204, 323/206. Compare Caputo, *Radical Hermeneutics,* pp. 153–154, 205 (n. 16), 288; Derrida, *Of Spirit: Heidegger and the Question,* pp. 47–57; Jim Cheney, "Postmodern Environmental Ethics: Ethics as Bioregional Narrative," *Environmental Ethics* 11 (1989): 117–134.

22. See my "Heidegger's Autobiographies," *Journal of the British Society for Phenomenology* (forthcoming); Theodore Kisiel, "Heidegger's Apology: Biography as Philosophy and Ideology," pp. 363–404 and his forthcoming "Edition and Übersetzung: Unterwegs von Tatsachen zu Gedanken, von Werken zu Wegen," in Dietrich Papenfuss and Otto Pöggeler, eds., *Zur philosophischen Aktualität Heideggers,* vol. 3 (Frankfurt: Klostermann); Sheehan, "Heidegger and the Nazis," pp. 38–47.

23. See my "Heidegger's *Sache:* A Family Portrait."

24. For example, the fragmentary explorations in Heidegger's youthful writings lack an intensive treatment of the nonpersonal depth dimension of *Ereignis,* they privilege human Dasein, and sometimes they express undertones of German nationalism and militarism. See Kisiel, "Heidegger's Apology: Biography as Philosophy and Ideology," pp. 363–404; Caputo, "Heidegger's *Kampf:* The Difficulty of Life," pp. 61–83 and his "*Sorge* and *Kardia:* The Hermeneutics of Factical Life and the Categories of the Heart," in Theodore Kisiel and John van Buren, eds., *The Early Heidegger: New Perspectives* (Albany: State University of New York Press, forthcoming).

Chapter 16. Sartre's First Two Ethics

1. This is clear in Sartre's statements about ethics at the end of *Being and Nothingness,* trans. Hazel Barnes (New York: Philosophical Library, 1956), pp. 625–626; hereafter cited as BN. See also *Critique of Dialectical Reason,* trans. Alan Sheridan-Smith (London: NLB, 1976), p. 800, hereafter cited as CRD; *On a raison de se revolter* (Paris: Gallimard, 1974), pp. 78–79, hereafter cited as OR. Also, of course, there is the title of his famous 1945 lecture, "Existentialism Is a Humanism."

2. In "L'Ecriture et la Publication," interview with M. Sicard, *Obliques,* nos. 18–19 (1979): 14–15, Sartre explicitly refers to three moralities. Other places where he refers to more than one of his moralities are *Sartre by Himself,* filmscript trans. R. Seaver (New York: Urizen Books, 1978), pp. 77–81; "Self-Portrait at Seventy," in *Life/Situations,* trans. P. Auster and L. Davis (New York: Pantheon Books, 1977), pp. 60, 74–75; OR, pp. 78–79; "An Interview with Jean-Paul Sartre," interview with L. Fretz in *Jean-Paul Sartre, Contemporary Approaches*

to His Philosophy, ed. H. Silverman and F. Elliston (Pittsburgh: Duquesne University Press, 1980), pp. 233–234.

3. *Imagination,* trans. Forrest Williams (Ann Arbor: University of Michigan, 1962), p. 116.

4. BN, pp. 25, 29, 176, 177, 181.

5. BN, pp. 440–441.

6. BN, p. 442.

7. BN, pp. 478–479, 481.

8. BN, pp. 61, 391, 472.

9. BN, p. 520. To be sure there are places in BN, IV, where Sartre speaks of the situation as the "common product" of freedom and the given objects (488). Nevertheless, even here, after asking whether "the given . . . conditions freedom?" He answers, "The given in no way enters into the construction of freedom since freedom is interiorized as the internal negation of the given" (486–487). Note also the following passage: "if consciousness exists in terms of the given, this does not mean that the given conditions consciousness; consciousness is a pure and simple negation of the given, and it exists as the disengagement from a certain existing given" (478).

10. BN, pp. 495, 489. See also pp. 498–499 and 509.

11. BN, pp. 509, 520–521, 529, 531, 549, 554.

12. BN, pp. 522, 549–550.

13. *Cahiers pour une morale* (Paris: Gallimard, 1983), pp. 406, 434; hereafter cited as CM. See also pp. 177 and 578. All translations from the *Cahiers* are my own. Actually, CM also says that creativity is the primary goal of ethics. I have argued elsewhere that it is ultimately reducible to the goal of human freedom. See my "Sartre's Early Ethics and the Ontology of *Being and Nothingness,*" in *Sartre Alive,* ed. R. Aronson and A. van den Hoven. (Detroit: Wayne State University Press, 1991).

14. *Existentialism and Humanism,* trans. P. Marret. (London: Eyre Methren, 1973), p. 51; hereafter cited as EH. Other works of this period where he states that freedom is his primary value are *What Is Literature?* trans. B. Frechtman (New York: Washington Square Press, 1966), pp. 108, 192; "Materialism and Revolution," in *Literary and Philosophical Essays,* trans. A. Michelson (New York: Collier Books, 1962), pp. 245, 253.

15. EH, p. 51. A similar argument is suggested in CM, pp. 465, 490, 498, 502, 514, 543. For more analysis of this argument, see Chapter 3 of my *The Foundation and Structure of Sartrean Ethics* (Lawrence: University of Kansas Press, 1979).

16. Sartre himself quotes variations of this Stoic dictum in CM, pp. 343, 352–353, and 406.

17. BN, Part III, Ch. 3, "Concrete Relations with Others." See especially pp. 526–527.

18. See Sartre's definition of authenticity in *Anti-Semite and Jew,* trans. G. Becker (New York: Schocken Books, 1948), p. 90. In that work he states that, although the choice of authenticity is a moral decision, it is not "a solution on the social or political level" (141). Also see p. 138. In BN Sartre states that one can never increase or diminish the freedom of others! (410).

19. EH, p. 52.

20. "The Obligation to Will the Freedom of Others According to Jean-Paul Sartre," Chapter 6 of *The Question of the Other,* ed. A. Dallery and C. Scott (Albany: State University of New York Press, 1989).

21. Sartre does identify his ideal city of ends with the classless society and true socialism. (CM, pp. 95, 170–174, 302, 421, 434, 487). But little concrete content is supplied to any of these notions.

22. OR, p. 79. See also, "L'Ecriture et la Publication," pp. 14–15.

23. CRD, p. 180.

24. CRD, pp. 34–38, 81–93, 180–185; *Search for a Method,* trans. Hazel Barnes (New York: Random House, 1963), pp. 87, 91ff., 150–151; hereafter cited as SM.

25. CRD, Book I, Ch. 1. SM pp. 150–151, 171.

26. CRD, Introduction. In fact, the entire *Critique* is a description of this dialectical interaction.

27. "Introduction to *Les Temps Modernes,*" trans. F. Ehrmann, in *Paths to the Present: Aspects of European Thought from Romanticism to Existentialism,* ed. E. Weber (New York: Dodd, Mead & Co., 1960), pp. 436–441. Sartre's approach to freedom in his early ontology seems clearly analytic according to this definition.

28. SM, pp. 92–94, 105, 111.

29. CRD, pp. 578, footnote 68, and 331.

30. Unpublished notes for a lecture given at the Gramsci Institute in Rome, 1964, p. 71 (all page references are to Sartre's handwritten manuscript available at the Bibliotheque Nationale, Paris); hereafter cited as Notes for Rome lecture. The translations are my own.

31. Notes for Rome lecture pp. 7ff. The entire second section of this lecture is entitled "The Experience of Morality." See also OR, pp. 45, 118.

32. Notes for Rome lecture, pp. 6–18, 63–73, 94–96.

33. Notes for Rome lecture, pp. 18, 64–65.

34. Notes for Rome lecture, p. 39. Also see the texts referred to in note 32.

35. Notes for Rome lecture, p. 55.

36. Notes for Rome lecture, p. 100. My analysis is based on pages 97–110 and 139–146.

37. *Integral humanity* is defined as the fulfillment of radical human needs, which needs, Sartre says are for "nude man," i.e., man defined as member of the human species not man defined by any particular social system. See Notes for Rome lecture, pp. 88, 102, 106, 109, 126, 139, 144.

38. Notes for Rome lecture, pp. 63, 66, 77, 81, 97-101, 133, 135, 164; "Self-Portrait at Seventy," pp. 63, 66, 78, 104. Unfortunately, Sartre does not explain how one would distinguish genuine from false needs, although he does refer to the former as more radical or fundamental, Notes for Rome lecture, pp. 139, 144.

39. Of course, because needs specify only the *general kind of* object that satisfies them (e.g., protein), we remain free to choose among *particular* things of this kind (e.g. to eat fish, or eggs, or grain, or meat). We can even choose not to satisfy a need.

40. Notes for Rome lecture, p. 67. See also pp. 98, 145.

41. Notes for Rome lecture, p. 98.

42. Notes for Rome lecture, pp. 101, 117–119, 134–143; OR, pp. 102, 108, 288–289, 300–307, 347; CRD, pp. 672–673.

43. *The Family Idiot,* trans. C. Cosman (Chicago: University of Chicago, 1981), vol. I. See for instance chapters 1, 2, and 3.

Chapter 17. Cognition and Morality: Lyotard on Addressors, Addressees, and Ethics

1. Jean-François Lyotard "The Sign of History," in *The Lyotard Reader* ed. Andrew Benjamin (Oxford: Basil Blackwell, 1989), p. 394.

2. Ibid., p. 394.

3. Jean-François Lyotard, "Sensus Communis," *Paragraph* 11, no. 1 (1988), p. 2.

4. Jean-François Lyotard with Jean-Loup Thébaud, *Just Gaming* (Minneapolis: University of Minnesota Press, 1985), pp. 22ff.

5. For discussion of this period of Lyotard's thought see Peter Dews, *Logics of Disintegration: Post-Structuralism and the Claims of Critical Theory* (London: Verso, 1987); Geoff Bennington, *Lyotard: Writing the Event* (Manchester: Manchester University Press, 1988); and David Carroll, *Paraesthetics: Foucault, Lyotard, Derrida* (New York: Metheuen, 1988).

6. Lyotard notes this point in his self-reflections in *Peregrinations: Law, Form, Event* (New York: Columbia University Press, 1988).

7. See Carroll, *Paraesthetics,* pp. 157, 164, for a discussion of Lyotard's relation to Wittgenstein.

8. Jean-François Lyotard, *The Differend: Phrases in Dispute* (Minneapolis: University of Minnesota Press, 1988), pp. 11, 14.

9. Jean-François Lyotard, "Levinas' Logic," in *The Lyotard Reader,* p. 287.

10. *The Differend,* p. 108.

11. Ibid., pp. 110–111.

12. See Lyotard's discussion in ibid., p. 51.

13. For discussion of the relation between Levinas and Buber, see Robert Bernasconi, " 'Failure of Communication' as a Surplus: Dialogue and Lack of Dialogue Between Buber and Levinas," pp. 100–135, and John Llewellen, "Levinas, Derrida and Others vis a vis," pp. 136–155, both in Robert Bernasconi and David Wood, eds., *The Provocation of Levinas: Rethinking the Other* (London: Routledge, 1988).

14. Consider in addition, Lyotard's conception of "the jew" as outsider. The lower case indicates not a specific group but the status of all groups that are outside established orders and treated as "Other." See Jean-François Lyotard, *Heidegger and "the jews"* (Minneapolis: University of Minnesota Press, 1990).

15. Emmanuel Levinas, *Totality and Infinity: An Essay on Exteriority* (Pittsburgh: Duquesne University Press, 1969), p. 194. I have also drawn on Levinas's *Otherwise than Being Or Beyond Essence* (Boston: Martinus Nijhoff, 1981).

16. *The Differend,* p. 116.

17. Ibid., p. 125.

18. *Just Gaming,* p. 35.

19. Ibid., p. 35.

20. Ibid., p. 37.

21. In some respects I follow Derrida's critique of Levinas in "Violence and Metaphysics: An Essay on the Thought of Emmanuel Levinas," in Jacques Derrida, *Writing and Difference* (Chicago: University of Chicago Press, 1978), pp. 79–153. As is obvious, however, I develop it in a different direction and from different theoretical assumptions.

22. Of course, Levinas could argue that the infinite is not outside the finite, but within it. But such an interpretation does not undermine the argument put forward here. Levinas still requires a transmundane awareness to be the basis of ethics. The argument that I put forward claims that, within mundane intersubjectivity, a social world is disclosed in which the otherness that Levinas and Lyotard want to recognize can be contained and interpreted.

23. Anthony Giddens, *The Constitution of Society: Outline of a Theory of Structuration* (Berkeley: University of California Press, 1981).

24. Anthony Giddens, *The Consequences of Modernity* (Stanford, Calif.: Stanford University Press, 1990), p. 36.

25. For a useful discussion of the problem of intersubjectivity in Husserl and beyond, see Michael Theunissen, *The Other* (Cambridge, Mass.: MIT Press, 1985).

26. Lyotard expands this critique in his essay "Grundlagenkrise" *Neue Hefte für Philosophie,* no. 21 (1986): 1–30. He essentially equates the critique of Apel and Habermas with that of Husserl. Transcendental subjectivity is replaced by transcendental intersubjectivity. Both, however, are essentially part of the philosophy of subjectivity stemming from Descartes, and both still seek a secure ground for knowledge. In part, such a position still holds for Apel. This can be seen in his essay "The Problem of Philosophical Foundations in the Light of Transcendental Pragmatics of Language," in *After Philosophy,* ed. Kenneth Baynes, James Bohman, and Thomas McCarthy (Cambridge, Mass.: MIT Press, 1987), pp. 250–290. Here, Apel argues for "the indubitability of certain paradigmatic evidence in the language game of philosophical argumentation" (p. 272). Although Apel criticizes Husserlian methodological solipsism as well as his notion of a monologic evidential consciousness, he does endorse a modified version of Cartesianism. The same cannot be said of Habermas's position as it is developed in *Theory of Communicative Action* and in the recent essays on morality and law. Habermas is critical of Apel's continuing search for an absolute foundation for ethics. See, for example, his critique of Apel's moral theory in "Diskursethik" now translated in *Moral Consciousness and Communicative Action* (Cambridge, Mass.: MIT Press, 1990). Habermas's notion of the social lifeworld takes its bearings from the practical intersubjectivity of participants, from the transcendental intersubjectivity of an individual or collective subjec

27. Anthony Giddens, *New Rules of the Sociological Method* (New York: Basic Books, 1976). Also see, Jürgen Habermas, "Reconstruction and Interpretation in the Social Sciences," in *Moral Consciousness and Communicative Action* (Cambridge, Mass.: MIT Press, 1990), pp. 21–42.

28. Certainly, we do not always engage in reflection quite as deliberately as this. When we become dissatisfied with the rationales for our action, however, we engage in a search for new rationales, though we may not do so in a systematic manner.

29. David Ingram's work has suggested such a linkage as well, although from a somewhat different point of view. See, for example, his *Habermas and the Dialectic of Reason* (New Haven, Conn.: Yale University Pres, 1987), for a hermeneutically informed reading of Habermas's notion of the life-world. Also see his "Legitimacy and the Post-Modern Condition: The Political Thought of Jean-François Lyotard," *Praxis International* 7, nos. 3–4 (1987–88): 286–305. Other treatments include Stephen Watson, "Jurgen Habermas and Jean-François Lyotard: Post-Modernism and the Crisis of Rationality," *Philosophy and Social Criticism* 10, no. 2 (Fall 1984): 1–24; and Seyla Benhabib, "Epistemologies of Post-Modernism: A Rejoinder to Jean-François Lyotard," *New German Critique* 33 (1984): 103–127.

Chapter 18. Deconstruction and Suffering: The Way to the Ethical

1. Drucilla Cornell, "From the Lighthouse: The Promise of Redemption and the Possibility of Legal Interpretation," *Cardozo Law Review* 11 (1990): 1687–1714; hereafter referred to as "Lighthouse."

2. The present chapter may be read as a response to John Caputo's *Radical Hermeneutics: Repetition, Deconstruction and the Hermeneutic Project* (Bloomington: Indiana University Press, 1987); hereafter referred to as *Hermeneutics,* and three presentations by Drucilla Cornell: "From the Lighthouse"; her talk at the 1989 SPEP Conference on "The Feminist Alliance with Deconstruction"; and "Post-Structuralism, the Ethical Relation, and the Law," *Cardozo Law Review* 9: 1587–1628, hereafter referred to as "Post-Structuralism." Some of the issues that I address in this chapter are succinctly articulated by Richard Bernstein in "Serious Play: The Ethical-Political Horizon of Jacques Derrida," *Journal of Speculative Philosophy* 1 (1987): 93–117.

3. Cornell, "Post-Structuralism," p. 1588.

4. Insofar as hope, as traditionally conceived and practiced, fastened on the possibility of avoiding rupture, it has been irreparably undermined by Heidegger's analysis of temporality and by the deconstruction of foundationalism. But this not necessarily mean that things are hopeless, only that the traditional

dichotomy between hope and despair (system-breach, structure-rupture, life-death) has been deconstructed. It is possible to place our hope *in* the rupture of deconstruction, instead of devoting our hopes to the possibility of avoiding such a rupture.

5. Drucilla Cornell makes this point repeatedly in arguing against both the legal positivists and the "irrationalists" of the Conference of Critical Legal Studies, whose nihilistic reading of Derrida she contests (see "Lighthouse").

6. Andrea Nye grapples with this dilemma continuously in *Feminist Theory and the Philosophies of Man* (New York: Routledge Chapman & Hall, 1989).

7. But to retrieve it would require more than returning to the womb. In Derridian terms, it would require retrieving from the past an experience of presence we never enjoyed; we have always been already beyond it, even when enwombed. In Freudian terms, too, life in the womb is already disruptive of the original homeostasis that can be retrieved only by going back to an inanimate condition that is indistinguishable from death. See *Beyond the Pleasure Principle,* Standard Edition (London: Hogarth Press, 1955).

8. Cornell, "Post-Structuralism," p. 1611.

9. One cannot let Being be, as Heidegger would have us do, without letting go of one's control of it; one cannot lose control without experiencing the loss of control as the end of one's world. In short, to let Being be, one must let the not not. By *suffering* I mean precisely this radical opening of oneself to the radical throe of the not; to describe this merely as a matter of "letting-be" obscures and occludes its deconstructive impact. It is crucially important to distinguish suffering in this sense from the *victim's* injury and experience of pain that Levinas discusses in "Useless Suffering" (*The Provocation of Levinas: Rethinking the Other,* ed. Robert Bernasconi and David Wood [London: Routledge, 1988], pp. 156–167). Levinas argues in this essay that we are always called not just to relieve such suffering, but in some sense to assume it. The process of doing so—the process of giving up one's own privileged position in which one is exempt from suffering to respond to the suffering of Others—is an example of suffering as I am defining it here. Indeed, the paradigmatic example of this kind of response to the Other would be for the violator to assume the suffering of those whom he has violated. This transformation of the self from violator into sufferer is the enactment of deconstruction; for that reason it is not a trans-form-ation at all, if by that one means the institution of a new structure, form, attempt at totality. It is, rather, a conversion that leads one to live in the rupture that is openness to the Other. (I try to describe this conversion in *The Way of Suffering: A Geography of Crisis* [Washington, D.C.: Georgetown University Press, 1988].)

10. Caputo, *Hermeneutics,* p. 258.

11. Caputo in fact argues that at least one version of a postmodern "ethics of dissemination" would focus on the elimination of suffering (see *Hermeneutics,*

pp. 273–282). This, it seems to me, is an incongruous conclusion to a book that argues that the purpose of deconstruction is to "make things difficult" for us. If this is its purpose, as I think Caputo himself convincingly demonstrates, should not deconstruction *open us* to suffering instead of leading us to work for its elimination? Caputo says, with Levinas, that we are called to respond to the suffering of the Other who has been victimized. But to do this one must let go of the desire to control that makes one a violator, and such letting go is itself an experience of suffering a mortal loss. Far from being something that the ethical life would lead us to eliminate, suffering this loss is, as I shall argue, the transcendental condition for the possibility of ethical relationship. But this condition is not a "ground" at all, much less an immovable arche; it is an irrevocable and inescapable throe.

12. Martin Heidegger, *Being and Time,* trans. John Macquarrie and Edward Robinson (New York: Harper and Row, 1962), pp. 293–304.

13. Jacques Derrida, *Of Grammatology,* trans. Gayatri Spivak (Baltimore: Johns Hopkins University Press, 1976), p. 183.

14. Wrong both in the sense of having wronged the Other and in the sense of having been radically wrong in my whole way of thinking of her. Such wronging and being wrong are implicit in each other: to make it possible for me to wrong the Other, I have to think of her as something other than the Other; and thinking of her as something other than the Other is itself a violation of her. If, as Levinas insists, noetic awareness of the Other does not contribute to the ethical relationship, but is in fact ruptured by it, it would not be appropriate to apologize for having been wrong in one's way of thinking of the Other. Rather, one would have to apologize for thinking of the Other at all because of the fact that thought is governed by the economy of the Same. This seems to me to deny that the ethical has the power to liberate noesis itself from the exigencies of totalization. The fact that *Totality and Infinity* exists seem to me to be evidence that such a liberation can occur.

15. As Cornell puts it, in commenting on Levinas's *Otherwise Than Being,* the self "is not born in an act of self-conscious assertion. He instead comes to himself in his proximity to Her" ("Lighthouse," p. 1695).

16. Thus, instead of modeling one's relationship to the Other after one's relationship to the self—which, it can plausibly be argued, was the inevitable tendency of metaphysics and foundationalist ethics—one can consider modeling one's relationship to oneself after one's relationship to the Other. For a magisterial treatment of the vicissitudes of the self in modern philosophy and culture and an evaluation of its crucial moral significance, see Charles Taylor's *Sources of the Self: The Making of the Modern Identity* (Cambridge, Mass.: Harvard University Press, 1989).

17. This, I would suggest, is the kind of categorical imperative that emerges from Levinas's thought. On the relationship between Levinas and Kant on this

issue, see Stephen Watson's "Levinas, the Ethics of Deconstruction, and the Remainder of the Sublime," *Man and World* 21 (1988): 35–64.

18. See, for example, Caputo, *Hermeneutics,* pp. 239 and 279.

19. In discussing Derrida's "Violence and Metaphysics," Cornell says: "Derrida shows us that there can and should not be an absolute priority of Levinas' Infinite over and against Heidegger's Being. Levinas' ethical philosophy cannot, in other words, just displace Heidegger's ontological project. More specifically, *'transcendental' ethics presupposes respect for the phenomena of the 'being' of the Other"* (Post-Structuralism, p. 1618, emphasis added). This could be construed to mean that Levinas tries but fails to liberate the ethical from its subordinate relationship to ontology. What makes it so difficult to clarify all of the issues involved here is Levinas's (in my judgment, mistaken) claim that ontology always operates within the economy of the Same. For Levinas to speak of the Other in ontological terms (as he sometimes and, I think, inevitably, does) is performatively inconsistent with this claim. Someone who wants to insist on the primacy of the ontological can point to this inconsistency as evidence that Levinas remains under the sway of that which he tries to subvert.

I would argue that (1) Levinas's thought subverts the economy of the Same and, in so doing, (2) it releases ontological thinking from the totalizing project. When Levinas speaks of the Other in ontological terms, it is *not* because the ethical has failed to free itself from ontological thinking, but because the ontological has been liberated from the economy of the Same by the ethical. I would therefore invert Cornell's commentary and say that respect for the being of the Other presupposes the breakthrough to the ethical.

Where would this place Levinas via-à-vis Heidegger? It might seem at first to bring them far more closely together than Levinas's attack on ontology would lead us to expect. I have explained the sense in which it seems to me that Levinas's thought is ontological; the more difficult issue is whether Heidegger's ontological thought is ethical. One way to focus this issue is to ask whether the Heideggerian thinker approaches Being from the perspective opened up by embracing his own destitution. I suggest (see *In the Throe of Wonder: Intimations of the Sacred in a Post-Modern World* [Albany: State University of New York Press, 1992]) that the tragic irony of Heidegger's thought is that, although *Being and Time* points the way to such an experience of radical destitution, it never gets there. In that book Heidegger is on the way *toward* the kind of rupture, the kind of nothingness, from which, I am arguing, the ethical arises; but he is never more than being-*toward*-rupture, never in the very throe of rupture, never *broken* by the ordeal of deconstruction. This leads me to fear that Heidegger's thought never reaches the breaking point that would be a breakthrough to the ethical. *Because of that,* it lacks the *ontological* richness of the infinite (in Levinas's sense) that such a breakthrough alone makes accessible. (In addition to the Cornell articles, Robert Bernasconi's "Deconstruction and the Possibility of Ethics" in *Deconstruction and Philosophy,* ed. John Sallis [Chicago: University of Chicago Press, 1987], pp 122–139, has been helpful to me in thinking out these issues.)

20. *Being and Time*, pp. 308–309.

21. See Plato's *Gorgias*, 469.

Chapter 19. Emmanuel Levinas: Ethics as Domination or Desire

1. The argument of this chapter is limited to an analysis of *Totality and Infinity* and *Collected Philosophical Papers;* Levinas's use of violent and totalizing language to describe responsibility that begins to emerge in these texts becomes greatly exaggerated in Levinas's more recent work, *Otherwise than Being or Beyond Essence*.

2. Emmanual Levinas, "Buber," in *Noms Propre* (Paris: Fata Morgana, 1976); Robert Bernasconi, "Failure of Communication as Surplus: Dialogue and Lack of Dialogue Between Buber and Levinas," in *The Provocation of Levinas*, eds. Robert Bernasconi and David Wood (London and New York: Routledge and Kegan Paul, 1988).

3. Emmanuel Levinas, *Totality and Infinity: An Essay on Exteriority*, trans. Alphonso Lingis (Pittsburgh: Duquesne University Press, 1969), p. 84; originally published in French as *Totaite et Infini* (The Hague: Martinus Nijhoff, 1961); further references to this work will be abbreviated as TI.

4. See Simone Weil, "Affliction and the Love of God" and "Human Personality," in *Simone Weil Reader*, ed. George A. Panichas (New York: David McKay Co., 1977); and Emil Fackenheim, *To Mend the World: Foundations of Future Jewish Thought* (New York: Schocken Books, 1982).

5. Emmanuel Levinas, *Collected Philosophical Papers*, trans. Alphonso Lingis (Boston: Martinus Nijhoff Publishers, 1987), p. 16; further references to this work will be abbreviated CPP.

6. My suspicions that Levinas is insufficiently attentive to the dangers of hierarchical thinking found support in a recent reading of "And God Created Woman" (*Nine Talmudic Readings*, trans. with an introduction by Annette Aronowicz [Bloomington and Indianapolis: Indiana University Press, 1990]; originally published in French as *Quatre lectures talmudiques* [Paris: Editions de Minuit, 1968], and *Du sacre au saint: cinq nouvelles lectures talmudiques* [Paris: Les Editions de Minuit, 1977]). Here Levinas defends the necessary inequality between men and women and the preeminence of man (173), arguing that the feminine is in "second place" (177). "Equality would end in immobility or in the bursting apart of the human being. The Gemara opts for the priority of the masculine. A man must not walk behind a woman, for his ideas may become clouded." "Essential point: in the interhuman order, the perfect equality and even superiority of woman, who is capable of giving advice and direction. According to custom, it is the man who must, nevertheless, regardless of the goal,

indicate the direction to walk." (174, 175). The humiliation these words convey is like a slap. To be subjected to another person, to be subjected to any form of domination entails the most burning pain; this pain is only increased when it is given an ostensibly religious or ethical justification. Just as one must "put a fence around Torah," to guard against accidental violations, one must likewise reject the logic and language of domination lest one find oneself justifying not only the domination of the command, but also the domination of the Other.

7. Levinas himself identifies the depiction of a transcendence of the logic of domination as a goal of *Totality and Infinity:* "The effort of this book is directed toward apperceiving in discourse a non-allergic relation with alterity, toward apperceiving Desire—where power, by essence murderous of the other, becomes, faced with the other and 'against all good sense,' the impossibility of murder, the consideration of the other, or justice" (TI 47).

Chapter 20. Facing Figures: Levinas and the Claims of Figural Interpretation

1. 1 Corinthians 10:11. The phrase *in a figure [typikos]* is variously translated as "in a warning," "as an example." Its force is monitory as well as typological. *The Anchor Bible: I Corinthians,* ed. William F. Orr and James Arthur Walther (New York: Doubleday and Company, 1976). On the privileged status of this passage within medieval biblical interpretation, on the way in which it has been used to authorize the figural interpretation of the Hebrew Bible as a whole, see Henri de Lubac, *Exégèse médiévale: Les quatre sens de l'écriture,* vol. 2, Part II (Paris: Aubier, 1964), pp. 60–84.

2. Levinas writes: "The other faces me, without any metaphor." "A priori et subjectivité," in *En découvrant l'existence avec Husserl et Heidegger* (Paris: Vrin, 1974), p. 186. Or, "the face is present in its refusal to be contained. . . . It is neither seen nor touched, for in visual or tactile sensation the identity of the I envelops the alterity of the object." *Totality and Infinity,* trans. Alphonso Lingis (Pittsburgh: Duquesne University Press, 1969), p. 194. This is just one of many examples that could be cited from this work.

3. Erich Auerbach, "Figura," trans. Ralph Mannheim, in *Scenes from the Drama of European Literature* (Minneapolis: University of Minnesota Press, 1984).

4. Thus Auerbach gives "literally" a figural history of the word *figura.* On literal and figurative in Auerbach's discourse, see Timothy Bahti, "Auerbach's *Mimesis:* Figural Structure and Historical Narrative," in *After Strange Texts: The Role of Theory in the Study of Literature,* ed. Gregory S. Jay and David L. Miller (University: University of Alabama Press, 1985), pp. 124–145.

5. Levinas distinguishes between his confessional writings and his philosophical works, as an adhesion to an exegetical tradition, on the one hand, and

an inquiry aware of its presuppositions, on the other hand. Yet the distinction between the two is not absolute because of the important way in which Levinas mobilizes the nonphilosophical—God, Judaic theology, empiricism—*within* his philosophical work. I show the necessity of Levinas's nonphilosophical work to a reading of the philosophical work in my "Alterity and the Judaic: Reading Levinas" in *Prodigal Son/Elder Brother: Interpretation and Alterity in Augustine, Petrarch, Kafka, Levinas* (Chicago: University of Chicago Press, 1991).

6. For an extended discussion of Levinas's writings on Judaism, see my review essay "An Inscribed Responsibility: Levinas's *Difficult Freedom*," *Modern Language Notes* 106 (1991): 1052–1062.

7. Emmanuel Levinas, *Difficult Freedom: Essays on Judaism*, trans. Seán Hand (Baltimore: Johns Hopkins University Press, 1990), p. 4, with occasional modifications of my own. All subsequent references will be given in the text, indicated by the abbreviation DF. The volume appeared originally as *Difficile liberté: essais sur le judaïsme* (Paris: Albin Michel, 1963; reprinted 1976).

8. Emmanuel Levinas, "The Temptation of Temptation," in *Nine Talmudic Readings*, trans. and with an introduction by Annette Aronowicz (Bloomington: Indiana University Press, 1990).

9. Geoffrey H. Hartman, "On the Jewish Imagination," *Prooftexts* 5 (1985): 201–220. Observing the Talmud's "associative way of going from topic to topic," Hartman also comments: "it . . . lacks that hypotactic unity of form or field characteristic of learned treatises in the West" (p. 209).

10. Deuteronomy 4:12. *The Torah* (Philadelphia: Jewish Publication Society, 1962). Cf. Exodus 20:4: "You are not to make yourself a hewn-image or any figure *[temunah]* that is in the heavens above, that is on the earth beneath, that is in the waters beneath the earth." *Now These Are the Names*, trans. Everett Fox (New York: Schocken Books, 1986). *Temunah* is often translated as "likeness," "representation."

11. Claudel relies extensively on the exegeses of the ninth-century commentator, Raban Maur, whose hermeneutics are discussed by de Lubac in *Exégèse,* vol. 1, part I, pp. 156–165.

12. Paul Claudel, *Emmaüs*, in *Oeuvres complètes de Paul Claudel*, vol. 23 (Paris: Gallimard, 1964), pp. 73–439, translation mine. The cited passages are found on pp. 154, 146, 191, 346, 246.

13. Levinas, *Totality*, p. 66.

14. Levinas writes: "It is as if our ancestors were dressed up in exotic costumes and made to speak in accents that render them, finally, unrecognizable" (DF 122).

15. Levinas, *Totality*, p. 66.

16. Claudel, *Oeuvres,* p. 107.

17. *Difficult Freedom* registers repeatedly, and in a manner more explicit than that of the philosophical works, the impact of the Nazi genocide of the Jews. The Holocaust is referred to as a passivity, a Passion, an event that "drains" the meaning of the suffering servant of Isaiah 53 (DF 12). It is a hidden center of the part of the book entitled "Polemics," where, in the essay "To Love the Torah More than God," it turns out that the real polemic is against God. But the polemic is also, and this applies to Levinas's essay on Claudel, against Christianity: "to find oneself Jewish in the wake of the Nazi massacres, mean[s] to take up once more a position with regard to Christianity" (DF xiii).

18. 2 Corinthians 3:12–16. On the importance of this scriptural passage for medieval biblical hermeneutics, see John Freccero, "Medusa: The Letter and the Spirit," in *Dante: The Poetics of Conversion,* ed. and with an introduction by Rachel Jacoff (Cambridge, Mass.: Harvard University Press, 1986).

19. This is not the only place in Levinas's work where an aesthetic category (like "the poetry which scans and bewitches our gestures") is invoked to make an ethical charge. The complex question of the place of the aesthetic in Levinas's ethical philosophy merits a separate discussion.

20. Robert Bernasconi has also noted this, with reference to a talmudic reading in which Levinas denounces those who sit in cafes. "The Ethics of Conscience," *Krisis,* forthcoming.

21. Jonas Barish, *The Antitheatrical Prejudice* (Berkeley: University of California Press, 1981), p. 79. My discussion of the tradition of antitheatricalism is indebted to Barish's book.

22. See Paul de Man, *Allegories of Reading: Figural Language in Rousseau, Nietzsche, Rilke, and Proust* (New Haven, Conn.: Yale University Press, 1979).

23. Paul de Man, *The Resistance to Theory* (Minneapolis: University of Minnesota Press, 1986), p. 10.

24. Alphonos Lingis, introduction to Levinas, *Collected Philosophical Papers* (Dordrecht: Martinus Nijhoff, 1987), p. xxx.

Index